Who Should We Be Online?

Why should we bother...?

Who Should We Be Online?

A Social Epistemology for the Internet

KAREN FROST-ARNOLD

OXFORD
UNIVERSITY PRESS

Oxford University Press is a department of the University of Oxford. It furthers
the University's objective of excellence in research, scholarship, and education
by publishing worldwide. Oxford is a registered trade mark of Oxford University
Press in the UK and certain other countries.

Published in the United States of America by Oxford University Press
198 Madison Avenue, New York, NY 10016, United States of America.

© Oxford University Press 2023

All rights reserved. No part of this publication may be reproduced, stored in
a retrieval system, or transmitted, in any form or by any means, without the
prior permission in writing of Oxford University Press, or as expressly permitted
by law, by license, or under terms agreed with the appropriate reproduction
rights organization. Inquiries concerning reproduction outside the scope of the
above should be sent to the Rights Department, Oxford University Press, at the
address above.

You must not circulate this work in any other form
and you must impose this same condition on any acquirer.

Library of Congress Control Number: 2022949319

ISBN 978–0–19–008918–4

DOI: 10.1093/oso/9780190089184.001.0001

1 3 5 7 9 8 6 4 2

Printed by Integrated Books International, United States of America

To my mother

Contents

Acknowledgments   ix

1. Introduction   1
   1.1. Frameworks for Social Epistemology of the Internet   6
      1.1.1. The Situated Knowledge Thesis   6
      1.1.2. Feminist Accounts of Objectivity   8
      1.1.3. Veritistic Systems-Oriented Social Epistemology   12
      1.1.4. Epistemologies of Ignorance   16
      1.1.5. Virtue Epistemology   19
      1.1.6. Epistemic Injustice   23
   1.2. Chapter Summaries   26

2. Moderators   29
   2.1. What Is Online Content Moderation?   29
   2.2. Varieties of Moderation and Censorship Debates   31
   2.3. The Epistemic Challenges of Moderation   33
   2.4. The Virtues of Moderators   35
   2.5. Constraints on Moderators   41
   2.6. Commercial Content Moderation, Epistemic Exploitation, and Epistemic Dumping   48
   2.7. Algorithms to the Rescue?   65

3. Imposters and Tricksters   71
   3.1. Objectivity and Truth   73
      3.1.1. Objectivity and Truth in Feminist and Veritistic Epistemology   73
      3.1.2. Objectivity, Truth, and Trust   75
   3.2. Imposters: Undermining Objectivity and Truth   77
   3.3. The Need for Trustworthiness   81
      3.3.1. Trust and Authenticity   82
      3.3.2. Practical Wisdom and Trustworthiness   94
   3.4. Tricksters: Resisting Oppression   97
      3.4.1. The Epistemic Benefits of Betrayal   99
      3.4.2. Internet Tricksters   101
      3.4.3. Changing Epistemic Landscapes and Trickery   108
      3.4.4. Who Should We Be Online?   109

4. Fakers   112
   4.1. What Is Fake News?   114

4.2. Causes of the Fake News Problem 118
    4.2.1. Cognitive/Psychological Causes 119
    4.2.2. Technological Affordances/Design Features 120
    4.2.3. Social Causes 124
4.3. The Epistemic Damage of Fake News 128
    4.3.1. Fake News and False Belief 128
    4.3.2. Fake News and Distrust 133
4.4. Fake News and White Ignorance 136
4.5. Fake News, Objectivity, and Neutrality 147
4.6. Conclusion 162

5. Lurkers   164
5.1. The Internet as a Medium for Unlearning Ignorance 164
5.2. What Is Lurking? 166
5.3. The Epistemic Benefits of Lurking 168
5.4. Epistemic Limitations of Lurking 174
5.5. Harmful Modes of Interaction: Ontological Expansiveness . . . 180
5.6. A Virtue Epistemology for Lurking and Online Engagement . . 184
    5.6.1. Virtues Relevant to Lurking and Engagement 184
    5.6.2. The Importance of Practical Wisdom 190
5.7. Applying the Virtue Epistemology of Lurking 193
5.8. Objections and Replies 196

6. Conclusion   203

Appendix: Internet Research Ethics for Philosophers: Privacy, Positionality, and Power   209
A.1. Purpose of this Appendix 209
A.2. Respecting Privacy 211
    A.2.1. Complications for the 'Public Data' Presumption 211
    A.2.2. Alternatives to Simply Quoting Material One Can Access Online 215
A.3. Protecting the Researcher in an Environment of Online Harassment 219
A.4. Avoiding Epistemic Appropriation 221
A.5. Cultivating a "Traitorous Identity" as a Researcher 223

References   227
Index   255

Acknowledgments

This book could not have been written without the help of many people in my personal and professional communities. My greatest supporter has always been my mother, Gillian. Mum was everyone's biggest cheerleader; she saw the best in people. She was also one of the most curious people I have ever known; Mum loved people and loved learning. I was set to finish this book in summer 2019, and Mum was reading drafts of some of the chapters around the time that she got sick. We found out that Mum had ALS. Despite her protests, I put the book on hold and took a leave of absence from work to care for her. I am so glad that I was able to spend that time with her, but it was a hard journey. I am eternally grateful to everyone who helped us care for Mum during her illness and for everyone who loved her throughout her life. This book would not have been finished without all the people who helped me after Mum's passing: my friends and family, as well as Judy Taylor and Marcy Little. This book is dedicated to my lovely mother.

Lucy Randall has been an incredible editor whose support and expertise made this project easier at every step of the process. I thank everyone at Oxford University Press and Newgen who worked on this publication. Cassie Herbert has given me fantastic feedback at many stages of this project. I am so grateful for her insights and support. I thank Lauren Collister for helping me get my feet wet in interdisciplinary internet studies, for thought-provoking conversations, and for her help as I negotiated my first book contract. I am immensely grateful to Sandy Goldberg and Michael Lynch for their ongoing support of my work and for their useful comments on a draft of Chapter 4. Dan Hicks, Kristen Intemann, and Inmaculada de Melo-Martín also generously gave me incredible feedback on Chapter 4. I thank Alessandra Tanesini for detailed comments on Chapter 2 that pushed the chapter much deeper. D. E. Wittkower's comments on an early draft of Chapter 5 were invaluable, as were the insightful notes from C. Dalrymple-Fraser. I am very grateful for Joshua Habgood-Coote's comments on Chapter 2 and for our ongoing discussions about internet epistemology. Regina Rini's comments at a presentation of Chapter 2 encouraged me to focus on the epistemic labor involved in epistemic dumping, and I am grateful for her support. Sarah Hoagland,

Jacqueline Anderson, and Anne Leighton generously gave me thoughtful feedback on an early draft of Chapter 3. Several conversations with Emmalon Davis at PRPSEW inspired some of my thinking in the research ethics appendix, and I am grateful to her. Two anonymous reviewers for Oxford University Press gave me incredible feedback on various stages of this manuscript, and I could not be more thankful for their insights and suggestions. I thank Michelle Martin-Baron for some suggestions of resources for the appendix. I am very grateful to Andrew Chalfen for letting me use his beautiful art for the cover.

A huge thanks goes to Veli Mitova, Abraham Tobi, Caitlin Rybko, David Scholtz, and everyone at the African Centre for Epistemology and Philosophy of Science at the University of Johannesburg for organizing a workshop on this book. I am grateful to the brilliant scholars who commented on chapters of the book: Abraham Tobi, Caitlin Rybko, Andrew (Akanimo) Akpan, Glenn Anderau, Daniel Barbarrusa, and Aisha Kadiri. Their work gives me hope for the future of internet epistemology, and their insights will shape the direction of my own research.

I want to thank my community at Hobart & William Smith, including my wonderful Philosophy department colleagues, the Women's Studies Program, and Judy Mahoney-Benzer. Thanks to my student research assistants: Cory Andrews, Tyler Maclay, Carly Petroski, and Edens Fleurizard. I thank the Provost and Dean of Faculty's office at HWS for research support. The works-in-progress group of feminist scholars at HWS has been a source of intellectual support for many years. I am also grateful to all my students at HWS from whom I have learned so much, especially the students in my senior seminar courses in 2015 and 2021.

I also wish to thank so many others for help along the way, including Lisa Parker, Todd Reeser, and the Gender, Sexuality, and Women's Studies Program at the University of Pittsburgh, Juliet Boisselle, Michael Hunter, John Monteleone, Stacey Goguen, Debra Jackson, and everyone at the 2018 Prindle Applied Epistemology Writing Retreat, Judith Simon (whose work on philosophy of the internet continues to inspire me), Veronica Ivy, Alison Reiheld, Heidi Grasswick (who has been so supportive and who was one of the first people to express support for the kind of philosophy of the internet I was undertaking), Peter Graham, Boaz Miller, Jennifer Nagel (an incredible mentor), Mary Kate McGowan, Laura Ruetsche, Sandra Mitchell, Kieran Setiya, David Papineau, Nicholas Rescher, Molly Doris-Pierce, and David Coady.

I thank audiences at the Penn-Rutgers-Princeton Social Epistemology Workshop; the Women's Rights National Historical Park; Northwestern University; Rochester Institute of Technology; SUNY Albany; three American Philosophical Association meetings; the Computer Ethics: Philosophical Enquiry conference; the University of Pittsburgh; two Feminist Epistemologies, Methodologies, Metaphysics, and Science Studies conferences; the Society for Analytical Feminism; the International Association for Computing and Philosophy; Cornell University, the Fake Knowledge Conference at the University of Cologne; University of Calgary; LeMoyne College, the Minds of Our Own Conference; University of Connecticut; SUNY Buffalo; Colorado State University; the Canadian Society for Epistemology; the Social (Distance) Epistemology Series; the University of Cincinnati, and the Beyond Fake News: Mitigating the Spread of Epistemically Toxic Content Workshop. I am grateful to everyone who told me this work was interesting and helpful to them. All of those comments sustained me in this project. I am also grateful to the organizers and participants of the All Things in Moderation conference at UCLA in December 2017 for creating a rich interdisciplinary space for conversations about content moderation. Chapter 2 benefited immensely from those discussions. I am especially thankful for everything Sarah Roberts does to support scholars in this area; her work has inspired so much of my thinking.

I am grateful to everyone using the internet to educate others and further social justice causes. I thank Leslie Mac, Didi Delgado, Rochelle LaPlante (who gave me detailed comments on Chapter 2), Rasalyn Bowden, Danny Ramadan, Aaron Bady, and Benny Vimes for looking at sections of the book and giving me permission to use their words or discuss their stories.

I am so grateful for all the support and patience I have received from my family all over the world. My research buddies Alla Ivanchikova and Leah Shafer have kept me going for years. Thanks to dear friends Emily Nacol, H May, Kelly Walker, and Jenny Goligoski. Greg Frost-Arnold is a lovely and wonderful husband and the most careful and thoughtful reader of my work.

Portions of this manuscript have appeared in different versions in some previous publications. Chapter 1, section 1.1.3 and Chapter 4, section 4.3.1 use material from "Trustworthiness and Truth: The Epistemic Pitfalls of Internet Accountability" (2014) *Episteme* 11 (1): 63–81 [available online: http://dx.doi.org/10.1017/epi.2013.43]. I am grateful to Cambridge University Press for permission to use this material. Chapter 3 is a revision and expansion of "Imposters, Tricksters, and Trustworthiness as an

Epistemic Virtue" (2014) *Hypatia* 29 (4): 790–807 [available online: https://doi.org/10.1111/hypa.12107]. I thank Cambridge University Press for permission to use this material. Chapter 5, sections 5.1 and 5.3, use material from "Social Media, Trust, and the Epistemology of Prejudice" (2016) *Social Epistemology: A Journal of Knowledge, Culture, and Policy* 30 (5–6): 513–31 [available online: https://doi.org/10.1080/02691728.2016.1213326]. I am grateful to Taylor & Francis for permission to use this material. Chapter 1, section 1.1.5 and section A.2.1 of the Appendix use material from "The Epistemic Dangers of Context Collapse Online" (2021) in *Applied Epistemology*, edited by Jennifer Lackey, 437–56, New York: Oxford University Press [https://global.oup.com/academic/?lang=en&cc=pl]. I thank Oxford University Press for permission to use this material.

1
Introduction

The Arab Spring uprisings, the 2016 U.S. Presidential election, and the COVID-19 pandemic, among other events, have thrown the promise and the peril of the internet into sharp relief. Many of us are acutely aware of how the internet shapes global events and our personal lives. Consider just some of the events of 2020 in the United States. The internet helped connect family and friends stuck at home during pandemic lockdown, it facilitated a shift from work outside the home to telecommuting for so-called non-essential workers, and it provided tools for sharing videos of police brutality and the violent suppression of protests for racial justice. In many ways, the internet helped connect loved ones, protect public health, and spread important information. But the internet also made possible the rapid dissemination of COVID-19 disinformation and conspiracy theories about election fraud, and it was used to coordinate militia groups who ultimately attacked the U.S. Capitol in 2021. The internet helped connect violent white supremacists, undermine public health messaging, and spread lies and misinformation. These examples illustrate how the internet presents opportunities and threats. Furthermore, the benefits and harms of online life are not distributed justly. Many professional workers were able to work safely from home, while low-wage grocery store and factory workers did not gain the benefits from online labor and were exposed to deadly health risks. Similarly, the harms of being online are not equally distributed—women, queer communities, and people of color are disproportionately targeted by online harassment. The internet is a complex, unjust sociotechnical system. From global incidents to small everyday interactions, it is woven into the fabric of our lives in constantly changing ways.

As an epistemologist, I have been researching how the internet shapes what we know (and what we don't know) since 2011. I started my work as a feminist philosopher of science and ethicist interested in the ethics and epistemology of trust. Then came the Arab Spring revolutions in 2011. Like many in the West, I tried to follow the events from afar, and I was fascinated by how the internet was being used by both activists in the Middle East to organize protests and people in the West to try to understand the rapidly changing landscape. During this time, I came across a hoax that brought together all my research interests. As I will discuss in Chapter 3, *A Gay Girl in Damascus* was a blog supposedly written by Amina Arraf, a Syrian-American lesbian activist in the Syrian uprising. Western journalists followed Amina and cited her as a hero of the Arab Spring. But it was later discovered that the blog was a fake—it was all written by an American, Tom MacMaster, who lived in Scotland. This hoax raised clear questions of trust, trustworthiness, power, privilege, and colonialism in online knowledge production. Since then, I have focused my work on internet epistemology, writing papers about online anonymity, Wikipedia as an epistemic community, internet imposture and trickery, the problems of online context collapse, and the power of social media to educate people about their prejudices. There are many fraught issues in internet epistemology. And feminist social epistemology has much to offer in tackling these problems.

This book uses a set of theoretical tools that illuminate some of the central problems of internet epistemology. My goal is to show how recent work in analytic social epistemology helps us understand online knowledge and online ignorance. I draw on feminist philosophy of science, veritistic systems-oriented social epistemology, epistemologies of ignorance, virtue epistemology, and epistemic injustice studies. I refer to the combination of these frameworks using the catchy acronym: the FOVIVI approach—for Feminist accounts of Objectivity, Veritism, Ignorance, Virtues, and Injustice. Using these FOVIVI epistemological frameworks, I tackle questions such as: How do social media companies silence marginalized people? How can we make online content moderation less exploitative? How do internet imposters erode epistemic trust? When is online trickery a valuable resistance strategy? What are the connections between fake news and white supremacy? Can feminist accounts of objectivity provide tools to solve some of the problems of online disinformation? Why is social media a powerful tool for educating people about their own prejudices and privileges? When, if ever, is lurking an epistemically responsible practice? How can each of us as users (and also as scholars) gain knowledge through (and about) the internet without engaging in voyeuristic, extractive modes of knowledge production? What do we need to do collectively to make our online structures and spaces more just?

This introduction provides an overview of the FOVIVI epistemological approach that will be applied throughout my analysis of the internet.

While it would be impossible to give a full explication and defense of each of these theories and still have space in the book to apply them to the internet, this introduction provides a basic explanation of the core concepts and commitments of each framework. Additionally, some of these theories might seem to be strange bedfellows to some epistemologists, so I show how they are compatible and provide an integrated and mutually supporting set of evaluative frameworks. After the introduction lays out the normative approach to be used throughout this project, the subsequent chapters focus on central topics of internet epistemology: content moderation, hoaxes, fake news, trust and testimony, and how to be a responsible knower in online spaces structured by injustice. But before I give an overview of the epistemological theories, I want to say a few words about the broad approach to studying the internet adopted here.

First, this book is interdisciplinary at its core. While I am a philosopher by training, I draw heavily on the work of sociologists, anthropologists, computer scientists, media scholars, and others from the field of internet studies. There are two reasons for this interdisciplinarity. First, scholars outside of philosophy have been writing about online knowledge production for years, and they have produced rich work that deserves more attention from philosophers. I have learned much from internet studies scholars, and their work influences my thinking immensely. Second, the scope and complexity of the problems we face with the internet require broad interdisciplinary conversations. As I argue in Chapter 4, mainstream social epistemology has a tendency to conceive of the empirical and formal fields relevant to its work narrowly. Analytic philosophers tend to draw on psychology, cognitive science, game theory, behavioral economics, and other related fields. Part of the goal of this book is to broaden the scope of social epistemology. To wrestle with the ways that inequalities shape online knowledge production, social epistemologists need to engage with scholars of race, gender, politics, media studies, and critics of capitalism, as well as computer scientists engaged in these issues.

Interdisciplinary conversations are notoriously difficult. Different disciplines speak different languages and rely on very different framing assumptions. This can often lead to misunderstandings and miscommunications. While I engage heavily with work in internet studies outside of philosophy, I approach this work as a philosopher. I have done my best to accurately represent the work in other fields, and I hope that this book helps facilitate future conversations across disciplinary boundaries. While I write primarily for epistemologists in my own field of philosophy, I have also attempted to write this book with an interdisciplinary audience of internet studies scholars in mind. Thus, this introduction provides a broad overview of the philosophical approaches that are used throughout the book. I have left more specialized discussion of debates within epistemology to parts of later chapters where philosophers' questions will naturally arise about certain points. In general, I have tried to provide enough background at those points so that interdisciplinary readers will be able to access those debates. My own expertise and life experience have led me to draw more heavily on work from various disciplines that analyze the internet as experienced in the Global North and the United States, in particular. So while global issues are discussed throughout the book, future interdisciplinary social epistemology needs to pursue a fully global perspective (cf. York 2021).

Second, this project approaches the internet as a complex sociotechnical system that disrupts many traditional binaries (cf. Nissenbaum 2010, 6). The digital era has blurred the distinction between virtuality and reality, and between humans, machines, and nature (The Onlife Initiative 2015). Thus, while I will often use common terminology that marks a distinction between online and offline, there is typically no such sharp distinction. Instead, most of us live in the "onlife"—a reality in which online and offline are blurred (The Onlife Initiative 2015). Of the global population, 59.5% are active internet users ("Internet Users in the World 2021"). While the majority of the world's population uses the internet, there are certainly disparities in access and use. Nonetheless, media systems cannot clearly be delineated between offline/old media and online/new media. As Andrew Chadwick puts it, we live in a period of hybridity where online and offline, new and old, are complexly interconnected (Chadwick 2017). To capture the interdependence and tensions between older and newer media, Chadwick uses the term the "hybrid media system," of which the internet is an important component. When it comes to the role of testimony and media, there is no clear distinction between offline knowledge production and dissemination and online knowledge production and dissemination.

This is an important point for epistemology: internet epistemology is not a niche field. We cannot fully understand how knowledge is produced and circulated in our era without understanding the role of the internet. What I witness online does not just shape some kind of online avatar that I shed when I log off. Instead, what I experience online shapes my sense of self, my beliefs, my background assumptions, my epistemic practices, and who I trust as a knower throughout my life, both online and offline. There are often no clear boundaries between my online epistemic community and my offline epistemic community. Under digital capitalism, the economy of the internet affects what I see, pay attention to, and ultimately believe. And the vast wealth of technology companies has important material and social implications for our political, scientific, and educational institutions. Social movements combine both social media work and street protests to spread knowledge (e.g., the Movement for Black Lives's attention to police brutality) and also ignorance (e.g., the "Stop the Steal" efforts to distribute disinformation about the 2020 U.S. Presidential election). In short, the internet affects so many aspects of our epistemic lives that internet epistemology is a key area of social epistemology.

Third, the social epistemology pursued in this book is thoroughly feminist and committed to theorizing in solidarity with all movements against oppression. I am interested in feminist theorizing that is anti-racist, anti-colonial, anti-capitalist, and works in solidarity with queer and trans activists, disabled activists, Indigenous activists, immigrant activists, and all who struggle against the many forms of intersecting oppressions we face. This kind of intersectional feminist epistemology is particularly useful for internet epistemology because it takes seriously the role of power in knowledge production. In philosophy, it is common to make a distinction between social epistemology and feminist epistemology, as though these are separate subfields. There are some good reasons for this, but ultimately I reject this distinction because feminist epistemology has always been about the social nature of knowledge. Some scholars erase important work when they promote histories charting the creation of a separate subfield of social epistemology that studies the social dynamics of knowledge without beginning with feminist epistemology and the work of other epistemologists who center the role of power in knowledge, for example, epistemologists of race. I claim for myself the title of social epistemologist, and I envision a field of social epistemology which recognizes the inherently political nature of knowledge and the political nature of epistemology. I envision a field of social epistemology committed to social justice, and I see much support for this approach in our discipline. My goal in this book is to draw together many theoretical tools of such a social epistemology and to demonstrate how they can be used to shed light on knowledge and the internet.

1.1. Frameworks for Social Epistemology of the Internet

The theoretical frameworks used throughout this book all reveal different facets of two important pursuits of internet epistemology: (1) the study of the online production and dissemination of knowledge and ignorance and (2) the investigation of how power and oppression shape online knowledge and ignorance. Normatively, this approach is committed to both knowledge and social justice as inherently valuable. Our online epistemic ecosystem is functioning well when it facilitates the spread of knowledge and when it treats users justly, and our online epistemic ecosystem is dysfunctional when it ultimately spreads ignorance and supports injustice in the world. Each of the social epistemological tools of the FOVIVI approach has been fruitfully used to study what makes epistemic systems work well to produce knowledge and work poorly to produce ignorance. And epistemologists (primarily feminist and anti-racist epistemologists) have used these frameworks to study how power shapes who is taken as a credible knower, how material structures shape people's access to knowledge, which knowledge is hidden, and which ignorance flourishes, among many other questions. Each framework reveals some features of our epistemic lives and obscures others. I do not envision a hierarchy of the FOVIVI frameworks, but instead deploy them as a set of mutually supporting theories that work together in a variety of ways to reveal and explain different aspects of internet epistemology.

1.1.1. The Situated Knowledge Thesis

The starting point of the social epistemology presented here is the situated knowledge thesis (Jaggar 1983; Harding 1991; Haraway 1988; Code 1995; Grasswick 2004; Toole 2019; E. Anderson 2020). Knowledge is socially situated. That is, what one knows depends on one's social location, and what knowledge (and ignorance) circulates within a community depends on the social structures, practices, institutions, and political economies operative at that time. As individuals, our race, class, gender, sexual orientation, disabilities, and other features of our social location shape our experiences and thus our knowledge. For example, online harassment disproportionately affects women, people of color, and queer users (Citron 2014; Pew Research Center 2014; Jeong 2015; Amnesty International n.d.); thus, members of these groups are more likely than white, straight, cisgender men to have experienced harassment and to know that harassment is a problem on social media. Our social location shapes what we know. Online harassment also illustrates the social situatedness of knowledge at the community level. Structural racism, misogyny, homophobia, transphobia, ableism, and other forms of oppression in our wider society fuel online harassment and influence social media platforms' failures to address harassment. As a result, marginalized people often withdraw from online spaces and stop sharing their knowledge through these media. Thus, social forces influence what is shared and known online.

This situated social epistemology rejects the abstract, Cartesian epistemological approach that dominated analytic philosophy before the rise of feminist epistemology. Using Lorraine Code's apt moniker, I call this Cartesian approach the "S-knows-that-p" approach to epistemology (Code 1995). The Cartesian "S-knows-that-p" approach embraces abstract individualism (cf. Jaggar 1983). Heidi Grasswick calls this the "atomistic view of knowers" and describes this view as characterizing "epistemic subjects as *generic* and *self-sufficient* individuals" (Grasswick 2004, 85). The "S-knows-that-p" approach is individualist in that it takes the individual, atomistic knower as the central epistemic agent. Descartes's epistemology was methodologically solipsistic and did not address issues of testimony or other ways in which knowledge is communally produced. While much social epistemology rejects this solipsism and focuses on testimony, collective knowledge, and group agents, much social epistemology nonetheless follows Cartesian epistemology in its high degree of abstraction. "S-knows-that-p" epistemology abstracts away from issues of race, class, gender, and other features of agents' social location, and discusses the epistemic challenges facing agents (various S's) regardless of their social position, social identities, or the social inequalities of the society they inhabit. And this approach also abstracts away from the content of the various propositions (p's) that the abstract agents know. As Charles Mills explains, the social world presented by many social epistemologists consists of "a societal population essentially generated by simple iteration of that originally solitary Cartesian cognizer" (Mills 2007, 15). To give some examples, the "S-knows-that-p" approach to epistemology presents us with accounts of the justification of testimony by generic testifiers providing generic testimony to generic hearers. It offers models of trust in science that refer to generic scientists trusting other generic scientists, without asking how the race, gender, class, historical location, or power relations of the agents involved shape trust or distrust. And in internet epistemology, the "*S*-knows-that-*p*" approach analyzes generic internet "users" interacting with other generic "users" online, rather than talking about how racism, misogyny, capitalism, transphobia, ableism, colonialism, and other injustices shape online knowledge production. Much social epistemology of the internet takes the knowers to be analyzed as essentially identical Cartesian cognizers with smartphones.

The problem with the "*S*-knows-that-*p*" approach is that, for some things for which we seek explanations, the level of abstraction is too high. This is not to say that all abstraction in epistemology is problematic, but just that we cannot explain some important phenomena adequately if we abstract away from race, gender, class, and other features of agents' social location. One of the central goals of this book is to show that we cannot adequately explain some of the most epistemically significant features of our online lives if we do not pay attention to the online dynamics of race, class, gender, sexual orientation, and so on. For example, we cannot understand Wikipedia's biases without acknowledging that its editors are (at least) 84% men and predominantly white (Hill and Shaw 2013; Murphy 2015). The gaps in Wikipedia's online encyclopedia are directly related to who feels welcome in the Wikipedian community, whose knowledge is taken as authoritative, which sources are granted credibility, and whose ignorance is supported and maintained. All of these features are structured by hierarchies of gender, race, and other forms of domination (Frost-Arnold 2018). The historical context of the contemporary internet also shapes us as knowers and shapes our modes of online engagement. For example, this book will pay particular attention to the epistemic significance of this era of monopolistic digital capitalism. In sum, I will show that abandoning "*S*-knows-that-*p*" epistemology, and turning instead to feminist epistemology, epistemology of race, queer epistemology, and other socially situated approaches, provides rich tools for social epistemology of the internet.

1.1.2. Feminist Accounts of Objectivity

Within situated epistemology, I will draw on feminist accounts of objectivity. In the sense under consideration here, objectivity is epistemic (a measurement of the degree to which bias is managed within a community of believers), rather than metaphysical (whether the objects of our beliefs exist independently of us) (cf. Lloyd 1995). The feminist literature on objectivity that inspires me has, unfortunately, been widely misunderstood. Anti-feminist critics have charged that feminists have completely abandoned notions of objectivity and truth in favor of harmful relativism. Such interpretations are often based on sloppy readings of feminist texts or outright willful ignorance of the literature (cf. Rooney 2011; Frost-Arnold 2016b). Rather than abandoning objectivity, many feminists have argued that the concept needs to be reconceptualized (Longino 1990, 2002; Harding 1991, 1995, 2015; Lloyd 1995; E. Anderson 2006; Solomon 2006; Douglas 2009). Feminists have critiqued problematic accounts of what it means to be objective, and they have shown that such accounts do epistemic and practical harm. But they have also provided alternative accounts of objectivity that I will show are useful for epistemology of the internet.

Feminists have long critiqued the value-free conception of objectivity. Broadly, the value-free conception of objectivity holds that social and political values have no legitimate place in knowledge production, and that objectivity depends on individuals detaching themselves from their own interests, values, and political commitments (cf. Lacey 2005; Douglas 2009). As early work in feminist science studies showed, the ideal that science should be value-free has for centuries proven inadequate to identify and remove biases grounded in sexism, racism, homophobia, and other prejudices. Instead, the ideal of dispassionate, disinterested, value-free, neutral, objective inquiry has functioned to undermine the epistemic authority of women and other groups stereotyped as emotional (Jaggar 1989). As Sandra Harding argued, the value-free conception of objectivity is both too narrow and too broad (Harding 1991, 143–44). According to the value-free ideal, individual members of the scientific community remove their own biases when they conduct their research. However, this fails to fully remove bias in the scientific community. By too narrowly conceiving of objectivity, this ideal does not address how science is biased when members of marginalized groups are excluded from membership in the community of inquirers. It is not enough to simply require those who are already granted epistemic authority to be disinterested inquirers—to remove bias, we also need to interrogate who is included in the community and granted authority (Harding 1991, 143). The value-free ideal is also too broad in that it views all social values and interests as inimical to the process of science. However, as more women entered science, their work, which was often motivated by feminist values, uncovered biases and produced more accurate and reliable research. Thus, some social values may help uncover previously unrecognized biases (Harding 1991, 144). A conception of objectivity is too broad if it discredits feminist scientists who uncover sexist assumptions that skew results.

These feminist critiques of traditional views of objectivity are often caricatured by their opponents as arguments against the very notion of objectivity, but many actual feminists did not take this route. There are good reasons for not completely abandoning an ideal of objectivity. Having a regulative ideal serves an important normative function. It provides the basis for judging biased knowledge practices as flawed. This is important for feminist projects. Being able to critique science and technology that is racist, sexist, and oppressive in other ways is important for the epistemological and political goals of feminism. Having a notion of objectivity that shows when science and technology have gone wrong is useful.

Two prominent strains of feminist philosophy of science propose different accounts of objectivity. *Feminist empiricism* views critical dialogue among members of a diverse epistemic community as a path to increasing the objectivity of knowledge produced in a community (Longino 1990, 2002; E. Anderson 2006; Solomon 2006). A community of inquirers who maintain a diversity of values and interests can make their inquiry more objective by subjecting the research to criticism from these diverse perspectives. This does not mean that complete objectivity is possible or that a community can achieve a value-free "view from nowhere" (cf. Haraway 1988). Instead, feminist empiricism maintains that objectivity comes in degrees and increases to the extent that it enables members of the community to engage in critical dialogue with others. Such critical dialogue can identify and weed out idiosyncratic biases. *Feminist standpoint theory* also rejects the notion of a value-free "view from nowhere," but it provides a different account of how to increase the objectivity of inquiry (P. H. Collins 1986; Harding 1991, 1995, 2015). Feminist standpoint theorists developed the ideal of "strong objectivity," which advocates starting inquiry from the lives of the oppressed and eschewing dominant frameworks in favor of frameworks developed from the standpoint of those outside the dominant norms (Harding 1991, 2015). Beginning inquiry from the lives of those outside power structures enables researchers to identify the common assumptions and biases that have persisted in research communities. Such biases have often persisted because these assumptions benefit the status quo, and because members of dominant groups have been unable (or unwilling) to recognize or challenge their validity (Harding 2015, 36). Often the perspective of the outsider reveals gaps, inadequacies, and distortions in the mainstream worldview (P. H. Collins 1986). Communities that include inquirers from marginalized groups who adopt the standpoint of the oppressed will be better able to identify the biases of dominant frameworks (Intemann 2010). This adoption of the standpoint of the oppressed is not an automatic epistemic advantage of belonging to an oppressed group; rather it is an epistemic achievement (Harding 1992; Wylie 2003; Intemann 2010; Crasnow 2013). Members of marginalized groups may find it easier to adopt the perspective of the oppressed, but members of dominant groups can work to achieve this standpoint in order to make their work more objective. Another important point that standpoint theorists have recognized is that the marginalized will tend to be fluent in both their own epistemic resources and also the conceptual tools of the dominant, which they will have to learn in order to survive in a world primarily shaped by dominant norms (Toole 2019). In contrast, members of dominant groups can often get by without learning about how marginalized people see and understand the world around them. Being able to see the world through multiple lenses is an epistemic advantage, and dominant groups who fail to acquire the standpoint of oppressed groups are thus often at an epistemic disadvantage (Medina 2013).

I will flesh out the details of these approaches to objectivity throughout the book, and I will draw on Kristen Intemann's argument that feminist empiricism and feminist standpoint theory have much in common (Intemann 2010). I will show that feminist approaches to objectivity are useful for epistemology of the internet, because they recognize that all knowledge is partial, objectivity comes in degrees, and bias cannot be completely eliminated—but it can be managed. Feminist epistemology shows how we can structure our communities to increase objectivity at the community level. And it suggests practices we can adopt as inquirers to check our own biases and find alternative conceptual frameworks. Feminist conceptions of objectivity help us avoid problematic claims that sociotechnical systems are neutral and value-free; such claims of neutrality serve to hide the politics of technology and the ways they often harm marginalized groups (cf. Winner 1980; Liao and Huebner 2021; Miller 2021). Having accounts of objectivity other than value-free neutrality enables critics to show how and why technology is biased and provide normative arguments that it ought to be changed.

1.1.3. Veritistic Systems-Oriented Social Epistemology

Systems-oriented social epistemology studies the epistemology of epistemic systems, which are social systems that include "social practices, procedures, institutions, and/or patterns of interpersonal influence that affect the epistemic outcomes" of their members (Goldman 2011, 18). Epistemic systems include formal social institutions, such as scientific or legal institutions, as well as informal or amorphous sociotechnical systems, such as the internet. As a normative enterprise, systems-oriented social epistemology evaluates epistemic systems according to their positive or negative epistemic outcomes. Since it evaluates the outcomes of systems, this epistemology is consequentialist. Assessing the epistemic consequences of various social systems requires a clear specification of the epistemic goods that well-functioning epistemic systems promote. On a veritistic social epistemology, the fundamental epistemic good is true belief. True belief is not only intrinsically valuable, but it is also instrumentally valuable for obtaining effective means to achieve our ends. Accordingly, this approach evaluates the impact of epistemic systems on the formation and dissemination of true beliefs within the community as a whole. This book follows Goldman in often referring to true belief as 'knowledge' in a weak sense. Instead of using a strong sense of 'knowledge,' according to which knowledge is non-accidental justified true belief, Goldman takes true belief as a type of knowledge. Thus, the veritistic systems-oriented social epistemology that I use evaluates the social systems of the internet in terms of its effects on the formation and dissemination of knowledge (true belief) within the community.

Veritistic systems-oriented social epistemology is a useful framework for studying the internet, because it focuses our attention on both the social structure of the internet and the normative value of truth.[1] To move beyond individualistic epistemology, we need to look at more than just individual users and their actions online. The social structure of the internet shapes what is known and what is not known. For example, as I will show in Chapter 2, the fact that social media platforms are owned by corporate monopolies that make their own rules for what kinds of speech are allowed has an immense impact on the kinds of claims users are exposed to online. Thus, the suppression of particular knowledge claims by corporate commercial content

---

[1] For other veritistic analyses of the internet, see Matthews and Simon 2012; Fallis 2007, 2011; Goldman 2008; Coady 2012; and Frost-Arnold 2014c, 2018.

moderation has significant epistemic consequences. Additionally, as I will argue in Chapter 4, a normative framework that accords value to truth is essential for uncovering some aspects of internet epistemology. For example, we cannot fully account for the damage done by fake news purveyors if we do not recognize that truth-conducive practices are superior to practices that spread false beliefs.

Some readers might imagine that veritism and feminist epistemology are strange bedfellows, but this is based in a misunderstanding of much feminist epistemology. Just as some have misinterpreted all feminist epistemology as rejecting objectivity, some imagine that feminism rejects truth as an epistemic value. This is mistaken. For example, many feminist epistemologists and science scholars have gone to great lengths to show the falsity of sexist scientific claims. And the feminist epistemic practices of diverse transformative criticism and starting inquiry from the lives of the oppressed are valuable tools for truth acquisition. As explained earlier, in scientific communities, diversity is epistemically valuable because biased background assumptions can be uncovered when research is subjected to conceptual and evidential criticism from scientists with diverse values, interests, and social identities. If the scientific community promotes such critical engagement within a diverse community, and if criticisms of bias are taken up, then the knowledge circulating in the community can become more objective (Longino 1990, 73–74). As Goldman notes, this feminist argument can be given a veritistic interpretation—critical discussion within diverse epistemic communities is an effective mechanism for error detection (Goldman 1999, 78). Thus, veritism is not incompatible with feminist epistemology.

That said, while Goldman acknowledges the compatibility of much feminist epistemology with veritism, he does present a supposedly apolitical epistemology which underestimates the social situatedness of knowledge. In the first chapter of *Knowledge in a Social World*, Goldman defends his veritism from a cluster of worldviews that he characterizes as "veriphobic":

> Although veriphobes differ from one another in the details of their preferred methodologies, they share the idea that the study of social "knowledge" should be confined to the interpersonal and cultural determination of belief: not true or false belief, just plain belief. . . . They deliberately bracket questions of truth and falsity, holding that nothing legitimate can come of any attempt to draw distinctions in those terms. (Goldman 1999, 7)

In his defense of a normative epistemology which centers (rather than brackets) questions of truth and falsity, Goldman presents objections to veriphobia. Goldman repeatedly presents veriphobia as the complete rejection of talk of truth. For example, he characterizes veriphobes as making such claims as the following: (1) "There is no such thing as transcendent truth.... So-called truths or facts are merely negotiated beliefs, the products of social construction and fabrication, not 'objective' or 'external' features of the world," (2) "Appeals to truth are merely instruments of domination or repression, which should be replaced by practices with progressive social value," and (3) "Truth cannot be attained because all putatively truth-oriented practices are corrupted and biased by politics or self-serving interests" (Goldman 1999, 10). The picture we get from Goldman is that veriphobes reject *all* truth claims as *merely* instruments of bias, social construction, or domination. Goldman's strategy for attacking this kind of veriphobia is interesting. He acknowledges that some veriphobes make some persuasive arguments that some truth claims are biased, socially constructed, or oppressive (Goldman 1999, 21, 34, 40). But he rejects the universal claim about all truth claims due to flaws in the specific arguments for veriphobia and because there are too many examples of truths which do not appear to be biased, socially constructed, or dominating. He asks, "Can one seriously maintain that every factual statement in everyday life cloaks a desire for domination, even such statements as 'There's a coyote behind that bush,' or 'Your friend Molly called this afternoon'?" (Goldman 1999, 36). Goldman repeatedly paints bias, social construction, and domination as rare aberrations. His use of a knife metaphor illustrates this: "Truth claims, like knives, can *sometimes* be used for lethal purposes, as when one culture claims cognitive superiority over another and uses this claim to justify political or economic domination. But knives are not always or normally used for lethal purposes, and truth claims are similarly not *normally* so employed" (Goldman 1999, 36–37, emphasis added). But notice that this approach centers certain people's experiences and certain kinds of truth claims as normal and other people's experiences as abnormal. In his depiction of oppressive, socially constructed, or biased knowledge as merely "occasional," Goldman centers specific questions and knowledge claims as the core of epistemological analysis. Beliefs such as "There's a coyote behind that bush" are moved to the center and beliefs such as "Women are more emotional than men" or "White people are intellectually superior to people of color" are moved to the margin. Goldman is making a deeply political move in centering some beliefs and moving others to the margins. Whose issues we center and whose problems we address are political decisions. When the lived experience of marginalized people, who confront a legacy of science and other knowledge systems biased against them, is relegated to the margins of epistemological analysis, their interests are ignored. As Charles Mills argues, Goldman's presentation of injustice as a deviation from the norm "turns things upside down" since "[s]exism and racism, patriarchy and white supremacy, have not been the *exception* but the *norm*" (Mills 2007, 17).

I said that Goldman presents a supposedly apolitical epistemology because he portrays both truth and epistemology as a neutral tool (like a knife), but socially situated epistemology rejects such claims of neutrality. Epistemology is political. It matters whose experiences and which knowledge claims we highlight in our analysis. Thus, while I agree with many of Goldman's arguments for a truth-based epistemology, I take a different political approach. A feminist veritistic social epistemology centers the kinds of knowledge claims that affect marginalized people's lives. It values truth and seeks to uncover the social practices that produce harmful falsehoods about oppressed people. Truth is important for social justice.

Some epistemologists might ask why I adopt veritism, which takes truth as the fundamental epistemic value, rather than epistemic value pluralism, which recognizes many primary epistemic goods (e.g., true belief, understanding, knowledge, objectivity, etc.; Kvanvig 2003, 2005). I take no stand on the epistemic value monism/epistemic value pluralism debate. Instead, I adopt veritism as a tool, rather than pluralism, for methodological reasons. Given the current debates about post-truth, "alternative facts," and misinformation, it is valuable to have an epistemology that places truth at its center. Many epistemologists agree that truth is an important epistemic value and that much of what we value about understanding, objectivity, and other epistemic goods stems from their connection to truth.[2] For example, having true beliefs about dependency relations is a type of understanding (i.e., I understand a topic if I have true beliefs about the relationships between propositions in that area). Objectivity is valuable because increasing the objectivity of knowledge-producing practices makes it more likely that the resulting beliefs will be true. So a truth-centered epistemology can capture much of what we value about other epistemic goods. This makes a truth-centered epistemology a good starting point for epistemology of the internet.

---

[2] For a dissenting view, see Elgin 2017.

I take truth to be the primary epistemic good and other goods (e.g., objectivity and understanding) to have value in terms of their connection to truth, but I do not think the core arguments in this book hinge on a particular answer to the epistemic value monism/pluralism debate. So I will not argue against pluralist approaches. My goal is simply to see how far we can get in internet epistemology by starting with true belief as the fundamental epistemic good. What I hope to show is that a feminist veritism can shed some light on important questions about the epistemology of online imposture, fake news, lurking, and more.

1.1.4. Epistemologies of Ignorance

The epistemologies of ignorance literature starts from the premise that ignorance is not just a passive, accidental absence of knowledge (Bailey 2007, 77). Instead, philosophers in this field identify practices that actively construct and preserve non-knowing (cf. Tuana 2004; Sullivan and Tuana 2012). Much work in this field also uses the term 'agnotology' to refer to the study of the production of ignorance (Proctor and Schiebinger 2008). The epistemologies of ignorance literature that I will focus on pays attention to the role of power and privilege in shaping ignorance at the individual and social level.

At the individual level, privileged people may engage in epistemically irresponsible practices of turning away from the truth or failing to learn the epistemic tools of the marginalized (Spelman 2007; Pohlhaus Jr. 2012; Medina 2016). Such habits do not just deprive the ignorant of knowledge, but they can also cause ripple effects of ignorance throughout other parts of a community. Kristie Dotson introduces the useful term 'pernicious ignorance' to refer to "any reliable ignorance that, in a given context, harms another person (or set of persons)" (Dotson 2011, 238). For example, pernicious ignorance by privileged people can have a stifling effect on communication by coercing marginalized people to censor themselves, thereby thwarting important knowledge exchange (Dotson 2011). Chapter 5 will show how privileged people can do harm by invading online spaces for marginalized people, derailing conversations among marginalized people, and disrupting networks of trust.

At the community level, the epistemologies of ignorance reveal how ignorance is created and sustained by institutions, corporations, cultural practices, scientific paradigms, and ideologies. Charles Mills's "White

Ignorance" and his discussions of ignorance in *The Racial Contract* are arguably the most influential works in this field (Mills 1997, 2007), and they inform much of my thinking about ignorance. Mills argues for an existential claim: there exists a phenomenon of white ignorance, which is a structural, group-based form of miscognition. White ignorance is a non-knowing that has its causal origins in white racism or white racial domination (Mills 2007, 20). In "White Ignorance," Mills draws on Goldman's veritism to define this non-knowing as including both false belief and the absence of true belief (Mills 2007, 16). Mills investigates the role of white racism in producing ignorance through perception, conception, memory, testimony, and motivational group interests. His work shows that ignorance is not just caused by individual psychological or cognitive phenomena, but it is also shaped by racist laws, institutions, economic arrangements, ideologies, and more. This framework is useful for social epistemology of the internet because it draws our attention to the role of power and domination in promoting ignorance and suggests many of the avenues through which this power operates online. Finally, it is impossible to fully understand the internet at this historical moment without addressing the role of digital capitalism, and the epistemologies of ignorance literature is helpful here also. Case studies of the role of corporations and corporate-funded think tanks in hiding truths and spinning falsehoods reveal many of the mechanisms by which corporate money fuels ignorance. I am particularly influenced by studies of the manipulation of science by corporate agents and special interests (Proctor 1995; Krimsky 2003; McGarity and Wagner 2010; Oreskes and Conway 2010). Seeing exactly how corporations have hidden scientific research and also how corporate funding turns scientific work away from the truth teaches us to look for similar strategies by social media companies. In Chapter 2, I argue that social media companies have actively hidden knowledge about the work of their content moderators. And in Chapter 4, I argue that these corporations have facilitated the spread of fake news. In sum, the epistemologies of ignorance literature adds important tools to a veritistic social epistemology of the internet—providing hints at how false beliefs and the absence of true beliefs are caused online.

Those familiar with the concept of strategic ignorance (Bailey 2007) and Cynthia Townley's argument for a reevaluation of the value of ignorance (Townley 2006) might wonder how a veritistic epistemology is compatible with some of the attention paid to the value of ignorance in this field. Veritism takes true belief (knowledge) to be the fundamental epistemic good. In apparent contrast, Townley argues that "ignorance is valuable to epistemic agents both instrumentally, as a tool for acquiring knowledge in certain contexts, and as part of inherently valuable epistemic relationships, for example, those involving trust or empathy" (Townley 2006, 38). Arguing for a reevaluation of the worth of ignorance, Townley shows that *epistemophilia*, an excessive love of knowledge, can make us overlook the problems with doggedly pursuing knowledge. For example, refusing to trust others' testimony and checking up on them can damage our trust relationships, thereby undermining important epistemic resources. Additionally, members of privileged groups who feel a sense of entitlement to gain knowledge about marginalized communities can engage in objectifying modes of extractive knowledge production. In another argument for the value of ignorance, Alison Bailey shows that the "ignorance [of dominant groups] can be wielded strategically by groups living under oppression as a way of gaining information, sabotaging work, avoiding or delaying harm, and preserving a sense of self" (Bailey 2007, 77). Similarly, Sarah Hoagland argues that keeping dominant groups in the dark about certain things can be an important part of an "ethics of survival" for oppressed people (Hoagland 2007, 106). In sum, several philosophers who have studied ignorance provide arguments that ignorance has important moral and epistemic value. Is this compatible with veritism?

The veritistic social epistemology presented in this book easily accommodates the value of ignorance: I argue that ignorance often has instrumental value as a means for producing true beliefs. Townley is right that epistemophilia can damage trust relationships. Excessively checking up on people, which might seem veritistically valuable in the short term, can undermine trust relationships, thereby destroying one's ability to gain true beliefs in the future. For example, if I install a camera to monitor my cat sitter while I travel, she may rightly come to think that I do not trust her. This may hurt our relationship, and she may not be comfortable telling me truths about changes in my cat's behavior that may indicate health issues. On social media, someone who persistently gaslights, nit-picks, and generally questions another person's testimony is likely to get themselves blocked, which removes opportunities for them to learn truths from the person they questioned. Similarly, as I will argue in more detail in Chapter 3, there can be veritistic value in practices of strategic ignorance. When marginalized people trick or temporarily keep privileged people in the dark, they can use this ignorance in a number of truth-conducive tactics. Finally, veritism maintains that true belief is the fundamental epistemic good; it does not argue that epistemic goods always trump ethical goods. Sometimes to secure ethical goods (such as privacy or justice) we might have to enact policies that sacrifice the attainment of some types of knowledge for some people. And oppressed individuals pursuing an ethics of survival might need to use strategic ignorance in order to thrive in an unjust world. Thus, my veritistic epistemology accepts that ignorance may have instrumental value in helping us attain important moral and epistemic goods. The philosophical tools provided by the epistemologies of ignorance literature, therefore, fit well with both veritism and feminist epistemologies grounded in the situated knowledge thesis. Providing concepts and frameworks to analyze how power and privilege create and maintain ignorance, this literature is useful for uncovering how both individual habits of online life and social structures (such as racist, digital capitalism) spread false beliefs via the internet.

1.1.5. Virtue Epistemology

Throughout this book, I will show that the concept of epistemic virtue can be usefully combined with systems-oriented social epistemology. Systems-oriented social epistemology examines a system "to see whether its mode of operation is genuinely conducive to the specified epistemic ends," and it also identifies "alternative organizational structures that might be epistemically superior to the existing systems" (Goldman 2011, 19). Realistic work in this area (i.e., non-toy models) can only be done with a conception of what the epistemic agents who interact in the epistemic system are like; for example, what faculties they tend to have, and what character traits they exhibit. In other words, we need to know what epistemic virtues the agents have in order to know what consequences will result from them interacting with each other within the epistemic system (cf. Alfano and Skorburg 2016).[3] Additionally, the organizational structures and virtues of the agents are not independent, but instead often interact in feedback loops such that certain kinds of social structures encourage agents to develop certain habits, and

---

[3] For a related argument that moral practices and virtues are always intertwined with technology, see Vallor 2016. As she puts it, "Technologies neither actively determine nor passively reveal our moral character, they *mediate* it by conditioning, *and* being conditioned by, our moral habits and practices" (Vallor 2016, 184). For related arguments about virtues and the internet, see Heersmink 2018 and Alfano and Klein 2019.

agents with certain habits are more likely to design systems with certain features. So investigating whether alternative epistemic systems might have superior epistemic outcomes sometimes requires investigating how they could change the habits of the agents involved. Conversely, systems-oriented social epistemologists should also study how changes in epistemic habits change the outcomes of epistemic systems. Thus, this book will ask whether the internet as a sociotechnical system might have different (and perhaps superior) epistemic results if the agents involved were to cultivate certain epistemic virtues.

Feminist epistemologists have investigated how the appropriate virtues often depend on the social location (e.g., the race, class, gender, etc.) of the knowers involved (Code 1987; Daukas 2006, 2011; Grasswick 2017). And they have studied how one's position in systems of domination affects one's ability to cultivate various virtues (Fricker 2007; Medina 2013). Thus, this book will also ask how online agents' social position shapes their epistemic virtue.[4]

Jason Baehr's proposal for applied virtue epistemology suggests other questions we might ask about the internet. Baehr argues that virtue epistemology suggests important questions about domains of human activity, such as:

> What exactly is the (intellectual character-relevant) structure of this domain? What sorts of demands does success in this domain make on a person's intellectual character? Which intellectual virtues are relevant to meeting these demands? And how exactly are they relevant? Are there potential *conflicts* between the requirements of intellectual virtue and the requirements for success in this domain? If so, how should they be understood and adjudicated? (Baehr 2011, 201)

These are pressing questions that can be asked of our online lives. While interacting with others via the internet may not constitute a crisply distinct and well-defined domain of human activity (as I argued by introducing the concept of the onlife), it is nonetheless an area of human life in which we can be more or less successful, evaluated by veritistic lights. And, as I will show

---

[4] There is not space in this introduction to discuss the situationist critique of virtue epistemology. For a useful discussion of how the kind of feminist virtue epistemology I adopt avoids the situationist critique, see Grasswick 2017.

throughout the book, there is an intellectual character-relevant structure to our online lives (cf. Heersmink 2018). There are a number of veristically damaging behaviors which can tempt us, and intellectual character virtues can prevent us from succumbing to these temptations. As I will show, there are several intellectual virtues which are relevant to avoiding veritistic harm and to maintaining epistemically beneficial trust in online communities. There are also many conflicts to understand and adjudicate (e.g., conflicts between the virtues). For these reasons, applied virtue epistemology is a useful tool for internet epistemology.

Providing and defending a full account of the intellectual virtues is an ambitious project and certainly outside the scope of this book. What I provide here is a brief introduction to the kind of virtue epistemology that I will use to analyze the internet. One common way of explaining what a virtue is depends on the responsibilist/reliabilist distinction. Responsibilists are interested in virtues as character traits (e.g., open-mindedness), while reliabilists focus on virtues as faculties (e.g., vision and memory) (Battaly 2008). According to this way of making the distinction, the approach I adopt is responsibilist, because the intellectual virtues I investigate are character traits. That said, Baehr argues that reliabilists have good reason to expand their analysis to include character traits among their analysis of the intellectual virtues (Baehr 2011, 47–67). Character traits like open-mindedness or intellectual courage can sometimes meet the reliabilist's formal requirements of an epistemic virtue. For virtue reliabilists, "intellectual virtues are personal qualities that, under certain conditions and with respect to certain propositions, are a reliable means to reaching the truth and avoiding error" (Baehr 2011, 52). Additionally, a personal quality counts as a virtue if it plays a critical (or salient) role in causing the person to form true beliefs. Baehr provides a nuanced argument that character traits can play a critical (or salient) causal role in getting a person to form true beliefs (Baehr 2011, 52–55). So limiting reliabilist focus to faculty virtues is unwarranted because character traits can be reliable as well. Furthermore, character virtues are particularly salient in domains where reaching the truth is difficult (Baehr 2011, 53). What best explains our getting to the truth in historical, philosophical, or religious matters is often not that our faculties are in proper working order but that we possess character traits such as carefulness, patience, and creativity, among others.

As I will demonstrate throughout the book, this is also true for the internet. Faculty virtues like vision, memory, and hearing are often not the most salient causes of getting to the truth online. Instead, character virtues like open-mindedness, thoroughness, perseverance, trustworthiness, and humility are often much more crucial (Heersmink 2018). Reason, our faculty for making inferential connections, is an important faculty virtue for our online lives, but even reason needs to be exercised in ways that reflect acts of personal agency by deliberating open-mindedly or choosing to humbly reassess the inferential connections we make between claims we read online. As Baehr puts it, "The situational relevance of character virtues often picks up precisely where that of many faculty virtues leaves off" (Baehr 2011, 65). For these reasons, the virtue epistemology I apply to the internet will focus on character virtues.

However, the account of the epistemic value of the character virtues that I favor is also consequentialist and reliabilist in another sense, namely seeing virtues as reliable means to reaching the truth. I follow Julia Driver's (2000, 2001) account of intellectual virtue: "A character trait is an intellectual virtue iff it systematically (reliably) produces true belief" (Driver 2000, 126). This is a form of epistemic evaluational externalism, according to which the epistemic value of a character trait is fixed by factors external to agency, that is, the consequences it produces (Driver 2001, 68). Since the consequences at issue are whether it reliably produces more true beliefs than not, this approach fits squarely with a veritistic epistemology.

In applying this approach to the internet, I will tend to focus on other-regarding epistemic virtues that produce true belief (and avoid error) in others. Much virtue epistemology has focused on the self-regarding epistemic virtues that help *S* attain knowledge for *S*. For example, intellectual courage can motivate an agent to doggedly pursue true beliefs for herself, even in the face of potential risks. In contrast, Jason Kawall describes other-regarding epistemic virtues as follows: "Such virtues are epistemic as they produce knowledge, but other-regarding as the knowledge is created in others, rather than in the agent herself" (2002, 257). Other-regarding epistemic virtues are central to thinking about the internet. The social epistemology of the internet has to include analysis of other-regarding epistemic virtues, because if we constrain our focus to self-regarding virtues that help agents attain knowledge themselves from what they observe online, we miss much of the epistemic work that agents are doing on the internet. Sharing, contributing content, and moderating online spaces are all shot through with epistemic significance. By engaging in these practices in epistemically virtuous ways, agents can reliably help members of their community attain knowledge, and their epistemic vices can be causes of false beliefs propagating throughout the community.

My virtue epistemology of the internet will also emphasize the importance of practical wisdom in our online lives. Practical wisdom is a unifying and sorting virtue that helps us resolve conflicts between virtues and also adapt our behaviors to the particularities of the situation at hand (Aristotle 1926; Zagzebski 1996; R. C. Roberts and Wood 2007; Vallor 2016). Finding the mean of the relevant virtues is important in our online lives because not all online spaces are alike, not all conversations are alike, and not all users are alike. I will show that often the virtues seem to conflict in the onlife, so we need practical wisdom to help us identify the salient features of the situation and decide what to do at each particular moment.

1.1.6. Epistemic Injustice

Epistemic injustice refers to "those forms of unfair treatment that relate to issues of knowledge, understanding, and participation in communicative practices" (Kidd, Medina, and Pohlhaus Jr. 2017a, 1). The epistemic injustice literature stands at the intersection of epistemology, political philosophy, and ethics. Grounded in a situated, non-ideal approach, the epistemic injustice field takes at its starting point that power relations, prejudices, and social structures shape what we know, what knowledge circulates in a community, who is taken as an authoritative knower, and so on. The starting point is that the injustices in our society shape our epistemic interactions. This has, of course, been widely discussed by feminist epistemologists, especially Black feminist thinkers, for decades. But this field has grown rapidly in the past fifteen years as philosophers have turned their attention to identifying specific types of epistemic injustices and suggesting ways that they might be overcome (Fricker 2007; Kidd, Medina, and Pohlhaus Jr. 2017b; Sherman and Goguen 2019). A plethora of types of epistemic injustices have been analyzed, including testimonial injustice (Fricker 2007; Wanderer 2017), hermeneutical injustice (Fricker 2007; Medina 2017), testimonial smothering (Dotson 2011), epistemic appropriation (E. Davis 2018), willful hermeneutical ignorance (Pohlhaus Jr. 2012), epistemic exploitation (Berenstain 2016), and gaslighting ([Ivy] McKinnon 2017), to name just few. I will show throughout the book how online users perpetrate these types of injustice on the internet, and I will investigate how institutional structures, economic arrangements, ideologies, and other features of the social context of the internet sustain systemic epistemic injustice. Rather than explain each type of epistemic injustice here, I explain two broad categories of epistemic injustice in order to preview how these issues arise online.

First, giving and taking testimony can be disrupted and corrupted by injustice. Testimonial injustice occurs when a speaker "receives a credibility deficit owing to identity prejudice in the hearer" (Fricker 2007, 28). For example, a woman who tweets about her experiences with sexual harassment and who is dismissed as an emotional, overreacting woman suffers a testimonial injustice due to the stereotype of the irrational woman. Testimonial injustice prevents hearers from giving due uptake to speaker's offered testimony, while testimonial smothering prevents the testimony from even being offered. Testimonial smothering occurs when marginalized people curtail their testimony in the face of pernicious ignorance on the part of potential hearers (Dotson 2011). Dotson explains testimonial smothering as a type of coerced "self-silencing" (Dotson 2011, 251). For instance, when women witness the online attacks on those who come forward with experiences of sexual violation, they may choose to stay silent about their own experiences. Pervasive ignorance about the reality of injustice can coerce those who experience injustice into withholding testimony.

Second, hermeneutical injustice relates to epistemic practices of meaning-making and understanding. José Medina defines it as follows:

> the phenomenon that occurs when the intelligibility of communicators is unfairly constrained or undermined, when their meaning-making capabilities encounter unfair obstacles or, as Fricker puts it, "when a gap in the collective interpretive resources puts someone at an unfair advantage when it comes to making sense of their social experience" (Fricker 2007, 163). (Medina 2017, 41)

Systemic injustice can prevent marginalized people from making sense of their lived experiences by denying them the necessary conceptual tools (Fricker 2007). But even when marginalized people develop their own tools for making sense of their own lives, they often experience the injustice of willful hermeneutical ignorance when privileged people fail to learn the conceptual tools of the marginalized (Pohlhaus Jr. 2012). This can lead to prevalent misunderstandings of the speech of marginalized people. For example, in Chapter 2 I will discuss how widespread misunderstandings of the speech of marginalized people can cause them to be misunderstood as harassing and attacking people on the internet, thereby leading to the removal of their posts by moderators.

The epistemic injustice literature has clear conceptual connections to the other FOVIVI epistemological frameworks. Work in epistemic injustice is socially situated and rejects the abstract individualism of Cartesian epistemology. Veritism provides a useful account of the negative epistemic consequences of epistemic injustice. Testimonial injustice is not only a hybrid moral/epistemic harm to the individual whose credibility is diminished (Fricker 2007, 120–28), but it also causes epistemic harm to the community as marginalized users curtail their testimony and even leave online spaces that they discover to be hostile. When readers fail to believe the online testimony of marginalized speakers, they can fail to form true beliefs that were offered through testimony. And when users smother their testimony, the community misses out on those true beliefs that could have been spread through their testimony. Similarly, misunderstandings caused by hermeneutical ignorance often lead to the adoption of false beliefs by privileged people. Thus, veritism helps us recognize the epistemic harms of epistemic injustice—epistemic injustice spreads false beliefs and also prevents agents from forming true beliefs.

Virtue epistemology provides a useful framework for identifying ways to prevent these harms. Miranda Fricker presents an account of the virtue of testimonial justice that outlines habits that help agents avoid doing others a testimonial injustice (Fricker 2007). For Fricker, some agents (e.g., children) have this virtue naively, while others can cultivate these habits over time. Testimonially virtuous agents take steps to correct for any prejudicial stereotypes that might affect their credibility assessments of others' testimony. Useful habits that help such agents avoid testimonial injustice include revising one's credibility assessments upward to compensate for the unjustly deflated assessments that the prejudice would cause, making one's judgments more vague and tentative, suspending judgment about the testimony, or taking the initiative to get further evidence for the trustworthiness of the testimony (Fricker 2007, 92). There are also many habits that agents can cultivate to avoid hermeneutical injustice. These include developing willingness to change one's views and schemata (Dotson 2014, 128), learning practices of active listening (Medina 2017, 48), and concentrating on the sense of a speaker's words as they mean them (Pohlhaus Jr. 2012, 730), among others. Throughout this book, I will discuss habits that we can cultivate to avoid epistemic injustice, and thereby avoid doing moral and epistemic harm to each other online. And, following the structural analysis suggested by systems-oriented veritistic social epistemology, I will also investigate what structural changes are necessary to support our cultivation of these virtues (cf. E. Anderson 2012). For example, in Chapter 2, I will argue that the virtues of testimonial and hermeneutical justice are critical for online content moderation, and that significant changes need to be made to the internal policies of social media companies and the labor model of content moderation in order to avoid the systemic epistemic injustice that currently pervades social media.

1.2. Chapter Summaries

Each of the following four chapters applies the FOVIVI epistemological frameworks outlined in this introduction to epistemic challenges raised by the internet. These four chapters each focus on one or two epistemically significant social roles and personas that populate the internet: moderators, imposters and tricksters, fakers, and lurkers. These chapters present the epistemic opportunities and problems posed by the persona at issue, explain how relations of trust structure the epistemic behavior of people occupying this social role, investigate the social structures and platform design features that both enable and constrain their behavior, explore the epistemic virtues and vices of the persona, and examine the epistemic consequences of these features of the internet in terms of truth. Each chapter provides practical guidance on how we should live our epistemic lives as we take on (or avoid) these roles, and how we should structure our online epistemic communities.

Chapter 2 investigates the epistemology of online content moderation, arguing that current corporate practices promote epistemic injustice and exploit workers in traumatizing ways. I argue that the labor model of commercial content moderation prevents workers from developing necessary epistemic virtues. I provide an account of the epistemic exploitation of moderators and suggest ways to make the work less exploitative. I then draw on this account and internet studies scholars' use of the metaphor of digital garbage to provide an account of a novel kind of epistemic injustice, which I call epistemic dumping.

In Chapter 3, I examine internet hoaxes. I argue for a crucial distinction between internet imposters who cause epistemic damage by violating norms of authenticity and internet tricksters who violate these norms in acts of resistance that encourage trust in the oppressed. I show that objectivity and truth depend on inclusive networks of trust. Next, I demonstrate that imposture can undermine trust, and that trustworthiness is a core epistemic virtue. However, trickery is an epistemically important resistance strategy. So we need a virtue epistemology that recognizes when violating norms of authenticity is veritistically valuable. I present some guidelines for virtuous online self-presentation that help us determine how to avoid the vices of imposters and decide whether and how to be tricksters.

Chapter 4 addresses fake news. I argue that normative social epistemology helps us understand *why* the fake news problem is a *problem*, a point that more descriptive studies lack the tools to show. I show how racism shapes online disinformation and how disinformation fuels racism. Fake news does not just generate a generic form of ignorance; instead, it often feeds a specifically racist form of ignorance: white ignorance. I argue that feminist accounts of objectivity can provide tools for platforms to avoid what I call 'a flight to neutrality' that prevents them from accepting responsibility for their role in the fake news problem.

In Chapter 5, I analyze how social media can play a powerful role in educating people about their own privileges and prejudices. I focus on the epistemic virtues and vices of lurkers, people who spend time in online epistemic communities without directly participating in them. I argue that, under the right circumstances, lurking can be an epistemically virtuous activity. However, lurking can also be an oppressive mode of knowledge production, one that treats marginalized subjects as objects of voyeuristic study rather than as epistemic agents. Often lurking should be avoided in lieu of active engagement or simply leaving epistemic spaces altogether. I develop a virtue epistemology that helps us discern when to engage in a conversation, when to be quiet and lurk, and how to avoid hijacking online spaces for marginalized people.

The research ethics appendix lays out several key ethical issues facing philosophers studying the internet, including privacy, protection of the researcher, and how to avoid epistemic exploitation of users. I explain my own choices in this project about when to anonymize users' content, when I ask permission before using someone's social media post as an example, and how I have attempted to avoid using my own lurking practices as a vehicle to exploit the labor of marginalized subjects. I discuss my own social location and how that has shaped my approach to this project.

The internet is thoroughly embedded in our lives as knowers. Our hybrid media system offers significant opportunities for sharing knowledge and liberatory practices. But it can also spread oppressive ignorance. Such ignorance has real, practical consequences. Many of the serious threats we currently face (e.g., white supremacy, global economic inequality, pandemics, and climate change) are fueled by pernicious ignorance. Under digital capitalism, the deck is often stacked against the majority of us. Our online epistemic communities are structured by injustice, and as a result oppressive ignorance is sustained. But this book avoids techno-pessimism or nihilism (cf. Vallor 2016, 127). There is real value in asking the perennial philosophical questions: How should we live? Who should we be? Pursuing these questions with an attitude of hope can sustain us as we work for social change. By applying the normative frameworks outlined here, we can develop answers for our online lives. We engage with each other online through many different personas. This book explores whether and how we ought to engage as moderators, imposters, tricksters, fakers, and lurkers. I offer practical suggestions for how to pursue a life of epistemic responsibility online. But asking who we should be online is not simply posing a question about individual choice. Who we are (and who we can be) online is shaped by broader social structures and dynamics. The social epistemology developed here suggests that we also need to work for greater structural change. I hope that this project contributes to that work and provides some models for collaboration across disciplinary boundaries to sustain liberatory knowledge in an online world.

2
Moderators

2.1. What Is Online Content Moderation?

In May 2017, Didi Delgado posted the following on their Facebook account: "All white people are racist. Start from this reference point, or you've already failed." In response, Facebook locked Delgado out of their account for seven days (Angwin and Grassegger 2017). In December 2016, Leslie Mac was banned from Facebook for twenty-four hours for posting "White folks. When racism happens in public—YOUR SILENCE IS VIOLENCE," although after a public outcry the ban was lifted and the post was restored (Dickey 2016; Angwin and Grassegger 2017). Both Delgado and Mac are Black activists who were silenced by Facebook. In October 2016, comedian Marcia Belsky sarcastically replied "men are scum" to a friend's Facebook post and was banned for thirty days. When Belsky publicized this event and reached out to other comedians, she heard similar stories of women being punished by Facebook for expressing frustration with men in the wake of #MeToo. When some women comedians tried posting "women are scum," there was no punishment from Facebook, despite the fact that those posts had also been reported by their friends to test Facebook's system (Lorenz 2017). These examples make vivid the fact that online platforms are often highly regulated spaces, contrary to a common myth of the internet as an unregulated free-for-all without gatekeepers (cf. S. T. Roberts 2018). Many people's speech is deleted from online platforms, and people are banned from online spaces on a regular basis.

This chapter focuses on the epistemic labor of the moderators who do this work. Thousands of people perform the work of online content moderation, which Sarah Roberts defines as "the organized practice of screening user-generated content (UGC) posted to Internet sites, social media and other online outlets, in order to determine the appropriateness of the content for a given site, locality, or jurisdiction" (S. T. Roberts 2017a, 1). Online moderators play a powerful role in shaping our online epistemic landscape, even if their work is frequently unrecognized and intentionally hidden by online platforms. Moderators shape our epistemic spaces not only by policing content but also by embodying the socio-epistemic norms and values of online communities (cf. Matthews and Simon 2012, 56). This chapter analyzes the epistemology of online content moderation using the tools of feminist epistemology, epistemology of race, epistemologies of ignorance, epistemic injustice, and virtue epistemology. Given just these few examples of posts selectively removed by Facebook, it is clear that online moderation raises pressing and troubling questions about bias and silencing of epistemic agents. I will show that the tools of social epistemology have much to contribute to addressing these issues.

Additionally, I will argue that if social epistemologists draw on the work of internet studies scholars studying the labor model of commercial content moderation (CCM) performed for companies such as Facebook and YouTube, there are rich possibilities for interdisciplinary conversations about epistemic injustice and the epistemic harms of digital capitalism. Consider the following descriptions of the work life of the moderators who perform the labor of deleting 'digital detritus' (Sarah Roberts's apt phrase for harmful online content [S. T. Roberts 2018]):

> Henry Soto worked for Microsoft's online-safety team, in Seattle, for eight years. He reviewed objectionable material on Microsoft's products . . . and decided whether to delete it or report it to the police. Each day, Soto looked at thousands of disturbing images and videos, which included depictions of killings and child abuse. Particularly traumatic was a video of a girl being sexually abused and then murdered. The work took a heavy toll. He developed symptoms of P.T.S.D., including insomnia, nightmares, anxiety, and auditory hallucinations. He began to have trouble spending time around his son, because it triggered traumatic memories. In February, 2015, he went on medical leave. (Chen 2017a)

> [Moderators] are often subject to metrics that ask them to process each piece of questionable UGC within a matter of seconds, resulting in thousands of decisions per day, in work that resembles a virtual assembly line of queued photos, videos and posts constantly fed to a worker for decision-making. (S. T. Roberts 2018)

Many thousands of moderators for social media companies work under low-wage, subcontracted, fast-paced, assembly-line conditions that expose them to extremely disturbing and potentially traumatizing content. I will argue that the labor model of CCM raises two pressing questions. (1) Is the commercial labor model conducive to epistemic virtue; that is, does it enable the workers to develop the kinds of epistemic habits (virtues) necessary for reliable and epistemically just work? (2) Does the risk of harm to moderators constitute a form of epistemic injustice; that is, is it an injustice that many of us are spared the knowledge of the worst of humanity via the internet only due to the fact that moderators are exposed to it under such concentrated and poorly compensated conditions? Addressing these questions will have to involve a kind of extreme non-ideal theory—our online platforms and modes of engagement are so broken that being a virtuous epistemic agent and making policy recommendations within this environment means confronting crushing constraints and an array of bad options. Nonetheless, I believe that the normative tools of social epistemology can usefully illuminate these constraints, provide structural critiques, and suggest some practical solutions and sources of hope.

2.2. Varieties of Moderation and Censorship Debates

Online moderation occurs in a variety of ways, and a variety of agents perform online moderation. Much of the work of online moderators involves viewing reported materials and deciding whether photos, videos, and text violate the platform's terms of service and policies. Moderators include volunteer moderators of Wikipedia, blogs, subreddits, Facebook groups, and Twitter accounts, as well as paid moderators of online platforms (e.g., those who work for Facebook or YouTube, often as outsourced contractors). In fact, I would argue that all of us who have social media accounts need to think of ourselves as performing a kind of moderation role and should cultivate some of the virtues of online moderators, since we can (and perhaps ought to) remove some comments or material others post on, for example, our Facebook timelines and posts.

As I will discuss, the labor practices and economics of online platforms shape and constrain the actions and virtues of all these online moderators. The kinds of freedoms I have as the moderator of my own blog's comment section differ significantly from the kinds of actions Wikipedia's moderators can take to ban users in their non-commercial, transparent, and democratically designed space of community-generated policies. And both of these occupy almost a different universe from the lives of social media moderators in places like the Philippines who often work under time pressures and heavy workloads, are required to view extremely violent and disturbing content (such as images of child sexual exploitation and beheadings), and make decisions within a matter of seconds about whether it should be taken down. While these are incredibly different social roles, shaped by different economies, design features, and governance structures, I will argue that there are some common features of the epistemic difficulty of online moderation that all online moderators face. These epistemic challenges inherent in the work shape the kinds of epistemic virtues necessary to do this work in ways that enable epistemic communities to flourish.

But before I analyze the epistemic challenges of online moderation, I want to acknowledge a question that plagues conversations about online moderation: is it even necessary and desirable, or is it a damaging form of online censorship? This question raises complex moral, legal, and practical questions about the limits of online free speech.[1] I cannot possibly address all those questions here, and even to broach some of them would distract from the epistemological aims of this chapter. As illustration of the complexity of the epistemological issues involved in the free speech debate, consider just some of the following considerations on either side. One might argue that moderation is necessary because without online moderation, online spaces become cesspools of harassment, spam, hate speech, disinformation, and conspiracy theories, all of which are epistemically corrosive and undermine marginalized groups' ability to participate in epistemic communities. In contrast, others might argue that while ideally moderation could function to protect diverse epistemic communities, in practice it is more likely to function to silence the speech of marginalized groups, since those with the power to determine moderation policies will tend to come from powerful groups.

Determining whether, how, and under which circumstances online moderation prevents or causes harm depends on empirical considerations. Resolving this debate is beyond the scope of this chapter, and I will not take a position on it. Fortunately, I think the arguments I present here are valuable regardless of where we come down on this debate. Whether or not online moderation is a good thing, it is pervasive, and we are stuck with it for the time being. That means it is worth investigating how it can go epistemically wrong and how it can be done better.

---

[1] For a comprehensive account of the history and legal context of free speech and content moderation, see Klonick 2018.

2.3. The Epistemic Challenges of Moderation

Given that moderation is a pervasive feature of online platforms, what kinds of virtues do online moderators need to perform this work well? Here I think it is useful to notice the ways in which online moderation is epistemically demanding and difficult work.

The first epistemically challenging feature of online content moderation is the initial identification of potentially problematic speech. The main problem is the sheer scale of online content. For example, 500 hours of video are uploaded to YouTube every minute (Roose and Conger 2019). To keep their users engaged, social media companies encourage the creation of more and more UGC, but this creates vast quantities of material to moderate (S. T. Roberts 2018). Even individual blog owners often struggle with the volume of reader comments when a discussion blows up. With significant scales of content, locating the items that need to be removed[2] poses an important epistemic challenge. One of the main mechanisms by which site owners manage this challenge is through the flag (Crawford and Gillespie 2016). By flagging content, users can report content that they deem offensive. As a means of identifying problematic content, flagging removes some of the epistemic burden and required labor from the site owner and places it on the shoulders of the users. As Crawford and Gillespie put it, "Flags, then, act as a mechanism to elicit and distribute user labor—users as a volunteer corps of regulators" (Crawford and Gillespie 2016, 412).[3]

Although flagging provides one kind of solution to the epistemic challenge of the scale of moderation, it generates other epistemic problems. First, "Flags are a thin form of communication, remarkable more for what they cannot express than what they can" (Crawford and Gillespie 2016, 413). Depending on how the reporting mechanism is constructed, a flag often carries with it very little information beyond the fact that someone has marked this piece of content as offensive. Moderators receiving the flag may not know which aspect of the content was considered offensive, who made the report, or what their intentions were for making the report (e.g., were they genuinely offended and flagging in good faith, or were they flagging content as part

---

[2] While I focus on removal of content and occasionally on the suspension and banning of users, removal of content or users is not the only means of moderation. For example, platforms can also make problematic content less visible or promote content that contradicts problematic material.

[3] This is by no means the only function flagging performs; see Crawford and Gillespie 2016 for a discussion of other functions, including rhetorical legitimation and avoidance of regulation.

of a coordinated campaign of harassment to silence someone? [cf. Brandom 2014; MacAulay and Moldes 2016; Hoffmann and Jonas 2017; York 2018]). This last point suggests the second problem with flagging as a mechanism of moderation: it is vulnerable to manipulation and systemic bias (Crawford and Gillespie 2016; Angwin and Grassegger 2017; West 2017; Kaye 2019). Groups of bad actors can disingenuously flag innocent content in order to have it removed, to silence the creator, and even to get them expelled from epistemic communities. These intentional abuses of flagging mechanisms often target members of marginalized communities. Additionally, marginalized communities often suffer the consequences of less intentional or unconscious biases that shape whose speech is flagged as inappropriate. Stereotypes can affect whether someone's online speech is interpreted as hostile, threatening, or violating of policies in other ways. Pervasive stereotypes of some groups as angry, emotional, and so on make it more likely that their speech will be flagged for removal. This bias in the application of flagging mechanisms is epistemically damaging since, as I argued in Chapter 1, diverse epistemic communities are better able to weed out false beliefs and attain true ones (cf. Frost-Arnold 2014c). To the extent that online moderation decisions are based on biased reports, members of marginalized groups will be disproportionately silenced, which is an injustice to them and a detriment to the epistemic community as a whole (cf. Hoffmann and Jonas 2017, 13).

Now one might hope that because some flagging mechanisms allow for anonymous reporting, the flag could level the playing field so that members of marginalized communities can report behavior that hinders their full participation in online epistemic communities. But often demographics and coordinated campaigns skew reporting mechanisms in favor of dominant groups. For example, in white-dominated epistemic communities, a person of color who publicly calls out racist speech may find their own posts attacking the hate speech reported as itself racist (Angwin and Grassegger 2017; Lorenz 2017). If the sheer number of white people flagging critiques of white racism as anti-white racism outweighs the number of reports of anti-Black racism, then there is a real risk that moderators who take the number of reports as indicative of the seriousness of the problem will disproportionately punish Black people who correctly call out anti-Black racism. Another level of bias exists where site owners' responses to accusations of bias in moderation decisions can themselves be biased: celebrities and influential individuals who complain after having their content removed for illegitimate or biased reasons receive apologies and redress, while other individuals who lack the social capital of celebrities do not have their concerns addressed (Angwin and Grassegger 2017; West 2017). So, in summary, moderators are faced which a host of difficult epistemic challenges. The flood of online content can overwhelm epistemic resources, but one way of managing this flood, namely relying on users to flag problematic content, can be biased and manipulated.

Two other related challenges facing moderators deserve mention: the ambiguity of online content and the paucity of contextual information available to moderators. Online speech is notoriously ambiguous (Jack 2017; Marwick and Lewis 2017; Phillips and Milner 2017; Grimmelmann 2018). Moderators often have to make difficult, if not impossible, decisions about whether a piece of content is advocating hate (and thus should be removed as a violation of community norms), or whether it is parodying or critiquing hate (and should not be removed). One of the many reasons why online speech is so ambiguous is that it is often stripped of context that would disambiguate its meaning.

2.4. The Virtues of Moderators

What kinds of character traits are most fitting to this difficult epistemic work of online moderation? Many of the common epistemic virtues of open-mindedness, humility, curiosity, and courage will be useful in this epistemic labor. But in this chapter, I focus on the virtues involved in epistemic justice: testimonial justice and hermeneutical justice.

Testimonial injustice, as explained in Chapter 1, occurs when a speaker "receives a credibility deficit owing to identity prejudice in the hearer" (Fricker 2007, 28). Stereotypes of women, people of color, queer people, and others as emotional and prone to overreacting frequently lead to their reports of harassing behavior being taken with less credibility than they deserve. This is testimonial injustice. This harms the individual whose credibility is diminished (Fricker 2007, 120–28). It also harms the community as marginalized users truncate their testimony (cf. Dotson 2011) and even leave hostile online spaces. Another epistemic harm to the community is that ignorance will be more pervasive in communities rife with testimonial injustice (Fricker 2016, 162).

While some early internet theorists imagined an online world free of the oppressive structures of race, gender, and other identity markers, the contemporary internet is rife with stereotyping and testimonial injustice (cf. Nakamura 2002). When all of us are conscripted into moderation work by platforms that ask us to report offensive material, we can be influenced by profile photos, author bios, speech patterns, and other ways that we determine someone's identity. Our judgments about their identity can trigger stereotypes that affect the credibility we assign to their speech. And even moderators who often do not receive full information about who posted a flagged comment can still be biased by unconscious assumptions they make about what kind of a person would post such a thing. Thus, testimonial injustice can skew moderation decisions.

Moderators who are motivated to avoid doing community members a testimonial injustice and who cultivate the virtue of testimonial justice are less likely to improperly dismiss a flagged report of harassment or hate speech targeted against a marginalized member of their community. The virtue of testimonial justice is generally a corrective virtue—the testimonially virtuous agent takes steps to correct for any prejudicial stereotypes that might affect their credibility assessments of others' testimony. For example, someone with this virtue might revise their credibility assessments upward to compensate for the unjustly deflated assessments that the prejudice would cause, they might make their judgments more vague and tentative, they might suspend judgment about the testimony altogether, or they could take the initiative to get further evidence for the trustworthiness of the testimony (Fricker 2007, 92). What does this look like in online moderation? What is the virtuous moderator doing? To consider a simple case, imagine that I am moderating the comment thread on my blog. If someone reports a comment to me as sexual harassment, I take the corrective steps Fricker suggests to correct for any sexist stereotypes I might have that might lead me to give less credibility to the reporter's testimony than they deserve: I could grant the reporter more credibility to compensate for my prejudice, I could be more tentative in my judgments, I could suspend judgment altogether, or I could take the initiative to get further evidence for the trustworthiness of the reporter (Fricker 2007, 91–92). In taking such steps, virtuous moderators could avoid doing a testimonial injustice to users whose speech they regulate.

A second useful virtue for online moderation is hermeneutical justice. While the full virtue of hermeneutical justice helps us avoid all forms of hermeneutical injustice, I take this to be an epistemic virtue that helps people avoid what Gaile Pohlhaus, Jr. calls 'willful hermeneutical ignorance'

(Pohlhaus Jr. 2012). This is a type of epistemic injustice in which "dominantly situated knowers refuse to acknowledge epistemic tools developed from the experienced world of those situated marginally" (Pohlhaus Jr. 2012, 715). The problem here is that dominant groups often fail to learn the epistemic tools necessary to understand the speech of marginalized individuals. In order to understand what someone is trying to say, I need to comprehend the language, concepts, and criteria this person uses. In other words, I need to learn their epistemic tools. As Pohlhaus points out, these epistemic tools are communally generated resources, often produced and shaped by lived experience. This means that differently situated groups often have different epistemic tools at their disposal to make sense of their different experiences. Members of dominant groups may draw on different language and concepts than members of marginalized groups whose experiences with oppression may require them to develop very different ways of understanding and talking about their lives. As standpoint theory predicts, the marginalized will tend to be more adept at using both their own epistemic resources and also the conceptual tools of the dominant, which they will have to learn in order to survive in a world primarily shaped by dominant conceptions and practices (Toole 2019). Conversely, the dominant will not be forced to develop fluency in the language and concepts of the marginalized, and, in fact, they often have an incentive to ignore the speech and knowledge of the oppressed since it challenges a social order from which the dominant benefit (Pohlhaus Jr. 2012, 719). Thus, members of dominant groups are often willfully ignorant of the epistemic tools of the marginalized—the dominant are not fluent in the language of the marginalized, and dominant groups often use their own ill-fitting concepts to understand marginalized people's speech. This leads to misunderstanding and ignorance—the marginalized find their speech willfully misinterpreted and cannot gain uptake among the dominant for the ideas and knowledge they wish to communicate (Medina 2017, 44). In Kristie Dotson's terminology, the marginalized suffer a 'contributory injustice' when "an epistemic agent's willful hermeneutical ignorance in maintaining and utilizing structurally prejudiced hermeneutical resources thwarts a knower's ability to contribute to shared epistemic resources within a given epistemic community by compromising her epistemic agency" (Dotson 2012, 32). As with testimonial injustice, this is a hybrid moral and epistemic harm to the individual whose speech is misinterpreted, but it is also an epistemic loss to the community as a whole, preventing testimonial exchange between differently situated groups.

Since the internet facilitates communication across boundaries (between social groups and around the globe), it is no surprise that online communication is rife with willful hermeneutical ignorance. I argue that we can see many examples of this with biased moderation decisions. As discussed earlier, one of the problems with bias in moderation is that the speech of marginalized users is often flagged and removed (and the authors often receive other sanctions such as temporary suspension of their accounts) because their speech is viewed as hostile, attacking, or in other ways in violation of community norms (cf. Hoffmann and Jonas 2017, 13–14). This can happen due to testimonial injustice when stereotypes cast the marginalized as angry or threatening, but it can also happen due to hermeneutical injustice because the person evaluating the speech is using epistemic tools which cause the speech to be interpreted as hostile. This is hermeneutical ignorance when the speaker is not understood due to the audience's ignorance of epistemic tools prevalent in marginalized communities. Consider two of the examples with which I began the chapter. These posts were removed by Facebook moderators: "All white people are racist. Start from this reference point, or you've already failed," and "White folks. When racism happens in public—YOUR SILENCE IS VIOLENCE" (both qtd. in Angwin and Grassegger 2017). Didi Delgado, the author of the first post, was locked out of their account for seven days, and Leslie Mac, the author of the second post, was banned from Facebook for twenty-four hours. Many of Facebook's moderation decisions are intentionally opaque, and the precise reasons why a post was removed or a user was banned are never made public. However, it is reasonable to assume that these posts were flagged for violating the rules against attacking people based on their "race, ethnicity, national origin, religious affiliation, sexual orientation, sex, gender, or gender identity, or serious disabilities or diseases" ("Community Standards" n.d.). But interpreting these statements as attacks against someone's race is hermeneutical ignorance. If these statements are interpreted using dominant conceptual tools, such as the spurious concept of 'reverse racism,' then they may appear to be racist attacks against white people. Facebook's moderation policies often encode this kind of interpretive framework. For example, it was leaked that Facebook took white men to be a protected category, while bizarrely denying this status to other groups, such as Black children (Angwin and Grassegger 2017). And Facebook's own civil rights audit recognized that "too many mistakes were being made removing content that was actually condemning hate speech" ("Facebook's Civil Rights Audit—Final Report" 2020, 45). Thus, the most plausible explanation for the removal of these posts is that they were interpreted as attacks against white people.[4]

However, there is another way to interpret these posts, one more in line with resistant knowledge and conceptual tools generated from the life experiences of the racially marginalized. Within this alternative interpretive framework, these statements are not attacks but are instead explanations of the pervasive and systemic nature of prejudice and privilege. One is likely to interpret these posts as racist attacks if one is willfully ignorant of the tools that racially marginalized people have developed to discuss the racist oppression with which they live and the common conversational moves they make to explain how racism operates and how it affects the lives of the oppressed. Thus, members of dominant groups who hear these statements as racist attacks often do so due to culpable willful hermeneutical ignorance. This is similar to Pohlhaus's description of the white jurors who misinterpret Tom Robinson's testimony in *To Kill a Mockingbird*: "The jurors are culpable since there is nothing forcing them to use faulty epistemic resources; rather, they lack such resources due to a prejudice against taking seriously the experienced world outside of white men and a refusal to enter into truly cooperative interdependence with knowers situated outside dominant social positions" (Pohlhaus Jr. 2012, 725). The same can be true for those who commonly flag (and remove) Black users' critiques of racism as anti-white racist attacks. They may do so due to faulty epistemic resources and a refusal to learn the epistemic tools of non-dominantly situated people. Relatedly, André Brock argues that "The callout, originally a practice of Black women signifyin', has occasionally been mistaken for Twitter's 'mob mentality,' but it is qualitatively different: it is often a critique of systemic inequality rather than an attack against specific, individualistic transgressions" (Brock 2020, 220). Thus, hermeneutical injustice threatens when non-Black users are unfamiliar with this practice and misinterpret structural critiques by Black people as personal attacks. In sum, hermeneutical injustice is a common problem in online moderation.

---

[4] Note that these posts were removed in 2017, which is before Facebook starting using algorithms to take down hate speech without being reviewed by a human moderator first. As I will discuss in section 2.7, algorithmic moderation is no panacea for avoiding these problems. Facebook's algorithms were set up to be "race-blind" in ways that "resulted in the company being more vigilant about removing slurs lobbed against White users while flagging and deleting innocuous posts by people of color on the platform" (Dwoskin, Tiku, and Kelly 2020). Facebook announced changes aimed at removing this bias in December 2020.

This is why the virtue of hermeneutical justice is so important for online moderators (and for all of us who have the power to flag speech for removal). As Medina argues, individual agency is an important part of avoiding hermeneutical injustice (Medina 2013, 2017). Individuals who cultivate sensitivity to differences in interpretive resources can avoid willful hermeneutical ignorance. This is a complex virtue. The literature on epistemic injustice suggests several dispositions and habits of the hermeneutically virtuous. First, although she doesn't use the term 'hermeneutical justice' in this context, Dotson's work suggests that someone with this virtue has a "willingness to change one's views and general ways of thinking," including changing one's "instituted social imaginaries and/or prevailing schemata" (Dotson 2014, 128). Second, Medina argues that the habits of virtuous listening needed to avoid hermeneutical injustice involve all of the following skills and habits of active and charitable listening: "knowing when to shut up, knowing when to suspend one's own judgment about intelligibility, calling critical attention to one's own limited expressive habits and interpretative expectations, listening for silences, checking with others who are differently situated, letting others set the tone and the dynamics of a communicative exchange, etc." (Medina 2017, 48). Third, drawing on her analysis of the virtues of Atticus and Scout Finch from *To Kill a Mockingbird*, Pohlhaus suggests that concentrating on the sense of the speaker's words "*as he means them* and actively blocking out the predominant epistemic practices of the . . . white audience" are useful habits for avoiding hermeneutical ignorance (Pohlhaus Jr. 2012, 730). There are affective, trustful, and attentive elements to this virtue. The hermeneutically just person "genuinely cares to know something about the world as experienced from social positions other than one's own," and they trust those from other positions to develop epistemic resources suited to their experiences and have an interest in attending to them and learning how to use them (Pohlhaus Jr. 2012, 731). With just this brief overview, we can see that this is a challenging virtue to cultivate. It involves much affective, cognitive, and relational work. It may seem a tall order for members of dominant groups to cultivate this virtue, but as Pohlhaus says, "entering less coercive and more symmetrical interdependent relations is not in principle impossible, just difficult" (Pohlhaus Jr. 2012, 722).

To provide an example of how this might work in moderation, consider how I might enact hermeneutical justice as the moderator of comments on my blog. To avoid willful hermeneutical ignorance by misinterpreting the speech of my marginalized readers, I engage in active listening, I humbly reflect on the limitations of my own epistemic resources from my social position, I build relationships with marginalized people so that I become familiar with their epistemic resources, and I check with others to make sure I have understood a comment before I delete it due to my own ignorance. Taking these steps and developing these habits will help me be a better moderator, and they will help me avoid biased moderation decisions that will damage the epistemic health of my online community. Thus, this section concludes on an optimistic note. There are things we can do and virtues we can cultivate to help us deal with some of the epistemic challenges of online moderation.

2.5. Constraints on Moderators

I now turn to a more pessimistic set of considerations, because, unfortunately, the economic model of much CCM is not conducive to these virtues. In fact, I would argue that our commercial social media platforms typically have a labor model that makes epistemically virtuous moderation practically impossible.

If we move from the blogging model of the early social internet to the labor of moderation as currently practiced by many corporate social media platforms, we immediately find a crushingly difficult environment for good epistemic practice. CCM is now frequently performed by contract labor in low-wage, low-status, outsourced jobs (S. T. Roberts 2017a). Social media platforms have gone to great lengths to hide the world of CCM from public view, cloaking the work of the laborers and the moderation policies by making moderators sign non-disclosure agreements and by moving the work at great distance from the U.S.-based companies (e.g., to the Philippines and India) (S. T. Roberts 2018). Nonetheless, due to the work of whistleblowers, journalists, and scholars, a picture of CCM has emerged.

As we saw earlier, one of the pioneering scholars on online moderation, Sarah Roberts, describes the speed with which these contractors work: "They are often subject to metrics that ask them to process each piece of questionable UGC within a matter of seconds, resulting in thousands of decisions per day, in work that resembles a virtual assembly line of queued photos, videos and posts constantly fed to a worker for decision-making" (S. T. Roberts 2018). Some CCM workers labor at home by picking up piecemeal work through Amazon Mechanical Turk, while others work in large office spaces surrounded by other CCM workers (Chen 2017a; S. T. Roberts 2017a). Despite these different environments, much of the CCM work of deleting or approving flagged content appears to be a relatively solitary endeavor in which workers are expected to make thousands of decisions by themselves, guided by the company's moderation policies and laws of the countries in which the site is based (S. T. Roberts 2017a). Burcu Gültekin Punsmann, who worked for a company to which Facebook outsourced moderation, reports that moderators are pressured to make decisions alone and not seek guidance from the subject matter experts, and moderators are told "Don't think too much" (qtd. in Kaye 2019, 61). As just one example of the scale and speed of the labor involved, one moderator interviewed for the documentary *The Cleaners* reported that their employer expected them to review 25,000 pictures per day (Block and Riesewieck 2018). While they may consult with peers and managers or push tricky cases to the next level up of scrutiny, the primary vision of the moderator's work is that it is something that can usually be done by an individual consulting their own judgment and the relevant policies. In *The Cleaners*, one moderator reports that the company's quality assessment involves a sampling of only 3% of a moderator's reviews (Block and Riesewieck 2018). If this is a common pattern, then much of this work depends on the individual moderator's judgment alone. In fact, Mary Gray and Siddharth Suri show that isolation, lack of guidance, and disincentives to ask questions are common features of the hidden "ghost work" of laborers powering websites, apps, and artificial intelligence (Gray and Suri 2019, 80–85).

In noting how much moderation work is largely a matter of solitary individual judgment, I do not mean to ignore the many people involved in the entire process of moderation and their collective decisions. I will return to this point about the many actors and levels of hierarchy involved in the making of policies and the review process for moderators work later in this section. Additionally, I do not want to erase the collective agency of on-demand laborers who have created their own forums for collaboration and mutual support (cf. Irani and Silberman 2016; Gray and Suri 2019). What I am emphasizing at this earlier point is the fact that many decisions at the level of deletion are made by the individual moderator alone.

A final point worth noting is the global and universalized nature of the work. CCM workers are often asked to moderate content from locations and communities far removed from their own. Ideally, this is done with the requisite knowledge, as Roberts puts it:

[CCM workers] must be experts in matters of taste of the site's presumed audience, have cultural knowledge about location of origin of the platform and of the audience (both of which may be very far removed, geographically and culturally, from where the screening is taking place), have linguistic competency in the language of the UGC (that may be a learned or second language for the content moderator), be steeped in the relevant laws governing the site's location of origin and be experts in the user guidelines and other platform-level specifics concerning what is and is not allowed. (S. T. Roberts 2017a, 3)

But as Roberts's own interviews with CCM workers show, this expert, localized knowledge is often more aspiration than reality (S. T. Roberts 2014, 2019). For example, Roberts interviewed one worker who often had to make decisions about videos from the Syrian civil war who had little knowledge of the conflict (S. T. Roberts 2014, 112; 2019, 102). This is a widespread problem, as shown in Mary Gray and Siddharth Suri's research on the globalized "ghost work" platform labor of sites such as Amazon's Mechanical Turk. Workers take on piecemeal tasks based on the initial description of the work posted to the platform, but "Workers don't know if they are technically or culturally competent for a task until they try to complete it" (Gray and Suri 2019, 81). Thus, moderation is often performed by workers with little knowledge of the communities they are moderating (cf. Kaye 2019; York 2021).[5]

To protect a profitable business model and to hide their moderation work from public scrutiny, social media companies have created a labor environment in which CCM work is low-status work, reflecting a lack of recognition of the skill involved in such labor. Additionally, the work is *fast, routine, solitary*, and *global*. This is in striking opposition to the picture of the virtuous epistemic agent that we receive from social epistemologists. The virtue epistemology I have outlined here suggests that this work often needs to be *slow, painstaking, relational*, and involve *local* engagement with multiple, especially marginalized, subcommunities. Put simply, it does not seem that CCM workers are given the time, the resources, or the local relationships to cultivate the skills necessary to avoid testimonial injustice and hermeneutical

---

[5] This is not to deny that social media companies may have some mechanisms to bring in local experts from time to time. For example, Facebook has some local content experts called their 'market team,' which a head of moderator training at the company described as "a body of professionals that specialize in certain markets and languages, and we often partner with them to make sure that our training has the most relevant examples" (Koebler and Maiberg 2019).

ignorance. This is a striking mismatch between where the epistemology literature has developed on how epistemically challenging and demanding it is to really hear and understand others' speech and the almost disdainful casualness with which the main social media platforms treat the labor of moderators. Given my analysis of some of the epistemic challenges involved in online moderation, and the complex virtues needed to do this work well, we can see that the current commercial practices of social media companies are antithetical to virtuous moderation.

This examination of the epistemic problems with the labor model of CCM shows the possibility for rich interdisciplinary conversations between internet studies scholars and social epistemologists. To its detriment, analytic social epistemology has not traditionally made the epistemological consequences of capitalism a central object of study. By drawing on the work of internet scholars who expose the labor model of CCM, and applying our own tools of normative analysis, social epistemologists can help articulate the epistemic harms of digital capitalism in general and the choices that social media companies have made to do moderation on the cheap in particular. I have shown that there are serious problems of epistemic injustice in moderation. Far too many marginalized users are experiencing testimonial injustice and hermeneutical ignorance in their online lives. Virtue epistemology is useful in providing a normative framework for habits that moderators can cultivate to avoid these epistemic and moral harms. Once we have a picture of these habits and the time and effort necessary for cultivating them, we can clearly see that the economic model of CCM fails to provide an environment conducive to these virtues. Thus, conceptual tools from virtue epistemology and the literature on epistemic injustice provide useful normative tools to evaluate the picture of social media provided by internet studies scholars.

At this point, I want to address an objection to this approach, because answering it will help complicate my analysis in important ways. One might worry that the virtue epistemology I have outlined here does not provide the right framework for addressing the problems with CCM. One might argue that the virtue approach individualizes the problems with online moderation by blaming the moderators rather than the structures and institutions in which they work. On this objection, virtue epistemology focuses on the wrong level of analysis, evaluating the habits of individual workers rather than the structures and policies guiding their actions. This virtue epistemology approach can seem unfairly moralizing because it might seem to place all the culpability on the individual for not cultivating good habits.

In response I argue that this objection is motivated, in part, by a misunderstanding of virtue epistemology. As we saw in Chapter 1, it is perfectly compatible with virtue epistemology that the social structures in which we live shape our ability and motivation to develop the relevant virtues. Judith Simon helpfully distinguishes between two relevant perspectives for analyzing epistemic responsibility in a hyperconnected era:

1. the individualistic perspective, focusing on individuals acting as knowers within increasingly complex and dynamic sociotechnical epistemic systems. The leading question here is: what does it mean to be responsible in knowing?
2. the governance perspective, focusing on the question how systems and environments should be designed so that individuals can act responsibly. The leading question here is: what does it take to enable responsibility in knowing? (Simon 2015)

Virtue epistemology has much to contribute to both levels of analysis for content moderation. From the individualistic perspective, we can investigate what habits moderators need to cultivate to be responsible knowers. From the governance perspective, we can investigate how systems and environments should be designed to enable responsible knowing for moderation. Thus, the objection is mistaken that virtue epistemology is a problematic framework for addressing these issues. Nonetheless, I think there is something insightful about this objection, in that I have focused my analysis on the moderators themselves and said relatively little about the other agents involved and the policies that structure the moderators' work. So let us enrich the analysis at this point by taking these features of the situation into account.

Many moderators do not, of course, work in isolation. There are many other agents involved in the process of moderation at social media companies who make decisions that shape the moderators' work. Many moderators report to supervisors, and there are often multiple levels of checking moderators' work (Klonick 2018, 1639–41). Difficult moderation decisions can often be "kicked up" a level of the company chain. Additionally, everyone who is involved in the crafting of the moderation policies and training of the moderators is a relevant epistemic agent, including team leaders, vice presidents, and lawyers (cf. Kaye 2019, 54–58). In May 2020, Facebook announced the first twenty members of its new Oversight Board, the goal of which Facebook says is "to promote free expression by making principled, independent decisions regarding content on Facebook and Instagram and by issuing recommendations on the relevant Facebook company content policy" ("Oversight Board" n.d.). This Board can choose cases of content removed from Facebook and Instagram to review, and it has the power to make moderation policy recommendations to the company. Analysts have raised numerous concerns about the diversity, power, independence, and efficacy of the Oversight Board (Klonick and Kadri 2018; Domino 2020; Douek 2020; S. Levy 2020; Swisher 2020; Vaidhyanathan 2020). But one thing is for certain, if members of the Board lack the virtues of testimonial justice and hermeneutical justice, biased decisions are likely to occur. Thus, it is not the moderators alone who need to cultivate the virtues of testimonial justice and hermeneutical justice; everyone in the process needs these virtues.

To complicate the analysis further, we can draw on the debate between Fricker and Medina about whether hermeneutical injustice is an agential or structural injustice (Fricker 2007, 2016; Medina 2012, 2013, 2017). In her original account of hermeneutical injustice, Fricker argues that it is a purely structural injustice, rather than a harm perpetrated by an agent who can be held responsible (Fricker 2007, 159). As Medina describes her position, "hermeneutical injustices are epistemic wrongs that simply happen, without perpetrators, without being committed by anyone in particular, for they result from lacunas or limitations in 'the collective hermeneutical resource' of a culture" (Medina 2017, 42). In contrast, Medina has argued that both individuals and entire cultures can be held responsible for hermeneutical neglect (Medina 2012, 2013, 2017). Medina calls on Fricker to recognize the multiplicity of social groups and cultures of meaning. He argues against a "monolithic conception of culture and its shared hermeneutical resources" and calls into question "blanket statements about the *impossibility* of expressing, understanding, or interpreting an experience, a problem, an identity, etc." (Medina 2017, 43). Drawing on Pohlhaus's account of willful hermeneutical ignorance, he argues that individuals can be held responsible for their failures to become familiar with the cultures of meaning of marginalized groups (cf. Mason 2011; Dotson 2012; Pohlhaus Jr. 2012). Fricker has responded to these criticisms by largely accepting the multiplicity of groups and cultures of meaning, although she still finds it useful to talk of a broadly shared 'collective hermeneutical resource' (Fricker 2016).

A sophisticated account of hermeneutical injustice on social media platforms calls for a combination of both structural and agential analysis.

There are policies at social media companies (contained in their moderation handbooks and training manuals) that structure the interpretive work of moderators. In order to know whether a post on Facebook, for example, is hate speech, a moderator needs to know Facebook's definition of hate speech and be familiar with the examples used to train moderators. Thus, in one sense, hermeneutical injustices can be caused structurally in Facebook moderation due to the lacunas and faulty tools of Facebook's 'collective hermeneutical resource.' In this sense, it is wrong to assign full responsibility for hermeneutical failures to the moderators. Instead, they are operating in a flawed interpretive culture.

Additionally, a structural problem facing moderation at the large social media companies is the lack of input that citizens have on the policies and moderation decisions made by Facebook, Twitter, YouTube, and other social media platforms. David Kaye, law professor and United Nations Special Rapporteur on the promotion and protection of the right to freedom of opinion and expression, was invited to attend one of Facebook's Content Policy Forum sessions, which is one of the joint meetings in which the employees responsible for speech policy meet. He describes the session as "impressive" and notes that the Facebook policymakers took their work seriously, but he also writes that no matter how impressive the meeting was, "that cannot obscure the reality of the legislative role they play for billions of users, who themselves lack input into rule development" (Kaye 2019, 58). The structure of Facebook's team at that time did not include local engagement by citizens who can identify problems with Facebook's hermeneutical resources. Jillian York's impressive account of global moderation problems in *Silicon Values: The Future of Free Speech under Surveillance Capitalism* is brimming with examples of activists around the world who had to resort to extreme lengths to get the attention of Facebook and other social media platforms when the companies' policies disrupted their work (York 2021). These internet studies scholars reveal a serious structural problem—it matters who is at the table, not just what decisions are being made by those already at the table. So a structural analysis is necessary for understanding hermeneutical injustice in social media moderation.

But there are also agents involved and agential responsibilities to assign. First, the Facebook policies did not "simply happen"; they were created by policymakers and lawyers at the company. Those agents bear some responsibility for the limitations of the interpretive resources provided to moderators. Second, while the Facebook policies structure the decisions made by moderators, no set of corporate policies can completely determine the meaning of online speech; moderators will often have to bring their own interpretive resources to the table in order to apply the policies to particular cases. Thus, they can be held responsible for willful hermeneutical ignorance when their own lack of familiarity with the available epistemic resources of marginalized communities leads them to interpret Facebook policies in ways that misunderstand the speech of marginalized users.

Thus, I argue that the virtue epistemology framework I have presented here can be defended from this objection. When we expand our analysis to include all the agents involved in the moderation process, and when we recognize both the structural and agential features of epistemic injustice in online spaces, this account no longer appears overly individualistic or focused on only one level of analysis.

2.6. Commercial Content Moderation, Epistemic Exploitation, and Epistemic Dumping

In this section, I argue that the labor model of CCM is not only epistemically flawed because it prevents the workers from developing epistemic virtues necessary for reliable and just moderation (as argued in section 2.5), but it is also exploitative in ways that inflict profound epistemic injustices on the workers who perform this labor. Recall the description from the beginning of the chapter of the effect moderation work had on Henry Soto, who is one of two Microsoft employees who sued the company after they developed posttraumatic stress disorder (PTSD) doing moderation work:

> Each day, Soto looked at thousands of disturbing images and videos, which included depictions of killings and child abuse. Particularly traumatic was a video of a girl being sexually abused and then murdered. The work took a heavy toll. He developed symptoms of P.T.S.D., including insomnia, nightmares, anxiety, and auditory hallucinations. He began to have trouble spending time around his son, because it triggered traumatic memories. In February, 2015, he went on medical leave. (Chen 2017a)

The everyday exposure to traumatizing material affects many CCM workers, including those Adrian Chen interviewed who work in the Philippines:

Every day they see proof of the infinite variety of human depravity. They begin to suspect the worst of people they meet in real life, wondering what secrets their hard drives might hold. Two of Maria's female coworkers have become so suspicious that they no longer leave their children with babysitters. They sometimes miss work because they can't find someone they trust to take care of their kids. (Chen 2014)

As another worker who removes terrorist material for a social media company recounts, "There was literally nothing enjoyable about the job. You'd go into work at 9am every morning, turn on your computer and watch someone have their head cut off. Every day, every minute, that's what you see. Heads being cut off" (qtd. in Solon 2017). Not only does this work have psychological costs, but it is routinely poorly compensated. For example, one worker, who earns roughly $15 per hour, says, "We were underpaid and undervalued" (qtd. in Solon 2017). Global pay inequalities also affect this labor model, as Chen describes:

[M]oderators in the Philippines can be hired for a fraction of American wages. Ryan Cardeno, a former contractor for Microsoft in the Philippines, told me that he made $500 per month by the end of his three-and-a-half-year tenure with outsourcing firm Sykes. Last year, Cardeno was offered $312 per month by another firm to moderate content for Facebook, paltry even by industry standards. (Chen 2014)

Given just the brief glimpse into the working lives of CCM moderators that I have provided in this chapter so far, I think we can intuitively recognize that it is an unjust set of labor practices for this significant epistemic work. CCM workers are "toiling largely in the shadows"; the social media companies that profit from their labor resist transparency about their working conditions (S. T. Roberts 2018). Exposed to disturbing content that can cause serious psychological harm, CCM workers are poorly compensated, and often poorly supported by their employers. In this section, I draw on the epistemic injustice literature and Ruth Sample's work on exploitation to provide a more detailed account of this intuitive epistemic exploitation involved in CCM. Having this detailed account of epistemic exploitation on the table enables us to see more clearly the contours and causes of the epistemic injustice involved in CCM, and it helps us understand precisely why this epistemic exploitation is wrong. It also suggests some practical solutions for a more just labor model for the moderation work that shapes our online epistemic landscape.

Pohlhaus identifies three categories of epistemic injustice related to epistemic labor and knowledge production: "*epistemic agential injustices*, those that directly and unfairly thwart epistemic labor; *epistemic labor invalidation*, those that disregard or systematically fail to acknowledge the epistemic labor of some; and *epistemic labor exploitation*, those that unjustly exploit epistemic labor" (Pohlhaus Jr. 2017, 21). Some of the problems I have already identified with the labor model of CCM fall under the category of epistemic agential injustices, since the labor model prevents CCM workers from developing and sustaining the epistemic virtues necessary to avoid testimonial injustice and hermeneutical ignorance. However, I will not develop that point here. Instead, I will focus on epistemic labor exploitation and, to a lesser extent, epistemic labor invalidation.

For Pohlhaus, epistemic exploitation takes place when "epistemic labor is coercively extracted from epistemic agents in the service of others" (Pohlhaus Jr. 2017, 22). Two of her main illustrations of epistemic exploitation are Rachel McKinney's account of extracted speech in which agents are coerced into providing testimony that may damage the testifier (McKinney 2016), and Nora Berenstain's account of epistemic exploitation as a type of epistemic oppression occurring "when privileged persons compel marginalized persons to produce an education or explanation about the nature of the oppression they face" (Berenstain 2016, 570). Both of these are useful additions to the epistemic injustice literature and highlight important forms of exploitation of the labor of marginalized subjects. However, I am not sure that Pohlhaus's gloss on epistemic exploitation as inherently coercive is the most useful framing of issues of epistemic exploitation, since often epistemic agents choose to provide the labor involved. Of course, specifying under what conditions agents' choices are constrained and manipulated in ways that make the situation coercive is a large and thorny question, one that it outside the scope of this chapter. Partially to avoid this question, and also because I find the account useful in other ways, I instead draw on Ruth Sample's account of exploitation in general, since coercion is not the central feature of exploitation on her approach.

Sample defines exploitation as "interacting with another being for the sake of advantage in a way that fails to respect the inherent value in that being" (Sample 2003, 57). The idea is that "human beings possess a value that makes a claim on us. In exploitation, we fail to honor this value in our effort to improve our own situation" (Sample 2003, 57). We can do this in three ways: "First, we can fail to respect a person by neglecting what is necessary for that person's well-being or flourishing. Second, we can fail to respect a person by taking advantage of an injustice done to him. Third, we can fail to respect a person by commodifying, or treating as a fungible object of market exchange, an aspect of that person's being that ought not to be commodified" (Sample 2003, 57). Although I suspect there may be ways of cashing out the nature of the exploitation faced by CCM workers according to all of these forms of exploitation, I will focus on the first.[6] Sample argues that interacting with someone for the sake of advantage in a way that neglects what is necessary for that person's well-being is exploitative. To avoid exploiting someone, we must "take their needs into account" (Sample 2003, 81). This is what has failed to happen in the development of the labor model of CCM; moderators have basic human needs that have not been taken into account. Thus, they have been treated with disrespect.

What kind of human needs does CCM neglect? Sample draws on Nussbaum's capabilities approach to flesh out a relevant notion of human well-being and flourishing, and I will argue that Nussbaum's approach highlights two important neglected needs in CCM. Nussbaum's capabilities approach to social justice provides an account of the basic activities or functions characteristically performed by humans, which all just societies ought to provide to their citizens. Without the availability of these functions, a human life is not fully human (Nussbaum 1999, 39). Thus, this list of capabilities provides Sample an account of the basic human needs which, if not respected, can create an exploitative relationship with someone. Nussbaum's list of capabilities includes (1) life; (2) bodily health; (3) bodily integrity; (4) sense, imagination, thought; (5) emotions; (6) practical reason; (7) affiliation; (8) other species; (9) play; and (10) control over

---

[6] Sample's second cause of exploitation, in which we take advantage of an injustice done to the other, seems to be at play in CCM because it is no accident that historically marginalized workers who are more economically vulnerable (e.g., women, people of color, workers from the Global South) are disproportionately represented in the low-paying CCM workforce (cf. Noble 2017; Gray and Suri 2019, 58; York 2021, 19). Thus, social media companies are benefiting from past injustices and being able to pay those workers less due to historical discrimination. As Sample notes, "[W]e can exploit persons by taking advantage of injustice, even when their threshold capabilities are met. If a person is in a weaker bargaining position because of past injustice, we stand to gain disproportionately in virtue of that injustice.... Thus historically whites have been able to pay blacks less money and men have been able to pay women less money for the same work because of a history of racial and sexual discrimination, respectively" (Sample 2003, 82).

one's environment (Nussbaum 1999, 41–42). The capabilities most relevant for assessing CCM are emotions and affiliation:

> *Emotions.* Being able to have attachments to things and persons outside ourselves; being able to love those who love and care for us; being able to grieve at their absence; in general, being able to love, to grieve, to experience longing, gratitude, and justified anger; not having one's emotional developing blighted by fear or anxiety . . .
>
> *Affiliation.* (a) Being able to live for and in relation to others, to recognize and show concern for other human beings, to engage in various forms of social interaction; being able to imagine the situation of another and to have compassion for that situation; having the capability for both justice and friendship. . . . (b) Having the social bases of self-respect and nonhumiliation; being able to be treated as a dignified being whose worth is equal to that of others. (Nussbaum 1999, 41)

The intense exposure to images of child sexual exploitation, beheadings, violence, and all the other forms of human cruelty does emotional harm that frequently damages moderators' relationships. Rasalyn Bowden, a former moderator at MySpace, recounts, "When I left MySpace I didn't shake hands for like three years because I figured out that people were disgusting. And I could just not touch people . . . I was disgusted by humanity when I left there" (Bowden 2017). The CCM work interfered with her basic needs for affiliation. She is not alone. Damage to relationships is a common theme in narratives of CCM work as workers struggle to talk to their friends and family about the violence and cruelty they view on a daily basis (Chen 2014, 2017a; S. T. Roberts 2014, 122–26). Recall that Henry Soto had "trouble spending time around his son, because it triggered traumatic memories" (Chen 2017a). Thus, CCM work damages relationships, thereby undermining Nussbaum's capability of affiliation, and the emotional trauma of PTSD reported by CCM workers and the emotionally desensitizing nature of the work interfere with the capability of emotion.

Why should we call this damage to CCM workers exploitative? Because the harm is being done by a system of employment set up by social media companies to generate profit without taking into account these workers' basic human functions. Sample defines an exploitative system as "one in which exploitative interactions are systematically favored and promoted" (Sample 2003, 61). Exploitation can be accepted as normal and can be unrecognized by agents who set up, maintain, and participate in exploitative systems. Thus, the fact that the labor conditions of CCM workers have been accepted as normal business practice at social media companies, and the fact that many executives involved in setting up this labor model may not have intended to exploit or harm the CCM workers, does not negate the exploitative nature of the system. Nor does the fact that many CCM workers freely choose this work and may in fact financially benefit from it (cf. Sample 2003, 61–62). They may have no better alternatives. Nonetheless, the fact that the social media companies profit from this labor system that shows lack of respect for their basic well-being makes it a labor system that shows disrespect for the workers.

What would make the labor model of CCM less exploitative? While many improvements could be made, I focus on three improvements that moderators and advocates have identified. First, let's consider better compensation. Social media companies have made the choice to pay low wages for moderation work and often subcontract out the work so that employees frequently do not receive health insurance and other benefits (S. T. Roberts 2014, 2019). Workers who perform CCM via Amazon Mechanical Turk can receive as little as 2 cents per task for labor that involves viewing disturbing content (LaPlante 2017). Pay on Mechanical Turk is generally low; one study found that "workers earned a median hourly wage of only ~$2/h, and only 4% earned more than $7.25/h" (Hara et al. 2017). In another example of the exploitative nature of moderation work on Mechanical Turk, Rochelle LaPlante describes moderation jobs that specifically direct workers how to categorize potentially harmful content (LaPlante 2017). In some cases these directions ask workers to label content as permissible or problematic and direct the worker that if they are not sure how to categorize the material to skip the task. But if a worker skips a task, then they are not paid for it. This is exploitative because the moderator has already performed the labor of looking at the potentially traumatizing material (e.g., a photo), but they are not compensated at all. This system shows no respect for the potential damage done to the worker who viewed the content and no respect for their epistemic agency in recognizing and reporting uncertainty about the nature of the material. The low pay of CCM is one of the features that makes it most exploitative; as Sample says, "If an employer fails to compensate an employee in a way that provides her with adequate income when such compensation is possible, then the relationship is exploitative" (Sample 2003, 81).[7]

A second way to reduce the exploitation in CCM work is to provide easy access to counseling to help moderators deal with the psychological costs of the work. This second improvement is related to the first, especially in countries like the United States where health insurance is tied to employers; the work would be much less exploitative if CCM workers were given health insurance that gave them access to mental health counseling that would meet their basic needs of emotional health and relational affiliation. Moderators using Amazon Mechanical Turk have no employer-provided medical insurance and no employer-provided counseling (LaPlante 2017). Moderators who do subcontracted work for social media companies are often not provided with health insurance, but are sometimes given access to counselors. However, how to access such counseling may not be clearly explained to workers, or they may fear losing their jobs if they seek help from company counselors (S. T. Roberts 2014, 124; 2019, 119; Solon 2017; Newton 2019a). Facebook, in particular, has been criticized for failing to take steps, such as intensive screening and training of new employees and mandatory counseling for moderators, adopted by other organizations such as Reddit and the National Center for Missing and Exploited Children (Solon 2017). In 2020, Facebook settled a class action lawsuit covering 11,250 current and former moderators in which the company agreed to pay $52 million to compensate the workers for mental health complications as a result of the work (Newton 2020). In the agreement, Facebook also committed to providing weekly counseling for its moderators. This is a small step in the right direction. In sum, ensuring that CCM workers have adequate mental health counseling is a second important way that social media companies can decrease the exploitative nature of the work.

A third way to reduce the exploitation of moderation work is of particular interest to epistemologists: bring CCM labor out of the shadows (S. T. Roberts 2018, 2019). As I briefly mentioned earlier, social media companies have shrouded CCM in secrecy through the use of nondisclosure agreements and moving work offshore from the countries in

---

[7] Some small progress was made toward less exploitative labor at Facebook in May 2019 when the company announced a pay increase to at least $18 per hour in North America for contractors, including moderators (Newton 2019b). However, this also shows the exploitative nature of the moderation model at Facebook because more adequate compensation was possible for Facebook previously, but it was not provided.

which the companies are based. Roberts describes platforms as operating under a "logic of opacity":

> [Platforms] are extremely reluctant to acknowledge, much less describe in great detail the internal policies and practices that govern what goes into the content ultimately available on a mainstream site.... Even when platforms do acknowledge their moderation practices and the human workforce that undertakes them, they still are loath to give details about who does the work, where in the world they do it, under what conditions and whom the moderation activity is intended to benefit. (S. T. Roberts 2018)

For philosophers, Roberts's "logic of opacity" will be reminiscent of an epistemology of ignorance, a set of practices that actively construct, produce, and preserve non-knowing (cf. Tuana 2004). Social media companies have worked to ensure that the public does not know or understand their moderation policies, practices, and labor conditions.[8] I argue that this epistemology of ignorance makes the work of CCM more exploitative and also contributes to epistemic invalidation, in Pohlhaus's sense. One of the reasons why CCM workers suffer psychologically, and their basic needs for emotions and affiliation are unmet, is because they find it difficult to explain their work to those around them. The general lack of knowledge and understanding of CCM makes these conversations difficult (if not impossible) for moderators, increasing their feelings of isolation (S. T. Roberts 2019, 210–11). As Roberts puts it,

> [C]ontent moderators are frequently required to sign non-disclosure agreements (NDAs) about the nature of their work in which they pledge to not reveal the particulars of their employment or job duties. This secrecy has many implications, but certainly the well-being of the workers, who contend with abhorrent material as a precondition of their continued employment, must be in question under policies that disallow them from speaking to anyone else about what they do and see, even when they do so for support. (S. T. Roberts 2016)

Additionally, lack of public familiarity leads people to ask moderators questions such as "What's wrong with you that you can do this type of

---

[8] This changed to some degree in 2018, as Facebook and YouTube released transparency reports (Gillespie 2018). But at the time of writing this chapter, there is still much that is hidden from view.

work?," a question which Mechanical Turk moderator and advocate Rochelle LaPlante reports making her feel like "a deer in the headlights" (LaPlante 2017).[9] Another aspect of the epistemology of ignorance surrounding CCM is that moderators have been denied gratitude and accolades for the difficult, skilled work they do to protect our epistemic spaces (S. T. Roberts 2017c). In a 2017 panel discussion at the *All Things in Moderation* interdisciplinary conference on moderation at UCLA, two moderators expressed how conscious they are of how their incredibly difficult and personally costly work protects the rest of us from an internet full of beheadings, child sexual exploitation, hate speech, and other upsetting content. These two moderators were keenly aware they are that they are not thanked or appreciated for this work, and several moderators in the audience demonstrated similar feelings (Bowden 2017; LaPlante 2017). This, I argue, is an example of Pohlhaus's 'epistemic labor invalidation' in which the epistemic labor of some people is disregarded or systematically not acknowledged (Pohlhaus Jr. 2017, 21). This invalidation also contributes to the epistemic exploitation of CCM workers, contributing to their psychological damage and unmet needs. As Naheed Sheikh, co-founder of the consulting company the Workplace Wellness Project, says, "You can get burnt out like with any field that draws on your emotional resources ... Particularly if the labor is not appreciated or rewarded" (qtd. in Solon 2017). Thus, bringing CCM work out of the shadows and helping the public understand and appreciate this work would make it more just because it would enable CCM workers to talk more openly about their work and gain the validation they deserve.

Reflecting on the particular type of epistemic exploitation found in CCM suggests that the following concept may be a useful addition to the lexicon of epistemic injustice: *epistemic dumping*. I tentatively define 'epistemic dumping' as a form of epistemic injustice in which the labor of sorting, handling, and disposing of the toxic epistemic trash of epistemic communities is disproportionately performed by some (typically traditionally oppressed) groups, while other (typically traditionally dominant) groups

---

[9] Rochelle LaPlante pointed out to me that this interaction between moderators and the public can also be seen as a reflection of the resiliency that some moderators display while doing this work (LaPlante, personal communication, November 17, 2018). While many of us imagine that we could never do this work of viewing so much disturbing content, some (but certainly not all) moderators are able to view this content with some resiliency. Perhaps if CCM were brought out of the shadows, then we might be able to learn more about what enables some moderators to do this work without experiencing the trauma that others suffer. I am grateful to LaPlante for her comments on a previous draft of this chapter.

benefit from this labor though usually being oblivious to its performance or dismissive of the epistemic labor involved in handling the trash. I propose this term because I have found it useful to analyze the injustice of the epistemic labor performed by CCM moderators through the metaphor of garbage provided by Roberts and Sarah Jeong. Roberts uses the language of "digital detritus" and "digital refuse" to refer to the harmful online content which moderators are charged with handling. In "Digital Refuse: Canadian Garbage, Commercial Content Moderation and the Global Circulation of Social Media's Waste," she draws an analogy between the illegal dumping of Canadian garbage (including dirty adult diapers) in the Philippines and the fact that much digital detritus is also transported to the Philippines where it is handled by CCM workers (S. T. Roberts 2016). Roberts draws important connections between the neocolonial practices of dumping physical garbage and the dumping of digital detritus on communities in the Global South. Jeong also uses the metaphor of garbage, using it to refer to "undesirable content" ranging from spam to online harassment (Jeong 2015, 11). Jeong's use of the metaphor is useful because it highlights the fact that some types of internet garbage (e.g., spam) have been somewhat successfully tackled, while for other types of garbage (e.g., online harassment) "the garbage disposal has broken down" (Jeong 2015, 8). Jeong's use of the trash metaphor directs us to ask whose interests are protected by the various garbage disposal mechanisms implemented in online spaces. For example, why was so much attention directed toward dealing with spam, while online harassment festers? I want to explore whether this garbage metaphor may be fruitful for epistemologists.

Epistemic dumping may be a useful concept because online communities are not the only epistemic communities that produce trash; in fact, all epistemic communities produce discarded and unwanted by-products of activities related to knowledge, understanding, and communication. Failed attempts at justification, false beliefs, misunderstandings, and miscommunications are all general types of what we might call 'epistemic trash.' Consider two examples of epistemic trash. (1) In a class discussion, students latch onto an example that they mistakenly believe illustrates the author's key claim; this false belief and misinterpretation keeps reappearing in discussion of the text, causing students to draw other faulty conclusions about the author's argument. The professor keeps working to disabuse them of this misinterpretation and eventually convinces them to toss out the example as an unhelpful distraction. (2) A faculty committee tasked with addressing a campus problem convinces themselves that a particular solution would never be accepted by the Board of Trustees, so they have several meetings in which they never look into the merits of that solution. At a later meeting, a committee member reports that the Board has been open to this suggestion all along; once they throw out the false assumption, the committee investigates the advantages of this solution. These are just two examples of unwanted epistemic trash that was usefully discarded.

I propose the following definition of 'epistemic trash':

Epistemic trash: x is epistemic trash for member(s) m of an epistemic community c iff:
  (1) x is an epistemic product of human epistemic activity.
  (2) x is useless for (or contrary to) m's epistemic interests and goals, and
  (3) due to (2), m wishes (or ought to wish) to remove x from circulation in c.

This definition captures several features of epistemic trash that I want to highlight. Let us start with the third criterion. With this condition, the definition emphasizes that trash is something to be discarded and removed from one's space; in this case, one's epistemic community. Next, the first condition distinguishes *epistemic* trash from other types of trash that should be discarded. Epistemic trash is an epistemic product. The idea here is that many of our activities have epistemic consequences; they generate beliefs, understandings, and so on. With the concept of epistemic trash, I want to capture the kinds of trash that are particularly interesting to epistemologists, and I want a concept that helps us focus on the epistemic features of unwanted items in circulation in a community. In contrast, one might argue that some online videos should be removed because they incite violence or violate the law in other ways. These videos might accurately be described as trash, but in emphasizing their incendiary or illegal nature, one would not be describing them as *epistemic* trash, but rather moral or legal trash. Additionally, I rely here on a distinction between a properly epistemic product of a practice and a non-epistemic product that nonetheless has 'secondary' epistemic effects. For example, an epistemic practice such as conducting an experiment might consume much of our grant funding. The scarce resources for more inquiry are a by-product of the epistemic practice of the experiment, but it would not be a properly epistemic product of the practice. One might cash out this distinction by forming a list of primary epistemic goods (e.g., knowledge, true belief, justified beliefs, understandings) and define things that directly increase or decrease the primary epistemic goods as properly epistemic products. In contrast, things that increase or decrease the primary epistemic goods only mediately (e.g., money, resources, time) are not properly epistemic products.

A further point to emphasize about this definition is that epistemic trash is interest relative: "one person's trash is another person's treasure" is a rough slogan here. Whether or not something is deemed useless or unproductive may not be the same for everyone in the community, because the judgment is made relative to one's epistemic goals. Some false beliefs may be valuable in certain contexts, and we may not want to discard them—or some members may have an interest in discarding them, while others have an interest in studying what others deem trash. For example, the false beliefs of past discarded scientific theories may be unwanted epistemic trash to contemporary scientists seeking to understand the world, but those same beliefs may be valuable epistemic treasure to historians of science (*qua* historians) seeking to understand the work of past scientists.[10] Moreover, consider what is happening when the students mistakenly believe an example illustrates an author's argument. The example they have latched upon is epistemic trash relative to the professor's goals of having the students understand the argument, but it could be epistemic treasure for the member of the Center for Teaching and Learning who is observing the class and whose goals are to understand how students make mistakes. This interest relativity of epistemic trash is one of the many reasons why moderation decisions are so fraught.

Importantly, some types of epistemic trash are more toxic than others; for example, the false beliefs of white ignorance, the misunderstandings of willful hermeneutical ignorance, and the damaging communication of hate speech are particularly toxic forms of epistemic trash. False beliefs, such as those embodying pernicious stereotypes, actively harm members of epistemic communities, causing such problems as stereotype threat and internalized oppression. These false beliefs are toxic epistemic trash. As a

---

[10] The historians (*qua* historians) may find the false theories useful for the goal of understanding science. However, as members of the general epistemic community, they have an interest in scientific literacy in the general public; so *qua* general epistemic agents, those same individuals can consider the false theories to be epistemic trash.

concrete example of toxic epistemic trash, consider the damage done to discussions of police brutality by the willful hermeneutical ignorance of misunderstanding the phrase "Black Lives Matter" as intended to mean "Only Black Lives Matter." This misinterpretation lurks around discussions of the issue (cf. L. Anderson 2017). Conversations about police brutality are frequently derailed by people in the grips of this misinterpretation who insist on "All Lives Matter" as an alternative. What epistemic communities discussing police brutality need is for this willful hermeneutical ignorance to be discarded as the toxic trash that it is. I define 'toxic epistemic trash' as follows:

Toxic epistemic trash: x is toxic epistemic trash for member(s) m in epistemic community c iff:
(1) x is epistemic trash for m, and
(2) x tends to cause practical or moral harm to some members of c; the more harm x causes, the more toxic x is.

The idea here is that some epistemic trash is trivial or harmless, while other epistemic trash does practical or moral harm to members of the epistemic community. Note that judgments about whether something is toxic epistemic trash will inherit some interest relativity, due to the interest relativity of epistemic trash. For example, racist, false conspiracy theories spreading through social media may be toxic epistemic trash that a community has an interest in discarding, because it decreases the veritistic value of the beliefs circulating in the community, while some sociologists (*qua* sociologists) may find that the unjustified claims provide a useful case study of online radicalization.

These concepts of 'epistemic trash' and 'toxic epistemic trash' are useful, especially in light of this chapter's analysis of the labor model of CCM. With this analysis in mind, many important questions of interest to both epistemologists and ethicists can be asked about the labor of handling epistemic trash: Who sorts and disposes it? How is that labor organized and compensated? Who benefits from the labor of disposal, and who is harmed by it? What kinds of harms does one suffer from handling toxic epistemic trash? Who is aware of the existence of epistemic trash? Who willfully ignores epistemic trash in their community? How do structures of social privilege or economic advantage shape who is aware of epistemic trash and who is blissfully ignorant of the trash? When is an epistemology of ignorance at play in hiding the fact of epistemic dumping and/or the nature of the labor involved in handling epistemic trash?

With these concepts in hand, we can identify a new form of epistemic injustice that will be of particular interest to epistemologists. This is 'epistemic dumping,' which, as I briefly mentioned earlier, I define as follows:

> *Epistemic dumping*: a form of epistemic injustice in which the labor of sorting, handling, and disposing of the toxic epistemic trash of epistemic communities is disproportionately performed by some (typically traditionally oppressed) groups, while other (typically traditionally dominant) groups benefit from this labor though usually being oblivious to its performance or dismissive of the epistemic labor involved in handling the trash.

The labor model of social media moderation is a clear case of epistemic dumping in which the toxic epistemic trash of online communities is dumped on CCM workers, but there are other examples of epistemic dumping that may be more familiar to academics. To illustrate the utility of these concepts of epistemic trash and epistemic dumping beyond CCM, consider the connections between the epistemic labor of CCM workers and the 'invisible labor' of faculty from marginalized groups. Just as the task of tidying up the hate speech of online platforms falls to CCM workers, the task of handling the aftermath of an act of hate speech at an on-campus lecture often falls to marginalized faculty. It is often faculty of color who are called upon to deal with the fallout when their white colleagues teach racist material. Homophobic or transphobic speech acts in classrooms are often brought to the attention of queer and trans faculty. In all these examples, toxic epistemic trash is disproportionately brought to marginalized faculty members. Just as much of the public remains blissfully unaware of the racist conspiracy theories, anti-vaxxer misinformation, and hate speech submitted to online platforms due to the labor of CCM workers, many faculty from dominant groups remain blissfully unaware of the hate speech and other epistemic trash that their colleagues from marginalized groups are handling. Sometimes this labor is funneled through exploitative institutional structures which call upon marginalized faculty to sit on committees or serve in administrative "diversity work" positions (cf. Bird, Litt, and Wang 2004; Fehr 2011; Joseph and Hirshfield 2011; Ahmed 2012; June 2015; Toole 2019). Other times, such as when institutions neglect to handle these issues, marginalized faculty pick up this labor themselves in informal groups or alone. In a final point of connection between the worlds of CCM and faculty labor, epistemic dumping on campus can be similarly exploitative in its pay structure and other harms, because it creates additional uncompensated labor that can undermine the well-being of marginalized faculty members, subjecting them to vicarious trauma and burnout. As Carla Fehr argues, academic institutions often act as "diversity free riders," by relying on the diverse perspectives of members of marginalized groups without actually adequately rewarding their epistemic labor and without increasing the total number of marginalized people in the community (Fehr 2011).

This invisible labor of dealing with epistemic trash has clear connections to other forms of epistemic injustice. For example, in the process of handling campus hate speech, marginalized faculty members are often called upon to educate members of dominant groups about the kinds of oppression faced by marginalized faculty and students; this is epistemic exploitation in Norah Berenstain's sense (Berenstain 2016). However, not all of the work involved in handling epistemic trash is education of privileged people, so the concept of epistemic dumping is broader than Berenstain's account of epistemic exploitation. Additionally, marginalized faculty are often called upon to do this work because they are granted token status and subject to prejudicial credibility excess, as discussed by Emmalon Davis (E. Davis 2016). But often marginalized people battle against credibility deficits when they try to handle toxic epistemic trash, so again the concept of epistemic dumping is broader than Davis's account.

I want to be clear that I do not include all of the additional, unrecognized, and uncompensated labor performed by marginalized faculty under the heading of 'epistemic trash.' For example, mentoring students from underrepresented groups is also often invisible labor performed by marginalized faculty, but I do not want to attach this negative label to that mentoring work. Instead, I want to draw attention to the ways in which the toxic by-products of epistemic communities (often produced by members of dominant groups) are disproportionately handled by members of marginalized communities in ways that are often exploitative. Additionally, I want to highlight the fact that much of the labor of dealing with epistemic trash is skilled epistemic labor, involving epistemic expertise, virtues, and talents. Often the labor of marginalized faculty members is described as "emotional labor" (Shayne 2017). Emotional skills and emotional efforts are certainly important parts of the labor of dealing with toxic epistemic trash in higher education, but simply labeling it as emotional labor may underestimate the full scope of the skills involved.

In what sense is epistemic dumping an *epistemic* injustice instead of a moral injustice? There is some disagreement among scholars in the epistemic injustice field about how narrowly to draw the boundaries of epistemic injustice as a concept. Some want to maintain a narrow use of the term, closer to what Fricker originally outlined, in order to focus on the particular phenomenon of people being disrespected in their capacities as knowers (Fricker 2007). Others see value in a broader use of the term. For example, in their introduction to the *Routledge Handbook of Epistemic Injustice*, Kidd, Medina, and Pohlhaus define 'epistemic injustice' broadly as "those forms of unfair treatment that relate to issues of knowledge, understanding, and participation in communicative practices" (Kidd, Medina, and Pohlhaus Jr. 2017a, 1). On this broader use, the discriminatory dumping of toxic trash relating to knowledge, understanding, and communication on certain groups seems to be a type of epistemic injustice. It seems unfair as a kind of distributive injustice relating to epistemic goods and unfair distribution of harms.[11] Epistemic dumping is a kind of *epistemic* injustice in this broader sense for two reasons: (1) it involves particularly epistemic objects, that is, the trash relating to knowledge, understanding, and participation in communicative practices, and (2) dealing with dumped epistemic trash involves a great deal of epistemic labor, for example, knowing when hate speech has occurred, understanding the meaning of marginalized people's reactions to hate speech, and participating in marginalized communities and being familiar with their communicative practices. As we have seen, many epistemic virtues are necessary for the proper sorting, handling, and disposing of epistemic trash. Thus, when epistemic trash is dumped on certain groups, it constitutes a particularly epistemic kind of injustice.

For those who wish to reserve the term 'epistemic injustice' for a narrower class of harms in which people are disrespected in their capacities as knowers, I think many (if not all) cases of epistemic dumping will count

---

[11] In her original account of testimonial injustice, Fricker argued that testimonial injustice is not a form of distributive injustice, but rather a distinctly epistemic type of injustice (Fricker 2007, 19–20). However, David Coady has argued that Fricker's accounts of testimonial injustice and hermeneutical injustice are, in fact, accounts of distributive injustices (Coady 2017). I am not convinced that Fricker's distinction between distributive justice and epistemic injustice can be clearly maintained, nor am I convinced that it benefits the field to engage in this boundary policing of the concept of epistemic injustice. Nonetheless, the field appears to disagree about how broadly to define this concept; thus, I offer multiple interpretations of epistemic dumping that I think will appeal to each camp.

as epistemic injustices in this narrower sense as well. In all the cases of epistemic dumping that I have in mind, the epistemic skills involved in dealing with toxic epistemic trash are not respected, valued, or compensated adequately (a sign of the lack of respect accorded to the work). CCM workers experience this disrespect as their epistemic skills are not valued. Social media companies have chosen to treat their labor as "low-skill" work that can be performed in an assembly-line format, paid poorly, and hidden from sight. Imagine another world in which the difficult work moderators perform was valued as skilled and nuanced and the resilience many moderators develop was heralded as an important moral, epistemic, and emotional skill on which the social media companies and their users depend. Joshua Habgood-Coote has suggested to me that moderators are treated as human computers, rather than as epistemic agents. This is a kind of epistemic objectification that disrespects them as knowers. This human computer analogy concurs with the analysis of Punsmann, the Facebook moderator mentioned earlier. She writes, "The mental operations [of moderation] are evaluated as being too complex for algorithms. Nevertheless moderators are expected to act as a computer. The search for uniformity and standardization, together with the strict productivity metrics, lets not much space for human judgment and intuition" (Punsmann 2018). Consider my other example of epistemic dumping: underrepresented faculty are disrespected in their capacity as knowers when the labor they perform handling toxic epistemic trash is not valued, it is dismissed as mere emotional labor, and it is not valued in tenure and promotion (cf. Bird, Litt, and Wang 2004). Underrepresented faculty are often treated by their peers as somehow more naturally suited to this kind of diversity work rather than the more valued scholarly work for which faculty from dominant groups have more time. To be treated by one's dominant peers as less of a scholar and more of guidance counselor or community organizer is often a sign of epistemic disrespect in academia. This is, of course, not to say that the work of guidance counselors or community organizers is inherently less valuable, but instead that traditionally it has not been accorded as much respect in academia relative to the work of scholarly publication. Thus, the dumping of toxic epistemic trash on marginalized faculty is a pervasive form of epistemic injustice, even in this narrower sense.

To summarize this section, I have argued that the labor model of CCM involves serious epistemic injustice. Focusing on epistemic exploitation, I have provided an account of the nature of epistemic exploitation involved as a relationship in which social media companies profit from the labor of CCM workers in ways that show disrespect for the humanity of the workers. CCM workers' basic human needs for emotions and affiliation are undermined by the poor compensation, lack of counseling support, and secrecy of their employers. Reflecting on the utility of the metaphor of garbage disposal for this difficult and exploitative labor, I have suggested the term 'epistemic dumping' to name a kind of epistemic injustice in which some groups are disproportionately charged with the handling of the toxic trash of epistemic communities. I believe this concept illuminates an interesting form of epistemic injustice and also suggests some fruitful points of solidarity between CCM workers and faculty from marginalized groups.

2.7. Algorithms to the Rescue?

Given the problems with bias and epistemic injustice that I have identified in the current labor model of moderation, one might be tempted to turn toward algorithms as a solution. If human moderators are biased in ways that generate problems of testimonial injustice and hermeneutical injustice, perhaps algorithmic moderation could avoid these human failings. And if human moderators are vulnerable to trauma from exposure to digital detritus, wouldn't it be better to spare humans this labor and have algorithms scan disturbing content instead? In this section, I consider whether algorithmic moderation would solve the problems I have discussed in this chapter. I follow several internet studies scholars in arguing that while algorithms can, and do, help mitigate some of these problems, there is a limit to what they can accomplish. Algorithmic moderation has serious limitations, and there are, in fact, reasons to want to keep humans in the loop. Researchers are currently developing proposals for how to best divide moderation between humans and algorithms; so instead of adopting what Evgeny Morozov calls a 'technological solutionism' that simply hopes algorithms will make all the epistemic problems go away, social epistemologists should be part of future discussions about how to best combine human and algorithmic solutions. Technological solutionism is "the idea that given the right code, algorithms and robots, technology can solve all of mankind's problems, effectively making life 'frictionless' and trouble-free" (Tucker 2013).

Algorithms are already significant players in online moderation (cf. Klonick 2018; Gorwa, Binns, and Katzenbach 2020). One disclosure by

YouTube suggests that algorithms play a large role in flagging videos for removal:

> In the three-month period between October and December 2017, 8.2 million videos were removed; 80 percent of those removed were flagged by software, 13 percent by trusted flaggers, and only 4 percent by regular users. Strikingly, 75 percent of the videos removed were gone before they'd been viewed even once, which means they simply could not have been flagged by a user. (Gillespie 2018)

Meanwhile on Twitter, "Between July 2017 and December 2017, a total of 274,460 Twitter accounts were permanently suspended for violations related to promotion of terrorism. Of those suspensions, 93% consisted of accounts flagged by internal, proprietary spam-fighting tools, while 74% of those accounts were suspended before their first tweet" (Global Internet Forum to Counter Terrorism 2019). Artificial intelligence (AI) software that identifies toxic comments has also helped publications like *The New York Times* turn back on comments for some of its articles (Sinders 2018). Social media platforms are increasingly incentivized to use algorithmic moderation as governments implement policies to regulate online speech that require short windows for removal of problematic content (e.g., Germany's NetzDG and the EU Code of Conduct on Hate Speech) (Gorwa, Binns, and Katzenbach 2020, 2). So algorithmic moderation is very much a part of the moderation landscape.

While algorithms can play a useful role in moderation, we should be suspicious of proposals to solve all epistemic problems with algorithmic moderation for the following three reasons. First, algorithms can be, and regularly are, biased (Duarte and Llansó 2017; LaPlante 2017; Noble 2018; Sinders 2018; G. M. Johnson 2021; York 2021). Second, AI technology is not currently at a level where it can reliably take over all moderation (Duarte and Llansó 2017; S. T. Roberts 2017b; Sinders 2018; York 2018; Llansó 2020). Third, algorithms are not ethical agents who can object and resist in ways human moderators can (S. T. Roberts 2018). I address each limitation in turn.

First, algorithms are not neutral, nor do they arrive on the scene without human intervention (cf. Noble 2018). As Caroline Sinders says, "To be clear, societal bias is already baked into machine learning systems. Data and systems are not neutral, and neither is code. Code is written by humans, algorithms are created by humans and products are designed by humans.

Humans are fallible, and humans make mistakes" (Sinders 2018). A move to algorithmic moderation just pushes the problems of bias to a different level. Instead of looking for bias in the actions of individual moderators (and platform policymakers) as the source of testimonial injustice and hermeneutical injustice, we need to investigate the design choices of engineers and the process that trains the algorithms on relevant data sets (cf. York 2021). Let's focus on the process of training algorithms. Biased input into an algorithm will generate a biased algorithm. For example, describing biased machine learning in predictive policing software designed to analyze gang activity, Sinders makes the point that the police department data used as input "is an example of the pre-existing bias in society, but when fed to an algorithm, the data actively reinforces this bias. The system itself becomes an ouroboros of dangerous data, and an ethical failure" (Sinders 2018). The image of the ouroboros is useful here. We cannot hope for algorithms to erase the problems of testimonial injustice and hermeneutical injustice in moderation if those problems exist in the data set on which the algorithm is trained. Consider one scenario in which these problems could creep into the data set. A social media company uses Mechanical Turk workers to generate the data set that will be used to train its moderation algorithm. Mechanical Turk workers are provided with examples of text and asked to label it as hate speech or not based on the platform's policies. If these workers lack the virtues of testimonial justice or hermeneutical justice, then the data set may be biased and the resulting algorithm will function to remove content in a biased manner. This is not simply a hypothetical concern. In 2019, Sap et al. found that two data sets of tweets widely used to train hate speech detection algorithms show strong correlations between a tweet containing African American vernacular English and that tweet's being labeled as toxic (Sap et al. 2019). Both data sets were created by researchers asking workers on a crowdsourcing platform to identify the toxic speech. Sap et al. showed how this bias in the initial training data percolated through the process of the creation of hate speech detection algorithms, resulting in the tweets of African Americans being more likely to be categorized as offensive (Sap et al. 2019, 1668). Thus, the issues of bias I discussed earlier cannot be eliminated simply through a move to algorithmic moderation—at some point, virtues of testimonial justice and hermeneutical justice will need to be cultivated by agents involved in the process, and the problems with human bias must be addressed.

In addition, problems related to the exploitative labor model of CCM reappear with this kind of training process as well. If moderation algorithms are trained on data sets created by workers on Mechanical Turk who are being paid as low as 2 cents per task, one might have concerns about the quality of the data set being created (LaPlante 2017). This poor compensation model creates perverse incentives for workers to rush through the tasks and not put in the time and careful epistemic labor necessary to avoid testimonial injustice and hermeneutical injustice. Similarly, the problems of epistemic exploitation reappear if we consider the psychological damage potentially done to those workers who view the content necessary for creating the data set. Thus, algorithmic moderation is limited in its ability to erase problems of bias and epistemic injustice.

A second reason to be skeptical of calls for pure algorithmic moderation is that we are a long way away from algorithms that can do this work well. Roberts summarizes:

> While some low-level tasks can be automated (imperfectly) by processes such as matching against known databases of unwanted content, facial recognition, and "skin filters," which screen photos or videos for flesh tones and then flag them as pornography, much content (particularly user-generated video) is too complex for the field of "computer vision"—the ability for machines to recognize and identify images. (S. T. Roberts 2017b)

Things are not much better when it comes to understanding text-based communication. A 2017 report by the Electronic Frontier Foundation found that "While AI algorithms can understand very simple reading comprehension problems, they still struggle with even basic tasks such as capturing meaning in children's books. And while it's possible that future improvements to machine learning algorithms will give AI these capabilities, we're not there yet" (Cope, York, and Gillula 2017; Eckersley and Nasser n.d.). One of the reasons for this is that context matters so much for understanding the meaning of human communication, which is often highly ambiguous (Singh 2019; York 2021). The COVID-19 pandemic presented a useful case study of the limits of algorithmic moderation (S. T. Roberts 2020). To protect human moderators, many social media companies sent moderators home and relied much more extensively on algorithmic moderation. A spike in the deletion of legitimate content immediately followed the decrease in human moderators (Dwoskin and Tiku 2020; S. T. Roberts 2020). In sum, current AI technology is not at the state where we can hope to avoid the epistemic problems I have identified simply by turning to pure algorithmic moderation (cf. S. T. Roberts 2019, 207; Duarte and Llansó 2017; Llansó et al. 2020).

Finally, even if the technology improves, Roberts makes a strong case that humans should stay in the loop of online moderation:

> While greater reliance upon algorithmic decision-making is typically touted as a leap forward, one that could potentially streamline CCM and reduce its vulnerability to human error (what, in other circumstances, we might think of as "judgment"), it would also eliminate the very human reflection that leads to pushback, questioning and dissent. Machines do not need to sign nondisclosure agreements, and they are not able to violate them in order to talk to academics, the press or anyone else. (S. T. Roberts 2018)

Unlike algorithms, human moderators are ethical agents who can choose to resist company policy and blow the whistle on unjust practices. Much of what we know about the moderation practices of social media companies comes from moderators who have talked to academics and the press. An algorithm could not have leaked the training materials for Facebook's moderators to *The Guardian*, and an algorithm would not raise questions and push back against moderation policies it is tasked to implement, as did some of the moderators whom Roberts interviewed in her research (S. T. Roberts 2017c, 107). Additionally, having humans in the loop helps keep salient the inherently sociopolitical nature of online moderation. Actions taken by AI can appear objective, technical, and depoliticized in the public's imagination (Elish and boyd 2018). Relying on algorithmic moderation enables social media companies to avoid responsibility for their weighty political interventions in speech communities (Gorwa, Binns, and Katzenbach 2020, 12). So there are serious advantages to having some agents in the loop who can exercise resistance and be seen to face accountability.

That said, the damage that moderation work does to the mental health of human moderators makes a compelling case for increasing algorithmic moderation where it can be effective and just. If platforms can find ways to reduce the number of humans who must be exposed to disturbing content while still recognizing and managing the bias that is an inherent risk in any moderation practice, a more just labor model may be possible. If the ethical and epistemic agency of the agents involved is respected, and there is transparency about the role and nature of the algorithms being used, then there is a legitimate place for algorithmic moderation.[12] While it is outside the area of expertise of most philosophers to provide specific recommendations for how best to design algorithms that can work symbiotically with human moderators, social epistemologists could make many useful contributions to these discussions. Feminist epistemologists and epistemologists of race have much to contribute about the nature of bias and how to manage it, and those working on epistemic injustice could contribute analyses of the kinds of epistemic harms that potential moderation practices could inflict. It is my hope that this chapter could inspire some of the future collaborations among social epistemologists, internet studies scholars, engineers, and moderation workers.

---

[12] On the need for transparency about algorithmic moderation, see "Santa Clara Principles on Transparency and Accountability in Content Moderation" 2018; York 2018, 2021; Sinders 2018; Gorwa, Binns, and Katzenbach 2020.

3
Imposters and Tricksters

On February 2, 2011, Amina Abdullah Arraf started a blog titled *A Gay Girl in Damascus*. For four months, Amina posted about her life as an openly lesbian Syrian-American living in Damascus during the Syrian uprising. Amina's blog was widely read in the West. On June 6, a blog post from Amina's cousin claimed that Amina had been kidnapped by armed men. A campaign sprung up to support Amina. A Facebook group demanding her release gained 14,000 followers, and the American embassy investigated her disappearance (Bell and Flock 2011). But after Syrian activists raised doubts about the accuracy of Amina's blog, an investigation began into the identity of the blogger (Abunimah 2011; Nassar 2011b). On June 13, Tom MacMaster, a white American living in Edinburgh, acknowledged sole authorship of the blog (The Telegraph 2011). MacMaster was an imposter, and Amina was an elaborate deception. MacMaster's imposture betrayed the trust of many people in ways that damaged Western understandings of Syrian activism.

This is not an isolated example of internet imposture. Sockpuppetry, the creation of fake internet identities for deceptive goals, has been recognized as a problem since at least the 1990s (Friedberg and Donovan 2019; Freelon et al. 2022). The creation of sockpuppet accounts that fake the identities of marginalized people has been a pervasive and damaging practice. For example, in 2014 anti-feminist 4chan users conducted a coordinated campaign to spread the fake hashtag #EndFathersDay (Todd, n.d.). Fake feminist Twitter accounts, particularly fake accounts of Black women, were used to post messages arguing that Father's Day should be abolished. The 4chan users also used the hoax and fake Twitter accounts to spread false claims aimed at pitting white feminists against feminists of color in a divide-and-conquer strategy. Black women on Twitter fought back by self-organizing to expose the imposters, using the hashtag #YourSlipIsShowing (Hampton 2019; Todd, n.d.). The failure of online platforms to deal with this coordinated imposter campaign targeted against Black women foreshadowed future harassment, including the Gamergate attacks on women in the video games industry later in 2014. Imposters have also received much attention in recent years as vehicles for mass disinformation, including the use of bots by the Russian Internet Research Agency to sow discord during the 2016 U.S. presidential election season (Friedberg and Donovan 2019; Freelon et al. 2022), and the influence of bots to spread COVID-19 conspiracy theories and fake cures (V. A. Young 2020). In this chapter, I argue that trustworthiness is an important epistemic virtue, and that imposters violate expectations of authenticity in ways that damage online epistemic communities.

However, while trustworthiness is an epistemic virtue, betraying expectations of authenticity is sometimes epistemically virtuous in communities structured by oppression. Not all cases of inauthentic online presentation are epistemically vicious. Consider activist tricksters who perpetrate hoaxes aimed at drawing attention to marginalized voices and exposing truths often hidden by dominant media practices. This chapter provides a case study of the Yes Men, a group of anti-corporate media activists whose pranks often depend on fake websites that mimic real corporate, government, or media sites (Reilly 2013, 1247). These fake sites impersonate powerful corporations and entities such as the World Trade Organization (WTO), Shell, Dow Chemical, or the Canadian government. These parody sites (and the Yes Men's offline impersonation of corporate and government figures at conferences and news appearances) draw attention to corporate greed, corruption, exploitation, and government inaction. These acts of imposture help spread truths about issues such as worker exploitation and climate change. The hoaxes also correct for the bias inherent in the domination of our media landscape by corporate agents. The Yes Men are not alone in using online trickery for epistemic and activist ends. The feminist artists from an organization called *FORCE: Upsetting Rape Culture* created two fake media campaigns using imposture on Twitter, fake Huffington Post sites, and other fake websites. First, in 2012 they spread a fake story that Victoria's Secret was coming out with a line of sexual-consent themed underwear (Baker 2012). Second, in 2013 FORCE convinced people that Playboy was promoting consensual sex in its annual guide to party schools (Ohlheiser 2013). The account I present in this chapter suggests that while these hoaxes may temporarily spread some false claims about Victoria's Secret and Playboy, they ultimately do epistemic good by spreading truths about rape culture and the possibility for better corporate policies. Thus, online trickery can have epistemic benefits. This means that we need a sophisticated account of trustworthiness as an epistemic virtue on the internet. We need theories that help us understand why the imposture of Tom MacMaster and others is epistemically harmful, but the activism of the Yes Men and FORCE is epistemically helpful.

This is one of the important roles social epistemology can play in internet studies: the normative role. While it is common in discussions of the internet to raise the complexities of online authenticity—to point out that inauthentic self-presentation can have both beneficial and harmful effects—many theorists balk at taking the next step and providing a normative analysis that helps us make judgments about those acts and the agents who engage in them. Social epistemology as a normative enterprise can help here, because it can provide normative tools that can hone judgment. A virtue-theoretic approach is particularly helpful in both using exemplars to illustrate good and bad habits of online agents, while also providing guidelines that can shape practical wisdom by showing which considerations are salient to a virtuous agent contemplating inauthentic online self-presentation.

My normative account makes a distinction between epistemically vicious imposters and virtuous tricksters. I define *imposters* as those who betray expectations of authenticity in ways that risk net harm to epistemic communities, and *tricksters* as those who intentionally betray such expectations in epistemically virtuous acts of resistance. Given these distinctions, a feminist account of trustworthiness must recognize that situatedness and positionality matter. It matters who is being trusted, by whom, to do what, for what reasons, and in what environment. But I want to go beyond simply acknowledging that situatedness matters. An account of the virtue of trustworthiness should guide epistemic agents about which features of the situation matter. So my central question is: *under what circumstances does the epistemically virtuous agent betray trust?* I answer that *a betrayal is epistemically vicious when it entrenches or promotes oppressive, exclusionary networks of trust, and a betrayal is epistemically virtuous when it undermines exclusionary practices and/or expands trust networks to involve the oppressed.* This account, I argue, correctly identifies the epistemic vice of MacMaster's imposture and the epistemic virtue of resistant tricksters, such as the Yes Men.

3.1. Objectivity and Truth

3.1.1. Objectivity and Truth in Feminist and Veritistic Epistemology

As discussed in Chapter 1, I am concerned here with epistemic objectivity (a measurement of how well bias is managed within a community of believers), rather than metaphysical objectivity (whether the objects of our beliefs exist independently of us) (Lloyd 1995). Objectivity comes in degrees (Longino 1990, 76), and the objectivity in a community increases (or decreases) exactly when the knowledge claims circulating in the community are evaluated in an increasingly (respectively, decreasingly) unprejudiced manner (Longino 1990, 63). I will not rehearse the feminist arguments that objectivity is valuable, nor will I address alternative conceptions of objectivity that do not identify objectivity with absence of bias (e.g., Scheman's account of objectivity as trustworthiness [Scheman 2001]). Instead, I will briefly summarize the two leading feminist accounts of what promotes objectivity. Kristen Intemann argues that in the past few decades, feminist empiricism and feminist standpoint epistemology have developed two similarities (Intemann 2010). First, both approaches are social epistemologies, because they maintain that objectivity arises from community interactions (Intemann 2010, 786). For feminist empiricists (e.g., Longino 1990, 2002; E. Anderson 2006; Solomon 2006), an epistemic community's objectivity increases to the extent it enables and responds to public, transformative criticism from a diversity of values and interests. For feminist standpoint epistemologists (e.g., P. H. Collins 1986; Harding 1991; Wylie 2003; Rolin 2006), objectivity requires that research start from the standpoint of the oppressed, where standpoints are achieved through critical reflection in which the "criticisms of 'insider-outsiders' are taken seriously" (Intemann 2010, 789). Thus, both epistemologies hold that objectivity arises from critical interactions between community members.

Second, both approaches value diversity within epistemic communities, though they value different kinds of diversity (Intemann 2010, 779). For feminist empiricists, objectivity requires a diversity of values and interests, because it provides checks and balances on idiosyncratic biases and widely held assumptions. Standpoint epistemologists maintain that diversity of social position is necessary for objectivity. Following Harding, standpoint epistemologists value strong objectivity, which not only requires systematic study of the ways in which embodied social location shapes background assumptions but also directs epistemic agents to "value the Other's perspective and to pass over in thought into the social condition that creates it—not in order to stay there, to 'go native' or merge the self with the Other, but in order to look back at the self in all its cultural particularity from a more distant, critical, objectifying location" (Harding 1991, 151). In sum, for both branches of feminist epistemology, objectivity requires critical dialogue within diverse epistemic communities. Social practices that impede critical dialogue within diverse communities will harm objectivity, on these theories.

As we saw in Chapter 1, there is a close connection between practices that support objectivity and practices of veritistic value that help cognizers form true beliefs and avoid errors. Thus, a veritistic systems-oriented social epistemology is useful for evaluating social practices, such as imposture. Systems-oriented social epistemology studies the epistemology of epistemic systems, which are social systems that include "social practices, procedures, institutions, and/or patterns of interpersonal influence that affect the epistemic outcomes" of their members (Goldman 2011, 18). As a normative enterprise, systems-oriented social epistemology evaluates epistemic practices according to their positive or negative epistemic outcomes for members. A veritistic approach takes true belief to be the fundamental epistemic good. Social practices are, therefore, evaluated according to their effect on community members' formation of true beliefs and detection of errors. In "Trustworthiness and Truth: The Epistemic Pitfalls of Internet Accountability" (Frost-Arnold 2014c), I argued that epistemic communities require diversity in order to form and disseminate true beliefs as well as detect errors. Following Alvin Goldman, I argue that we can give a veritistic interpretation of the feminist empiricist argument that transformative criticism within diverse communities promotes objectivity (Goldman 1999, 78). When knowledge claims are subjected to scrutiny from a variety of perspectives, it is not only bias that can be detected but also errors. Diverse communities that include members of the oppressed are more likely to identity falsehoods than homogenous communities that exclude the oppressed. Thus, social practices that impede critical dialogue within diverse communities will impede truth acquisition.

3.1.2. Objectivity, Truth, and Trust

For objectivity and truth-promoting social practices to flourish, members of oppressed groups must be involved in the trust networks of epistemic communities. This requires three types of trust:[1] (1) *self-trust*—members

---

[1] More precisely, since trust comes in degrees, each type of trust is required to the proper degree. It is possible to have excessive trust of each type, but usually only privileged groups are excessively trusted (Jones 2012a, 246).

of oppressed groups must trust themselves (Mills 1997, 119; Daukas 2011; Jones 2012a; El Kassar 2020); (2) *trust in others*—they must be trusted by fellow community members (Daukas 2006, 2011; Fricker 2007); and (3) *trust in practices*—community members must trust the practices, institutions, and social structures that create avenues for critical discourse (Scheman 2001). Trust is a complex affective, cognitive, and conative state that involves dispositions to rely upon the trusted with an attitude of confidence that the trusted will act as expected (Jones 2012a, 245). Why do objectivity and truth acquisition within a community require these three types of trust? First, if members of oppressed groups lack self-trust, they are unlikely to proffer criticisms or have confidence in the insights gained from their standpoint. Second, if the criticisms of the oppressed are not heard as authoritative and taken up, objectivity fails to flourish and the errors that the oppressed have identified are unlikely to be rejected. Transformative criticism does not result, nor do community members succeed in adopting the standpoint of the oppressed through critical engagement. Finally, if community members lose faith in the public avenues for critical discussion, then they are less likely to participate in critical dialogue.

One major mechanism of oppression is the exclusion of oppressed groups from trust networks. As work on epistemic injustice has shown, stereotypes that cast oppressed people as untrustworthy constrict trust networks and preclude the oppressed from having their knowledge claims trusted by others and themselves (Jones 2002; Daukas 2006, 2011; Fricker 2007). Such exclusionary, oppressive networks of trust impede critical community interactions from a diversity of values and social locations. For instance, it damages objectivity and truth when agents diminish trust in oppressed groups and the public avenues through which such groups voice potentially transformative criticisms. And strong objectivity is hindered when an oppressed group loses the self-trust necessary to construct separate "worlds" of meaning (cf. Lugones 2003), or others lose confidence in the value of traveling to these "worlds."

My claim that exclusionary, oppressive networks of trust undermine objectivity is not an argument against conceptual separatism. Feminists have shown the epistemic value of separate spaces and conceptual schemes that enable the oppressed to construct separate "worlds" of meaning (e.g., Hoagland 1988, 2001, 2007; Lugones 2003). When oppressed groups choose to separate, they create opportunities for strong objectivity. In contrast, excluding oppressed groups who wish to participate in dominant epistemic communities undermines objectivity, as do practices that damage self-trust in separate spaces. I now argue that imposture can entrench exclusionary, oppressive networks of trust in these ways. My argument proceeds through a detailed, ecological analysis of the MacMaster/Amina imposture (cf. Code 2006).

3.2. Imposters: Undermining Objectivity and Truth

MacMaster's imposture illustrates three ways imposters can undermine objectivity and truth.[2] First, imposters impede diverse transformative criticism by taking space away from marginalized voices. Second, imposters can decrease the quality of transformative criticism by promoting stereotypes that decrease trust in the oppressed. Third, imposters undermine confidence in the social practices that generate objectivity and truth.

MacMaster caused epistemic harm by decreasing the diversity of voices in multiple communities' critical dialogue. MacMaster excused the imposture by positioning the fake blog as an act of advocacy for marginalized people:

> I do not believe that I have harmed anyone—I feel that I have created an important voice for issues that I feel strongly about.

> I only hope that people pay as much attention to the people of the Middle East and their struggles in this year of revolutions. The events there are being shaped by the people living them on a daily basis. I have only tried to illuminate them for a western audience. (MacMaster 2011; Read 2011)[3]

Advocacy can have many epistemic benefits, including giving the claims of silenced testifiers a hearing (Code 2006, 179). However, the practice of speaking for others can also do significant moral and epistemic harm when

---

[2] In this chapter, I focus on MacMaster's imposture as a Syrian activist. In contrast, much public discussion focused on a presumed gender imposture. Discussion of gender imposture requires responsible analysis that was missing from much of the media attention and is beyond the scope of this chapter. There is a long-standing history of transphobic representations of transgender people as evil-deceiver gender imposters (Bettcher 2007). Additionally, the internet provides a powerful medium for transgender people to explore their identities, express themselves, and build community (Whittle 1998; Haimson et al. 2021). Thus, discussion of MacMaster's gender presentation on the blog demands careful analysis to avoid playing into transphobic narratives.

[3] Post-exposure, MacMaster deleted the blog. Where online documents disappeared, I have provided alternatives quoting the original.

advocates speak "in place of" marginalized others (Alcoff 1991, 9). Not only can advocacy on behalf of marginalized others buttress the social standing and epistemic credibility of privileged advocates at the expense of those with less privilege (cf. E. Davis 2018), but it can further silence the marginalized by occupying space in trust networks. The advocate runs the risk that their speech will be attended to in place of the speech of the marginalized others on whose behalf they are advocating. Middle Eastern LGBTQ activists raised this concern at the time. As Syrian activist Danny Ramadan (writing under the pseudonym "Daniel Nassar") wrote, "You took away my voice, Mr. MacMaster, and the voices of many people who I know. To bring attention to yourself and blog; you managed to bring the LGBT movement in the Middle East years back" (Nassar 2011a).[4]

MacMaster's entrance into the public dialogue took the place of marginalized voices. Western audiences interested in the Syrian uprising or LGBTQ life in the Middle East spent time reading Amina's blog instead of the blogs, tweets, or Facebook posts of nonfictional Syrians. Journalists covered Amina when they could have interviewed others. That said, it is also possible that had Amina's blog never appeared, Western audiences would not have given attention to other, authentic Syrian voices. Part of Amina's appeal was surely the Western tendency to find the Other erotic and exotic. MacMaster's blog played into these tropes, which may have made it more attractive to Western audiences than other authentic social media accounts. So although we cannot be certain that Syrian activists would have received more attention in Amina's absence, it is likely that MacMaster's speech took some space from others who could have contributed more diversity to the discussion. The imposture was central to MacMaster gaining access to the space—in fact, MacMaster admitted that one reason for pretending to be Amina was the lack of attention MacMaster's views on the Middle East received when writing under a Western masculine name ("Gay Girl in Damascus: Tom MacMaster Defends Blog Hoax" 2011). As Lisa Nakamura puts it, "Tom MacMaster was tempted by and ultimately gave in to his desire to speak literally *as* the subaltern—as the queer female Asian-Islamic subject—for many reasons, but perhaps the most obvious one is his conviction that he was the victim of reverse racism" (Nakamura 2011). By illegitimately gaining access to the critical dialogue, MacMaster decreased the diversity of the trust networks that

---

[4] I thank Danny Ramadan for permission to use this quote and for his work on this issue. I have learned a lot from his writings on the Amina hoax.

comprised that epistemic space. Thus, MacMaster's imposture undermined the diversity needed for objective and truth-conducive dialogue about the Arab Spring.

Additionally, MacMaster undermined the quality of transformative criticism by promoting Western prejudices. For example, in an online interview with CBS, MacMaster, under the guise of Amina, called on LGBTQ Syrians to come out of the closet. In response to a query about what Amina had to say to closeted Syrians "afraid to share their sexuality," Amina said:

> Don't be: The worst thing we face is our own fear. If we want to be free, we must first overcome our own worst enemy, which is the one within us. It is that fear that has allowed the dictators to rule; it is that fear that keeps us as Arabs, as Muslims, as women and as lesbians trapped. If we stop being afraid within ourselves, we can achieve freedom. The prison of our own minds is the darkest place. (qtd. in Lazar 2011)

An American chastising Syrian lesbians for living in the closet is morally appalling, but it is also epistemically harmful. MacMaster's intervention undermines objectivity in the dialogue about the Middle Eastern LGBTQ community because Amina's perpetuation of Western stereotypes prevents transformative criticism of Western bias. Amina criticizes Syrian lesbians for passively living in fear. In doing so, she feeds into a long-standing Western narrative presenting non-Western marginalized groups as unempowered, passive, and in need of Western help in their liberation (e.g., the help of an enlightened Syrian-American like Amina) (cf. Mohanty 2003). News of Middle Eastern uprisings had the potential to challenge Western assumptions about Middle Eastern women, but Amina reinforces those stereotypes (Bady 2011). Thus, MacMaster's imposture gave credibility to pernicious stereotypes— when MacMaster spoke under a Western masculine identity, the speech received less credibility. In this way, MacMaster follows the tradition of what Lisa Nakamura calls "identity tourism," in which users take on non-white identities online that do not match their offline identities (Nakamura 1995, 2002, 2011). For example, in the text-based role-playing communities of MOOs (the acronym for multi-user domain, object oriented), Nakamura found users playing as stereotypical Asian characters. She calls this a form of tourism to emphasize the "superficial, reversible, recreational play at otherness" involved (Nakamura 2002, 55). The imposture allows MacMaster to speak as a Syrian lesbian online without having to live the risks and dangers that people who live these lives offline have to endure (Nakamura 2011). And like many other identity tourists, MacMaster uses the credibility stolen by appropriating this identity to perpetuate damaging stereotypes about marginalized others.

To summarize so far, MacMaster's imposture undermined transformative criticism. First, by taking the place of marginalized others, MacMaster excluded them from the networks producing knowledge about Syrian activism for Westerners. Second, the stereotypes of marginalized groups (in this case non-Western women) as passive and unempowered diminish trust in the abilities of the oppressed. Both the self-trust of the oppressed and the trust others place in them are damaged by stereotypes that construct them as less authoritative and autonomous than the privileged. Thus, MacMaster's imposture threatened the first two types of trust necessary for objective international understanding of Syrian activism.[5]

Finally, imposters can also threaten objectivity and truth by undermining the third type of trust mentioned earlier: trust in the social practices that promote objectivity. MacMaster's imposture fueled doubts about the trustworthiness of social media in general, which could potentially undermine trust in all bloggers, but the stakes were higher for marginalized users. MacMaster's imposture raised suspicions about practices that both feminist empiricists and standpoint epistemologists endorse as objectivity-enhancing and truth-conducive, if done properly. Blogs and other social media can generate community-level transformative criticism and opportunities to start inquiry from the standpoint of the oppressed. For example, social media was used at the time to critique and provide alternatives to dominant conceptions of the Arab Spring (Khondker 2011). In addition, blogs can create smaller epistemic communities by hosting active comment threads. Commenters often engage in a critical dialogue with one another, another potential objectivity-enhancing practice. Of course, much depends on how comment threads are moderated, and whether uptake, shared standards, and equality of intellectual authority are present (Longino 1990). But for these practices to play any positive role, community members must think it worthwhile to engage with social media. If I want a from-the-ground perspective of the Syrian uprising instead of the mainstream media's

---

[5] To avoid a one-sided narrative of victimhood, I should mention that activists and journalists used the Amina controversy to draw attention to their causes and to challenge Western coverage of the Middle East (e.g., Abbas 2011; Nassar 2011b). On the damage done by narratives that ignore resistance, see Lugones 2003, 53–63, and Hoagland 2007, 102.

coverage, then I will not subscribe to a purportedly Syrian blog if I have no confidence that a Syrian actually wrote it. Thus, MacMaster's imposture undermines trust in the avenues for public dialogue that activists often use to disseminate alternative messages (cf. Friedberg and Donovan 2019). In sum, this case study shows that imposture has the potential to undermine the trust necessary for diverse networks of trust that promote objectivity and truth acquisition.

3.3. The Need for Trustworthiness

Recall that objectivity and truth acquisition are sustained by social practices (e.g., critical dialogue, transformative criticism, and starting from the oppressed's standpoint). Inquirers who hold objectivity and truth as ideals rely on one another to engage in these practices. But because inquirers do not live in a panopticon of complete surveillance, they must take it on some degree of trust that others are upholding their end of the social practices. Distrust is poison; it spreads throughout the body of epistemic communities, destroying members' faith in one another and their confidence in the social practices that support knowledge production. Therefore, objectivity and truth acquisition depend on members' trustworthiness.

A trustworthy person is someone who can be counted on to avoid unduly violating the normative expectations that others rely upon her to meet. More precisely, the trustworthy person takes the fact that others are relying on her to fulfill these expectations as a reason to avoid violating them (Jones 2012b). This brief account of trustworthiness is based on two features of trust. First, trust involves reliance. Reliance on another involves making plans based on the assumption that the trusted will perform a particular action. This makes the truster vulnerable. If I rely on you to tell the truth, then I am vulnerable to forming a false belief if you lie. Because of this vulnerability, unquestioning and ungrounded trust is the exception, rather than the rule. We usually rely on people because we have some evidence that they will act as we expect. Second, trust involves normative expectations. Trust involves vulnerability to feeling betrayed when the relied-upon party fails to act as expected (Baier 1996, 99). These feelings of betrayal are reactive attitudes that link trust to practices of holding people morally responsible for their actions (Walker 2006, 80). Thus, when I trust someone to do something, I make plans based on the assumption that they will do it, and I do so with normative expectations (Frost-Arnold 2014b).

The trustworthy person cultivates habits to avoid unduly betraying the trust others place in them. The "unduly" here is important because, as I argue in section 3.4, trustworthy people sometimes betray trust. Part of the virtue of trustworthiness involves determining whose trust should be betrayed and under what circumstances. But without some disposition to avoid betraying others' trust, one does not have the character trait of trustworthiness. Note that I follow Annette Baier in using 'betrayal' to refer to failure to uphold the expectations someone trusts one to fulfill (Baier 1996, 16). This use has a neutral moral valence—some betrayals can be virtuous (e.g., betrayal of an exploiter's trust), whereas others are not.

3.3.1. Trust and Authenticity

3.3.1.1. What Is Authenticity?

In cases of imposture, the truster's normative expectations of authenticity are violated. We often rely on one another to signal truth from pretense. In trusting others to be authentic, we trust them to avoid deceptive self-presentation. Communities often have prescriptive norms of authenticity, and members trust each other to live up to normative expectations of authenticity. But what is authenticity? Authenticity is a complex concept with a long and varied history. Meredith Salisbury and Jefferson Pooley trace the modern concept of authenticity back to Jean-Jacques Rousseau's account of an authentic self that we can discover in ourselves and work to express in the face of social conventions (Salisbury and Pooley 2017, 5). Sarah Banet-Weiser charts shifting conceptions of authenticity from Rousseau to Marx to Thoreau and examines contemporary debates about the possibilities of authenticity in a consumer, brand culture (Banet-Weiser 2012). As the varying histories of the term show, 'authentic' has many meanings, and norms of authenticity are context dependent and constantly shifting. As Alice Marwick and danah boyd put it, "the authentic is a localized, temporally situated social construct that varies widely based on community" (Marwick and boyd 2011, 124).

Expectations of (and attempts to manage) authenticity online have been extensively investigated by internet studies scholars, and in this section I discuss features of online authenticity that are relevant for my analysis of imposture. I argue that norms of authenticity can play important roles in protecting us from deception and harm, and I show that trustworthiness is a key epistemic virtue by showing how, in many contexts, living up to the expectations of authenticity within an epistemic community is vital to protect the objectivity and truth conduciveness of that community's epistemic practices. However, authenticity is not a pure concept—it can also function in oppressive ways, and it has been used by technology companies to push oppressive policies that serve corporate interests at the expense of marginalized communities. These problems motivate my argument that trustworthiness is a complex virtue. Trustworthy agents will be attentive to the ways that norms of authenticity can be oppressive. Thus, full trustworthiness demands that we live up to norms of authenticity when imposture threatens vulnerable members of our community who are counting on us, but it also requires that we sometimes violate expectations of authenticity and resist policies and discourses that oppress marginalized communities.

Salisbury and Pooley identify several different meanings of 'authenticity' in social media contexts (Salisbury and Pooley 2017, 2–3). Most commonly, (1) *consistency* is taken to be authentic. Consistency in match between one's online and offline self (Sessions 2009; Haimson and Hoffmann 2016; Salisbury and Pooley 2017), consistency in presentation across different platforms (Marwick 2015; Salisbury and Pooley 2017), and consistency in online presentation over time (J. L. Davis 2012; Marwick 2015; Haimson and Hoffmann 2016; Uski and Lampinen 2016; Salisbury and Pooley 2017) are all taken as signals of authenticity. Additionally, (2) *spontaneity* (Sessions 2009; Uski and Lampinen 2016; J. L. Davis 2012; Salisbury and Pooley 2017), (3) *sharing personal details* (Marwick and boyd 2011; Salisbury and Pooley 2017), and (4) *amateurism* (Duffy and Hund 2015; Salisbury and Pooley 2017) are types of authenticity valued in different social media contexts. Thus, there are several different conceptions of authenticity at play in online environments—presenting an online self that is inconsistent with one's offline self is quite a different kind of inauthenticity than carefully and deliberately crafting an online branded self. The former violates expectations of consistency, while the latter violates expectations of spontaneity and amateurism.

In this chapter I am primarily concerned with authenticity as consistency (which I will call 'consistent authenticity' or simply 'authenticity'). Internet imposters violate expectations of presentation of a self that is consistent across contexts, most commonly expectations of presentation of an online self that is consistent with one's offline self. MacMaster violated expectations of consistency between one's online persona and one's offline identity. MacMaster did not signal that the blog was written in a fictional voice or that Amina did not exist in the offline world. Thus, the blog violated norms that held bloggers accountable for accurately signaling whether a blog was written in a fictional voice or a pseudonym was being used.

3.3.1.2. The Value of Authenticity

What are the functions of these norms of authenticity? This is a complicated question, and I will argue that expectations of authenticity play both valuable and harmful roles. I begin with the valuable role of authenticity. First, norms of authenticity help ground our practical reasoning and inductive inferences about whom to trust. Norms of consistent authenticity often hold people responsible for conforming to socially constructed boundaries of identities. The reason for this is that we take some signals that a person belongs to a social group as evidence that they are likely to have other characteristics or behave in certain ways. Thus, our trust in others to maintain stable social identities within expected boundaries grounds our inductive inferences and practical reasoning. Importantly, these expectations of authenticity can either protect the vulnerable or oppress individuals who do not conform to dominant social boundaries (I will discuss the latter problem in section 3.3.1.3). To see the protective function of authenticity, consider the modern predicament of trust in professionals and experts. Modern life involves being caught up in complex systems of expertise that we neither fully understand nor completely control (Giddens 1990, 2–3; Barber 1983; Pellegrino, Veatch, and Langan 1991). We cannot avoid relying on the work of doctors, lawyers, engineers, and other professionals as we navigate lives structured by these systems. Try as we might to gain evidence that the professionals on whom we rely are trustworthy, there is a limit to our ability and resources to fully gauge their trustworthiness. Thus, we are extremely vulnerable to betrayal of this trust in the form of medical malpractice, poor legal representation, and engineering disaster. Part of what we trust professionals to do is accurately represent their expertise. For instance, expectations of authentic medical practice hold doctors accountable for conforming to expectations of safe, expert treatment of vulnerable patients. To protect vulnerable patients, we expect that doctors' presentation of their qualifications be consistent with the qualifications they actually possess. Thus, when we are in positions of vulnerability, we often have to trust others' authenticity.

Although particular norms of authenticity are context dependent, if community members trust one another to engage in joint epistemic projects, the community often has norms of authenticity. This is because knowing a person's identity carries significant weight in assessing their epistemic authority. Information about someone's identity (and information about whether they are engaged in deceptive self-presentation) is relevant to judging whether their testimony is competent and sincere. For example, whether the author of the blog or Twitter account I am reading to learn about the Syrian civil war is actually a person living in Syria or not is relevant to my judgment of whether the author is a competent eyewitness testifier to events on the ground. Thus, in many contexts, expectations of consistent authenticity are epistemically reasonable. Of course, prejudices about certain groups can be triggered by information about the identity of a testifier, and this can impair one's assessment of the competence and sincerity of the testifier (Fricker 2007). This is a testimonial injustice for which virtuous epistemic agents will try to correct. Nonetheless, members of epistemic communities often reasonably trust one another to uphold norms of consistent, authentic self-presentation so that they can make accurate assessments of the trustworthiness of testimony.

That said, in some contexts we expect others to deceive us and pretend to be something other than they are. Imagine a dinner theater murder-mystery play in which audience members know that actors are scattered throughout the audience. The actors are intentionally pretending to be someone else, but this is unobjectionable because the audience is not relying on them to do otherwise. Now, an objector to my case study might advocate for a similar attitude to people's online self-presentation. Knowing that some blogs were fake, a reader in 2011 might take a playful attitude to blogs. Like a dinner theater audience member, this reader might have no normative expectations of truth-telling. In fact, this is one view of the internet that MacMaster used to defend the blog. Post-exposure, the following subtitle appeared under the blog's heading: "The Image is not the Real; When you realize that you were reading a story, rather than the news, who should you be angry at? The teller of tales that moved you?" (MacMaster 2011; U. Friedman 2011). On this view, the internet is a space for moving stories, rather than a community (or set of overlapping communities) bound together by trust in members' authenticity.

But the reason MacMaster's subtitle was a gross evasion of responsibility is that people do not always take such a casual, playful attitude to what they read online. Nor should they, if the internet is to have some epistemic value (beyond the value fiction has). Many readers of Amina's blog relied on it for news about Syrian activism. And their normative expectations of authenticity were reasonable given the social-epistemic environment of blogging on the Arab Spring. Why? Blogs and other forms of social media had taken a place among the social-epistemic practices by which various overlapping epistemic communities attempted to produce knowledge. This was especially true during the Arab Spring, when activists used social media to organize and spread their message in an environment of state censorship (Khondker 2011; Tufekci 2017).[6] Additionally, in the case of Syria, the Assad regime had closed the country off from Western journalists (Zuckerman 2011). In this atmosphere of censorship, Western journalists bolstered the credibility of social media by citing blogs and tweets as sources and reporting on the ways activists used them. This made it reasonable for readers to read purportedly Syrian blogs with epistemic aims (to get an alternative take on the news). In addition, given both the importance of the information conveyed and the risks to activists, it was reasonable to hold certain bloggers to norms of authenticity.

Let me forestall a few objections at this point. First, since MacMaster's blog played on many stereotypes, perhaps some readers enjoyed the blog because it confirmed their previously held worldview, for example, one in which Western activists save non-Western peoples. I agree that this plausibly describes many readers. But this does not diminish my claim that if blogs are to provide an opportunity for learning, rather than just confirmation bias, readers are sometimes warranted in expecting authenticity. That readers often do not avail themselves of opportunities to challenge their beliefs does not mean that the opportunities are not, or should not, be there. Second, when I claim that it was reasonable to hold Arab Spring bloggers to norms of authenticity, I argue that this is a reasonable normative expectation, not a warranted prediction that everyone will uphold these norms. Third, my argument that the expectations of truth-telling were reasonable is indexed to

---

[6] This is not to say that the sharing of knowledge is the only purpose for which social media was used during the Arab Spring. Zizi Papacharissi argues that much use of Twitter during the Arab Spring was affective, as tweets were used to share and galvanize affective engagement (Papacharissi 2016, 57–58). Additionally, I do not want to overstate the role of social media in the political landscape of North Africa and the Middle East during this period. Siva Vaidhyanathan argues that "The reductive narrative of the power of social media to energize and organize from below prevented serious and sensitive analysis of crucial political movements and events" (Vaidhyanathan 2018, 138).

this particular community of blogs. Certainly, expectations of truth-telling are unreasonable in other areas of social media (e.g., fan-fiction blogs).

Recall that trust involves vulnerability. When one trusts someone, one is vulnerable to betrayal. This is true for trust in someone's online authenticity. Unable to check up on all social media postings to determine whether every word written is true, and unable to fully investigate the background of all social media authors, readers are in a position of relative ignorance. If readers' attempts to engage in objectivity-enhancing and truth-conducive practices are to be successful, readers have to trust the authors.

Of course, readers also bear responsibility for using their critical skills. As Lisa Heldke and Mariana Ortega argue, privileged knowers who attempt to correct for their biases by reading marginalized others' texts need to check and question what they read (Heldke 1997; Ortega 2006). Thus, Western readers who failed to question their own ready acceptance of Amina's words were not fully epistemically virtuous. That said, in claiming that readers needed to trust the blog's author, I argue that features of the social-epistemic environment of the blog (e.g., the difficulty of determining the real-world identities of bloggers, activists' need for protective anonymity, and the widespread [and culpable] Western ignorance of the Middle East) put the readers in a position of vulnerability with limited ability to detect betrayal. A trustworthy blogger would recognize this vulnerability and not exploit it in ways that damage objectivity. MacMaster failed to do this.

One might wonder why my analysis of the epistemic harm of imposters has not focused on the lies MacMaster told. Lying is perhaps the most obvious epistemic harm of imposture, and it is of particular interest to veritists. Imposters like MacMaster certainly do epistemic harm by disseminating falsehoods online. But if we limit our analysis to the falsehoods that MacMaster typed into the blog and focus on the epistemic harm that many people believed the falsehoods, we lose sight of what is often a more long-lasting and pervasive epistemic harm—the betrayal of reasonable trust that undergirds epistemic practices themselves. This betrayal erodes people's willingness to take the risk of making themselves vulnerable. The more people are betrayed by imposters (and the more reports, especially sensational reports, of imposture they hear), the more people avoid relying on each other in these ways, and the more cynical they are likely to become. For example, they may lose trust in the social media presence of Arab Spring activists and stop turning to social media to gain an alternative, potentially less biased account of current events. Imposters thus spread poison within an epistemic community; their untrustworthiness undermines members' willingness to engage in practices of objectivity. In sum, given my earlier argument that objectivity depends on networks of trust, the objectivity of a community depends on the trustworthiness of its members, so betrayal of trust in ways that constrict trust networks to exclude marginalized people is an epistemic harm.

3.3.1.3. The Harms of Authenticity

In recognizing the harms imposters do by violating norms of authenticity, we have to be careful not to uncritically endorse all norms of authenticity. Authenticity is a complex concept, and often expectations of authenticity are unreasonable and oppressive. I now turn to the problems with norms of authenticity. My goal here is to complicate the earlier account and motivate the need for practical wisdom in our epistemic lives.

First, let us return to my earlier point that norms of consistent authenticity often hold people responsible for conforming to socially constructed boundaries of identities. I argued that these expectations of authenticity can protect the vulnerable, but they can also oppress individuals who do not conform to dominant social boundaries. For example, oppressive expectations of authentic gender presentation or racial identity hold people morally blameworthy if their behaviors transgress boundaries and are taken as deceptive signals (Bettcher 2007; Lee 2011). Such oppressive expectations limit natural fluidity and change in self-presentation, coerce individuals into conforming to traditional or normative boundaries (often constructed to privilege dominant groups), and expose marginalized people to harassment or erasure. As Oliver Haimson and Anna Lauren Hoffmann argue, "Identities necessarily change as a person ages, learns, and moves around in the world" (Haimson and Hoffmann 2016). So expectations of consistent self-presentation can punish people for changing self-presentation in response to fluid changes in their sense of self. But even beyond considerations of fluidity, norms of authenticity can be problematic when what is taken as normal reflects the life experiences of dominant groups.

A perfect example of how expectations of authenticity can oppress marginalized groups is Facebook's "real-name" policy. Facebook has a long history of requiring users to present personas consistent with their offline identities (Haimson and Hoffmann 2016). Its real-name policy has mutated over the years and has been enforced to varying degrees. As of this writing, the policy states: "Facebook is a community where everyone uses the name they go by in everyday life" ("What Names Are Allowed on Facebook?" n.d.), it outlines several types of names that are not allowed (e.g., "unusual capitalization"), and it requires that Facebook names match names on Facebook's list of identity documents ("What Types of ID Does Facebook Accept?" n.d.). In 2014, drag queens in San Francisco were locked out of their accounts for violating the policy, and their public protests drew increased attention to the discriminatory policy (K. V. Brown 2014; MacAulay and Moldes 2016). Drag queens, LGBTQ users, and victims of stalking and harassment are all harmed by Facebook's policy. Facebook's policy assumes that it is normal for people to use the same name in every context, and it excludes from Facebook's community those whose everyday lives involve using names that do not match the names on their identity documents.

A second and related problem with norms of authenticity is that, in atmospheres of fear of deception by imposters, the language of online authenticity can be wielded to push for surveillance cultures which disproportionately target those with non-normative identities (Chun 2006, 2016; Haimson and Hoffmann 2016; MacAulay and Moldes 2016). In the face of fear of a dangerous "other," securitization frameworks argue for increased transparency and often use consistency in self-presentation as a sign of safety. For example, in the post-9/11 United States, fear of terrorism was used to justify the installation of body scanners at airports. These scanners, which require Transportation Security Administration (TSA) agents to push a pink or blue button based on the agent's perception of the gender of the traveler, regularly lead to transgender travelers being subject to invasive pat downs ("New TSA Policy Codifies Discrimination Against Transgender People" 2016). Maggie MacAulay and Marcos Moldes ask the following questions about such technologies: "What happens when technologies recognize the wrong person? Or, when the name and face do not match—in other words, *when someone fails to compute*? The individual and social costs of these failures are real, and the price paid too often by those with non-normative names and bodies" (MacAulay and Moldes 2016, 7). They focus on Facebook's real-name policy as a powerful example of the role that norms of authenticity play in the policing and surveillance of non-normative identities. As we saw in Chapter 2, platforms often outsource the labor of surveillance to users by asking users to report ("flag") suspicious behavior. In the case of online authenticity, this turns users into monitors of each other's authenticity (cf. York 2021, 17). This situation is ripe for bias, since members of dominant groups can disproportionately flag as inauthentic members of marginalized groups whose self-presentation is inconsistent with dominant expectations (Haimson and Hoffmann 2016). This explains why so many drag queens, transgender people, and Native Americans were reported to Facebook as having fake names. For example, given the dominance of white users on Facebook and the lack of racial diversity in Silicon Valley tech workers who write policies such as the real-name policy, it is no surprise that Native American names were flagged as inauthentic. Not only were typical Native American names likely unfamiliar to non-native users who Facebook asks to report fake profiles, but also the policy itself encodes white naming norms by banning "unusual capitalization" ("What Names Are Allowed on Facebook?" n.d.). For example, Kimberly TallBear, a member of the Sisseton-Wahpeton Oyate and a professor at UT Austin at the time, was locked out of her Facebook account for violating the policy and reported that the capitalization of her last name was considered problematic by Facebook (Bowman 2015).

The problem here is not just the bias but also the ways in which norms of authenticity are often connected with what Wendy Chun has criticized as the "epistemology of outing," which she defines as "a mode of knowledge production that focuses on the exposure of 'secrets,' open or not" (Chun 2016, 150). Chun draws on Eve Kosofsky Sedgwick's *Epistemology of the Closet* (Sedgwick 1990) and Michel Foucault's account of the pleasures that come from "a power that questions, monitors, watches, spies, searches out, palpates, brings to light" (Foucault 1978, 45). Chun charts the familiar phenomenon of people's confessional 'outing' of themselves online (e.g., by posting a YouTube video confessional video describing their pain at being bullied) followed by suspicion from other users who challenge the authenticity of the confession (Chun 2016, 135–65). This suspicion is often accompanied by amateur sleuthing by other users who attempt to hold the suspected imposter accountable for their inauthenticity by digging up evidence of inconsistencies, a method of accountability that I have elsewhere dubbed "investigative accountability" (Frost-Arnold 2014c). Investigative accountability is a problematic epistemic practice which is based on the assumption that the way to encourage trustworthiness in online activity is through threat of punishment. On the reasoning behind investigative accountability, if agents know that suspicious activity on their part will trigger the uncovering of their offline identity, then they will be less likely to spread falsehoods and engage in imposture. Without attention to problems of bias, investigative accountability can diminish the diversity of epistemic communities as members of marginalized groups withdraw in order to protect themselves from being exposed (Frost-Arnold 2014c). In sum, the pleasures of detecting an imposter can be great, but these pleasures can also feed a culture of paranoid distrust and damaging investigations disproportionately targeted against those from non-dominant groups.

A third, connected problem with norms of authenticity is that they can be used as a cudgel against those who, for good reason, want to maintain some privacy by withholding information online or using online personas that do not match their offline lives (Marwick 2015, 235). Living an authentic online life is often considered the same as living a fully transparent online life. Secrecy is viewed as suspect. "The idea that privacy is only necessary for those engaging in illegal activities is, unfortunately, widespread in the general U.S. population, yet it does not hold up under scrutiny" (Marwick 2015, 235). Not only do people have good reason to construct different online identities in order to facilitate different kinds of relationships with different people online (just as we regularly do offline [Rachels 1975]), but also vulnerable populations often need to create pseudonyms and conceal information online in order to avoid stalking, harassment, and to protect themselves from offline abusers (Frost-Arnold 2014c; Haimson and Hoffmann 2016; MacAulay and Moldes 2016). This is where standpoint epistemology is particularly useful; beginning inquiry into the value and function of norms of authenticity from the lives of the oppressed reveals truths that are lost from a privileged perspective. As Marwick puts it, "Promoting absolute openness disregards the privilege of most people in the tech scene. It is one thing for a wealthy, white male programmer to admit that he sometimes smokes pot. It is another for an undocumented worker to publicize his immigration status, or for a woman escaping a domestic violence situation to reveal her home address" (Marwick 2015, 236).

A fourth problem with norms of authenticity is that they can be used to foreclose opportunities for experimentation and play. First, consider experimenting with one's identity. Sarah Roberts recounts how the internet allowed her "to experiment with identifying as gay well before I was able to do so 'IRL' (in real life, in internet parlance). Having had the opportunity to textually partake of the identity made the real-world embodiment much easier than it might have been" (S. T. Roberts 2019, 10). Roberts's narrative reminds us to be cautious of the fiction of a clear, rigid boundary between the online and offline self. Online experimentation with identities that may not initially match one's offline presentation can nonetheless help one explore identities that then shape one's sense of self and presentation both online and offline. Second, consider online play. Playfully violating expectations and pushing boundaries is a pleasurable form of self-expression and a way of resisting confining social norms. Online spaces with stronger norms of authenticity (e.g., Facebook with its real-name policy) are often less playful and creative, in some respects, than spaces with fewer expectations of consistency between one's online and offline identity (e.g., Twitter). Zizi Papacharissi studies how Twitter users playfully act out fantasies online, and she argues that "experimenting with potential of behaviors in an 'as-if' mode [is a] strategy for dealing with the fixity of norms" (Papacharissi 2016, 95). Play can be a way of constructing a story of who one is that pushes beyond traditional boundaries: "Play enables experimentation with language and aesthetics toward the construction of everyday narratives that support the lifelong storytelling of the self (Hamera 2006)" (Papacharissi 2016, 98). The value of online play is even recognized by internet scholars, such as Nakamura, who critique oppressive, irresponsible cultural appropriation of marginalized identities (Nakamura 2002). As I discussed in section 3.2, Nakamura's influential 1995 analysis of "identity tourism" in text-based online communities commonly referred to as MOOs uncovered the racist Orientalism of much role-playing of stereotypical Asian characters by predominantly white users. Despite focusing on the problems of this role-playing, Nakamura finishes the piece with the following hopeful vision of a positive function for role play:

> Player scripts which eschew repressive versions of the Oriental in favor of critical rearticulations and recombinations of race, gender, and class, and which also call the fixedness of these categories into question have the power to turn the theatricality characteristic of MOOspace into a truly innovative form of play, rather than a tired reiteration and reinstatement of old hierarchies. Role playing is a feature of the MOO, not a bug, and it would be absurd to ask that everyone who plays within it hew literally to the "rl" ["real life"] gender, race, or condition of life. A diversification of the roles which get played, which are permitted to be played, can enable a thought provoking detachment of race from the body, and an accompanying questioning of the essentialness of race as a category. Performing alternative versions of self and race jams the ideology-machine, and facilitates a desirable opening up of what Judith Butler calls "the difficult future terrain of community" (Butler 1993, 242). (Nakamura 1995, 191)

Thus, we need to be careful that we do not take the desire for consistency and accurate self-presentation so far that we remove the possibility for resistant online role play.

Given all of these problems with norms of authenticity, why do they persist? The answer is complicated. First, norms of authenticity are practically and epistemically useful—they ground our inductive inferences. Second, they can be ethically warranted—authenticity can protect vulnerable individuals and populations from deception by those they need to trust. So there are epistemic and ethical reasons why communities would promote norms of authenticity.

But another cause of the persistence of these norms in online contexts is that norms of authenticity serve corporate interests by facilitating tracking. Alice Marwick observes that "[W]hat is high status in social media is often that which benefits technology companies and sustains neoliberal discourse," and she points out that users who maintain consistent identities across websites are easier for technology companies to track (Marwick 2015, 17). Thus, the support for consistent authenticity from companies like Facebook is likely driven more by their profits from mining the data from our online profiles and connecting them to offline identities than from these companies' professed concerns for user safety (Chun 2016, 109; MacAulay and Moldes 2016, 11).

In sum, expectations of consistent authenticity are practically and epistemically useful as they ground our practical reasoning and testimonial practices, but they are morally complex—depending on the context and nature of the norms, expectations of authenticity can protect vulnerable people or oppress marginalized populations, fuel a culture of surveillance, and deter experimentation and playfulness. My goal here is not to provide a comprehensive account of the conditions under which norms of authenticity are ethical, nor is it to use this complexity to advocate throwing up our hands and saying, "Who's to say what's ethical? There's just no answer." Instead, I want to recognize this ethical complexity in order to lay the groundwork for an account of the role of practical wisdom in trustworthiness. Trustworthiness is a complex virtue, one that requires practical wisdom and attention to not only the ethical dilemmas of online authenticity but also epistemic considerations of epistemic vulnerability and the efficacy of strategic deployments of ignorance. We need an ethics and epistemology that can hold nuance and complexity within its scope. And we need an ethics and epistemology that can recognize both the harm done by imposters such as MacMaster while also recognizing the harm of securitization frameworks, real-name policies, and investigations to "out" fakers that disproportionately target marginalized people in the name of rooting out any threat of imposture. I think a virtue approach can do this. This is where thinking about the need for practical wisdom and structural change is necessary to ensure true trustworthiness in online spaces.

3.3.2. Practical Wisdom and Trustworthiness

According to Aristotle, practical wisdom (*phronesis*) is both a moral and epistemic virtue (Aristotle 1926; cf. Zagzebski 1996, 211). Practical wisdom is a unifying and sorting virtue which involves "a facility for switching from one [virtue] to another as occasion requires, for blending the considerations characteristic of one virtue with those of others, and for adjudicating between the different appeals of virtues when they seem to conflict" (R. C. Roberts and Wood 2007, 311). Zagzebski provides two relevant theoretical reasons why practical wisdom is necessary to make sense of our moral and epistemic lives. First, since some virtues are Aristotelian means between extremes, we need practical wisdom to determine the mean (Zagzebski 1996, 220). Courage is such a virtue. We can be excessively courageous (foolhardy) or insufficiently courageous (cowardly). The person of practical wisdom can find the amount of courage appropriate to the situation at hand, which can be different depending on the person (Zagzebski 1996, 221). Second, practical wisdom is the "ability to mediate between and among the individual moral virtues" (Zagzebski 1996, 222). We need this virtue "to sift through all the salient features of the situation—that is, all those features that are pertinent to *any* of the virtues—and to make a judgment that is not simply the judgment of a person qua courageous, qua generous, or qua humble but is the judgment of a *virtuous* person" (Zagzebski 1996, 222).

We need practical wisdom to mediate between the virtue of trustworthiness and the virtue of justice. Virtuous agents are not just sensitive to whether others trust them to do something; they are also sensitive to whether the trust placed in them is reasonable and just. It is unreasonable for someone to trust me to flap my arms and fly, because I cannot. It is also unreasonable and unjust for someone to trust me to live up to expectations that oppress me and others like me. Practical wisdom can help agents decide when considerations of justice trump considerations of trustworthiness. In those situations many courses of action are available to people who want to avoid living up to unjust expectations: they can opt out, voice their rejection of oppressive norms, or sometimes engage in acts of trickery to make the injustice of the norms visible. Trickery can be one course of action chosen by the person of practical wisdom who knows that trustworthiness is not always the foremost virtue in online life.

On Aristotle's account of the Doctrine of the Mean, the virtuous person has the right emotions and engages in the right actions to the proper degree "at the right times, about the right things, toward the right people, for the right end, and in the right way" (Aristotle 1969, 1106b15–25). Thus, the fully virtuous person does not live up to all normative expectations that others rely on her to uphold. When it comes to norms of authenticity, this means that the trustworthy agent will live up to expectations of authenticity in many, but not all, circumstances. This does not mean that failure to engage in trickery is a vice because trickery is only one possible course of action when justice conflicts with expectations of trustworthiness.

But how do we know when expectations of authenticity are unjust? This is where standpoint epistemology is helpful. Investigating the effects of norms of authenticity by beginning with the effects on the lives of the oppressed reveals the conditions under which norms of authenticity protect vulnerable people, and when they perpetuate oppression. I have argued that we need to pay attention to the ways that oppression functions by circumscribing fixed boundaries of identities, rejecting fluidity, and encouraging surveillance of marginalized groups. Additionally, standpoint epistemology draws our attention to the value of privacy for oppressed groups and the ways in which playfulness can be a useful form of resistance to oppressive norms.

To summarize this section, I have argued that trustworthiness is an important epistemic virtue that undergirds the objectivity of a community and facilitates members' ability to form true beliefs. Virtuous epistemic agents will pay attention to others' epistemic vulnerabilities and when others are justly trusting them to maintain a consistently authentic online identity. In many contexts, epistemically trustworthy agents will live up to community norms of authenticity. But this does not mean that virtue always demands that we live up to others' expectations of authenticity. Sometimes norms of authenticity are oppressive, and sometimes the value of authenticity is trumped by other considerations, such as privacy. In the next section, I further explore these questions of when to violate expectations of authenticity. In addition to the ethical reasons for questioning the value of upholding norms of authenticity that I presented in this section, I show that, under the right circumstances, inauthentic self-presentation can have epistemic value.

But before I move on to the epistemic value of online trickery, I want to address one objection to the virtue theory presented here. One might worry that a virtue-theoretic approach to these complexities of authenticity is overly individualistic and places the onus on individuals to avoid harm while letting the corporations who set policies and the governing agencies who have resisted regulating online spaces off the hook. To make this objection concrete, MacAulay and Moldes criticize Facebook for attempting to shift the blame for the harms of the real-name policy from Facebook onto individual bad actors (MacAulay and Moldes 2016). In the wake of public protest by drag queens and others against the policy, Chris Cox, vice president at Facebook, apologized for the harm caused, but defended the policy by arguing that imposters are responsible for "mass impersonation, trolling, domestic abuse, and higher rates of bullying and intolerance" (Cox 2014). But as MacAuley and Moldes point out, Cox and Facebook were attempting to shift responsibility for these problems onto bad-acting imposters, rather than Facebook's own privacy policies that fail to protect users from the problems of impersonation, domestic abuse, and bullying (MacAulay and Moldes 2016, 15). Thus, one might worry that a virtue approach that recognizes the harm of imposture and argues for individuals to adopt the virtue of trustworthiness might provide cover for such moves by Facebook and others.

In response, I argue that a virtue approach does not support such an individualistic ethics and epistemology because a full virtue theory recognizes that all of us are embedded in social histories and institutions that shape our ability to be virtuous and which need to be properly virtuous themselves. We are constructed as online agents by platforms that influence our conceptions of what is right, what is real, and what we can do. Nancy Potter argues that a requirement that is necessary for us to be fully virtuous is that "our institutions and governing bodies be virtuous" (Potter 2002, 29). She takes this to be an Aristotelian point that "we are political by nature (Aristotle 1969, 1253a2), and how good we are is a matter of how good our institutions are (Aristotle 1969, 1103b3, bk. VII. 7, 1179b31–1180a20)" (Potter 2002, 29). She provides concrete case studies of ways in which institutional policies both prevent certain agents from being trustworthy and also cast other agents as inherently suspicious and untrustworthy. My analysis of the complexity of norms of authenticity is an attempt to raise the same concerns about the need for institutional and structural reform online. We need to look at the particular policies of social media platforms and organize collectively to make them more just, and we need to dismantle the structures of monopolistic digital capitalism, which organizes our epistemic landscapes around corporate profit for a small number of technology companies. Concretely, this means that we need to resist oppressive policies like Facebook's real-name policy and resist Facebook's attempt to conscript us into agents of surveillance for its data-mining operations. To address MacAuley and Moldes's concerns, we can hold Facebook accountable for its own failures, while simultaneously recognizing that imposture can be harmful. With these considerations of the need for resistance in mind, I now turn to my argument for the epistemic value of online tricksters who strategically betray expectations of authenticity in ways that resist oppression.

3.4. Tricksters: Resisting Oppression

The trickster is a powerful archetype who appears in many cultures and art forms. The trickster often appears as a wily prankster who fools others in ways that teach lessons of human folly. Tricksters are subversive. As Gabriella Coleman describes, "Tricksters are united by a few characteristics, such as the burning desire to defy or defile rules, norms, and laws" (Coleman 2014, 34). Coleman cites Native Americans' Coyote, the Nordic Loki, and Shakespeare's Puck as examples of tricksters. Her account of Anansi from West African and Caribbean folklore particularly captures the spirit of the trickster I have in mind: Anansi is "a spider who sometimes imparts knowledge or wisdom—and sometimes casts doubt or seeds confusion" (Coleman 2014, 33). The trickster is a fascinating epistemic character. On the one hand, the trickster is untrustworthy and deceptive. But on the other hand, the trickster's pranks often create opportunities for grasping knowledge and wisdom otherwise inaccessible. Thus, analyzing the trickster illuminates the complexity of trustworthiness as an epistemic virtue. As I will show, the internet is fertile ground for epistemically intriguing trickery.

This section focuses on trustworthiness as a complex virtue for tricksters who intentionally betray expectations of authenticity in virtuous acts of resistance against oppression. For example, the trickster may take advantage of a privileged group or person's ignorant and oppressive expectations of the oppressed's behavior. María Lugones describes her playful trickery as follows:

I can be stereotypically intense or be the real thing and, if you are Anglo, you do not know which one I am *because* I am Latin-American. . . . I can see that gringos see me as stereotypically intense because I am, as a Latin-American, constructed that way but I may or may not *intentionally* animate the stereotype or the real thing knowing that you may not see it in anything other than in the stereotypical construction. This ambiguity is funny and is not just funny, it is survival-rich. (Lugones 2003, 92)

Navigating "worlds" in which they are constructed according to stereotypes, oppressed people sometimes animate the stereotypes in order to get along with privileged others. But trickily playing off the ignorance of the privileged is not merely a survival tool; it can also be a means of challenging and educating the privileged. When telling the truth is dangerous, there are "truths that only the fool can speak and only the trickster can play out without harm" (Lugones 2003, 92). Sarah Hoagland notes that in lesbian communities, a working-class or Black lesbian might pull the leg of a privileged lesbian who is in the grip of dominant values (Hoagland 1988, 245–46). Such tricksters' presence in the community prompts privileged lesbians to work to unlearn their ignorance to avoid being tricked. The privileged, if they do not take themselves too seriously, can laugh at themselves when a trickster pokes fun at their ignorance.

But often, the privileged react with anger at the betrayal of expectations involved in trickery. For example, when Coco Fusco and Guillermo Gómez-Peña's counter-Columbus-quincentenary performance art piece titled "Two Undiscovered Amerindians Visit . . . " was discovered as an act of trickery, it was condemned for being deceptive (Fusco 1995; Hoagland 2007, 104–5). The piece was staged at art and natural history museums and public squares in the United States, United Kingdom, Australia, Spain, and Argentina. Fusco and Gómez-Peña lived in a cage and presented themselves as members of a newly discovered Amerindian tribe. Signs around the cage provided fake facts about the tribe, and visitors were allowed to interact with the caged people by having their photos taken with them or paying them to dance. Many audience members believed the fake signs and taunted or simply gazed at the supposed museum specimens. Fusco recalls, "As we assumed the stereotypical role of the domesticated savage, many audience members felt entitled to assume the role of colonizer, only to find themselves uncomfortable with the implications of the game" (Fusco 1995, 47). Fusco and Gómez-Peña tricked visitors into believing they were seeing human specimens,[7] and the visitors ignored evidence to the contrary. When the trickery was revealed, many felt betrayed by the manipulation of expectations of truth-telling within scientific museums. But the piece ingeniously reveals those expectations and asks challenging questions about whose story is presented as truth. Thus, trickery can be an important resistance tool.

3.4.1. The Epistemic Benefits of Betrayal

As discussed in section 3.3.2, the trustworthy person follows the Doctrine of the Mean (Potter 2002, 14–16). Recall that on Aristotle's account, the virtuous person has the right emotions and engages in the right actions to the proper degree "at the right times, about the right things, toward the right people, for the right end, and in the right way" (Aristotle 1969, 1106b15–25). Can anything more substantive be said about the appropriate circumstances for betraying trust? In this section, I offer the following criteria that flesh out the Doctrine-of-the-Mean account of trustworthiness: *A betrayal is epistemically vicious when it entrenches or promotes oppressive, exclusionary networks of trust, and a betrayal is epistemically virtuous when it undermines exclusionary practices and/or expands trust networks to involve the oppressed.* Since there are epistemic goods other than objectivity and truth, objectivity-decreasing betrayals are vicious only ceteris paribus (mutatis mutandis for virtuous betrayals). I argue that these criteria properly distinguish between imposters (like MacMaster), who are untrustworthy, and tricksters (like Fusco and Gómez-Peña), who virtuously betray oppressive expectations.

Recall the two points of agreement between feminist empiricist and feminist standpoint epistemologies: objectivity requires diversity and critical community interactions. Exclusionary, oppressive networks of trust impede critical dialogue from a diversity of values and social locations. Thus, oppressive norms that promote a climate of distrust in oppressed groups threaten

---

[7] One might object that Fusco and Gómez-Peña did not trick the public, since Fusco claims that "[o]ur original intent was to create a satirical commentary on Western concepts of the exotic, primitive Other," and that the audience's acceptance of the performance as literal was unexpected (Fusco 1995, 37). But although their initial intent may not have been to trick the public, they did refuse to correct the audience's misinterpretations once it became clear from the first performance that many were confused (Fusco 1995, 50). Thus, I interpret their decision to continue the performance without clarification as a case of trickery.

objectivity. Acts of betrayal that undermine these oppressive norms can promote an inclusive climate of trust and thereby promote objectivity. To put the point somewhat paradoxically, acts of betrayal can actually in the long run promote trust, when they are betrayals of oppressive norms that constrict networks of trust. For this reason, tricksters who betray others' trust in them to be authentic are displaying practical wisdom by choosing a just course of action, when pursuing justice trumps the virtue of living up to others' expectations. Such tricksters should not be condemned as unethical, nor praised merely for strategic cunning, when their acts of resistance expand trust networks. Such resistance can strengthen the oppressed's self-trust, and also challenge the stereotypes and conceptual frameworks that prevent others from trusting the oppressed. In "Imposters, Tricksters, and Trustworthiness as an Epistemic Virtue," I argued that two types of tricksters meet my criteria from earlier: revealed tricksters (whose betrayal is eventually recognized) and stealth tricksters (whose trickery remains hidden) (Frost-Arnold 2014a). Both display practical wisdom, but in different ways. In this chapter, I focus on revealed tricksters because epistemically interesting types of online hoaxes often use this form of trickery.

Revealed tricksters often resist oppression by making the privileged aware of their oppressive norms. They trick the privileged into seeing how their ignorant expectations of oppressed people promote exclusionary trust networks, constructing only the privileged as trustworthy and credible. Fusco and Gómez-Peña betrayed the expectations of visitors to the museums that everything can be taken literally. Many visitors and officials condemned their betrayal as immoral. But this reaction ignores the virtue of resisting oppressive norms. Fusco and Gómez-Peña expose the cultural imperialism that both allows white settlers to erase others and excludes colonized people from the production of knowledge about them. Norms of expertise and expectations of detached inquiry support the position of settler elites as knowers and undermine the authority of colonized people. In tricking spectators into examining their expectations of what is in museums, who put it there, and whose conceptions of knowledge and expertise ought to be trusted, Fusco and Gómez-Peña resist the exclusion of colonized people from the trust networks that constitute the scientific community. In response to museum representatives who asked the artists to correct the audience's literal interpretation, Fusco says, "We found this particularly ironic, since museum staffs are perhaps the most aware of the rampant distortion of reality that can occur in the labeling of artifacts from other cultures. In other words, we were not the only ones who were lying; our lies simply told a different story. For making this manifest, we were perceived as either noble savages or evil tricksters, dissimulators who discredit museums and betray public trust" (Fusco 1995, 50). The performance piece provides a powerful opportunity for strong objectivity. Audience members who were "taken in" and later realized that the piece was satirical can reflect on how they appeared to the artists. This enables a reflective audience member to "pass over in thought" to the world of the artists—"to look back at the self in all its cultural particularity from a more distant, critical, objectifying location" (Harding 1991, 151). From this location, audience members might see their patterns of trust and distrust (e.g., their trust in museums where the knowledge of colonized people is excluded).[8]

I say that audience members who were tricked *can* reflect and gain a more objective view of the world because there is of course no guarantee that people *will* take this opportunity to reflect and gain an epistemically superior perspective. Motivated reasoning and ego-protective defensiveness often kick in and prevent people from updating their beliefs in the face of new evidence. So I am not claiming that trickery will always have an epistemically beneficial effect on their audience, but trickery can provide valuable opportunities for positive epistemic change.

In contrast, MacMaster's imposture does not expand networks of trust. Instead, it further constricts trust networks, and thus cannot be excused by my argument here. Because MacMaster speaks in place of authentic Syrian activists, this imposture further denies them participation and credibility in the epistemic community. Not only does speaking in place of others exclude marginalized people from trust networks, but the exposure of MacMaster's imposture casts suspicion on these marginalized others and the social media networks through which they speak. Thus, there is no epistemic virtue in this act of betrayal, according to my account of trustworthiness.

3.4.2. Internet Tricksters

The internet provides fertile ground for tricksters. The availability of some degree of anonymity, the ability to easily mimic markers of an identity (e.g.,

---

[8] By focusing on the value of revealing the trickery, I do not claim that this exhausts the epistemic value of the performance. Audience members who knew it was satire could also learn something from the piece; for example, by reflecting on why they found the satire unsettling.

photos, usernames, website design, URLs), and the place of humor in internet culture all encourage internet trickery.[9] And the relative difficulty in detecting hoaxes, the scope of the audience, and the speed with which hoaxes can travel all contribute to online trickery's effectiveness. In her study of the hacker group Anonymous, Coleman describes the internet as "a petri dish for pranking" (Coleman 2014, 35). In this section, I show that this petri dish has cultivated some epistemically fascinating culture jammers and media activist tricksters. I argue that internet tricksters have made useful epistemic contributions that are worth distinguishing from the harms of internet imposters.

Consider the Yes Men, a group of anti-corporate media activists who have been using the internet (and other media) to pull off pranks since the late 1990s. Starting with a partnership between Mike Bonanno and Andy Bichlbaum (pseudonyms used by Igor Vamos and Jacques Servin), the Yes Men's general recipe for successful internet trickery involves using fake websites that mimic real corporate, government, or media sites (Reilly 2013, 1247). The fake websites have URLs and design that trick readers into believing they are looking at the actual site for the World Trade Organization (WTO), Shell, Dow Chemical, or the Canadian government, for example. The content of the fake sites parodies the real organizations in order to draw attention to the corporate greed, corruption, exploitation, and government inaction against which the Yes Men agitate. While careful readers of the fake sites find the parody clear at some point, the site often tricks people for a while, and even fools some completely. This often leads officials to contact the Yes Men through the sites to invite representatives of the real organizations to conferences and media interviews. The Yes Men then show up at these events pretending to be representatives from the real entities, and pull off further outlandish pranks. For example, due to a fake website, the Yes Men received an invitation to appear on BBC World TV. The producers

---

[9] While it is common to use the term 'internet culture,' I use this term with some caution. There is, of course, no *one* internet culture, and it is inaccurate to describe online culture as something distinct from an imagined offline culture. Additionally, the notion of internet culture is often coded white, straight, and masculine. And people labelled as "social justice warriors" are often charged with misunderstanding internet humor and taking online harassment too seriously. In this way, the concept of internet culture is harmful when it is conceived of as entirely unserious and harassment is excused as playful lulz. This rhetorical move is often made in association with the term 'trolling,' with harassment being excused as 'just trolling.' For this reason, I follow several internet scholars in avoiding using the term 'trolls' to refer to internet tricksters (Phillips 2015a, 2015b; Phillips, Beyer, and Coleman 2017). That said, humor does play a large role in internet communication and our expectations of what we will encounter online (e.g., memes).

thought they were inviting a representative from Dow Chemical to talk about the twentieth anniversary of the Bhopal disaster, a chemical industrial accident which killed over 3,000 and injured over 500,000 Indians in 1984. In the BBC interview, Bichlbaum, posing as the Dow representative, took responsibility for the incident, pledging to dedicate $12 billion to fully compensate the victims and remediate the site (Reilly 2013, 1248). The TV appearance had a dramatic impact, with Dow's stock dropping $2 billion in the hours before Dow issued a correction. The hoax drew attention to Dow's failure to take responsibility and compensate the victims who continue to live with devastating health effects. It also showed that it was completely within Dow's power to do something to redress the harms of the Bhopal disaster.

The Yes Men use the term "identity correction" to refer to their strategy with such hoaxes. In the documentary *The Yes Men*, Mike Bonanno explains this strategy in relation to their pretense of representing the WTO:

> We're calling that basic idea 'identity correction'. Like saying, ok, these things that are not really presenting themselves honestly or that hide something about their nature that is really scary, we want to bring that out, we want to show that . . . For the WTO, we think that the WTO is doing all these terrible things that are hurting people, and they're saying the exact opposite. And so we're interested in correcting their identity: in the same way that an identity thief steals somebody's identity in order to basically engage in criminal practices, we target people we see as criminals, and we steal their identity to try to make them honest, or to try to present a more honest face. (Ollman, Price, and Smith 2003)

The real WTO presents itself as a legitimate, neutral institution ensuring that "trade flows as smoothly, predictably and freely as possible" ("What Is the WTO?" n.d.). But the Yes Men aim to correct this deceptive self-presentation by revealing the WTO as a tool that richer nations use to exploit poorer ones. Their goal is to present a truer picture. Additionally, the Yes Men seek objectivity. They want to balance out the disproportionate voice that rich nations and corporations have in the media by hijacking their identities to give voice to alternative perspectives. In just this brief description, we can see the seeds of these internet tricksters' epistemic contributions to truth acquisition and objectivity. To see how this works in detail, let us look at a Yes Men climate-change-related hoax.

The documentary *The Yes Men Are Revolting* presents this hoax as formulated in response to a call from a Ugandan climate activist, Kodili Chandia from ActionAid, who invited the Yes Men to come to Uganda to plan an action in advance of the 2009 UN Climate Change Conference in Copenhagen (referred to as COP15). This resulted in a Yes Men hoax perpetrated at COP15 in collaboration with Ugandan, Canadian, and European activists. The activists' goal was "to highlight the most powerful nations' obstruction of meaningful progress in Copenhagen, to push for just climate debt reparations, and to call out Canada in particular for its terrible climate policy" ("Activists Come Clean," n.d.). The hoax began with fake Canadian government websites, a fake Twitter account, and fake press releases announcing that Canada was taking dramatic steps in emission reduction and was initiating a climate debt reparations program for African countries. Later in the day, a fake press release drew attention to media response to the announcement by linking to a fake *Wall Street Journal* article. And an elaborate fake live press conference was streamed online in which a fake Ugandan government representative praised the Canadian actions while sitting next to a fake Canadian official. The activists continued to circulate fake press releases throughout the day to continue to draw attention to the concerns of the Ugandan activists ("Canada Freaks out the World," n.d.; Reilly 2013; Bichlbaum, Bonanno, and Nix 2014). This hoax drew the ire of Canadian officials at COP15, who decried the hoax, a response that furthered the activists' agenda by making it clear that Canada was not making significant cuts in emissions and that it was not committed to taking responsibility for the harm its actions cause poorer nations (Taber 2009).

Using this prank as a case study, how does the trickery of the Yes Men increase objectivity? First, recall that ignoring, silencing, and denying epistemic authority to marginalized people hinders objective knowledge production. This has been a persistent problem in climate change deliberations with the voices of disproportionately affected poorer nations from the Global South being drowned out by wealthier Global North countries and their multinational corporations.[10] The COP15 prank counters this silencing by drawing attention to the work of Ugandan activists. This is a fascinating use of identity correction in which activists steal the identity of government

---

[10] This erasure was highlighted when The Associated Press published a story on youth climate activism at the World Economic Conference in Davos that failed to mention the presence of Ugandan activist Vanessa Nakate and also cropped her out of a picture of activists posing with Greta Thunberg (Okereke and Burari 2020).

institutions and use the epistemic authority and media attention traditionally granted to such entities to give voice to typically unheard groups. Much of the Yes Men's media activism is aimed at upending the status quo in which corporations and governments with expensive public relations agents can drive policy conversations and negotiations. The ability to engage in internet trickery is crucial to their activism. As Mike Bonanno says,

> [T]he internet made it possible for us bottom-feeders to do it at a scale that was compared to what [PR agents] were doing. We had this outsize or disproportional ability to act in an arena that used to be reserved for these huge companies, or these very powerfully connected people, the Roger Ailes of the world. So, for a brief window, we had this possibility of being these really small fish, but having the effect of the bigger fish—at least in terms of the media. (qtd. in McLeod 2020b, 304)

Not only do these acts of trickery help marginalized activists gain access to networks of epistemic authority in which corporate elites have an outsized voice, but they also challenge stereotypes that function to discredit activists. When activists are stereotyped as hysterical, unsophisticated agitators who do not understand the realities of public policy and who make unreasonable demands, their voices are easily ignored. The COP15 hoax challenges this stereotype by showing that activists can craft policy and set agendas that are, in fact, credible—credible enough to fool many into believing that they come from government agencies. These hoaxes show that another world is possible, a world in which non-elites craft policy. This possible world is so close that it does not take much of a hoax for us to hear these policies and not immediately reject them as unreasonable. Thus, the Yes Men's internet trickery meets my account of trustworthiness by helping to increase networks of trust to include the oppressed, and this increases objectivity.

This trickery is also veritistically valuable, and veritism helps us see another important difference between the trickery of the Yes Men and the imposture of MacMaster. This quote illustrates the Yes Men's veritistic goals:

> The critical difference with what we do is we're telling stories to reveal more information, not to obscure it ... There is a phase in which you reveal [the trickery], and then we get more attention and get to tell the whole story—you get to get the facts and information in that you want to. What we're

doing is not really 'fake news,' although it uses trickery to get there. It fits in better with traditions of satire, where the goal of satire is not to make people believe something that is false, but rather to get them interested in discovering the truth. (qtd. in McLeod 2020a, 310)

The COP15 hoax uses internet trickery to get facts and information to more people and motivates them to discover the truth about climate reparations and Canada's climate debt. Undermining exclusionary practices, expanding networks of trust to include the oppressed, motivating truth-seeking, and disseminating facts are all veritistically valuable because they help members of an epistemic community form true beliefs and avoid errors. While the Yes Men's hoaxes may temporarily disseminate false beliefs, their revelation of the trickery undercuts the epistemic harm of the deception. As Andy Bichlbaum puts it, "There has to be a distinction between what we do, which is to tell a few lies in order to reveal a bigger truth, and what this other fake news is doing" (qtd. in McLeod 2020a, 311).

Social epistemology helps us unpack several different ways in which trickery can tell "a few lies in order to reveal a bigger truth." First, the bigger truth may be a more interesting truth. Goldman's veritism accords more veritistic value to true beliefs that answer questions that interest the inquirer (Goldman 1999, 87–96, 351–52). For example, the question "What is the number of hairs on my head?" is likely to be of much less interest to inquirers than the question "Is climate change a pressing threat?" The details of how Goldman cashes out the notion of interest are not important here, but his account does allow that democracies have an interest in an informed citizenry. This means that even though individual community members may not be initially curious about their country's climate change policies, the community has an interest in them knowing about the policies. Thus, one way to interpret the claim that the trickery reveals bigger truths through a few lies is that the trickery may temporarily spread some false beliefs about less interesting propositions (e.g., that such-and-such office released such-and-such press release on this particular day), but that these lies help reveal more interesting truths (e.g., that the Canadian government has an ongoing policy of refusing to acknowledge its climate debt).

Second, a "bigger truth" might be a more fundamental truth that helps cognizers infer or draw connections to other truths. True beliefs about root causes of disparate problems would seem particularly veritistically valuable in this regard, because forming true beliefs about fundamental causes can help cognizers see truths about connections between phenomena and also reveal further phenomena that might remain hidden. The Yes Men's hoaxes reveal much about who has the power to make policy, what their values are, who has easy access to the media, and who does not. These are all 'big' truths that, when grasped, help citizens come to see how governments, corporations, and the media function together to maintain the status quo. A Yes Men hoax can be incredibly powerful at helping us grasp the relationships among governments, corporations, and the media in capitalist systems. While a hoax may temporarily spread some isolated false beliefs about a Canadian press release, the hoax can still be veritistically valuable because it helps many people form true beliefs about the relationships between often-hidden structures of power in policy production, epistemic authority, and knowledge distribution.

One might argue that MacMaster's imposture also has epistemic value because in tricking the public it reveals some bigger truths about the nature of the media. For example, one might argue that MacMaster's imposture revealed how Western media relied on Arab Spring social media accounts that were hard to verify. Coming to understand how the media and the public can be fooled can provide some understanding of the relationships between the media and various entities. Thus, one might argue that MacMaster's imposture had epistemic merit. In responding to this objection, I want to highlight what I take to be a fundamental difference between epistemically harmful imposters and beneficial tricksters. Notice that the Yes Men always "punch up" while MacMaster "punches down." In other words, the Yes Men target powerful entities who have an outsized dominance in the trust networks that produce knowledge. They aim to correct the identity of powerful entities who have gained access to these trust networks through deceptive self-presentation. In so doing, they both give room for marginalized voices, and they help us understand how it is that such voices are routinely marginalized. In contrast, MacMaster and other internet imposters (such as fake Black twitter accounts) target those with less power, those who are already marginalized in trust networks. They attempt to steal what little credibility those marginalized voices do have. It is true that once this imposture is exposed, there may be greater understanding of how the media and the public can be fooled. However, in MacMaster's case this understanding comes at the expense of even further undermining the trust in marginalized people. The Yes Men's activism teaches this lesson without perpetuating the exclusion of oppressed people from networks of trust. This is a crucial difference. Having argued for criteria that mark the distinction between harmful imposters and beneficial tricksters, I now turn to guidelines that help agents decide when to engage in trickery. These guidelines help agents determine which features of the situation are epistemically relevant to the choice at hand. But before we can begin to outline these situational considerations, we need to recognize that epistemic landscapes can change in ways that shape the epistemic outcomes of trickery.

3.4.3. Changing Epistemic Landscapes and Trickery

One of the reasons that I break up my discussion of online disinformation into two chapters (this one and the next on fake news) is that there has been a significant shift in both expert and public perception of internet trustworthiness. This is something of an oversimplified generalization, but in 2011 MacMaster's imposture appeared on the scene at a time of optimism about the power of the internet to share knowledge and empower democratic activism. MacMaster's imposture was particularly shocking against the backdrop of this optimism, based on a significant degree of trust in the internet. But as I will argue in the next chapter, 2016 saw the rise of concern about fake news and a concomitant increase in pessimism and distrust in the internet as a space for truth and bias correction.[11] There are many reasons given for why the internet became less trustworthy during this period, including increasing sophistication in state and corporate actors with disinformation agendas, the increasing monopolization of online platforms that created financial incentives for fakery, and a general erosion of norms of trustworthiness and truth-telling. Whatever the cause, this apparent shift in the epistemic landscape of the internet presents interesting questions for social epistemologists. In particular, how does internet trickery have different epistemic consequences in different epistemic contexts? And what features of the situation should a virtuous trickster pay attention to in deciding whether and how to engage in a prank?

Since the Yes Men have been in the trickery business since the late 1990s, their work provides a window into how changing epistemic landscapes may change the effectiveness of online trickery. Since 2016, the Yes Men have

---

[11] As noted earlier, there were many signs of online fakery earlier than 2016, such as the attacks on Black women surrounding #EndFathersDay and #YourSlipIsShowing, but these signs were often ignored in the mainstream in ways that exacerbated the problems.

worried that their pranks are having less of an effect. For example, in the midst of the Black Lives Matter uprising of July 2020, Andy Bichlbaum wrote an essay titled "Creative Trickery Is Dead, Long Live Creative Trickery" in which he urged activists to get out into the streets and raised concerns about the value of trickery during the Trump era: "nothing creative I've done in the past four years has felt useful. It's as if our brand of trickery only serves to expose hidden truths, and when nothing is hidden—when the emperor already has no clothes, and nobody cares—exposure is useless" (Bichlbaum 2020). In an interview from 2018, Bichlbaum wondered whether their kind of trickery works best when the trickster can shock people by violating norms or widely held values. Presenting an extreme version of their target "doesn't work anymore. It's not guaranteed that it will offend people, and you can't rely on universals like human rights" (qtd. in McLeod 2020a, 311). For example, Bichlbaum says that it used to be the case that "You couldn't say, 'I want to enslave people' or 'I want to imprison immigrants in concentration camps'" (qtd. in McLeod 2020a, 310). But given how desensitized the public had become by 2020 to Trump's racist policies and rhetoric, and given the complete abandonment of human rights in his agenda, people would not be shocked if a Yes Men prank revealed the imprisonment of immigrants in concentration camps as Trump's agenda. It may be that identity correction only works when the target's true identity is somewhat hidden. The epistemic landscape may need to suffer from an epistemology of ignorance about the target. And perhaps there need to be some shared values (e.g., respect for human rights) or expectations that, when flagrantly violated in a prank, create a sense of shock that motivates curiosity about the truth. This potentially makes trickery less effective in an era of widespread fake news, which, as I will argue in the next chapter, increases polarization. In a polarized society, there may be insufficient shared values and expectations that tricksters can violate for shock value. This descriptive analysis of the relationship between changing landscape and effectiveness of trickery raises many interesting epistemic questions, but how should a virtuous trickster think through how to act in light of these considerations?

3.4.4. Who Should We Be Online?

I have shown that my criteria for the epistemic appraisal of betrayal capture the epistemic virtue of many acts of trickery and the vice of impostures. Thus, my account provides guidelines for agents considering betraying others' expectations of authenticity. But such guidelines cannot alone determine whether a betrayal is warranted. Instead, they direct the virtuous agent's attention to the most epistemically relevant features of the situation: namely, the effects of betrayal on the diversity of trust networks. Detailed information about the particular situation at hand is needed to determine whether any particular case will constrict trust networks or expand them to involve the oppressed. And often the effect of a betrayal on the three types of trust (self-trust, trust in others, and trust in practices) can be mixed (e.g., it increases self-trust but decreases some groups' trust in others). The epistemically responsible agent must attend to the details of the situation and must also make difficult judgments about which act has the most trust-increasing effect. Therefore, our epistemic communities require members with virtuous characters that include wise judgment and well-honed epistemic sensibilities to identify the relevant particularities of the situation.

My examples of tricksters illustrate the complexities such wise tricksters must confront. First, possible side-effects of the prank that increase distrust in the marginalized must be investigated. Suppose that Fusco and Gómez-Peña had the opportunity to perform at a museum that was simultaneously presenting an exhibit curated by members of a real Indigenous population from South America. Should they present the piece? Making this decision requires determining whether their piece would undermine trust in the other exhibit. In wrestling with these complexities, the virtuous trickster should consider how the trickery affects the networks of trust necessary for objectivity and truth. Second, since my account of virtue is consequentialist, virtuous tricksters will attend to whether their trickery will be effective. Thus, they will ask themselves whether the prank will shock its intended audience. Thus, attention to the audience's background beliefs and values is necessary. As part of these considerations, virtuous tricksters should ask themselves whether their target's nature is hidden. For social justice activists, the answer to the question "Who should we be online?" may depend on the epistemic landscape. When powerful entities have been successful at hiding their true exploitative and oppressive natures, trickery may be a useful and virtuous tool for spreading knowledge and opening up networks of trust. But when powerful agents dispense with subterfuge and make their oppressive agenda blatantly obvious, trickery may not be effective. In those circumstances, activists may want to follow Bichlbaum's advice and get out into the streets, rather than engage in online pranks.

In conclusion, trustworthiness is a complex epistemic virtue. Untrustworthiness in epistemic communities can damage social practices that enhance objectivity and truth acquisition. Untrustworthy imposture can be an arrogant act of privilege, further silencing marginalized voices. It can thwart their efforts to enter epistemic communities that have previously excluded them. But sometimes betraying the trust of others is useful for disrupting systems that exclude oppressed groups from networks of trust. Some who are castigated as imposters are in fact engaging in epistemically beneficial acts of resistance. By challenging stereotypes or undermining structures that promote distrust in the oppressed, such tricksters are epistemically virtuous.

The internet provides rich opportunities for imposture and trickery. Epistemically virtuous agents will eschew the damaging practice of adopting fake identities of marginalized people in order to spread an agenda or gain credibility and/or access to conversations. And virtuous tricksters will carefully assess the epistemic landscape and the consequences of pranks to ensure that any hoaxes work to resist oppression by undermining exclusion and/or expanding networks of trust. Unfortunately, in the post-2016 internet we see far too many acts of vicious imposture. But, as I will argue in the next chapter, the problem of online disinformation ranges further than simply problems with inauthentic self-presentation—there are a host of causes of the fake news problem, and understanding the epistemology of fake news requires additional tools from social epistemology.

4
Fakers

In January 2017, four teenagers used Facebook Live to broadcast themselves physically and verbally attacking a teenager with intellectual disabilities whom they had kidnapped (Yan, Jones, and Almasy 2017). Following the incident, alt-right blogger Mike Cernovich and his followers created a fake news story that Black Lives Matter supporters had orchestrated the attack.

> [Cernovich] and his followers 'brainstormed' the hashtag #BLMKidnapping and coordinated to make it trend on Twitter; it was used 480,000 times in 24 hours and trended across the United States. While police and BLM advocates decried the connection, the theory spread widely and was mentioned in most of the mainstream media stories about the kidnapping. (Marwick and Lewis 2017, 36)

The false account of a "Black Lives Matter Kidnapping" is just one example of what is now widely referred to as 'fake news.' While, as we saw in the previous chapter, the problem of online disinformation has been discussed by scholars, journalists, and the public for years, concern about fake news exploded during the 2016 U.S. presidential election. Outlandish stories gained widespread attention, such as the Pizzagate conspiracy theory that members of the Democratic party were involved with a human trafficking and child sexual abuse ring run out of a pizza restaurant in Washington, DC (Kang 2016). Evidence that Russian 'troll farms' of paid operatives planted and disseminated fake stories fueled investigations into foreign interference in the U.S. election, as well as the British Brexit vote (Booth et al. 2017; B. Collins and Cox 2017; Timberg and Dwoskin 2017). In 2020, concerns about disinformation rose again in public discourse, as the world wrestled with the COVID-19 pandemic alongside an 'infodemic' of conspiracy theories, snake oil salesmen, and dangerously inaccurate public health information spread throughout the hybrid media system (AFP et al. 2020; DiResta 2020; Donovan 2020; Ingraham 2020; Kreps and Kriner 2020; V. A. Young

2020). In recent years, the public has been exposed to such a bewildering array of false news stories, exposés of hoaxes, allegations of media bias, and manipulation of internet platforms that many people feel that they have lost a grip on what to believe and how to tell truth from fiction in the media. The internet and its role in our media landscape are at the heart of discussions of what has come to be known as "the fake news problem."[1]

This chapter presents a social epistemology of the fake news problem as it appeared during and after the 2016 U.S. election period. I begin by clarifying terminology, defining 'fake news,' and discussing problems with this term. Then I summarize some of the recent literature on the causes of the host of problems associated with fake news. This is an extremely rich and burgeoning body of scholarship, which I cannot possibly comprehensively encapsulate in one chapter. My goal with this section is to provide a taste of the complexity and scope of the challenges we face in our media landscape. Understanding some of the purported causes of the dissemination and uptake of fake news helps us grasp its many manifestations and the ways in which important features of human psychology, technological design, and social structures are mutually implicated in news media manipulation.

Once the scale and complexity of these problems are clear, the obvious next question to ask is: what should we do about this? Which interventions will be most effective is largely an empirical question. We need more research to determine which of the proposed causes of our predicament are the most significant drivers of the problems. As Shao et al. explain, the nature of the cause determines the appropriate solution:

> If the problem is mainly driven by cognitive limitations, we need to invest in news literacy education; if social media platforms are fostering the creation of echo chambers, algorithms can be tweaked to broaden exposure to diverse views; and if malicious bots are responsible for many of the falsehoods, we can focus attention on detecting this kind of abuse. (Shao et al. 2018, 2)

This crucial empirical work is being pursued by sociologists, anthropologists, computer scientists, media scholars, and many others. Social epistemology

---

[1] While it is commonly referred to as *the* fake news problem, there is not just one problem, but a host of interrelated epistemic problems. Nonetheless, I use the phrase 'the fake news problem' in this chapter, in part, because it is a helpful shortcut for referring to our current epistemic predicament.

also has much to offer in understanding the fake news problem. This chapter presents three different contributions made possible by the Feminist accounts of Objectivity, Veritism, Ignorance, Virtues, and Injustice (FOVIVI) epistemological frameworks introduced in Chapter 1. First, I argue that social epistemology helps us understand *why* the fake news problem is a *problem*, a point that more descriptive studies lack the tools to show. The normative frameworks of social epistemology are needed to show why a media landscape with high levels of disinformation is epistemically inferior to one with lower levels of disinformation. Second, the FOVIVI frameworks show that context matters for understanding fake news. In particular, racial context matters to fake news. By drawing on work by Charles Mills, I show that fake news does not just generate a generic form of ignorance; instead, it often feeds a specifically racist form of ignorance: white ignorance. Third, I illustrate one way in which social epistemology can be useful in suggesting solutions to the fake news problem: feminist accounts of objectivity offer ways that Facebook could have avoided disseminating fake news through its "Trending Topics" news feature. By adopting feminist approaches to objectivity, we may be able to address one of the many causes of online disinformation.

4.1. What Is Fake News?

'Fake news' is far from a precise term. A myriad of concerns about online disinformation, journalistic practices, and media manipulation have been widely discussed under this heading since use of the term exploded around the 2016 U.S. presidential election. This has led some scholars to attempt clarificatory projects to define the term and distinguish it from other related terms, such as 'disinformation' ("information that is deliberately false or misleading" [Jack 2017, 3]), 'misinformation' ("information whose inaccuracy is unintentional" [Jack 2017, 2]), and several other related terms like 'propaganda' and 'information operations' (cf. Jack 2017; N. Levy 2017; Rini 2017; Aikin and Talisse 2018; Gelfert 2018; Mukerji 2018; Fallis and Mathiesen 2019; Pepp, Michaelson, and Sterken 2019a). I do not have space in this chapter to substantively engage with all the debates surrounding how to cash out these terms and determine which one is most appropriate to describe any particular instance of what I am calling 'fake news,' nor is there space to articulate a stipulative definition that covers all of the phenomena I wish to capture in my account of the epistemology of fake news. Instead, to clarify how I use this term, I present two definitions that each capture aspects of our epistemic predicament that I will discuss.

Axel Gelfert defines 'fake news' as "the deliberate presentation of (typically) false or misleading claims *as news*, where the claims are misleading *by design*" (Gelfert 2018, 108 emphasis in original). This definition has several virtues for my purposes. First, it allows for multiple ways in which fake news is "unconstrained by the truth" (Gelfert 2018, 108). Some fake news stories are almost entirely factually inaccurate, but much of what fakers circulate is not wholly false news stories. Instead, as Benkler et al. point out, much fake news is "the purposeful construction of true or partly true bits of information into a message that is, at its core, misleading" (Benkler et al. 2017). Second, Gelfert emphasizes the deliberate ways in which fakers craft and disseminate stories to mislead the audience. This chapter focuses on fake news as a problem of intentional misleading of audiences. Thus, I do not consider accidental or unwitting false news reports as instances of fake news, nor do I label as 'fakers' satirists who produce intentionally recognizable satirical false news stories (e.g., writers at *The Onion* or *The Daily Show*). A third virtue of Gelfert's definition is that it does not build any particular motivation for fakery into the definition. For example, unlike 'propaganda,' which is often taken to refer to manipulation for an ideological agenda, 'fake news' has been usefully used to refer to disinformation disseminated for political, financial, or mischievous motivations (Gelfert 2018, 110).

One complicated feature of Gelfert's definition, and other uses of the term 'fake news,' is that it is premised on a distinction between 'real' and 'fake' news. On the one hand, this is a helpful feature of the term because one of the elements of our epistemic predicament is the mimicry of markers of traditional news media by agents who, unlike the epistemic ideal of journalists, feel unconstrained by the truth. Websites that intentionally adopt the stylistic conventions of traditional news sites in order to exploit the trust of readers are faking in a way that *The New York Times* website is not. Ideally, reports and sites that present themselves as news would contain truths rather than falsehoods. Gelfert's definition is useful because it highlights the fact that our current epistemic landscape often falls short of this ideal. On the other hand, this distinction between 'fake' and 'real' news can have negative consequences, when traditionally recognized news outlets make a rhetorical appeal to their status as 'real' news in order to bolster their credibility in the face of legitimate criticism (Coady 2019). This effect is especially powerful if fake news is framed as a new problem that arose in 2016 with Russian bot election interference or fake news sites created by Macedonian teens to make money from clickbait. In such discussions of fake news, traditional mainstream media sources (e.g., *The New York Times*) often figure as the old-guard, reliable foil to the new, unreliable internet sources. This is problematic when it obscures the history of unreliable reporting in traditional news media, such as during the buildup to the Iraq war (Coady 2019). Of course, this does not mean that *The New York Times* and *Breitbart* are equally reliable on average (cf. de Ridder 2019). I try to mitigate the problem Coady identifies by avoiding attributing the terms 'real' and 'fake' to sources as a global assessment of their reliability (i.e., I avoid phrases such as "real news sites/sources" and "fake news sites/sources"), and I instead focus on fake news stories, which can appear on any site or be disseminated by any sources, including mainstream media. Any source that promulgates a fake news story can (and should) be held accountable for any resulting harms. A third complication with Gelfert's definition for my purposes is that it does not highlight that part of the problem of fake news is the concerted effort to push and exploit the unclear boundaries of what news is at this moment in our media era. Gelfert's definition requires that fake news involve the presentation of claims "*as news*." This is useful for identifying the sites that mimic the traditional markers of news journalism to trick readers into sharing and believing false stories. But much of what is discussed under the heading of the "fake news problem" is the blurring of journalistic boundaries, such that it is unclear whether something is being presented *as news*, and the ways in which various actors manipulate this situation. This problem of confusion is part of what Michael Lynch calls the 'internet shell game' (Lynch 2018, 2019; Gunn and Lynch 2021). He notes that "Propagandists often don't care whether everyone, or even most people, really believe the specific things they are selling (although it turns out that lots of people always do) . . . They just have to get you confused enough so that you don't know what is true" (Lynch 2018).

For this reason, I also find Andrew Chadwick's definition of 'fake news' helpful: "the exploitation of the technological affordances and incentive structures of social media platforms, online search engines, and the broader news media industry to spread fabricated information for financial and/or political gain" (Chadwick 2017, 272). More simply, Chadwick characterizes the fake news problem as the hacking of the "hybrid media system," which, as we saw in Chapter 1, is a useful term he introduces to capture the media environment in which older and newer media are complexly interwoven and interconnected (Chadwick 2017). This chapter has a broader focus than just those websites designed to look like news sources but which are full of misleading stories. I am also concerned with attempts by media manipulators to push the boundaries of what is perceived as news, to confuse audiences about the nature of news dissemination in the hybrid media system, and to exploit the blurred journalistic boundaries to advance various agendas or profit financially.

Finally, I want to address an objection to the very use of the term 'fake news.' Several critics have argued that this term should be abandoned because it has been thoroughly captured by a right-wing, authoritarian agenda (Zuckerman 2017; Coady 2019; Habgood-Coote 2019, 2020; Freelon and Wells 2020). According to this objection, continuing to use the term keeps the authoritarians' framing of the issues at the forefront of the public's attention in damaging ways, undermining trust in media institutions (Zuckerman 2017; Habgood-Coote 2019). During his presidency, Trump attacked as 'fake news' any news reports or media entities which presented stories that angered him or countered his interests. This is such an egregious attack on an independent press that it must be opposed. For example, while CNN may certainly be an occasional purveyor of misinformation, the facts just do not support accusing it of intentionally exploiting the media landscape to spread disinformation; thus, it is just not appropriate to label it 'fake news' in the way Trump did. According to this objection, the best way to deal with such attacks on the press is to stop playing into Trump's narrative and to stop contributing to the fake news discourse. Additionally, David Coady argues that governments and corporate media entities have exploited the moral panic over fake news to censor speech that challenges powerful entities and orthodoxies (Coady 2019). Coady cites examples of 'fake news' discourse being used to legitimize anti–fake news laws and censorship efforts by Malaysia, Brazil, India, Germany, France, and the United Kingdom. On this objection, scholars who refer to "the fake news problem" add to this moral panic and provide justificatory tools to authoritarian censorship regimes.

I am very sympathetic to this objection. However, two considerations have led me to stick to 'fake news' here. First, part of what I want to analyze is the discourse surrounding 'fake news' that appeared in discussions of the 2016 internet. As discussed in previous chapters, it is important to recognize that social epistemology of the internet is historically contextual—different issues are taken to be epistemic problems at different times, partly due to changes in language and conceptual framings. In discussing issues of veracity, authenticity, and disinformation online, I have found it helpful to distinguish between the 2011 concerns about imposters and the 2016 concerns about fake news. Without using the term 'fake news,' I could not find an efficient way to discuss the differences between these historical moments and their associated sets of scholarly and popular analysis. Second, I am less pessimistic than the critics about the possible liberatory potential of the term. It is certainly true that Trump and other authoritarians have made much progress through the 'fake news' discourse, but I feel reluctant to concede this term to Trump and his ilk. As I will discuss in section 4.3, 'fake news' is a contested term that is used in multiple discourses to draw attention to several important challenges of our epistemic landscape. While critics of the term argue that left-wing uses of the term have been outpaced by right-wing success with it, I think they ignore a use of the term identified by Johan Farkas and Jannick Schou (Farkas and Schou 2018), who identify a discourse of critique of digital capitalism as a use of the 'fake news' term. Using the public's attention to the so-called fake news problem, critics of digital capitalism (including its racist and misogynistic dimensions) have found traction for addressing some of the epistemic harms of capitalism in an online age. I am interested in the liberatory potential for such discussions, and I am reluctant to drop the term and the attention to these issues that comes from using the most publicly recognizable term for a set of issues (cf. E. Brown 2019; Pepp, Michaelson, and Sterken 2019b). Of course, it may be that right-wing authoritarians have so captured this term that this potential is small and may have disappeared by the time this book is published. While it is somewhat outside the scope of my professional expertise as a philosopher, I have attempted to investigate whether this is the case at the time of writing. Not being convinced that this discursive battle has been definitely lost, I continue to use the term. However, I recognize that there are risks in my use of 'fake news,' and I accept responsibility for my mistake if I am proven wrong. Having clarified and defended my use of the term 'fake news,' I now turn to analyzing the literature on the purported causes of the fake news problem.

4.2. Causes of the Fake News Problem

In this section I outline some of the many proposed causes of our fake news predicament found in the literature on this topic that has exploded since the 2016 U.S. presidential election, but which was already growing before then. By 'causes' of the fake news problem, I mean factors that contribute to, maintain, or make possible the high levels of dissemination and uptake of fake news stories in our current information ecosystem. I cannot hope to give a comprehensive account of the proposed causes of the fake news problem in this chapter. Instead, I will highlight some of the purported causes that identify some of the key agents, structures, and technologies that sustain this problem. I have roughly categorized these alleged causes into three very broad categories to provide some structure that helps us see that these causes are not all alike in nature. The three categories are (1) cognitive/social psychological causes, (2) technological affordances/design features, and (3) social causes. Many of these causes are interrelated and mutually reinforcing. A brief introduction to these causes helps us understand the scope and complexity of the epistemic challenge facing us with fake news. I spend some time outlining many different types of cause of the fake news problem so that social epistemology, as a field, recognizes the scope and complexity of this problem that requires broad interdisciplinary conversations. Mainstream social epistemology has a tendency to narrowly conceive of the empirical and formal fields relevant to its work, for example, psychology, cognitive science, game theory, and behavioral economics. But recognizing the complexity of the fake news problem makes it clear that social epistemologists need to engage with scholars of race, gender, politics, critics of capitalism, and media studies, as well as computer scientists and engineers. Part of the feminist goal of this book is to broaden the scope of social epistemology. So outlining these connections motivates the need for broad, socially engaged interdisciplinary scholarship in social epistemology of the internet.

4.2.1. Cognitive/Psychological Causes

Cognitive science and social psychology have identified several cognitive tendencies and biases that make us particularly vulnerable to believing fake news stories. First, we are liable to *confirmation bias*, which is "the seeking or interpreting of evidence in ways that are partial to existing beliefs, expectations, or a hypothesis in hand" (Nickerson 1998, 175). Users tend to seek out media sources that make them feel comfortable and agree with their views, and they give undue weight to evidence that supports their previously held beliefs (Hendricks and Hansen 2014; boyd 2017; Shu et al. 2017). This makes us vulnerable to believing fake news stories that confirm our expectations. Boyd (2017) also argues that it makes fact checking a risky enterprise, since some studies show that we have a tendency to double down on our beliefs when provided with evidence against them (cf. Nyhan and Reifler 2010).[2]

A second troubling result of social psychology is the phenomenon of *group polarization* (Sunstein 2006, 2008; Silverman et al. 2016; Benkler et al. 2017; boyd 2017; Shu et al. 2017).[3] The cognitive problem here is that "members of a deliberating group typically end up in a more extreme position in line with their tendencies before deliberation began" (Sunstein 2006, 92). When users join online political groups, they join deliberating assemblies which, given group polarization, are likely to make their political views more extreme. This makes users more vulnerable to accepting outlandish, conspiratorial fake news stories.

Internet users' reliance on heuristics in evaluating online content also plays a role in the fake news problem. Internet users deploy an *endorsement heuristic*, which means that "people are inclined to perceive information and sources as credible if others do so also, without much scrutiny of the site content or source itself" (Metzger, Flanagin, and Medders 2010, 427). This makes users vulnerable to taking fake news as credible if others are endorsing and sharing it online (cf. Rini 2017). Another heuristic, the *frequency heuristic*, leads media consumers to form a positive opinion of information they come across frequently (Shu et al. 2017, 25). In a disinformation-rich environment in which fake news is trending, consumers may come across fake news stories often and thereby may come to accept them.

4.2.2. Technological Affordances/Design Features

Many have argued that the internet amplifies the epistemic impact of these cognitive tendencies and biases (Sunstein 2008; Pariser 2011; Miller and Record 2013; Simpson 2012; Hendricks and Hansen 2014; boyd 2017; Shu et al. 2017; Lynch 2019; Gunn and Lynch 2021; Nguyen 2020, 2021). Thus, some of the specific design features of internet platforms and the affordances

---

[2] Some studies have failed to replicate the "backfire effect." For a literature review of problems with the "backfire effect" research, see Swire-Thompson, DeGutis, and Lazer 2020.

[3] Polarization is one of the purported causes of fake news that is hard to capture in my tripartite framework of cognitive/psychological, technological affordances/design features, and social causes. Caitlin O'Connor and James Own Weatherall argue for an account of polarization as a social phenomenon, rather than a matter of psychological bias (O'Connor and Weatherall 2018).

they provide are also commonly cited causes of the fake news problem.[4] Many of these design choices are intentional, and companies, executives, and engineers can be held accountable for these choices. For example, the internet makes it easy for people to find groups of others who share their beliefs. It also makes it easy for people to personalize their news sources (e.g., by curating whom they follow on Twitter, creating news feeds, or liking pages on Facebook). Thus, the internet is an incredibly effective technology for creating an echo chamber, which as Shu et al. explain, drives polarization: "this echo chamber effect creates segmented, homogeneous communities with a very limited information ecosystem. Research shows that the homogeneous communities become the primary driver of information diffusion that further strengthens polarization" (Shu et al. 2017, 25; cf. Nguyen 2020). That said, empirical work in this area provides mixed results; for example, challenging the assumption that the internet is a major cause of increased political polarization (J. A. Tucker et al. 2018, 16).

The reliance of Twitter, Google, Facebook, and other search engines and platforms on *algorithms* that can be gamed and exploited to promote fake news is another technological source of the problem (Marwick and Lewis 2017; Mustafaraj and Metaxas 2017). I will examine a detailed case study of algorithm-driven disinformation on Facebook in section 4.5, but the general point here is that social media algorithms are designed to show users more of the information they find interesting (so that they will spend more time on the site and the social media companies can deliver more attention to their advertisers) (cf. Wu 2016). Since users often find fake news stories interesting, social media algorithms often end up prioritizing the fake stories in users' feeds. This means that users are exposed to more fake news stories than they would with alternative methods of presenting feeds, for example, chronological display of posts. Furthermore, Mustafaraj and Metaxas (2017) discuss the vulnerability of Google's algorithm to fake news stories. For example, a previous version of Google included a "real-time search results" feature that placed social media posts in some of the top positions of search results. This was a boon to fakers, as they could ensure that their message received high ranking in Google search results by repeatedly tweeting their message (Mustafaraj and Metaxas 2017, 4).

---

[4] There are many different accounts of the concept of affordance. I use Davis and Jurgenson's definition of affordances as "the architectural components of an object which guides—but does not determine—user practices" (J. L. Davis and Jurgenson 2014, 484).

Another affordance of the networked publics that the internet facilitates is *searchability*, which also plays a role in misinformation campaigns. In online networked publics, content can be found via online search tools (cf. boyd 2011, 46). According to Mustafaraj and Metaxas, searchability gives a new tool to propagandists and fakers: "before the development of search engines it was not easy *for propaganda to discover you*" (Mustafaraj and Metaxas 2017, 4). They show how the ability to locate people interested in a topic can be used by fakers to "bomb" Facebook, Twitter, and Google. Here is the recipe they outline for a Facebook fake news bomb:

> Step 1: Register web domains for lots of related websites, with catchy names such as: http://TrumpVision365.com . . . Step 2: Create Facebook accounts of fictitious people, e.g., Elena Nikolov or Antonio Markoski . . . Step 3: Identify and join a Facebook group about a political candidate, e.g., "Hispanics for Trump" or "San Diego Berni[e]crats" . . . Step 4: Target members of the Facebook group with posts, by linking to the fake news website stories . . . Step 5: Wait for members of the group to spread the fake news in their organic subnetworks, by sharing and liking it. (Mustafaraj and Metaxas 2017, 3)

The ability to search for Facebook users who are likely to be interested in a fake news story allows fakers to target their campaign and exploit users' endorsement and frequency heuristics to gain acceptance of their fake story. As fellow members of the Facebook group share the story, users are exposed to it more frequently and by users whose judgment they are more likely to trust.

The deployment of *social bots* and *cyborgs* has been held responsible for many cases of fake news spreading like wildfire (Marwick and Lewis 2017; Shu et al. 2017; Shao et al. 2018). Platforms that allow for anonymity can make it easy for users to deploy fake accounts to signal-boost fake news stories. In one of the first studies of the role of social bots in spreading misinformation during the 2016 election, Shao et al. provide evidence of likely bots spreading fake news. Their data suggest that "Relatively few accounts are responsible for a large share of the traffic that carries misinformation" (Shao et al. 2018, 5). They also uncovered the following strategic uses of bots by fakers: "First, bots are particularly active in amplifying content in the very early spreading moments, before an article goes 'viral.' Second, bots target influential users through replies and mentions" (Shao et al. 2018, 5). It is difficult for regular users to identify bots, so the fact that they are particularly active during the initial phases of a fake news story going viral means that their role in pushing the story may be initially widely unrecognized. Notice also that by targeting influential users, bots take advantage of the endorsement heuristic by attempting to get trusted and influential people to share the misinformation.

Many authors point out that a major driver of the fake news problem is *profit* and the design of the *online ad market* (Jack 2017; Kantrowitz 2017; Marwick and Lewis 2017). Much has been made of the "Macedonian teens" who made money during the 2016 election by posting fake news stories on their websites, seeding links to them in Facebook groups related to American politics, and collecting ad revenue from Google (Silverman and Alexander 2016; Tynan 2016; Subramanian 2017). Of course, fakers are not confined to the Balkans, and the post-election coverage of fake news has been full of stories of individuals who profited from sharing fake news (e.g., Silverman 2016a). The common economic thread here is that website owners can earn advertising revenue through Google's AdSense service, which enables them to earn money when visitors to their site click on an ad placed on the site by Google (Vaidhyanathan 2012, 34). Now this role of online advertising in the fake news problem may seem to be more of a social cause than a technological/design cause, but Mustafaraj and Metaxas argue that there is also a connection to the design of algorithmic web search (Mustafaraj and Metaxas 2017, 4). They argue that Google's adoption of the AdWords and AdSense advertising models was, in part, an attempt by Google to defend the integrity of its search results from attack by the Search Engine Optimization (SEO) industry. This industry is geared around finding ways to get certain pages top ranking in search engine results. Using the techniques of "Link Farms" and "Mutual Admiration Societies," SEO spammers worked to game Google's PageRank algorithm. Search engines were engaged in a cat and mouse game of trying to stay one step ahead of spammers by tweaking their algorithms to return valuable results rather than manipulated results. This is where AdSense comes in: "Google's solution was the advertising model AdWords and AdSense that gave spammers an opportunity to make money while following the rules" (Mustafaraj and Metaxas 2017, 4). Thus, the need for corporations like Google to maintain the integrity of their product (i.e., web search) led them to make significant interventions in the online advertising models that had the by-product of creating profitable revenue streams for fakers. Of course, the need to protect the integrity of search was only one of the motivations for the move toward AdSense. Tim Wu details the internal deliberations within Google that pushed it toward this highly profitable business model (Wu 2016). Understanding the profit incentives and ad platforms as a hybrid technological/design and social cause of the fake news problem provides a nice segue into the social causes of our predicament.

4.2.3. Social Causes

A commonly cited cause of the fake news problem is pervasive *distrust* of the media and other institutions (e.g., educational institutions and expertise in general) (boyd 2017; Marwick and Lewis 2017; D. Roberts 2017; Nguyen 2020). A 2016 Gallup poll reported the lowest levels of trust in the media in Gallup's polling history: only 32% of Americans polled trusted mass media "to report the news fully, accurately and fairly" (Swift 2016). Low levels of trust in the media, as well as scientific and educational institutions—traditional sources of fact checking—mean that the public is in an increasingly difficult position from which to locate reliable information (D. Roberts 2017).

This distrust in mainstream media has been exploited and exacerbated by the rise of political groups who use fake news to spread their message. The existence of loosely organized *alt-right groups* that have intentionally developed strategies for media manipulation is an important social cause of the problem (Marwick and Lewis 2017). Several scholars of the alt-right argue that charting their changing dynamics is crucial to understanding their role in the fake news problem (Marwick and Lewis 2017; Phillips, Beyer, and Coleman 2017). These groups engage in coordinated campaigns to spread fake news stories by, for example, making a hashtag trend on Twitter (e.g., #BLMKidnapping) or creating and spreading memes (Marwick and Lewis 2017; Broderick 2017). Alt-right groups actively research media manipulation techniques and share books and research with each other (Marwick and Lewis 2017).

Some critics charge that the mainstream media has let itself be goaded into *giving the alt-right and other fakers a platform* (Marwick and Lewis 2017; Phillips 2018; Phillips and Milner 2020). When the lines between news and entertainment are blurred, media entities will cover salacious, surprising, or funny fake news stories. Often articles about fake news are merely entertaining clickbait, but the fact of the virality of a fake news story can also be a legitimate current event worth covering (Jack 2017; Marwick and Lewis 2017). Thus, the fake news problem derives, in part, from the economic incentives for infotainment in a capitalist media system. As Marwick and Lewis discuss, there can be significant incentives for mainstream media to cover fake news: "Mainstream media profits from conspiracy theories: Mass media has greatly profited off the appeal of conspiracy theories despite their potential for harm. Network news channels feature 'documentaries' investigating theories without fully refuting them" (Marwick and Lewis 2017, 19).

Even if we set aside the blurred lines between news and entertainment, there is a difficult *epistemic double bind facing the media*. On the one hand, it is journalists' job to inform the public about current events, including events in the media, and fact checking is a central journalistic function. So when a notable fake news story gains traction, the fact of its popularity may be worth covering and journalists may have a responsibility to demonstrate its falsity. But on the other hand, reporting on a fake news story gives fakers a larger platform. It allows them to drive the media narrative. This has been identified as a causal factor in the 2016 election (Benkler et al. 2017; Marwick and Lewis 2017; Phillips 2018; Phillips and Milner 2020). Marwick and Lewis explain:

> For manipulators, it doesn't matter if the media is reporting on a story in order to debunk or dismiss it; the important thing is getting it covered in the first place. The amount of media coverage devoted to specific issues influences the presumed importance of these issues to the public. This phenomenon, called agenda setting, means that the media is remarkably influential in determining what people think about. The media agenda affects the public agenda. In this sense, by getting the media to cover certain stories, even by debunking them, media manipulators are able to influence the public agenda. (Marwick and Lewis 2017, 39)

Thus, one of the social causes of the fake news problem is that fakers have figured out how to exploit this conflict at the heart of the media's epistemic responsibilities. For each individual trending fake news story, it may appear that journalists have a responsibility to report and debunk it. However, in a disinformation-rich environment that is being manipulated by organized groups to promote certain messages, reporting and debunking may ultimately serve to more widely disseminate and entrench falsehoods.[5]

---

[5] Phillips provides a detailed analysis of this double bind, interviews with journalists who face it on a daily basis, and a plethora of useful solutions for dealing with it in (Phillips 2018). For strategic silence and strategic amplification by journalists as a solution to this double bind, see Donovan and boyd 2019.

Fakers have successfully exploited the double bind facing a media landscape with infotainment pressures, but they have also taken advantage of the inherent *ambiguity of online communication*, which is another source of the problem (Jack 2017; Marwick and Lewis 2017). Note that internet studies scholars use 'ambiguity' in a broader sense than analytic philosophers tend to. 'Ambiguity' in this sense includes both cases where readers are uncertain about the intentions of the author of a communication and cases of multiple meanings. Whitney Phillips and Ryan Milner argue that online communications are more ambiguous than offline speech (Phillips and Milner 2017). It is much harder to determine whether someone is being sincere in online communication. Caroline Jack argues that one of the causes of the fake news problem is that bad actors exploit journalists' hesitancy to attribute malevolent intentions to deceive (Jack 2017). Without being able to definitely attribute the intent to deceive, journalists are more likely to label fake news as unintentional misinformation rather than intentional disinformation. Additionally, fakers may try to deflect responsibility for spreading fake news by claiming it was "just a joke" (Jack 2017, 12). Thus, the ambiguity of online communication makes it difficult for fact checkers to identify fakers and hold them responsible.

While many lay blame at the feet of the media who give a platform to fake news, others also point out that *individual users also share some blame* for sharing these stories. For example, boyd notes how during the 2016 election left-wing users gleefully shared right-wing fake news stories to show how "stupid and backwards" Trump supporters are (boyd 2017). It seems worth exploring to what extent liberals shared these stories because they were in the grips of elitist stereotypes about the stupidity of working-class, rural voters who were, according to dominant media narratives, more likely to vote for Trump. Boyd's point is that if repeated exposure to fake news is epistemically harmful, then liberal voters should be careful about sharing fake news stories, even if they are only sharing them in order to mock them or express outrage at the fakery. Phillips makes a similar point about individual responsibility: "Every retweet, comment, like, and share extends the life of a given story. So we need to pay careful attention to what we share and spread online" (Phillips 2015b). These points raise important questions about epistemic responsibility. There may be a difference between any liberals who unwittingly passed on fake news due to their anti-rural, working-class bias and those who knew the stories were fake and shared them to mock rural, working-class conservatives (Inmaculada de Melo-Martín, personal communication, June 15, 2018).

The lack of *media literacy* among internet users is also frequently cited as a cause of the fake news problem. This is a social cause because many claim that our educational institutions have failed to provide adequate media literacy education for the internet age (Domonoske 2016; Marwick and Lewis 2017; Heersmink 2018). But it is also a cognitive cause in that the concern here is with the individual critical thinking resources of readers and consumers of online communications. Critics have also raised concerns about the content of media literacy education (boyd 2017; Phillips and Milner 2020). For example, boyd notes that students were told for years not to trust Wikipedia and that it would be more reliable to use Google to search for sources; however, it now appears that Wikipedia with its gatekeeping methods may be less vulnerable to manipulation by fakers than Google's algorithm. So it may be that the advice given to students has raised a cohort that is more vulnerable to fake news than would be the case with different media literacy education (boyd 2017).

Finally, research shows a social dimension to the group polarization problem in the form of *asymmetric polarization* (Benkler et al. 2017; Benkler, Faris, and Roberts 2018). Benkler et al. studied the patterns of language, topics, hyperlinking, and sharing of Twitter and Facebook users during the 2016 election. Their research showed that there was a greater amount of polarization in right-wing media consumers: "Pro-Clinton audiences were highly attentive to traditional media outlets, which continued to be the most prominent outlets across the public sphere, alongside more left-oriented online sites. But pro-Trump audiences paid the majority of their attention to polarized outlets that have developed recently" (Benkler et al. 2017). Benkler et al. conclude that "internal politics in the right" are responsible for some of the fake news problem. In other words, it is not the fault of the internet by itself:

> Our analysis challenges a simple narrative that the internet *as a technology* is what fragments public discourse and polarizes opinions, by allowing us to inhabit filter bubbles or just read "the daily me." If technology were the most important driver towards a "post-truth" world, we would expect to see symmetric patterns on the left and the right. Instead, different internal political dynamics in the right and the left led to different patterns in the reception and use of the technology by each wing. (Benkler et al. 2017)

This analysis of asymmetric polarization nicely captures why we need to look at all three types of causes of the fake news problem: polarization may result from cognitive vulnerability, and the internet as a mode of information dissemination may amplify its effects, but there are also social dynamics within political groups that shape the kind of polarized beliefs formed in various communities. Finally, to foreshadow my argument for a social epistemology in which race is taken into account, researchers found that racial dynamics may be driving asymmetric polarization (Freelon et al. 2022, 573). In their study of Russian Internet Research Agency disinformation spread by imposter Twitter accounts, Freelon et al. found that pretending to be a Black activist was "the most effective predictor of disinformation engagement by far" (Freelon et al. 2022, 560). It is worth noting that Freelon et al. only detected this result when they disaggregated the data on Black-presenting accounts from non-Black liberal accounts. Previous work on asymmetric polarization did not disaggregate this data. So understanding fake news requires attention to the ways racial dynamics influence the interplay among cognitive, design, and social causes.

In concluding this section, we can see that the causes of the fake news problem are numerous, complex, and mutually reinforcing. Simply trying to describe what is happening in our hybrid media landscape that makes disinformation so prevalent is a daunting task. But at this point, I move from the descriptive to the normative, where the tools of social epistemology are most useful. I begin with the normative question: why is fake news epistemically damaging?

4.3. The Epistemic Damage of Fake News

4.3.1. Fake News and False Belief

Beginning with a veritistic social epistemology framework, we can easily recognize that disseminating false news stories is veritistically damaging because it facilitates the spread of false beliefs throughout a community. For a veritist, a disinformation-rich media landscape is obviously epistemically dangerous, especially given the influence of our cognitive heuristics and other features of our psychology that make it likely that we will give uptake to the false claims to which we are exposed. The value in adopting Goldman's veritistic social epistemology for thinking about fake news is that it provides a normative framework that recognizes the value of truth (cf. Goldman 1999, 6–7). This is not to say that hoaxes, tricks, and strategic deployments of ignorance are always ethically or epistemically wrong; in fact, I argued for the contrary position in Chapter 3. But we do need a normative framework in which truth has epistemic value, if we are to capture one of the central features of what is epistemically damaging about our current media landscape.

While Chapter 1 argued that Goldman goes too far in his attacks on veriphobia, he is right that we need a distinction between accepted belief and true belief as part of our social epistemology (Goldman 1999, 7–40). If we do not make that distinction, then we cannot fully articulate what is epistemically broken about our current media landscape. In 2017, I attended the Association of Internet Researchers (AoIR) conference in Estonia where fake news was a hot topic of research and discussion. This is a highly interdisciplinary conference with scholars from a variety of fields using a plethora of methodologies to study the mechanisms of fake news dissemination, among many other topics. A non-negligible number of the presenters and discussion participants expressed discomfort with (or desire to avoid) talk of the truth or falsity of the messages whose dissemination they studied. Some presenters and audience members preferred to simply understand how the messages were being disseminated without distinguishing between true and false messages. This is akin to what Goldman attacks as the veriphobic move: to simply study the social dynamics of belief and not distinguish between true and false belief.

> Although veriphobes differ from one another in the details of their preferred methodologies, they share the idea that the study of social "knowledge" should be confined to the interpersonal and cultural determination of belief: not true or false belief, just plain belief. . . . They deliberately bracket questions of truth and falsity, holding that nothing legitimate can come of any attempt to draw distinctions in those terms. (Goldman 1999, 7)

I agree with Goldman that we lose something if we bracket questions of truth and falsity. For example, one can imagine a nearby possible world in which many of the same features of our media landscape obtain but with different epistemic effects. In this world, agents have figured out how to take advantage of search engine and social media platform algorithms as well as human cognitive tendencies (etc.) to spread their messages, except in this world the messages that are most widely disseminated are almost always true. The plethora of tools of the internet researchers are just as useful for studying how the agents disseminate their messages in this alternate world; we can still study which beliefs become accepted in this society and how they become accepted. But there is a crucial epistemic difference between these worlds; namely, the alternate world is epistemically superior to ours, because the media landscape is disseminating more true beliefs than ours does. Without a truth-based epistemic normative framework, we cannot make this evaluation.

At this point, one might argue that this kind of counterfactual assessment is only of interest to philosophers. One might wonder whether there are any practical uses of a veritistic epistemology for fake news. First, I argue that without a distinction between true and false belief it is harder to identify changes we can make to bring our actual world closer to the epistemically superior possible world in which true beliefs are more widely disseminated. To the extent that we can change some of the technological and design features of our hybrid media system to reduce the spread of false beliefs, change our social institutions and social prejudices to remove some of the social causes of fake news, or find ways to shift or adapt to our cognitive tendencies that make us likely to believe false stories, veritism accords those efforts epistemic value. Thus, veritistic social epistemology is one useful tool we can use for epistemic appraisal and remediation of our fake news problem. It tells us that fake news is epistemically damaging because spreading false beliefs diminishes the epistemic value of our online communities. It gives us a theoretical tool to identify practices that reduce the spread of disinformation. If internet researchers lump together both true and false news stories in their studies of online content dissemination, then, by working with theoretical tools that make no distinction between true and false news story dissemination, they cannot identify which practices are epistemically superior. Second, a veritistic framework is useful for holding fakers accountable for the epistemic damage they do. We need a truth/falsehood distinction in order to identify those who intentionally disseminate falsehoods. This is the first step toward holding them epistemically and morally responsible for harm.

Of course, these practical goals might not be part of the research agenda for a particular internet researcher. All research involves bracketing some questions, so my point here is not that all research on internet news dissemination needs to distinguish between true and false stories. My point is not that *all* internet scholarship needs to be based on a veritistic framework; it is hardly my place as a philosopher to make this judgment for other fields. Instead, my point is simply the normative, epistemic claim that if *none* of the internet scholarship makes a true/false distinction, then we lose important insights and we cannot achieve important practical goals. Thus, while any individual researcher may have good methodological reasons for choosing not to include in their analysis whether the news stories they study are true or false, it would be damaging for the community as a whole to adopt veriphobia.

In taking a veritistic approach to the fake news problem, we cannot avoid the fact that drawing the line between truth and fakery often involves difficult normative and political judgments. As Farkas and Schou argue, "attempts to categorise, classify and demarcate between 'fake' and 'true' must be a deeply political practice, whether conducted from the context of journalism or academic interventions" (Farkas and Schou 2018, 309). According to one set of conceptual tools, frameworks, background assumptions, and methods of verification, a particular claim may be accorded the status of truth, while it would be denied this status according to a different set of conceptual tools, frameworks, and so on. For example, in identifying fake news, we have to make normative judgments about which fact-checking sources are reliable. And in a political environment in which the process of fact checking itself is seen as politically biased in some conservative circles, engaging in any kind of demarcation between truth and fiction may have political consequences (cf. Graves 2016, 218–22).

Farkas and Schou analyze 'fake news' as a floating signifier, a "signifier used by fundamentally different and in many ways deeply opposing political projects as a means of constructing political identities, conflicts and antagonisms" (Farkas and Schou 2018, 300). They identify three political projects in which participants mobilize a discourse of 'fake news' to promote their goals: (1) critics of digital capitalism, (2) critics of right-wing media and politics, and (3) critics of the mainstream media's 'liberal bias.' Critics in the first camp discuss fake news as an inevitable problem of our capitalist media system which creates profit incentives to spread disinformation that threatens democracy (Farkas and Schou 2018, 303–4). The second political project lays the blame for the fake news problem at the feet of right-wing media and political groups who, the critics claim, show disdain for truth, promote irrationality, and spread fake news in order to score political points (Farkas and Schou 2018, 304–6). The third use of the 'fake news' signifier is deployed by Trump and right-wing critics who wield the term as a cudgel against the mainstream media, attacking them as biased in favor of liberals (Farkas and Schou 2018, 306–7).

Farkas and Schou's analysis helps us to look beneath the surface of the discourse of 'fake news' to find the political agendas and uses of the term. This is the kind of analysis of the consequences and political meanings of our work which analytic social epistemologists often eschew. My own rationale for using the term 'fake news,' my summary of the purported causes of fake news, and my veritistic analysis of fake news as a problem of disinformation make this chapter most closely aligned with the first two camps of critics. Thus, my analysis has political implications: it supports the critique of digital capitalism that makes disinformation profitable, and it is consistent with the critique of the right-wing, white supremacist, misogynist politics that use disinformation as a weapon.

That said, I want to resist what I take to be a set of implications of Farkas and Schou's analysis—that talk of truth is merely a political tool wielded by some political camps against others, that noting the harms of disinformation is merely a political strategy, that these three political projects are to be analyzed as operating on the same level, and that instead of evaluating which of these political projects is superior, we should focus on charting their various discursive strategies. Farkas and Schou write, "Instead of simply lamenting and condemning the spread of false information, research might try to explore and understand *how* and *why* such information gains traction" (Farkas and Schou 2018, 309). I agree that understanding *why* false information gains traction is important, and Farkas and Schou's analysis is helpful in this regard, but I think that lamenting and condemning disinformation is also important. Social epistemologists need to do both. Truth has epistemic, ethical, and practical value. So while it is helpful to understand that discourses lamenting 'fake news' are associated with different political agendas, it is also important to note that these political agendas are not all epistemically, ethically, or practically equal. This is a point Farkas and Schou never make. They present all three political uses of 'fake news' as equally political, but they fail to note the ways in which Trump's agenda has been epistemically damaging and ethically suspect. Journalist Lesley Stahl reports that in July 2016 she asked Trump why he constantly attacked the media. According to Stahl, "He said you know why I do it? I do it to discredit you all and demean you all, so when you write negative stories about me no one will believe you" (qtd. in Rosenberg 2018). When he was president, Trump's discourse of 'fake news' was epistemically pernicious when it prevented people from attaining true beliefs about negative stories about him and other matters. And his attack on the freedom of the press was ethically suspect, since a free press is essential to a just society with some accountability for powerful agents. For these reasons, we need a politically engaged feminist veritistic analysis of fake news, one which recognizes the epistemic harm of fake news (and damaging uses of the term itself) while also self-reflexively acknowledging the political implications of this analysis.

4.3.2. Fake News and Distrust

In addition to veritism, a second useful set of theoretical tools for epistemic appraisal of fake news comes from the epistemology of trust and trustworthiness. We can draw on Chapter 3's analysis of the distrust spread by internet imposture to understand the epistemic harms of fake news in general. This analysis also shows how epistemology can, and needs to be, responsive to the changing dynamics of online information and how such dynamics alter our epistemic predicament. The epistemic landscape of the 2011 internet is different than the internet of the 2016 election period. This has to be part of our analysis.

Recall that one of the ways MacMaster's 2011 *A Gay Girl in Damascus* imposture did epistemic harm was through undermining trust in the social practices that promote objectivity and truth acquisition. Distrust in our social epistemic practices is corrosive and epistemically harmful when it discourages people from engaging in practices that promote objectivity and help them acquire true beliefs. As we saw in Chapter 3, the exposure of American Tom MacMaster's fake blog masquerading as the testimony of a Syrian activist caused suspicion of the blogs, Facebook accounts, and Twitter accounts of real Syrians and other Arab Spring activists. To the extent that this led Western audiences to rely less on the testimony of these activists and more on, for example, the verified Twitter accounts of Western reporters, a potential decrease in objectivity resulted (due to lack of diversity of testifiers), and some true beliefs were potentially lost to users. Thus, in the 2011 epistemic landscape of the internet, MacMaster's imposture caused harm by decreasing trust in many trustworthy epistemic agents. Similarly, in 2016 fakers and media manipulators undermined many people's trust in the practice of reading about current events on the internet. This does epistemic damage because the internet provides a platform for a diversity of voices to provide testimony about a wide array of current events; when users do not trust these voices, a potential decrease in objectivity results (due to lack of diversity of trusted testifiers), and some true beliefs about events that would otherwise remain uncovered or not widely disseminated are lost to users. Thus, one of the epistemic harms of the proliferation of fake news is that it gives us reason to distrust potentially epistemically useful sources.

Thus, the fake news problem, like MacMaster's imposture, promotes suspicion and distrust, but the appropriateness of this distrust marks a potential difference between the problems and a change in the epistemic landscape of the internet. There has been a marked decrease in trust in mass media between 2011 when a Gallup survey found "44% of Americans who have a great deal or fair amount of trust" in the media (Morales 2011) and 2016 when that number dropped to 32% (Swift 2016). Anecdotally, it was even more common in 2016 than it was in 2011 to hear people express skeptical opinions about news stories by saying, "Well, you know you can't believe anything you read on the internet." Now whether this increased attitude of generalized distrust in the media system is epistemically harmful depends, in part, on whether the distrust is appropriate. If the hybrid media system has indeed become less trustworthy, then increased distrust is appropriate. While empirical work is still being done in this area, this seems to be the general attitude of scholars in this area: the fakers and media manipulators have become more numerous and more sophisticated than they were in 2011 and platform monopolization has increased, such that there is more online disinformation than in earlier periods of the internet. For example, Zeynep Tufekci provides a useful analysis of changes in the social and technological landscape between the optimism of the power of the internet in Arab Spring era and the increase in disinformation in the ensuing years. One of her key arguments is that powerful bad actors and authoritarian governments learned how to use the internet to their advantage: "Power always learns, and powerful tools always fall into its hands" (Tufekci 2018). So there is a difference between the attitude of distrust toward online Arab Spring activists in 2011, which may have been a hasty generalization from the sensational *A Gay Girl in Damascus* case and others, and the increased attitude of distrust in the hybrid media system in 2016, which may be appropriate, given the increased unreliability of the system. Changes in the reliability of the hybrid media system will change whether or not generalized distrust is appropriate for some of our epistemic goals.

At this point, it is helpful to draw on the distinction between error-avoiding veritism and truth-seeking veritism: *error-avoiding veritists* prioritize avoiding false belief, while *truth-seeking veritists* prioritize attaining true belief (Coady 2012, 5–7; Frost-Arnold 2014c). These different versions of veritism, thus, place different weight on our two epistemic duties, as outlined by William James: "*We must know the truth*; and *we must avoid error*" (James 2007, 17–18). If we prioritize avoiding error, then it would seem that the increased distrust in our hybrid media system, given the revelations of increased levels of disinformation, is appropriate. But James's insight that avoiding error often comes at the cost of attaining fewer truths helps us see why there is an epistemic cost to this increased distrust—it may lead us to rely less on online media, which as I argued earlier, provide access to diverse voices that may help us attain true beliefs that would otherwise be inaccessible. In sum, while the changing epistemic landscape of the internet and the increased awareness of disinformation make distrust more reasonable, there is nonetheless an epistemic cost, and this is why the erosion of trust in the hybrid media system is one of the epistemic harms of fake news.

I want to preempt a misinterpretation of my argument in this section. As several authors have argued, discussions of the fake news problem and the supposed "post-truth society" often adopt a wistful, conservative attitude (Mejia, Beckermann, and Sullivan 2018; Habgood-Coote 2019). Those who raise alarms about fake news and the post-truth society argue that we are facing a new problem in which large swaths of the public no longer care about truth and no longer trust (purportedly) neutral institutions (e.g., the media and higher education); they worry that we are facing what David Roberts calls "an epistemic crisis" (D. Roberts 2017). In this alarmist discourse, fake news and post-truth are framed as a new crisis, one which is best resolved by a return to better critical thinking skills, respect for truth, and general trust in institutions (Habgood-Coote 2019). But such nostalgic narratives of a time when truth was generally respected erase the long history of promulgated ignorance, such as false racist ideologies (Mejia, Beckermann, and Sullivan 2018). As Mejia, Beckermann, and Sullivan put it, "[O]ur argument is this: because of the general ignorance about the scholarship, literature, and experiences of people of color, it is not surprising that so many of our post-truth critics think that the post-truth [era] begins with the Internet; or more simply, American racial politics have never been concerned with the 'truth'" (Mejia, Beckermann, and Sullivan 2018, 111). Similarly a call for return to the days when we all supposedly trusted neutral institutions is misguided.

Elite institutions have never been neutral, and many marginalized groups have had good reasons to distrust them (cf. Scheman 2001). This distrust is often epistemically and practically valuable for marginalized groups. For example, Sarah Florini notes how Black activists' "healthy skepticism about newcomers, given the history of government informants and agent provocateurs penetrating past movements" made them less trusting of fake Russian Facebook accounts that were used to stoke tensions prior to the 2016 election (Florini 2019, 195–96). So in arguing that fake news has negative epistemic consequences when it spreads false beliefs and undermines truth, I do not join these nostalgia narratives of a time when everyone was more trusting.

My position is that truth matters, and that trust in trustworthy people and trustworthy institutions matters. But we do not need an ideal theory that ignores that manufactured ignorance is an old problem, one which has all too often targeted marginalized people. What we need is a non-ideal theory of fake news that recognizes the history and mechanisms of ignorance and shows how these are newly manifesting themselves in a digital age. I provide one such account in section 4.4. And we do not need a decontextualized theory of trust that erases the very good reasons that marginalized people have had over the years for distrusting institutions that present themselves as neutral while often failing to address the needs of the oppressed. Instead, we need a theory that provides an account of objectivity and ways to make institutions more objective and trustworthy for everyone, including the marginalized. This is what I provide in section 4.5.

To summarize, this section has shown how the theoretical tools of both veritistic social epistemology and the epistemology of trust and trustworthiness provide insight into the nature of the epistemic harms of fake news. The next section presents a second contribution from social epistemology to the study of fake news: the epistemologies of ignorance literature illuminates the racial dynamics of fake news. Specifically, Charles Mills's work on white ignorance helps us understand how racism in our collective memory and testimonial practices shape online disinformation.

4.4. Fake News and White Ignorance

In Chapter 1 I outlined the differences between abstract, Cartesian "S-knows-that-p" epistemologies (Code 1995; Grasswick 2004) and epistemologies based on feminist theory and philosophy of race that take seriously the social situatedness of knowledge. Recall that an "S-knows-that-*p*" approach abstracts away from issues of race, class, gender, and other social inequalities, and discusses the epistemic challenges facing agents regardless of their social position, social identities, or the social inequalities of the society they inhabit.[6] We are now in a position to see why context matters to the fake news problem. An "S-knows-that-*p*" approach to the fake news problem may be able to grapple with some of the causes of our epistemic predicament, but it is ultimately inadequate to the task. I am not denying that social epistemologists can make progress by giving analyses of fake news that ignore issues of race, gender, and other social inequalities. Drawing on the social psychological literature on confirmation bias, polarization, and more, philosophers can provide useful accounts of how the internet magnifies these problems and leads to the proliferation and uptake of many false stories. So good work can be done with a more abstract approach. However, this kind of analysis will completely miss some epistemically crucial aspects of the problem. For example, asymmetric polarization can only be recognized as a problem if we look into the social dynamics within political groups. If we just take the agents involved to be identical Cartesian cognizers with smartphones, then we will miss the fact that agents with different political identities and media consumption behaviors will be differentially polarized.

We can go further in understanding the social dynamics of online knowledge if we recognize that much fake news promotes not just a generic ignorance but a specifically *white ignorance*, to use a concept introduced by Charles Mills's ground-breaking contribution to the epistemologies of ignorance literature (Mills 2007). A detailed account of how white ignorance shapes (and is shaped by) fake news provides a model for investigating how

---

[6] Recall also that Code's name for this abstract Cartesian approach (i.e., the "S-knows-that-*p*" approach) targets the high level of abstraction away from social context deployed by many mainstream epistemologists; it is *not* a critique of the choice to use variables to express one's view or abstraction per se (Code 1995). An epistemologist who writes about the epistemology of race and who, for example, points out that knowers of different races (different *S*'s) might know different propositions about issues of racial inequality (different *p*'s) is not an "S-knows-that-*p*" epistemologist in my sense, even if their work contains the phrase "*S* knows that *p*." This point is important in forestalling misunderstandings of my claim that an "S-knows-that-*p*" approach *cannot* account for issues of white ignorance in fake news. Of course, one *could* write about issues of white supremacy shaping fake news and use variables in one's writing (e.g., "If *S* lives in a white supremacist society, then *S* is vulnerable to white ignorance"), but an epistemologist who accounts for race in epistemology in this way is not an "S-knows-that-*p*" epistemologist, in Code's sense. So the problem with the "S-knows-that-*p*" approach is that, for some things for which we seek explanations, the level of abstraction is too high. This is not to say that all abstraction in epistemology is problematic, but just that we cannot explain some phenomena adequately if we abstract away from race, gender, class, and so on.

other socially situated forms of ignorance are part of the fake news problem, for example, misogynist ignorance, homophobic ignorance, and capitalist ignorance.

Mills delivers a blistering attack on the abstract, Cartesian approach to epistemology:

> [B]lithely indifferent to the possible cognitive consequences of class, racial, or gender situatedness (or, perhaps more accurately, taking a propertied white male standpoint as given), modern mainstream Anglo-American epistemology was for hundreds of years from its Cartesian origins profoundly inimical terrain for the development of any concept of structural group-based miscognition. (Mills 2007, 13)

While mainstream Anglo-American epistemology has wrestled for centuries with the problems of individual miscognition caused by hallucinations, illusions, and dreams, it had, prior to Mills's work, never systematically addressed sources of miscognition grounded in systemic white racism and white supremacy (Mills 2007). Part of the reason for this gaping hole is that mainstream social epistemologists had taken a generic "*S*-knows-that-*p*" approach. As Mills puts it, the social world imagined by many social epistemologists consists of "a societal population essentially generated by simple iteration of that originally solitary Cartesian cognizer" (Mills 2007, 15). To fill this gap, and to recognize that the race of cognizers and the racial hierarchies of their communities make an epistemic difference, Mills argues that there exists a phenomenon of white ignorance, which is a structural, group-based form of miscognition. White ignorance is a non-knowing that has its causal origins in white racism or white racial domination (Mills 2007, 20). Mills defines this non-knowing as including both false belief and the absence of true belief (Mills 2007, 16).[7] Mills outlines several causal mechanisms linking white racism or white racial domination to the

---

[7] Mills follows Goldman in adopting a 'weak' account of knowledge as true belief. Thus, Mills's discussion of ignorance does not address true beliefs that fail to be knowledge. In later works, Mills expands his account of ignorance beyond false belief or the absence of true belief to include "a pervasively deforming outlook" (Mills 2018, 217), which he describes as "a particular optic, a prism of perception and interpretation, a worldview" (Mills 2018, 218). Thus, white ignorance can be theorized as an ideology, discourse, habitus, or "white racial frame," to draw on the work of Marx, Foucault, Bourdieu, and Feagin (Mills 2018, 218). For the purposes of this chapter, it will be sufficient to focus on white racism as the cause of false belief or the absence of true belief. But keeping this broader conception of white ignorance as a perceptual and interpretive frame may be useful for future investigations of fake news (cf. El Kassar 2018).

acquisition and dissemination of false beliefs, as well as showing how white racism/domination has been causally responsible for agents failing to form any beliefs at all about certain topics. I will focus on his analysis of how white racism in our collective social memory and testimonial practices produces ignorance.

Social memory determines which historical events and figures are remembered, and this memory shapes social identities and subjectivities. Our sense of who we are as a social group is determined, in part, by what we collectively recollect. Social memory is "inscribed in textbooks, generated and regenerated in ceremonies and official holidays, concretized in statues, parks, and monuments" (Mills 2007, 29).[8] White racism has had a profound effect on what, and whom, people remember and celebrate. Mills cites several cases where white racism clearly shaped efforts to produce a forgetting and the absence of true beliefs about historical events. For example, official records of King Leopold II's colonial regime in the Belgian Congo were burned, and exhibition galleries in Brussels fail to commemorate the 10 million people who died in the brutal regime (Mills 2007). Adam Hochschild describes the "deliberate forgetting" as so effective that in the 1970s a Belgian ambassador to West Africa was surprised to learn of the genocide from a newspaper: "I learned that there had been this huge campaign, in the international press, from 1900 to 1910; millions of people had died, but we Belgians knew absolutely nothing about it" (qtd. in Mills 2007, 30). Absence of true beliefs about historical events is also caused by white racist suppression (and discrediting) of testimony of the victims of white racial domination. Witnesses to racist crimes were often terrorized into silence or denied the ability to testify in court. For example, a Black woman from the Jim Crow era describes an environment of suppression: "My problems started when I began to comment on what I saw. . . . I insisted on being accurate. But the world I was born into didn't want that. Indeed, its very survival depended on not knowing, not seeing—and certainly, not saying anything at all about what it was really like" (qtd. in Mills 2007, 32). Even fifty years after the Tulsa race massacre, Ed Wheeler, a white scholar, found that Black witnesses feared retribution if they spoke about what they had seen (Mills 2007, 32). Thus, when the testimony of people of color about historical events is suppressed,

---

[8] Mills draws on Maurice Halbwachs's account of collective, social memory (Halbwachs 1992). The field of memory studies has grown in recent decades; for useful accounts of memory that address the role of new media, see Hoskins 2018b, 2018a; Tirosh 2017.

the collective memory about what occurred is inaccurate. While witnesses and members of the community who have heard tales passed down through word of mouth may hold events in their local social memory, that knowledge is often lost to the national memory.

Not only does white racism/dominance generate gaps in collective memory, but it also produces false beliefs. Add gaps in the historical record to racist framings of slavery and we can understand the causal mechanisms behind false beliefs that slavery was a benign, rather than horrific, institution. Examples of such framing narratives include textbook depictions of happy enslaved people (Mills 2007, 30). Additionally, failure to fully grasp the racism that runs throughout U.S. history is one of the causes of the prevalence of the myth of meritocracy. When white people lack true beliefs about the many ways in which institutionalized racism has worked to advantage white Americans at the expense of people of color, whites are likely to believe that their accomplishments are due solely to their own merits and efforts. Thus, many white Americans have the false belief that white privilege does not exist. In sum, Mills's explanation of the role that white racism plays in the reception of testimony and the construction of collective memory helps us understand the causal mechanisms behind an important form of miscognition.

So what is the connection to fake news? I argue that to understand the kind of miscognition spread through fake news in our current epistemic landscape, we need to see how white racism and white racial domination are shaping key features of our collective memory and testimonial practices. We cannot ignore that the alt-right, white supremacists, and racist narratives are major drivers of the problem. Let's not overstate this: of course, there are many fakers who do not self-identify as white supremacists, and racist narratives are not the only framing devices for many fake news stories. But as Marwick and Lewis (2017) argue, members of the alt-right (and other allied groups who may be radicalized into white supremacist thought) are major players in the fake news ecosystem. White racism and rhetorics of white domination are an undercurrent running through alt-right online communities:

> Many alt-right actions—propagating Nazi symbols, using racial epithets, or spreading anti-immigrant ideology—support white nationalist ideologies. Whether undertaken sincerely or ironically, the outcome is the same. There seems to be a coherent willingness to act in support of white nationalism,

even in the parts of the alt-right that do not explicitly adopt or claim it as an ideological commitment. (Marwick and Lewis 2017, 12)

It is no surprise then that we find racism as a major driver of fake news stories, be it attacks on Black Lives Matter, anti-immigrant stories, or Islamophobic narratives. The false account of a "Black Lives Matter kidnapping" discussed at the beginning of the chapter is just one example of this genre of racist fake news stories.

Fake news stories such as the Black Lives Matter kidnapping are one means by which white supremacists push their political agenda, but racist narratives are also attractive to fakers with other motivations. In a racist society, many users are more vulnerable to believing fake news stories with racist undertones due to confirmation bias. Thus, fakers with profit motivations or political motivations will find it to their advantage to add a racist dimension to their fake stories because it is likely to drive uptake and dissemination. For example, there is ample evidence that Russia used fake news, imposter Twitter and Facebook accounts, and online political ads to sow racial discord before the 2016 election (B. Collins and Cox 2017; Starr 2017; Watts 2017; DiResta et al. 2018; Howard et al. 2018; Freelon and Lokot 2020; Freelon et al. 2022).

So I think Mills helps us understand fake news better: Mills's epistemology draws attention to the mechanisms by which white racism shapes the creation and dissemination of fake news. But I also want to argue that thinking about white ignorance in fake news helps us extend Mills's analysis in new directions. To analyze fake news as an online manifestation of white ignorance helps us see new ways that collective memory and testimonial practices operate online. Consider social memory, which, as we saw, is "inscribed in textbooks, generated and regenerated in ceremonies and official holidays, concretized in statues, parks, and monuments" (Mills 2007, 29). In an online world, we have to add to this list the role of internet archives, web search results, and autocomplete suggestions in creating and sustaining collective memory. This is because the internet plays an important role in the construction of social memory. As Noam Tirosh puts it, "Society remembers by being exposed to media content" (Tirosh 2017, 648). In an online world, new media and search engine results are important mechanisms of the creation and maintenance of collective memory. Boyd's analysis of networked publics highlights *persistence* and *searchability* as key features of online communication (boyd 2011). Much online content is archived and accessible for future retrieval by web search. This means that we have to think about the role of online fake news in shaping our collective memory. Which stories are archived and how they appear in search engine results shape which events and figures in our history we will recall. While many fake stories are debunked, the original fake story can still persist in search engine results. Thus, fake stories can persist in the collective memory for years after the supposed event. This adds an additional dimension to the difficult epistemic bind facing mainstream media that we discussed in section 4.2.3. When mainstream media cover fake news stories, it amplifies their message: as the story circulates through cycles of coverage, debunking, and coverage of the debunking, more and more users are repeatedly exposed to it. Earlier we discussed this as a problem because, due to the frequency heuristic, people are led to believe stories they hear frequently. But now we can recognize that this problem shapes our collective memory as well. When mainstream media outlets cover fake news stories, they add searchable content to search engine databases that refers to the fake news story. This content becomes material that search engines are likely to recall when related terms are searched for, especially since respected outlets like *The New York Times* are already likely to rank highly in search engine results. For example, given the extensive coverage of the Pizzagate fake news story, we can safely assume that even if many of us forget about this bizarre story, we will be reminded of it when we Google certain terms. The spurious connection between Hillary Clinton's campaign and child abuse will be remembered in Google's archives for years to come. Of course, Google could take active steps to sever the connection between Clinton's campaign and child abuse, but this seems unlikely.

This means that to understand the mechanisms for white ignorance in an internet age, we need to pay attention to how white supremacists can manipulate mainstream media into covering fake stories that perpetuate racist narratives, and we need to recognize how these racist narratives can saturate our collective memory for years through web search. Thus, understanding fake news requires understanding racist bias in web search, a topic which internet scholars have studied extensively (Daniels 2009a, 2009b, 2013; Noble 2013, 2018). Safiya Umoja Noble gives a detailed analysis of racism within search engine results in *Algorithms of Oppression* (Noble 2018) and other works where she argues that "cultural images and symbols inject dominant social biases into search engine results by transmitting a coherent set of meanings that evolve historically" (Noble 2013). Critiquing the racism and sexism of digital capitalism, Noble shows how Google profits from web search rankings that give legitimacy to racist content by ranking it at the top of search results (Noble 2018, 31). Both Noble and Jessie Daniels challenge the notion that web search results are, as Noble puts it, "a simple mirror of the collective" (Noble 2018, 36; Daniels 2009a, 169–71). The mirror metaphor frames Google as a passive reflection, rather than a designed tool for which the company and its engineers can be held accountable, and which can be manipulated by racist agents. Noble provides an example of activism that held Google accountable for search results associating Black teens with criminality (see Noble 2018, 80). In response to this social media activism, Google appeared to tweak the algorithm to make it less racist, thereby demonstrating that Google is not a simple mirror and can be pushed away from racist results. Daniels provides useful examples of racist manipulation of search engine results, such as the racist fake Dr. Martin Luther King, Jr. site (www.martinlutherking.org), which racists worked to make one of the top search results for his name (Daniels 2009a, 141–47; 2009b). Both Noble and Daniels draw on Mills's earlier work from *The Racial Contract* in which Mills argues that whites produce an "inverted epistemology" of ignorance (Mills 1997, 19) which prevents white people from understanding the world created by racism (Daniels 2009a, 20; Noble 2018, 60). I build on this important work by using the details of Mills's elaboration of this epistemology of ignorance in his "White Ignorance" paper, where he develops the account of the mechanisms of white ignorance in memory and testimony.

Search engine autocomplete plays an important role in maintaining racist fake news stories in our social memory. The fake #BLMKidnapping story that I introduced at the beginning of the chapter illustrates this point. On November 6, 2017, I entered "BLMK," "BLM K," or "Black Lives Matter K" into the Google search bar, and I received "BLMKidnapping," "BLM Kidnapping," or "Black Lives Matter Kidnapping," respectively, as autocomplete suggested searches. This is not simply due to the personalization of my web search. I received the same suggestions when I googled these terms in Chrome's Incognito mode. Cernovich's fake story lived on in Google's autocomplete results. Notice that I did not have to be intentionally searching for the historical record of a Black Lives Matter kidnapping to come across the story; all I needed to do is enter "Black Lives Matter" and the letter "K" and Google suggested this fake historical event to me. This is an important feature of racist web search: Google will often suggest racist content to you, even if you do not enter search terms intended to illicit racist content. As Noble observes, "a [Google] search on Black girls without including the word porn still gets you porn" (Noble 2013). These autocomplete results are similar to the kinds of embodiments of social memory that Mills considers: I may not be intending to bring to mind the confederate General Robert E. Lee, but if I go for a walk in the park and come across a monument to him, I will recall him. The causal mechanisms and entities involved in such moments of recollection are different in the online and offline cases, but both are instances of white racism playing a role in which historical events and figures are remembered.

Uncovering the specific impact of white racism in web search and autocomplete results is a difficult task, given the shifting and opaque nature of web search algorithms. For example, on November 6, 2017, Google's autocomplete suggested "Black Lives Matter Kidnapping" to me when I entered "Black Lives Matter K," but the same search on July 31, 2018, did not suggest the fake news story. Search algorithms are often changed in response to many factors. So different people who conduct the same search at different times can be reminded of different events. Thus, web search does not provide a static archive of collective memory. This presents challenges to tracking and understanding racism's influence on our online collective memory, especially given the lack of algorithmic transparency by corporate search engine providers. It is difficult, if not impossible, to know how many people's knowledge and understanding of history was shaped by the autocomplete results I observed in 2017, and also perhaps impossible to know whether the algorithm will be changed again so that the effect recurs in the future.

The personalization of web search complicates its relationship with collective memory. Since 2009, Google has filtered its search results based on the data that Google has on file about the user making the request (this includes their location, search history, and other information) (Miller and Record 2013, 119). Two users who search for the same terms can receive very different results based on the information Google has about them. This has led Cass Sunstein to raise concerns about the loss of a shared public sphere and collective understanding of current events (Sunstein 2008). If each of us is trapped in our own filter bubble or a news stream that Sunstein calls our "Daily Me," then is there any sense in which we share a collective public sphere? Is there any sense in talking about a collective memory shaped by web search?

There are two reasons why I think it still makes sense to apply Mills's concept to this situation. First, we should not overstate the "Daily Me" metaphor. Sunstein's "Daily Me" is an exaggeration if it implies that there are no similarities among users' web search results. Algorithms such as Google's PageRank rely on categories to filter results, so I will not be the only user to whom "Black Lives Matter Kidnapping" is suggested as a result. Other users who belong to whatever category Google has sorted me into will also recall this fake news story. So while web search may not provide collective memory at the level of a nation, there will be smaller collectives who will recall the same fake news stories. We can then sensibly talk of collective memories. Second, even if the first response is unpersuasive, I think we could still talk about a related concept that we might call "perceived collective memory." Many users do not know that web search is personalized (Powers 2017), or they forget that it is while they are engaged in a search. Google does not highlight its personalized nature when you interact with the search engine. Thus, we are often given the illusion of a collective memory when we search for historical events. Due to the lack of algorithmic transparency, we cannot really know whether the memory presented to us in any instance of web search is representative of the memory others will recall when they search similar terms.[9] This certainly adds some opacity to online collective memory, and I think this opacity has interesting epistemic implications that could be explored in future work. However, I do not think this means that it makes no sense to talk about the internet's role in shaping social memory.

The highly contextual and personalized nature of web search also provides a reply to an objection that I have painted an overly pessimistic picture of autocomplete results and web archives. Often when someone searches for a racist fake news story, they will be presented with results that debunk the false history. Thus, one might object that web search archives need not always harm our collective memory; they can often help it by debunking false beliefs (Inmaculada de Melo-Martín, personal communication, June 15, 2018). This is certainly true, and I do not take myself to be arguing that online archiving of racist fake news stories will always cause epistemic damage. My argument is simply that it *can* do harm, and we need to take the role of white ignorance in online collective memory seriously. While some users will search for terms that suggest a racist fake news story and receive debunking results that they believe, others will reject the debunking sources as biased or implausible (given their background beliefs) and still more others will not receive

---

[9] See Miller and Record 2013 for a discussion of how lack of algorithmic transparency threatens the justificatory status of our beliefs, and see Noble 2018, 54, for discussion of users' attitudes toward opaque, personalized search results.

the debunking sources at all due to the personalized nature of search or the specific key word terms they entered (cf. Noble 2018, 110–18; Tripodi 2018, 27–34). As Noble says, "What we find in search engines about people and culture is important. They oversimplify complex phenomena. They obscure any struggle over understanding, and they can mask history" (Noble 2018, 116). Mills's "White Ignorance" paper focuses our attention on how this masking of history can be due to white racism.

Let us now turn to Mills's other mechanism of white ignorance: testimonial practices. Recall that Mills explains how the silencing and discrediting of the testimony of people of color helps create white ignorance. What I want to add here is a new testimonial practice that plays a significant and somewhat opposite role in the fake news problem: the proliferation of racist testimony through the use of social bots. While Mills is concerned with how the testimony of people of color is given less of a voice than it deserves (something that is certainly a problem in online spaces), I am proposing that an additional cause of white ignorance is a type of amplification of white racist voices. I have in mind a different type of amplification than the phenomenon of credibility excess that José Medina has studied, because I am not discussing how a single speaker gains *excess credibility* that they do not deserve due to stereotypes that privilege them (Medina 2011, 2013). Instead, the problem here is the *excess number* of speakers that social bots and fake accounts provide to white supremacists. In an internet age, one person with the technological skill (or money to pay someone else with the skill) can commandeer an army of fake Twitter accounts to spread their racist message. This army can be deployed in many ways to spread false beliefs, such as making a fake news story trend, thereby prompting media coverage and debunking efforts, and the cascade of other epistemic effects we have discussed. Note that while I have described this as the proliferation of white racist voices, it can often happen through imposture, making it seem as if the racist messages are being spoken by people of color. As I discussed in Chapter 3, there are many documented cases of alt-right trolls orchestrating campaigns to create fake accounts with non-white identities, and members of the Black Twitter community regularly share alerts to new campaigns of imposture and advice about how to identify fake accounts (Rashid 2017). Thus, the epistemic problems with imposture that we encountered in Chapter 3 also shape the problem of online white ignorance spread through fake news.

In summary, Mills's concept of white ignorance and his account of how memory and testimony are implicated in this type of race-based miscognition are useful in understanding the epistemology of fake news. Additionally, our analysis of fake news adds new dimensions to our understanding of the mechanisms of white ignorance in an online world. Neither of these two sets of insights is accessible to an "S-knows-that-*p*" epistemology which abstracts away from the race of the various *S*'s who comprise the society analyzed by social epistemologists and the often-racist content of the *p*'s that circulate within that society. We need an epistemology that accounts for (rather than abstracts away from) race and racism in order to fully grasp the causes of fake news and the role that memory and testimony play in our fake news predicament. My analysis of online racism has a U.S. focus, but as Mills argues, white ignorance is a global problem (Mills 2018), and many scholars are studying how racism manifests itself online in other countries (Matamoros-Fernández 2017; Farkas, Schou, and Neumayer 2018; Siapera 2019). My hope is that this section might provide some tools to analyze the role of other social inequalities and oppressions in the fake news problem (e.g., sexist ignorance and fake news, capitalist ignorance and fake news).

4.5. Fake News, Objectivity, and Neutrality

The social epistemology presented in this book can also show how flawed conceptions of objectivity feed the problem of fake news. In this section, I argue that feminist accounts of objectivity provide resources to manage some of the distrust in the media that has been identified as one of the key causes of the fake news problem. In fact, a good case can be made that decades of persistent, misinformed attacks on feminist epistemology are partly responsible for the situation we find ourselves in now. As I discussed in Chapter 1, sloppy readings of feminist epistemologies are among the reasons why feminist accounts of objectivity remain relatively sidelined (cf. Rooney 2011; Frost-Arnold 2016b). Had these accounts received wider uptake, many segments of society, from journalists to social media companies and the public, might have had a more productive understanding of the nature of bias and ways to manage it. I will argue that failure to adopt feminist accounts of objectivity created missed opportunities to (1) prevent the spread of particular instances of fake news and (2) buttress responsible trust in the media.

While I argue that ignoring feminist epistemology is part of the cause of these problems, feminist epistemology is by no means the only potential source of critiques of online content providers' claims to objectivity and neutrality. Internet studies and Science and Technology Studies (STS) scholars have a rich literature in this area (cf. Winner 1980; Noble 2018). For example, Tarleton Gillespie makes the influential argument that by positioning themselves as 'platforms,' online content providers problematically present themselves as neutral and apolitical (Gillespie 2010). Feminist philosophy of science can add much to these conversations because philosophers have studied for decades both the promise and pitfalls of claims to objectivity. While the production of scientific knowledge and the dissemination of knowledge online are different phenomena, there are important similarities. Bias is inevitable in both, and attempts to manage bias are inherently social phenomena suffused with power relations. Both scientific institutions and online platforms claim neutrality in order to prove their trustworthiness. The analyses of feminist philosophers who have critiqued flawed conceptions of neutrality and who have provided accounts of better ways to manage bias are useful in the social media sphere, as they have been in science.

Let's start with an example to illustrate the role of conceptions of objectivity in the fake news problem. From 2014 to 2018, Facebook had a "Trending Topics" section, which presented a sidebar list of news topics that were being discussed on Facebook. Prior to 2016, the trending news feature was curated by humans who were former journalists (Nunez 2016a). The section was managed through a team of what Facebook called 'news curators' who played a significant role in filtering and editing the news stories that appeared as trending news. The news curators' job was to look over the list of topics that were trending on Facebook, write headlines and summaries, and provide links to news stories. The list of trending news stories that formed the basis for their work was provided by a Facebook secret proprietary algorithm that ranked news stories according to various measures of user engagement (Nunez 2016b). Facebook is an extremely influential source of news in the United States. This was true in the year of the 2016 U.S. presidential election: according to a 2016 Pew Research Center study, 66% of Facebook users got news from Facebook (Gottfried and Shearer 2016). This translates to a large segment of the U.S. media market: "Facebook is by far the largest social networking site, reaching 67% of U.S. adults. The two-thirds of Facebook users who get news there, then, amount to 44% of the general population" (Gottfried and Shearer 2016). Given its wide reach, Facebook had a large impact on the dissemination of fake news. How much of this impact was generated from the Trending section is unclear. When Facebook shut down the section in 2018, it reported that "From research we found that over time people found the product to be less and less useful" and that on average it accounted for less than 1.5% of clicks on news publishers (Hardiman 2018). While people may not have clicked on the associated articles, who knows how much simply seeing the titles of the trending topics influenced people's perceptions of what newsworthy events were occurring.

In retrospect, Facebook's early approach of human curation of the news algorithm was probably the right approach, since it added a layer of human moderation that could identify fake news stories that had floated to the top of the algorithmic ranking (Frenkel 2016; Chen 2017b; Mustafaraj and Metaxas 2017). The human news curators, who had a journalistic background, could blacklist a news topic if they could not find at least three traditional news sources covering the story (Nunez 2016a). This provided a valuable check on fake news stories.

However, in 2016 *Gizmodo* published a story with allegations from an anonymous former news curator claiming that news of interest to conservatives was being suppressed by the curation team (Nunez 2016b). The source maintained that stories about Mitt Romney, Rand Paul, and other conservatives were removed from the Trending news list, despite being highly ranked by the algorithm. *Gizmodo* also cited news curators' reports that they inserted news stories into the Trending list when they had not been suggested by the algorithm. There were additional allegations that trending stories covered by conservative media outlets were not listed unless they were also covered by more mainstream outlets. Facebook denied these allegations (Wagner 2016), but there was an uproar about the alleged bias. This appears to have caused great concern at Facebook. Mark Zuckerberg met with a dozen conservative leaders to rebuild their trust in Facebook (Kantrowitz 2016). Most importantly, in the wake of this scandal, Facebook fired the news curation team and moved to an algorithm-driven source of Trending news topics. Unsurprisingly, fake news stories started appearing in the Trending news section following this move (Silverman 2016c). For many of the reasons discussed in section 4.2, fake news purveyors were able to game the algorithm.

So what does this example teach us about the role of conceptions of objectivity in the fake news problem? My argument is that Facebook was in the grips of a problematic view of objectivity: the neutral/biased binary. What do I mean by the neutral/biased binary? When we think that there are only two alternatives for some institution, knowledge claim, or other entity (1) for it to be neutral or (2) for it to be biased, then we are in the grips of the neutral/biased binary. On this flawed conceptual framework, objectivity does not come in degrees; something is either biased or it isn't, and the only way for it to avoid being biased is for it to be neutral. This framework is not only flawed in its failure to identify degrees of objectivity but also in its identification of objectivity with neutrality (a conception of objectivity that I explain in due course). The neutral/biased binary caused Facebook to overreact to the *Gizmodo* allegations, and the view of objectivity as neutrality was inappropriately deployed in this context.

Consider Facebook's public response to the *Gizmodo* charges of anti-conservative bias. Facebook released the following statement:

> We take allegations of bias very seriously. Facebook is a platform for people and perspectives from across the political spectrum. Trending Topics shows you the popular topics and hashtags that are being talked about on Facebook. There are rigorous guidelines in place for the review team to ensure consistency and *neutrality*. These guidelines do not permit the suppression of political perspectives. Nor do they permit the prioritization of one viewpoint over another or one news outlet over another. These guidelines do not prohibit any news outlet from appearing in Trending Topics. (qtd. in Constine and Buhr 2016, emphasis added)

Facebook presents itself as a "neutral pipeline for news" (Nunez 2016b). By stating its goal as "consistency and neutrality," Facebook attempts to garner the trust of its diverse users. One marker of trustworthiness is objectivity (cf. Scheman 2001; Douglas 2009). So it is no surprise that social media companies have worked hard to cultivate the perception that their practices of content moderation are objective. Facebook embraces a conception of objectivity as neutrality. Facebook clearly wants users to trust its Trending News section because its guidelines are 'neutral.' Additionally, in its public presentation of the Trending section, Facebook downplayed the role of the curators and focused on the role of the algorithm, thereby bolstering the public perception of the section as neutral (Duguay 2018).

Neutral objectivity is just one of the many types of objectivity. In the context of scientific objectivity, Heather Douglas describes neutral objectivity as a complex balancing act:

[Neutral objectivity] focuses on scientists taking a position that is balanced or neutral with respect to a spectrum of values. In situations where values play important roles in making judgments but there is no clearly 'better' value position, taking a value-neutral position allows one to make the necessary judgments without taking a controversial value position and without committing oneself to values that may ignore other important aspects of the problem or that are more extreme than they are supportable. . . . Thus, with value-neutral objectivity, 'objective' can mean reflectively centrist. (Douglas 2009, 123–24)

When agents try to obtain neutral objectivity, they refrain from making judgments on difficult value choices. Facebook's statement signals that it avoids making judgements; recall its claim: "Nor do [the guidelines] permit the prioritization of one viewpoint over another or one news outlet over another." In this respect, Facebook appears to be claiming neutral objectivity.

Douglas argues that there are times when neutral objectivity is appropriate. For example, when values appear on a spectrum between extremes, and when there are legitimate debates surrounding which value to adopt, then it may be appropriate to adopt a neutral position that presents all sides without taking a position. A scientific literature review may legitimately adopt such a neutral form of objectivity by presenting all sides to ongoing scientific debates without privileging any one view (Douglas 2009, 124). But neutral objectivity is inappropriate when the values on the spectrum are unacceptable: "For example, if racist or sexist values are at one end of the value continuum, value-neutrality would not be a good idea. We have good moral reasons for not accepting racist or sexist values, and thus other values should not be balanced against them" (Douglas 2009, 124). So when individuals or groups want to present themselves as objective by occupying a neutral position, they have to carefully evaluate whether being neutral in this case abdicates an important moral or epistemic responsibility to take a stand.

Facebook claims a kind of neutrality by saying that it does not privilege one viewpoint or news outlet over another. Most clearly, in response to the Trending Topics controversy, Sheryl Sandberg, Facebook's chief operating officer, claimed, "We don't have a point of view. We're not trying to make you have a point of view" (qtd. in King 2016). This might seem to be an appropriate use of neutral objectivity because it is not obviously Facebook's job to make judgments about whether *The Wall Street Journal* is more reliable than

The New York Times, or whether news of interest to conservatives is more important than news of interest to liberals. But given our analysis of the limits of neutral objectivity, we can see that Facebook's approach is flawed. First, recall Douglas's argument that neutral objectivity is inappropriate when some of the values on the spectrum are unacceptable. Neutral objectivity is simply inappropriate in an epistemic landscape as disinformation-rich as our current media environment. Facebook should not remain neutral about truth as an epistemic value. If Facebook presents itself as a destination for news by presenting a list of news stories that its users are talking about, then it has to grapple with the existence of fake news. If it presents itself as a news provider, then it has to take a stand for true news stories and against false news stories. Facebook has attempted to avoid this responsibility by publicly rejecting the notion that it is a news organization. In the aftermath of the Gizmodo controversy, Sheryl Sandberg denied that Facebook had immense power over news by saying, "We're clear about the industry we're in—we're a tech company. We're not a media company, so we're not trying to hire journalists, and we're not trying to write news" (qtd. in King 2016). But this is a clear abdication of responsibility and an attempt to have it both ways.

Now Facebook does sometimes claim to take a stand for truth in its presentation of the Trending feature (Carlson 2018). For example, in response to the *Gizmodo* story alleging anti-conservative bias, Tom Stocky, the vice president for search at Facebook whose team was in charge of the Trending Topics, posted a public message denying the allegations. Stocky's post included the following, "We have in place strict guidelines for our trending topic reviewers as they audit topics surfaced algorithmically: reviewers are required to accept topics that reflect real world events, and are instructed to disregard junk or duplicate topics, hoaxes, or subjects with insufficient sources" (qtd. in Nunez 2016b). Similarly, after it fired the news curators, Facebook's newsroom posted an explanation of the new algorithm-driven process saying, "There are still people involved in this process to ensure that the topics that appear in Trending remain high-quality—for example, confirming that a topic is tied to a current news event in the *real* world" ("Search FYI: An Update to Trending" 2016, emphasis added). With these public statements, Facebook is signaling that it values truth and will take steps to exclude fake news from the Trending Topics feature.

However, when we look at the guidelines Facebook provided the engineers who trained the algorithm and "ensure[d] that the topics . . . remain high quality," we find that neutrality hampered their ability to weed out fake news. Facebook published the guidelines for the engineers who made up the Trending Team ("Trending Review Guidelines" 2016). While these guidelines do not present a completely clear picture of what was happening at Facebook, what appears to have happened at this stage is as follows. The engineers used a tool that presented the results from the Trending algorithm that collected the topics that were trending and provided access to the articles users were sharing about the topic and Facebook posts they were making about it. The guidelines set out two criteria that a story must meet in order to qualify as a current news event in the real world:

1. If the topic contains at least three recently posted articles (<48 hours old) in the articles feed focused on the same real-world event, the topic should be accepted.
2. If the topic does not meet condition (1), review the public posts section of the feed. If the feed contains at least five recent public posts (<48 hours old) related to a recently posted article above, the topic should be accepted. ("Trending Review Guidelines" 2016, 2)

If at this time Facebook was true to its presentation of itself as neutral, then there was no filtering of the list of articles users were sharing or filtering of their posts about a topic. This shows how easy it would be for a faker to game this system. If I could produce three articles on my three different websites (or produce one and inspire at least two other fake news purveyors to cover the fake story) and get those articles widely shared on Facebook, then my fake news story would be likely to pass Facebook's test for a news story in the real world.

Reporters studying fake news on Facebook reported an increase in the number of fake news stories that appeared in the Trending section after Facebook fired its news curators (Silverman 2016b). Days after the news curators were let go, a fake story about former Fox News host Megyn Kelly appeared as a Trending topic. This story came from Endingthefed.com, a hyperpartisan site that published many false and misleading stories. Fake news in such hyperpartisan sites is likely to spread like wildfire on Facebook because it confirms people's partisan beliefs. Craig Silverman explains why this means that an algorithm-driven approach is liable to spread fake news:

> Any Facebook algorithm looking for news stories with strong engagement signals is going to surface these stories, and they are going to look *great*. The

algorithm might check how many other sites have published a story about the same thing—multiple sources, right!—and it will find lots of other articles, because hyper-partisan sites and fake news sites constantly republish (or steal) each other's content. There's a good chance the copycat stories may be doing well on Facebook, too. (Silverman 2016b)

One solution would be to use human curators or train the algorithm to filter out or demote stories published in disreputable sources such as Ending the Fed, but this is where Facebook's commitment to neutrality lets it down. Silverman reported that Facebook employees were unwilling to take such a stand because they viewed it as censorship (Silverman 2016b).

So what we have here is a situation in which understanding objectivity as neutrality has led to an increase in disinformation on social media. This is just one example of a larger problem of media obsession with neutrality which, as others have pointed out, leads to the false balance in which news channels endlessly present "both sides" of a debate, even if one side is pushing disinformation or misinformation (McGarity and Wagner 2010, 223; Oreskes and Conway 2010). This has been epistemically damaging in the climate change debate. I hypothesize that one of the reasons this happens is that both older and newer media lack alternative viable conceptions of objectivity by which to demonstrate their trustworthiness to the public and other stakeholders. And this is where I think feminist accounts of objectivity are helpful. Let us look at one.

Consider what it would mean for Facebook to implement procedures aimed at increasing what Douglas calls 'interactive objectivity,' which is objectivity generated through the kind of transformative criticism endorsed by feminist empiricists (cf. Longino 1990, 2002; Douglas 2009; Intemann 2010). On this approach, objectivity arises at the level of the community. Feminist empiricists argue that the objectivity of a community increases to the extent that it enables members of the community to engage in critical dialogue with others that identifies and weeds out idiosyncratic biases. Helen Longino's influential four criteria necessary for facilitating transformative criticism are helpful here:

(1) [T]here must be recognized avenues for the criticism of evidence, of methods, and of assumptions and reasoning;
(2) there must exist shared standards that critics can invoke;

(3) the community as a whole must be responsive to such criticism;
(4) intellectual authority must be shared equally among qualified practitioners. (Longino 1990, 76)

A community will have interactive objectivity to the extent that it meets each of these criteria. Longino agrees with many other feminist epistemologists discussed in Chapter 1 that objectivity comes in degrees (i.e., she rejects the neutral/biased binary). So the more transformative criticism produced, the more weeding out of bias the community collectively accomplishes.

To see how this can happen, consider the following abstract scenario that mirrors many improvements in objectivity due to feminist scientific critique. Imagine a community of scientists working in a particular subfield. This community has recognized avenues, such as journals and conferences, that enable them to learn about each other's work, assess its merits, and share criticisms with their colleagues. This community also has some widely shared standards for what constitutes acceptable research in this area (e.g., standards for empirical success, favored statistical models). Now imagine that at a conference, a scientist makes a well-supported criticism of a colleague's work by pointing out how a bias in the work prevents it from adequately meeting the relevant shared standards in the field. We now have a potential transformative criticism that could move the community toward weeding out this bias, if the criticism is given uptake. Stubbornness or unwillingness to accept such criticism will prevent the potential transformation from being actualized, thus the need for Longino's third criterion. A further barrier to uptake is prejudice and testimonial injustice (cf. Fricker 2007)—if the critique is made by a member of a marginalized group, then their criticism may not be given due uptake due to the other scientists' prejudices. Thus, Longino's fourth criterion is required because a community in which all qualified researchers are given the proper amount of respect and their criticisms are given due uptake is one in which biases that they identify can be weeded out. In sum, a community that meets Longino's criteria is more likely to give space for, and give due uptake of, criticisms that identify biases that skew research. Thus, Longino's criteria provide a useful evaluative framework for analyzing the extent to which a community can be objective, and they can also suggest steps that communities can take to increase their chances of weeding out bias (e.g., clarifying shared standards, increasing equality of intellectual authority by including a diversity of voices and challenging prejudiced community cultures).

How does this framework apply to Facebook? Let's examine how Facebook could have responded to the allegations of anti-conservative bias in its news curation team, if it had used interactive (rather than neutral) objectivity. If we take the news curation team and its supervisors as the relevant community to assess in terms of whether trending topics were being selected according to an objective method, then Facebook could have evaluated to what extent its methods and structures facilitated transformative criticism to weed out the idiosyncratic and political biases of its news curators. Did the news curation team have avenues for discussing decisions that their colleagues were making about whether a particular event was a real-world event worthy of inclusion in the Trending section, or whether a particular news source should be selected for the posted news article or trusted to corroborate the event? In any such discussions, were there shared standards to which participants could appeal to demonstrate that a decision to exclude (or include) a story or source was based on political bias (or other bias)? Did criticisms of bias gain uptake in the community; were reasonable, well-supported criticisms of bias taken seriously? What about the composition of the news curation team—was it diverse? Did it include a variety of values and political commitments? Were criticisms of some members of the team unfairly dismissed due to biases or stereotypes? Conducting an 'objectivity audit' of the news curation team, reporting the results to the public, and making any necessary changes could have provided Facebook with alternatives to simply firing the team. By making a commitment to addressing questions of bias by recognizing the ways in which objectivity is a product of communal interactions, Facebook could have taken a public stand for objective, trustworthy news curation. By acknowledging that its individual employees are, like all of us, likely to have their own political values and idiosyncratic biases, but ensuring that it has in place mechanisms for weeding out these biases through critical dialogue, Facebook could have restored trust in its methods after the allegations of bias.

I think this approach could have been a useful alternative to Facebook's flight to the algorithm-driven method that proved to be so vulnerable to fake news stories. To some extent, misinterpretations of feminist epistemologies have led to an impoverished understanding of objectivity—one which presents neutrality as the only alternative to subjective bias run amok. Perhaps a return to this vibrant feminist literature might help us out of the predicament we find ourselves in. Not only could interactive objectivity have prevented some instances of fake news, but perhaps it could have avoided the cycle of scandals with the Trending features that are so corrosive of trust in the media. When the public sees first allegations of bias, then stories of firings at Facebook, only to be followed by new scandals of fake news stories, it is no surprise that their trust in our hybrid media system is shaken. As we have seen, fakers and media manipulators exploit this trust. Thus, I think the benefits of a media landscape that moves beyond the neutral/biased binary and adopts methods of interactive objectivity could both help avoid some fake news scandals and also restore some trust that our media institutions sorely need.

This is not to say that implementing interactive objectivity at Facebook would be easy or uncontroversial. As a corporation, Facebook is concerned with public perception. And in a public environment in which the neutral/biased binary is pervasive, Facebook could find it difficult to 'sell' interactive objectivity as a solution. Firing the news curation team and moving to the algorithm-driven approach makes public-relations sense in an environment in which the public views algorithms as neutral and all humans as tainted with bias. Thus, it might have been that conservatives would not have considered my objectivity audit sufficient to address their concerns of bias. However, I think the public is increasingly aware of the problem of algorithmic bias, and this may provide an opening to make alternatives, such as interactive objectivity, more plausible.

Other challenges to my approach come from limitations of Longino's account that have been widely debated in the feminist literature. First, consider the debate surrounding the inclusivity of Longino's account. Feminist standpoint epistemologists have long argued that feminist empiricists, such as Longino, are too inclusive when they argue that all values and interests are useful in weeding out bias (cf. Intemann 2010, 790–94; 2011). Many feminists have worried that requiring a diversity of values means requiring that scientific communities include racist, sexist, and other oppressive values (Intemann 2017; Rolin 2017). Daniel Hicks argues for a particular version of this objection by presenting the "Nazi problem" for Longino's fourth criterion (Hicks 2011).[10] The motivation for Longino's fourth criterion is the historical exclusion of women and racial minorities from science, which prevented critical analysis of the sexist and racist assumptions that were shared by members of the scientific community. Thus, Longino includes the fourth criterion as a mechanism for actively cultivating the inclusion of

---

[10] Hicks credits Natalia Baeza and Janet Kourany with first developing the "Nazi problem" objection in a seminar at the University of Notre Dame.

women and other underrepresented groups. But Hicks argues that Longino's reasoning for her fourth criterion also justifies actively cultivating the inclusion of racist and sexist groups, such as Nazis. Longino's argument that we need to cultivate diversity of viewpoints to provide critical examination of the common beliefs of an epistemic community may, according to Hicks, justify including Nazis in an epistemic community:

> [Longino's argument] applies *mutatis mutandis* to views antithetical to those of feminists and other progressives and leftists: the exclusion of groups who hold misogynist and racist beliefs means certain feminist and anti-racist beliefs will be shared by all (or almost all) members of the community, and hence these beliefs cannot be subject to the critical scrutiny that objectivity requires; to prevent this, active steps must be taken to include members of these misogynist and racist groups. (Hicks 2011, 337)

Hicks is thus concerned that Longino's account of objectivity may ultimately be unfeminist, because it seems to require the inclusion of anti-feminist groups.

This suggests a pressing question to the application of Longino's criteria to Facebook's Trending Topics news curation team: does applying Longino's framework require Facebook to include Nazis (and other oppressive groups) in its news curation team? That this is a pressing problem, and not merely a philosopher's idle thought experiment, should be immediately clear from my discussion of the role of racism in the fake news problem. Do we really want Nazis influencing the decisions about which stories make it into the Trending Topics feature? Fakers often use racist narratives to exploit the mechanisms of confirmation bias in a public where racist biases are common. Having members of the Trending Topics team who are ideologically committed to racism could create a situation in which they accept racist fake news as legitimate and include it in the Topics feature. Thus, if Longino's criteria require us to cultivate representation from such groups on the news curation team, then there is a legitimate concern that Longino's criteria are not what we want in this area.[11]

However, Longino's framework provides an initial answer to this concern in this applied context. Recall that Longino's fourth criterion does not exist

---

[11] The Nazi problem bears similarities to the ways in which the language of "viewpoint diversity" has been used in Silicon Valley by conservatives to argue for the inclusion of misogynistic and white supremacist viewpoints; see Jack, Lewis, and Dave 2018.

in isolation—a community is objective to the extent that it meets all four criteria. The second criterion requires that the community adhere to shared epistemic standards. As we saw, for Facebook, this would require members of the news curation team to adhere to epistemic standards for determining which news stories are "events in the real world" and which are fake news. Nazis who do not adhere to such standards and who instead are ideologically committed to promoting racist fake news stories do not belong on the news curation team and may be excluded based solely on Longino's second criterion. Similarly, the third criterion requires uptake of legitimate criticisms based on the shared epistemic standards. Nazis who refuse to give due uptake to the well-grounded criticisms of members of the community would be in violation of the third criterion (and also the fourth, if their failure to give uptake is due to prejudice against the critics' racial or other social group) (Daukas 2011, 63; Intemann 2011, 121; Rolin 2017, 123–24). In sum, the kinds of behaviors Nazis tend to engage in—that is, failing to adhere to norms of truth and accuracy (violations of criterion two), stubborn refusal to accept legitimate criticism (violations of criterion three), and denial of epistemic authority to marginalized groups (violations of criterion four)—preclude them from legitimate membership in an objective community of gatekeepers. Thus, Longino's criteria provide multiple reasons to exclude Nazis (and other epistemically pernicious and oppressive groups) from the Facebook news curation team.

Hicks recognizes this possible response to the "Nazi problem," but Hicks thinks there is still room for concern that Longino's criteria do not provide the resources for excluding a more sophisticated bad-faith Nazi who adheres to the shared standards of the community and follows Longino's criteria, even though these standards conflict with their deeply held Nazi values (Hicks 2011, 338). I think the bad-faith Nazi presents an interesting hypothetical challenge to Longino, but (fortunately) dealing with this philosophical hypothetical is largely unnecessary for answering the real-world applied epistemological question of whether Facebook should have Nazis on its news curation team. Sophisticated bad-faith Nazis are just not individuals we meet in this world; they are a philosophical thought experiment who will not apply for jobs at Facebook. Thus, given what we know about the epistemic practices of actual Nazis, they do not meet the epistemic qualifications for objective appraisal of news. Thus, they should not be part of the news curation team.

Hicks rejects my suggestion that bad-faith Nazis are a mere philosophical thought experiment (Daniel Hicks, personal communication, May 29,

2018). Hicks notes that members of the alt-right, such as Milo Yiannopoulos, deploy the rhetoric of 'free speech' and thus may appear to endorse liberal values consistent with Longino's criteria. Cloaking their illiberal agenda in liberal rhetoric has been a successful strategy for members of the alt-right, encouraging many people, even outside the alt-right, to resist their exclusion from epistemic communities (cf. D'Ancona 2017). Thus, Hicks argues that the concerns about inclusion of bad-faith Nazis raise a very practical problem that must be addressed by attempts to draw on Longino in this area.

In response, Hicks is right that bad faith and misleading rhetoric is a significant problem in our current epistemic landscape. The example of Yiannopoulos is an apt one insofar as Yiannopoulos represents the kind of bad-faith actor who should be excluded from inclusion in Facebook's news curation team. However, I do not think this example exactly fits the contours of the sophisticated bad-faith Nazi from Hick's original paper, and I also believe that Longino's criteria can provide tools for excluding such actors from the team. The sophisticated bad-faith Nazi not only "talks the talk" of Longino's liberal criteria, but they also "walk the walk"; that is, they adhere to the standards in their epistemic practices. Yiannopoulos simply does not do this. As Hicks acknowledges, Yiannopoulos does not grant women equality of epistemic authority (Yiannopoulos 2016; Daniel Hicks, personal communication, May 29, 2018). This is one hint at just how hard it would be to pull off being a sophisticated bad-faith Nazi in actual practice (rather than philosophical thought experiment); one would have to consistently act in accordance with epistemic criteria to which one is vehemently opposed. For this reason, actual agents such as Nazis and members of the alt-right do not consistently meet Longino's criteria, and thus they are not fit members of an objective epistemic community. The fact that they sometimes strategically deploy misleading and bad-faith rhetoric is cause for concern because it means that it will often take much vigilance and critical analysis to detect bad-faith actors. But this is a reason why it will be sometimes difficult in practice to determine who meets Longino's criteria; it is not a reason why Longino's criteria cannot, in principle, exclude members of the news curation team who would undermine its objectivity.

While I think Longino's account can address the Nazi problem for Facebook news curation, I do think Facebook could also learn some lessons from the standpoint epistemologists who criticize Longino's framework. As we saw in the previous chapter, Intemann argues for a consensus view in feminist epistemology that she calls "feminist standpoint empiricism" (Intemann

2010). This theory draws on Longino's feminist empiricist insights that objectivity arises through critical engagement within a diverse community. It joins with Longino in identifying the historical exclusion of women and minority groups as an impediment to the transformative criticism that improves objectivity. So to that extent, it agrees with all of Longino's four criteria for objectivity. But feminist standpoint empiricism rejects Longino's conception of diversity as diversity of values and interests and the claim that all values are equally useful in weeding out bias (Intemann 2010, 791–92). In part for the reasons discussed earlier as the Nazi problem, Intemann maintains that Longino's criteria are too inclusive. Instead, her feminist standpoint empiricism adheres to the fundamental insight of standpoint theory that, in some contexts, the standpoints of the oppressed offer epistemic insights typically inaccessible from the standpoints of the privileged (Wylie 2003, 28; Intemann 2010, 783). For this reason, feminist standpoint empiricism maintains the following thesis of epistemic advantage: "epistemic communities that *include* members of marginalized groups will have epistemic advantages, or more rigorous critical consciousness, than communities that do not (at least in *some* contexts)" (Intemann 2010, 787). I argue that this normative principle provides a useful tool for an objectivity audit of news curation teams at social media companies like Facebook. An objectivity audit should evaluate whether members of Facebook's news curation team are a diverse group of agents in which the *epistemic expertise* of marginalized members is included and respected in contexts where it is relevant.

This is where my analysis of fake news as a problem of white ignorance intersects with my analysis of the value of interactive objectivity in news curation. Fake news is not a problem of generic ignorance. Fake news often targets marginalized communities and trades on a society's prejudices. As a result of living in an oppressive society, members of marginalized communities are more likely to be attuned to these prejudices and the tactics often targeted against their communities. That means that members of marginalized groups may have an epistemic advantage in identifying fake news stories targeted against their community. Thus, a news curation team that includes and respects the insights of marginalized curators will be more critically attuned to fake news stories and better able to weed out any biases in the news curation process.

One might argue that Nazis would be epistemically well-positioned to identify fake news stories targeted against their community; thus, they should be included in the news curation to weed out these fake news stories

(Kristen Intemann, personal communication, June 6, 2018). However, recall my previous arguments that Nazis tend to have other epistemic vices and fail to follow Longino's criteria. Additionally, following Intemann's feminist standpoint empiricism, we should recognize that Nazis, who have not achieved the standpoints of the oppressed, lack the epistemic advantages that standpoint epistemologists have demonstrated accrue to these standpoints.

To summarize this section, one of the causes of the fake news problem is a failed conception of neutral objectivity on the part of social media companies and other internet platforms. I have argued that instead of a flight to easily manipulated algorithms as a way to avoid challenges of bias, companies like Facebook should adopt interactive objectivity to weed out bias and buttress trust in their content. By conducting an objectivity audit of their news curation teams, social media companies can demonstrate that their processes of removing fake news are increasingly objective because they are increasingly able to detect and remove biases. I have outlined several specific criteria (based on Longino's feminist empiricism and Intemann's feminist standpoint empiricism) that can provide a detailed framework for an objectivity audit. In this way, the decades of feminist analysis of methods for improving objectivity can help us make progress in addressing the fake news problem.

4.6. Conclusion

Let us return to the framing premise of this chapter that social epistemology has much to contribute to the ongoing analysis of the fake news problem. From my summary in section 4.2 of the purported causes of the fake news problem, we can see that this is a complex problem requiring interdisciplinary analysis. What social epistemology can contribute to this interdisciplinary work is a set of normative tools for analyzing why fake news is a problem, understanding what kind of a problem it is, and suggesting solutions to the problem. In section 4.3, I argued that veritism and the epistemology of trust help us recognize that fake news is a problem because it spreads false beliefs and undermines trust in the social practices of objectivity and truth acquisition. In section 4.4, I argued that the fake news problem is closely tied up with our problems with racism (and other forms of oppression). So my use of Mills's "White Ignorance" supports those scholars of cyber racism who argue that racism and our hybrid media landscape shape and co-constitute each other (Daniels 2009a, 2009b, 2013; Noble 2013, 2018; Matamoros-Fernández

2017; Farkas, Schou, and Neumayer 2018). We need to work on multiple fronts to confront the *epistemic* threat that racism poses and the *racist* threat posed by our online epistemic ecosystem. As Noble argues, "What we need is a way to reframe, reimagine, relearn, and remember the struggle for racial and social justice and to see how information online in ranking systems can also impact behavior and thinking offline" (Noble 2018, 117–18). A social epistemology that accounts for (rather than abstracts away from) race and racism illuminates more of the causes of fake news and the role that memory and testimony play in our fake news predicament. Finally, in section 4.5, I argued that one of the causes of the fake news problem is faulty thinking about objectivity and neutrality in Silicon Valley. A feminist social epistemology provides a solution to this lack of understanding of the interactive nature of objectivity. With these feminist tools in hand, social media companies could make significant progress toward weeding out bias and buttressing trust in their epistemic practices. This is important work because, as I will argue in the next chapter, social media provide real, positive epistemic opportunities. While this chapter has drawn attention to social media's vulnerabilities to disinformation, the next chapter argues that social media can be a useful epistemic tool for addressing the epistemic challenges of prejudice and ignorance of privilege.

5
Lurkers

5.1. The Internet as a Medium for Unlearning Ignorance

One of the great epistemic benefits of the internet is that it enables us to learn from people very distant, both geographically and socially, from ourselves. Of course, these benefits do not come without risks—opportunities to learn are often thwarted by biased moderators, untrustworthy imposters, and manipulative fakers. And we do not always bother to take advantage of the opportunities to learn from people different than us—we stay in echo chambers, and we engage in willful ignorance. But opportunities to learn exist. The internet can connect us across lines of difference, and we can take this opportunity to unlearn some of our socially constructed ignorance.

In a 2016 paper, "Social Media, Trust, and the Epistemology of Prejudice," I investigate these issues through the epistemic persona of the sharer, someone who wants to share their experiences with others in order to educate them (Frost-Arnold 2016a). In that paper, I show that a certain kind of sharing, coupled with a powerful kind of trust, can reduce socially constructed ignorance of privilege and prejudice. The internet is full of blog posts, tweets, Facebook posts, and subreddits in which people discuss privilege and prejudice. People have many reasons for engaging in such discussions. Some want to share their experiences (de Laat 2008) and form community with other activists, while others enjoy being provocateurs, discussing prejudice to get a rise out of their audience. However, much online discussion is not simply self-expression, community building, or provocation; instead, many people discuss privilege in order to help others unlearn their privileged habits and prejudiced stereotypes (Kahn, Spencer, and Glaser 2013, 208). And this online sharing is often successful—sharers can be powerful educators whose testimony reduces pernicious ignorance.

In this chapter, I flip the focus from my previous work on sharers, and I analyze the epistemic persona of the one who wants to learn. One type of online learner is the lurker. Lurkers are people who listen to or read communications without participating in the conversations themselves. The internet provides unprecedented opportunities for lurking. And lurking is a complex epistemic activity. Deciding when and where to lurk is epistemically consequential. Those of us who identify as lurkers in some online spaces face tricky decisions. In which spaces do I want to lurk? Am I welcome to lurk there? When should I lurk, and when should I participate? When should I shut up, listen, and stay out, and when should I engage, share, and join? As with all the epistemic questions studied in this book, these dilemmas are not merely matters of individual choice operating in a vacuum. Instead, the very persona of the lurker is made possible by platform design decisions made by large corporations for profit. Additionally, the individual decisions made by lurkers are influenced by lurkers' social locations, and the inequalities of the surrounding society shape the consequences of these decisions. Thus, the complicated epistemic dilemmas of lurking practices are ripe for analysis with the kind of social epistemological approach offered in this book. We need to pay attention to power and privilege in an epistemology of lurking—an abstract epistemology that ignores racial oppression, for example, will miss some crucial dynamics of online knowledge.

To pursue these issues, I start with a line of argument that might seem to naturally follow from my analysis in "Social Media, Trust, and the Epistemology of Prejudice." In that paper, I argue that when marginalized people share their stories of oppression, it can provide a powerful opportunity for privileged people to unlearn their ignorance. Consequently, one might be tempted to advocate for lurking as an epistemic practice. One might argue that privileged people ought to try to unlearn as much of their ignorance of their privileges and prejudices as they can by lurking in online spaces where marginalized people congregate. This makes sense as an attempt to learn from listening. And it is certainly true that privileged people can learn much from lurking in these spaces. An additional epistemic benefit of lurking is its potential to reduce the undue epistemic burden often placed on the shoulders of marginalized people. This burden frequently arises from privileged people's demands for education (cf. Berenstain 2016). I will argue that lurking can decrease this unjust epistemic burden on marginalized people by giving privileged people opportunities to listen and learn quietly.

But lurking is not an epistemically or ethically unproblematic practice. I will argue that lurking is often an oppressive mode of knowledge production, one that treats marginalized subjects as objects of voyeuristic study rather than as epistemic agents. We need an epistemology that recognizes the value of learning from people different than oneself without legitimating privileged people's invasion of marginalized spaces. Many spaces where marginalized people congregate online do not exist for the education of members of dominant groups, and this needs to be respected. Another problem with lurking is that it can be a cowardly practice of hiding to protect oneself from critique and thus be epistemically vicious. Courageous engagement across lines of difference is often necessary for unlearning ignorance. Thus, respectful habits of lurking must be carefully balanced with habits of online critical interaction across lines of difference. That said, there are also dangers in these critical dialogues. For example, what Shannon Sullivan calls 'ontological expansiveness' is a habit of white privilege that poses a threat to cross-racial online interaction: ontological expansiveness encourages white people to expect control, to focus on their own interests, and to assume that they have the right to enter any public space (Sullivan 2006). These habits of privilege manifest themselves in common practices of whites derailing or hijacking online spaces and conversations for people of color. While well-intentioned whites may aim to unlearn their ignorance by interacting with people of color in online conversations, these epistemic practices need to be developed in the context of an epistemically virtuous character that can discern when to engage in a conversation, when to be quiet, and how to avoid white habits of ontological expansiveness. This chapter argues that to address these challenges we need a virtue theory for lurking, and it presents one such approach.

5.2. What Is Lurking?

Lurking, in my sense, is regularly reading online communications of an online community without participating in the conversations oneself. Lurkers might be engaged in activities other than reading. In the case of lurking in someone's YouTube channel, one might be viewing, rather than reading, online content; however, I will focus on cases of reading. Malin Sveningsson defines a lurker as "one who watches what happens in the environment without being seen her/himself" (Sveningsson 2004, 49). Thus, lurking involves a number of features. First, the concept of lurking involves an element of *persistent* reading of online content. If one simply reads one random blog post (or tweet, Facebook post, or Reddit thread, etc.), then one is not a lurker. Lurkers are, in some sense, lingering in an online community without fully participating in it. A lurker on a blog may often read the posts and discussions that comprise the online discussion occurring within the community of people who gather around the blog. But what distinguishes lurkers is that they do not comment themselves. As D. E. Wittkower puts it, "A lurker remains party to an interaction without signaling her presence within it" (Wittkower 2016). So a second important feature of lurking is *not contributing* to the community. This is where one of the affordances of the internet becomes significant: online anonymity makes online lurking possible. In offline spaces, it is extremely difficult to persistently and undetectably listen in on the conversations of a community to which one does not belong. But many online platforms make lurking easy. An important aspect of the connection between lurking and anonymity is that the lurker is almost entirely invisible and unaccountable. Other community members probably do not even know that a lurker is reading the discussion. While a listserv moderator has access to the list of subscribers, often other members do not know the full list of who receives the messages. There can be even greater anonymity for lurkers on a blog. People with public Twitter feeds may know the names or pseudonyms of everyone who is following them, but one does not need to click 'follow' in order to read public tweets, so lurkers may be completely unknown to the author and her followers. The anonymity of the internet provides safety to the lurker, but it also makes them unaccountable eavesdroppers on others' conversations. Thus, the character of the lurker is socially and ethically interesting and complex. In what follows, I argue that it is also epistemically complex.

There are many reasons to lurk in online spaces. Some are non-epistemic, such as lurking in a community with which one identifies but is afraid to join publicly. Voyeurism and the pleasure of watching while invisible are also reasons for lurking. But there are also many epistemic reasons why people lurk in online spaces. For example, to deal with the polarization of our media, one might lurk in Facebook groups of people with different politics than oneself to learn about what motivates them. One might lurk in these conversations rather than participate to avoid the tensions (or worse) that often arise from dialogue across lines of political difference. Lurking can also provide some measure of safety to those, both researchers and members of the public, who wish to learn about powerful, privileged, or threatening groups. For example, lurking in online gathering places for white supremacists can be an important and more protected way that members of oppressed groups can learn about the beliefs and tactics of these dangerous groups. Thus, lurking can potentially provide many kinds of epistemic benefits to different groups.

This chapter will focus on lurking by privileged people as a means to unlearn their socially constructed ignorance. This focus connects to important questions in the epistemology of ignorance literature. How is ignorance unlearned? What do lurkers learn? How do they learn it? When is lurking a voyeuristic, creepy, and oppressive invasion of marginalized spaces? If lurking is ever epistemically responsible, what epistemic practices and virtues do privileged lurkers need? The next section begins by outlining a preliminary argument that lurking can provide the privileged with some epistemic benefits. Future sections will complicate this argument by discussing some of the epistemic limitations of lurking and its oppressive manifestations.

5.3. The Epistemic Benefits of Lurking

The epistemologies of ignorance and epistemic injustice literature detail the many causes of socially constructed ignorance of privilege and prejudice. Willful ignorance (Pohlhaus Jr. 2012), white ignorance (Mills 2007, 2018), testimonial smothering (Dotson 2011), testimonial quieting (Dotson 2011), testimonial injustice (Fricker 2007, 2016; Wanderer 2017), hermeneutical injustice (Fricker 2007, 2016; Mason 2011; Dotson 2012; Pohlhaus Jr. 2012; Medina 2013, 2017), meta-blindness (Medina 2013, 2016), a logic of purity (Lugones 2003; Bailey 2007), lack of 'world' traveling (Lugones 2003), lack of epistemic friction (Medina 2013, 2016), and implicit bias (Brownstein and Saul 2016) are just some of the causes of this type of ignorance. As remedies to these problems, philosophers have uncovered habits and strategies that epistemically virtuous agents can use to unlearn ignorance. These habits are too numerous to review exhaustively in this chapter, but it will be helpful to summarize two of them. First, José Medina advocates seeking beneficial epistemic friction, which can force one to be "self-critical, to compare and contrast one's beliefs, to meet justificatory demands, to recognize cognitive gaps" (Medina 2013, 50). Someone who seeks beneficial epistemic friction is open to alternative social imaginaries and standpoints. These alternatives "can serve as correctives of each other, epistemic counterpoints that enable people to see limitations of each viewpoint" (Medina 2013, 78). Second, recall María Lugones's argument for the epistemic benefits of 'world'-traveling discussed in Chapter 3 (Lugones 2003). A 'world' in Lugones's sense is a society or part of a society, and worlds can differ depending on whether they are given a dominant or non-dominant construction (Lugones 2003, 87–88). Lugones notes that we are different people when we occupy different worlds; for example, she describes herself as having the qualities of playfulness or being at ease in some worlds, but not in others. When we "shift from being one person to be a different person," we are 'world'-traveling (Lugones 2003, 89). Marginalized people are forced to 'world'-travel as a result of moving between dominant and non-dominant 'worlds.' This 'world'-travel is epistemically beneficial—by traveling to someone else's 'world,' we can come to know and understand them in a way inaccessible to the non-traveler (Lugones 2003, 97). Cultivating habits of seeking beneficial epistemic friction and playful 'world'-travel are steps epistemically virtuous agents can take to reduce their ignorance.

Lurking online can be one avenue for pursuing epistemic friction and engaging in some degree of 'world'-travel. When privileged people lurk in online discussions between marginalized people, the privileged can gain epistemic benefits and unlearn some of their ignorance. Social media can be a powerful tool for educating privileged people about their privilege and prejudice. In my previous work on sharing, I argue that when members of marginalized groups make themselves vulnerable by telling their stories of oppression in attempts to educate their audience, they can engage in a powerful form of hopeful trust—a kind of trust which encourages the trustee to live up to the truster's trust (Frost-Arnold 2016a). By telling their stories with an attitude of hopeful trust in their audience, these oppressed speakers can motivate their audience to push past some of the barriers to unlearning one's prejudice. For example, if I read a Twitter thread by a woman of color describing her interactions with white feminists and revealing some of the unconscious biases they possess, I may be touched by the power of her story and moved by the trust in me that she demonstrated by making herself vulnerable on Twitter. This may motivate me to push past the defensive reactions I may initially feel in learning of biases people like me are liable to possess, and reading this thread may help me unlearn some of my ignorance.

Put in Medina's terms, lurking on Twitter may create some beneficial epistemic friction for me—as a white woman, I am liable to view myself as a good person, but reading tweets by people of color may create friction with this self-conception. It may make me aware of unflattering biases I hold. In Lugones's terms, reading Twitter threads can give us some of the benefits of 'world'-traveling. Some authors give us opportunities to witness the 'worlds' of others as they invite us into their lives through their writing. In describing how traveling to her mother's 'world' helped her develop a greater understanding of her mother, Lugones says, "Loving my mother also required that I see with her eyes, that I go into my mother's 'world,' that I see both of us as we are constructed in her 'world,' that I witness her own sense of herself from within her 'world' (Lugones 2003, 85–86). If a privileged person lurks on a thread by a marginalized woman, it may provide an opportunity to "see with her eyes" and to "see both of us as we are constructed in her 'world.'" As a white woman lurking on Black Twitter, I can experience moments of seeing how I am constructed in the 'worlds' of some Black women. It is worth emphasizing the 'some' in the previous sentence. As André Brock observes, "That Black Twitter is often portrayed as representative of the entire Black community despite the heterogeneity of Black culture speaks to the power of American racial ideology's framing of Black identity as monoculture" (Brock 2020, 124). White lurkers who are attentive to diversity within racially marginalized communities can learn something, as long as they keep in mind the limitations of what they learn. And trending hashtags like #SolidarityIsForWhiteWomen can expand these opportunities to more lurkers. In sum, when people with privileged identities lurk in social media spaces targeted toward marginalized people, they can encounter perspectives that help them unlearn their ignorance.

An additional epistemic benefit of lurking is its potential to reduce the undue epistemic burden often placed on the shoulders of members of marginalized groups. This burden frequently arises from privileged people's demands for education. Norah Berenstain uses the term 'epistemic exploitation' to refer to this type of epistemic injustice (Berenstain 2016). For Berenstain, epistemic exploitation happens "when privileged persons compel marginalized persons to produce an education or explanation about the nature of the oppression they face" (Berenstain 2016, 570). Unlearning one's socially constructed ignorance is often a developmental process. At some stages in the process, the privileged person may become cognizant that their social location puts them at an epistemic disadvantage, but they may not yet know the full scope of their ignorance or how to resolve it. They may be aware enough of the social situatedness of knowledge to realize that members of oppressed groups may have insights that are different and epistemically superior in some respects. While these are epistemically beneficial realizations for a privileged person to have, since they reflect virtuous epistemic humility and appropriate levels of distrust in one's own epistemic abilities (cf. Jones 2002), they frequently cause privileged people to request that oppressed individuals educate them about the issues. Of course, listening to the testimony of oppressed people is an important part of unlearning the ignorance of privilege. However, this places an undue epistemic burden on the oppressed. Sharing one's experiences or insights in ways that may educate the privileged is epistemically demanding, emotionally draining, and time-consuming. When privileged people ask members of oppressed groups to educate them, they are asking the oppressed to perform epistemic labor that will very rarely be asked of the privileged. But members of marginalized groups can also take on this undue epistemic burden themselves. Some members of marginalized groups choose to share their stories as supererogatory acts of epistemic heroism (cf. Medina 2013). However, other members of oppressed groups may not see these acts as supererogatory; they may believe that they ought to educate the privileged, thereby taking the undue epistemic burden on themselves.

One of the epistemic benefits of online lurking is its potential to alleviate some of that burden. The internet provides the potential for one blog post, Facebook post, or tweet to reach many people. This potentially reduces the epistemic burden for marginalized people in their everyday lives, since they can direct privileged people to online spaces where they can be educated through lurking. Consider the following dynamic that I have witnessed in my classroom: a student with a privileged identity asks for education on an issue (or on privilege in general) from their marginalized peers. They may direct this request to their peers generally, or they may direct it to a particular peer. In response, another student with a marginalized identity suggests an online source that could provide the education requested, by saying something such as "So-and-so talks about that a lot. You should look her up on YouTube," or "You really need to hang out more on disability Twitter to learn why that's wrong." By responding to a demand for education with a quick referral to an online space where the privileged person can lurk and learn, a marginalized person has an easy way to deflect the epistemic burden. While sometimes specific recommendations for spaces can be useful, one can use the mere presence of online spaces where lurking is possible to remind the privileged that they can educate themselves—they do not need to, and ought not, demand that the marginalized people around them educate them. So, for example, sometimes my students will simply reply to a demand for education with something like "You need to educate yourself. That's what the internet is for." Thus, the internet serves a useful epistemic function by providing a medium through which material that can educate the privileged can reach a large audience, thereby alleviating the burden on individuals to constantly take on this task in their offline lives.

To summarize so far, I have argued that lurking is a practice that can reduce the ignorance of the privileged in a way that does not place an undue epistemic burden on the marginalized. Analyzed using Goldman's standards for veritistic social epistemology, lurking can be a *reliable*, *powerful*, and *efficient* practice. The reliability of a social-epistemic practice is measured by the ratio of true beliefs acquired to the total number of beliefs produced by a practice (Goldman 1992; Thagard 1997). Lurking can be *reliable* because it can increase the ratio of true beliefs to false beliefs circulating in the community as privileged people replace their false beliefs with truths learned from the marginalized people in whose spaces they lurk. The power of a social-epistemic practice is assessed by how well it helps affected individuals acquire true beliefs about issues that matter to them (Goldman 1992; Thagard 1997). Lurking can be a *powerful* practice when it helps privileged people find true answers to their questions. The efficiency of a social-epistemic practice is measured by how costly it is for cognizers to acquire true beliefs. Lurking can be *efficient* because it limits the costs the community bears for this education of the privileged; the epistemic burden in terms of energy, time, and resources that it costs the marginalized to provide this educational opportunity is reduced by the large audience of lurkers who can read their content. So there are many veritistic advantages to lurking.

But I think additional epistemic advantages to lurking appear when we look to the literature on epistemic injustice and 'ally' epistemology.[1] The work of Veronica Ivy (publishing as McKinnon 2017) on the epistemic harms perpetuated by 'allies' is particularly useful here. 'Allies' are "generally conceived as dominant group members who work to end prejudice in their personal and professional lives, and relinquish social privileges conferred by their group status through their support of nondominant groups" (K. T. Brown and Ostrove 2013, 2211). While 'allies' may have good intentions, Ivy argues that they often cause harms to the nondominant groups they claim to support. Consider gaslighting, which Ivy analyzes as a form of epistemic

---

[1] I follow Ivy's practice of putting the term 'ally' in quotes to reflect skepticism about whether those who call themselves 'allies' are truly living up to the ideals of social justice which they profess to hold ([Ivy] McKinnon 2017).

injustice. In gaslighting, a hearer of a piece of testimony raises doubts about the speaker's credibility (McKinnon 2017, 168). Gaslighting is often deployed as a way of discrediting the testimony of oppressed people about the injustices they face. One common problem with 'allies' is that they often react defensively to being told that they have committed an injustice. Since they self-identify as good 'allies,' they may reject testimony by marginalized people about harms they have caused. By drawing on stereotypes that cast the marginalized testifier as unreliable (e.g., casting a trans woman testifier as emotional and "overreacting"), the 'allies' gaslight and harm the testifier by perpetuating a testimonial injustice. So while an 'ally' may often participate in conversational spaces for marginalized people because the 'ally' is attempting to provide support, the 'ally' may often do harm by joining those communities. Ivy's work is a particularly vivid contemporary account of the practical and epistemic harms privileged 'allies' can cause when they try to unlearn their ignorance and act upon newly acquired awareness of their privilege.

Ivy's analysis stands on the shoulders of the long history of scholarship and activism among women of color that point out these dynamics among white feminism. Women of color have repeatedly documented the ways white women tend to do epistemic harm when they reach beyond the scope of their own experience and try to represent the lives of women of color. The analyses of loving, knowing ignorance (Ortega 2006), exclusionary, racist feminism (hooks 1984; Lorde 1984), testimonial quieting and testimonial smothering (Dotson 2011), cultural imperialism (Lugones and Spelman 1983), and the problem of speaking for others (Alcoff 1991) are all useful concepts for understanding some of the epistemic damage that privileged people can do when they attempt to replace socially constructed ignorance of the marginalized with knowledge.

One of the main recommendations for how white women can avoid these harms is for them to listen and check their assumptions. Ortega's detailed analysis of loving, knowing ignorance gives a particularly useful summary of the many solutions proposed for white feminists' epistemic failings. In particular, she uses Marilyn Frye's notion of arrogant perception (which produces inaccurate representations) and loving perception (which is more accurate) to reveal the arrogant and inaccurate scholarship of white feminists. Ortega cites the following passage from Frye: "The loving eye knows the independence of the other. . . . It is the eye of one who knows that to know the seen, one must consult something other than one's own will and interests and fears and imagination. One must look at the thing. One must look, and listen and check and question" (Frye 1983, 75). Arrogant perceivers rely only on their own imagination or experiences to form beliefs about others. Examples include cis, straight 'allies' who consult only their own imagination for their understanding of queer lives or white 'allies' who know few people of color and who can "just imagine" how terrorizing it would be to live under constant fear of police brutality. Arrogant perception produces false representations. In contrast, the loving perceiver recognizes the limitations of their own viewpoint and takes steps to correct for their biases. As both Frye and Ortega emphasize, some of the key steps toward loving perception (and less ignorance) include looking, listening, checking, and questioning.

Lurking can be a somewhat risk-free opportunity for this listening. Lurking greatly reduces the risks because it is a practice of silence, of non-engagement. Privileged people who adopt a practice of lurking can do so as an attempt to take time to listen, check, and question. They can do so while directly avoiding the harms that women of color have identified as so pervasive when white women speak and write without first listening enough. Thus, by anonymously lurking—by silently listening—privileged people can take steps to unlearn their ignorance without engaging in the practical and epistemic harms that often accompany the blunderings of the privileged who have not yet learned enough to avoid injuring others. This is a significant affordance of online anonymity—it provides a space for privileged people to lurk and be largely invisible and less dangerous to marginalized people. Lurking can be a way for privileged people to learn without doing epistemic damage by gaslighting, speaking for others, smothering, or dominating discussion, practices which do significant epistemic harm to the marginalized and the broader community as a whole. As a means to reducing ignorance while avoiding these harms, lurking can be epistemically beneficial.

5.4. Epistemic Limitations of Lurking

That said, there are significant epistemic and ethical problems with lurking. First, when privileged people lurk in online spaces primarily for marginalized people, they can enact what Cynthia Townley describes as a "spectator-collector model" of knowledge production (Townley 2006, 43). Townley argues that "Colonialism often imposes practices and procedures on an individual (or group) who becomes an object for others' knowledge, assessment, and even manipulation" (Townley 2006, 43). There is a long history of dominant groups treating marginalized communities as exotic spectacles and subjecting them to voyeuristic treatment as objects of study. While it might be a helpful educational experience for a privileged person to lurk in an online space for marginalized people, one needs to ask what right they have to enter this space and whether it is disrespectful for them to lurk there. Lurking can be a form of epistemic irresponsibility when it treats others merely as tools, rather than epistemic ends in themselves. One way to deny the epistemic agency of marginalized people is to treat them the way we treat thermometers—as passive tools from which we collect information (Townley 2006, 40). Townley argues that a more responsible, empathic, and less oppressive mode of knowledge production involves "a broader range of responsibilities: knowing and understanding in a way that recognizes others' authority and right to say 'You don't know'" (Townley 2006, 46).

Two responses to this problem include (1) encouraging privileged people to stay out of spaces marked for marginalized people and (2) advocating engagement across lines of difference, rather than voyeuristic passive watching. Whether lurking is appropriate and non-oppressive or whether one of these alternatives is superior depends on the context. Some marginalized spaces welcome lurkers, while others do not. Sometimes lurking is a respectful way to learn from others, and sometimes it is a passive, objectifying practice which should be replaced with active engagement.

Consider first the wisdom of encouraging privileged people to pay attention to signals that certain spaces are not for them. As I will discuss in detail in section 5.5, one of the habits of privilege is feeling entitled to enter any space. I will argue that this is a habit of white privilege, in particular, that needs to be unlearned. The virtuous online agent pays attention to cues that a certain space is intended as a safe space for marginalized people; and if the agent does not belong to that group, they stay out. These cues often appear in the "About" pages on blogs and Facebook groups, on pinned tweets, and in general discussion. If marginalized people signal that they do not welcome privileged lurkers, then those lurkers should stay out as a sign of respect.

Now consider the second response to lurking as an oppressive mode of knowledge production: engagement. When a privileged person finds a marginalized space that welcomes outsiders, then the privileged person needs to consider when to lurk and when to engage in dialogue across lines of difference. As mentioned earlier, Townley advocates active, collaborative knowledge production rather than treating marginalized people as mere objects to be observed. If, instead of lurking, a white person engages in a Twitter conversation about race with people facing racial oppression, the white person can say, "Here's what I know, but you can tell me that I'm wrong" (cf. Townley 2006, 45). This is often morally and epistemically superior than simply observing marginalized people and producing knowledge about them without holding oneself accountable to the people from whom one learns. By engaging in online dialogue across lines of difference in respectful ways that acknowledge the autonomy and authority of others, privileged people can build relationships of trust which can be rich sources of learning in the future (cf. Townley 2006, 42).

This recognition of the value of relationships in epistemic endeavors echoes Lugones and Spelman's argument that friendship is crucial to epistemically and ethically sound feminist theorizing (Lugones and Spelman 1983). Their paper is an influential critique of cultural imperialism in white feminism. They argue that white/Anglo feminists have tended to make theories that purport to be about the lives of all women that silence, ignore, and misrepresent the lives of women of color. Instead of universalizing their own experiences, white/Anglo feminists need to theorize jointly with women of color. For Lugones and Spelman this process requires a careful balance of *unintrusive learning* ("So you need to learn to become unintrusive, unimportant, patient to the point of tears, while at the same time open to learning any possible lessons" [Lugones and Spelman 1983, 580]) and *interaction and relationship* ("So the motive of friendship remains as both the only appropriate and understandable motive for white/Anglo feminists engaging in the task [of theorizing jointly with women of color]. If you enter the task out of friendship with us, then you will be moved to attain the appropriate reciprocity of care for your and our wellbeing as whole beings" [Lugones and Spelman 1983, 581]). They reject mere "passive immersion" in others' cultures in favor of friendship between white/Anglo women and women of color in which reciprocity is central. While Lugones and Spelman's focus is on the epistemic enterprise of feminist theorizing, which is not my topic in this chapter, they also provide a helpful model for the epistemic enterprise of unlearning socially constructed ignorance. The value of this approach becomes clearer when we look at the second and third problems with lurking as an epistemic practice.

A second problem with merely lurking is that it does not necessarily involve the kind of change in one's self that is central to Lugones's fully fledged notion of 'world'-traveling. 'World'-travel involves shifting to become a different person. When one travels to a 'world,' "one is someone who has that personality or character or uses space and language in that particular way" (Lugones 2003, 90). A white person who tries to unlearn their ignorance by merely lurking in Black Twitter is not fully living in community with Black people. If they merely lurk, they are missing out on opportunities to be a different person than they are in white-dominated spaces. They lose out on the opportunity to notice how they act, speak, or move differently when interacting with people of color than they do with white people. This is an epistemic loss, and it prevents them from noticing aspects of their privilege and unlearning some prejudices. Put in Ortega's terms, merely lurking can be a route to loving, knowing, ignorance: "Theorizing about women of color without checking and questioning about their actual lives, without actively trying to participate in their lives, without knowing any flesh-and-blood women of color, or without practical engagement with them, is loving, knowing, ignorance" (Ortega 2006, 68). True 'world'-traveling which avoids loving, knowing, ignorance requires interaction with people different than oneself. Thus, silently lurking will not provide all the epistemic benefits that interaction can provide.

A third limitation is that lurking can be motivated by epistemically harmful cowardice or defensiveness. To protect ourselves from what we perceive to be attacks, we may lurk rather than engage in a conversation. But often the most useful epistemic friction comes from having our beliefs and actions openly challenged. Prejudice and the habits of privilege are often so thoroughly hidden from us that it may take someone explicitly pointing them out to us for them to rise to the level of awareness. This kind of direct epistemic friction is not available to lurkers.

Seeking epistemic friction and living in community with people different than oneself are important practices that decrease willful hermeneutical ignorance. As I argued in Chapter 2, willful hermeneutical ignorance is a significant cause of misunderstandings of the speech of marginalized people. When members of dominant groups fail to learn the language of marginalized people, they can misunderstand marginalized speech. This is a problem that lurkers can face. If one merely lurks in marginalized spaces, one may not fully understand what one reads. Jacob Hale discusses this kind of misunderstanding in his suggested rules for non-transgender people writing about transgender issues:

> Be aware that our words are very often part of conversations we're having within our communities, and that we may be participating in overlapping conversations within multiple communities, e.g., our trans communities, our scholarly communities (both interdisciplinary ones and those that are disciplinarily bounded), feminist communities, queer communities, communities of color. Be aware of these conversations, our places within them, and our places within community and power structures. Otherwise, you won't understand our words. (Hale 1997)

Cisgender people who lurk in trans spaces are at risk for misunderstanding what they read if they do not carefully check and question their assumptions, and if they do not take the time to learn the languages trans people use in different spaces. This means that mere lurking is no simple epistemic solution to ignorance—lurkers also need to cultivate the virtue of hermeneutical justice and also live in community with marginalized people.

These practices will also help lurkers avoid another potential problem: lurking in the wrong spaces. As I discussed in Chapter 3, internet imposters who impersonate marginalized people spread misinformation online. Imposters, such as Tom MacMaster, can create (and participate in) online spaces which provide inaccurate information about marginalized people. Identifying reliable marginalized voices to follow is an important step for privileged people who want to unlearn their ignorance. But this can sometimes be difficult for privileged people who are just beginning to unlearn their ignorance. Such privileged people are likely to be vulnerable to the stereotypes and tropes that imposters trade upon to gain uptake from people who cannot distinguish them from authentic marginalized people. Under non-ideal conditions, there is not going to be a perfect solution to these problems, but the practices of seeking epistemic friction and building relationships can help with this challenge to lurking. Consider a cisgender person trying to wade into trans Tumblr during the period when Tumblr was a thriving place for trans community (cf. Haimson et al. 2021). If the cisgender person has some relationships with trans people whose judgment they trust, then they can rely on those trusted experts in the community as a guide. For example, they might get their footing in trans Tumblr by following those accounts that they see their trans friends follow. A cisgender person who does not have such relationships will be in a much more difficult epistemic position. For them, carefully paying attention to the multiplicity of trans voices and seeking out epistemic friction between their assumptions and what they read will provide some help.[2] This is just another way in which lurking is a complicated, limited, and epistemically challenging epistemic practice.

To summarize my argument so far, people of privilege can fruitfully unlearn their ignorance through a thoughtful balance of unintrusive lurking in spaces that welcome it and friendly interaction with marginalized people. Lurking can be a way of unintrusively and patiently opening oneself up to epistemic friction and learning about the lives of others. As I have argued, especially at early stages in their process of unlearning ignorance, privileged people can be dangerous to marginalized people (cf. Hoagland 2001). Lurking is a way of learning while avoiding doing harm.[3] But lurking has limitations, both epistemic and ethical. It provides limited epistemic friction and 'world'-traveling, it can be a cowardly way of avoiding having one's beliefs challenged, and it can irresponsibly and oppressively treat marginalized people as mere tools or instruments whose lives are to be viewed and used to the advantage of the privileged. So lurking has to be balanced with relationships of trust in which the privileged live in community with marginalized people, and privileged people need to learn when to stay out. Lurking should not be the only online mode of engagement between the privileged and the marginalized. However, as we shall see in the next section, matters grow more complicated when we investigate some of the epistemically damaging ways that the privileged interact with the marginalized on the internet.

---

[2] I will discuss the importance of epistemic virtues later in the chapter, but it is worth noting that epistemic virtues will also help privileged people with these challenges. The virtue of epistemic humility will be important, as privileged people may need to accept that they may initially lack the epistemic resources (such as the hermeneutical skills) to make accurate judgments about who is sharing reliable information and who is an imposter.

[3] The following passage in Lugones and Spelman is suggestive of the obligation privileged people have to sometimes stay out of the way and avoid harm: "Out of obligation you [white/Anglo feminists] should stay out of our [women of color's] way, respect us and our distance, and forego the use of whatever power you have over us—for example the power to use your language in our meetings, the power to overwhelm us with your education, the power to intrude in our communities in order to research us and to record the supposed dying of our culture, the power to engrain in us a sense that we are members of dying culture and are doomed to assimilate, the power to keep us in a defensive posture with respect to our own cultures" (Lugones and Spelman 1983, 581).

5.5. Harmful Modes of Interaction: Ontological Expansiveness

While the call for interaction and friendship in our epistemic lives sounds promising, unfortunately, power and privilege tend to mar our relationships both online and offline. An important consideration to weigh in our online lives is the problem of ontological expansiveness. Ontological expansiveness is one of the habits of racial privilege. According to Shannon Sullivan, "As ontologically expansive, white people tend to act and think as if all spaces—whether geographical, psychical, linguistic, economic, spiritual, bodily, or otherwise—are or should be available to them to move in and out of as they wish" (Sullivan 2006, 10). To illustrate these habits of white privilege, Sullivan draws on Patricia Williams's story of a tour of Harlem she took with an otherwise all-white tour group (P. J. Williams 1995, 71). The tour guide asked whether the group wanted to stop inside some Black churches to experience the "show," and none of the white people questioned whether they had the right to enter this space or whether the Black churchgoers welcomed being stared at by white tourists. Ontological expansiveness is a complex suite of behavioral scripts that whites are socialized into, as they learn to expect that the world is open to them. Whites are taught that they can and should have mastery over their environment (Sullivan 2006, 10), and they have a tendency to recognize only their own interests, needs, and projects (Sullivan 2006, 25). While my primary example in this chapter is racial privilege, and Sullivan's account of ontological expansiveness focuses on it as a habit of whiteness, other groups are also socialized into ontologically expansive behavioral scripts. For example, straight people often feel entitled to enter queer physical and virtual spaces (Vimes 2016).

While Sullivan focuses on white habits of taking up physical space, ontological expansiveness also encourages whites to feel entitled to occupy virtual space. Habits of privilege manifest themselves in common practices of whites derailing or hijacking online spaces and conversations for people of color. Read any Facebook thread, blog post comment thread, Twitter conversation, or subreddit populated by a significant number of people of color, and you are likely to come across a moment when a white person intervenes to derail the conversation away from the topics the people of color were discussing and direct it to the concerns of white people. Common derailing moves include white people directing the conversation toward their own feelings of being attacked or their requests for further education on the issues from people of color. Sometimes these requests are motivated by a genuine desire to learn, but other times they are malicious acts of sealioning. Amy Johnson explains sealioning as "an intentional, combative performance of cluelessness. Rhetorically, sealioning fuses persistent questioning—often about basic information, information easily found elsewhere, or unrelated or tangential points—with a loudly-insisted-upon commitment to reasonable debate. It disguises itself as a sincere attempt to learn and communicate" (A. Johnson 2016, 13).

Consider one example that I have anonymized in order to follow guidelines of internet research ethics (Townsend and Wallace n.d.; A. Markham 2012). A Black woman activist wrote a blog post on a blog for women of color. The blog post described a recent painful incident, and the post discussed issues of men's allyship in the Black community. The post gathered many comments of support and discussion. This blog is a space for women of color to build community. And yet in the comment thread, we find a comment that I have paraphrased as follows: "I am sorry this happened. Thanks for posting about it. I know this post is not focusing on white women's allyship. But as a white person, I don't know how to join this discussion. How can white people be useful? How can we help without taking over? How can we avoid doing more harm? ... I hope I could have done something useful to help you in this situation." As later commenters pointed out, this comment derails the conversation away from the discussion among people of color to steer it toward the concerns of white people. A later anonymous commenter who identifies herself as a white woman asks why the earlier commenter tried to make this post an educational exercise for herself, and she entreats white women to stop making everything about themselves. On a charitable interpretation, the first white woman may be trying to unlearn her ignorance and become a supportive 'ally.' This act of interaction rather than merely lurking may, as I discussed earlier, have some epistemic benefits. But her intervention into this conversation is an example of ontological expansiveness. It demonstrates a sense of entitlement to enter the conversation and direct it to her needs and interests and away from the needs and interests of the woman of color who wrote the blog for herself and her community.

Ontological expansiveness is such a common online problem that people of color often are forced to expend significant energy in claiming and maintaining spaces free from white intervention. Moderators for blogging communities of color have to spend time deleting or responding to derailing comments by white people. People of color on Twitter often have to invest time blocking abusive or simply time-wasting white users whose sense of entitlement to enter any conversational space leads them to take up space in a person of color's mentions and to expect (and often demand) responses to their tweets. For example, Sarah Florini provides a detailed case study of white intrusion into a network of Black podcasters and Twitter users that occurred following the creation of the hashtag #BernieSoBlack by Rod Morrow of The Black Guy Who Tips podcast (Florini 2019, 89–99). Morrow used the hashtag to criticize Bernie Sanders's handling of a Black Lives Matter protest at a town hall. Sanders supporters harassed Morrow on Twitter, hijacked the hashtag, and intruded into the Black community spaces of the podcast's live chatroom and private Facebook community.

Ontological expansiveness is certainly annoying and ethically suspect,[4] but why is it an epistemic problem? The simplest initial response is that it wastes epistemic resources and distracts efforts from knowledge production and dissemination. For example, if women of color have to spend time dealing with the white derailers to their online conversations, they are wasting time and energy that could instead be spent in sharing and co-producing knowledge within their community. Thus, ontologically expansive practices are inefficient, in Goldman's sense, because they increase the costs of knowledge production (Goldman 1992, 195).

A second, more complex reason why ontological expansiveness is epistemically harmful is that it disrupts networks of trust in which knowledge production and dissemination flourish. Sometimes knowledge is best produced within a closed community of marginalized people. For example, marginalized people may need to create their own language in which to describe their oppression (Spivak 1988; Fraser 1990; Jaggar 2004; Fricker 2007). And, given the power dynamics of dialogue (such as testimonial injustice or testimonial smothering [Fricker 2007; Dotson 2011]), this language and knowledge creation can be deterred by outsiders. Several internet studies scholars (Steele 2018; Florini 2019; Brock 2020) draw on Catherine Squires's notions of 'enclave publics' and 'satellite publics' to analyze how Black internet users form somewhat closed deliberative

---

[4] Wittkower's account of the ethically problematic nature of online 'creepers' is useful for thinking about the ethical problems of ontological expansiveness. For Wittkower, a creeper "signals presence within too many interactions, interactions of the wrong sort, in a way disproportionate to interactants' responses" (Wittkower 2016). It might be fruitful for ethically analyzing online ontological expansiveness to think about how white people (and other privileged people) are socialized into becoming creepers.

communities (Squires 2002). For Squires, forming (or being forced into) an enclave involves "hiding counterhegemonic ideas and strategies in order to survive or avoid sanctions, while internally producing lively debate and planning" (Squires 2002, 448). Satellite publics are also separate communities, but they interact more with other publics. Satellite publics separate "to maintain a solid group identity and build independent institutions," but they "enter into wider public debates when there is clear convergence of their interests with those of other publics or when their particular institutions or practices cause friction or controversies with wider publics" (Squires 2002, 463). In these ways, modulating interaction with members of dominant groups protects and epistemically enriches marginalized communities.

There is an important connection to trust here: knowledge creation within a community often requires that we have some degree of trust in members of our community to not take advantage of the vulnerability we demonstrate in sharing our ideas with each other. And, given legacies of exploitative appropriation and silencing of the knowledge of marginalized people, they often have justified low levels of trust in members of dominant groups. Thus, there are good reasons why members of marginalized groups create online spaces and networks of trust in which to have conversations among themselves.

When dominant groups intrude in these spaces, they disrupt those networks of trust and conversations. As we have seen, privileged people have tendencies to engage in many disruptive behaviors, such as gaslighting and derailing ontological expansiveness. These behaviors can stifle conversations among marginalized people. Additionally, as Dotson argues, the mere presence of perniciously ignorant members of dominant groups can smother the testimony of marginalized subjects (Dotson 2011). When marginalized people have well-founded distrust of members of dominant groups, they have good reason to perceive them as a dangerous audience and will often curtail their speech accordingly. This is an epistemic loss to the marginalized community, which may be prevented from accessing useful truths that would be shared if the dominant members had not intruded. Thus, ontological expansiveness is not only an epistemically inefficient behavior (in Goldman's sense), but it also disrupts the networks of trust that allow marginalized people to produce and disseminate knowledge, which undermines its power to produce true beliefs (i.e., it is not a powerful practice, in Goldman's sense).

5.6. A Virtue Epistemology for Lurking and Online Engagement

Having laid out some of the epistemic opportunities and challenges presented by online lurking, the rest of the chapter develops a virtue epistemology that can provide a useful normative framework for evaluation and practical application.

5.6.1. Virtues Relevant to Lurking and Engagement

Trustworthiness, open-mindedness, curiosity, inquisitiveness, humility, and courage are all virtues implicated in the ethics of lurking. Trustworthiness is a virtue that has both moral and intellectual forms (cf. Zagzebski 1996, 159). Many virtues are definable in terms of their particular motivation. In moral trustworthiness, the particular motivation is to not betray others' trust in us—to not take advantage of the vulnerability of those who trust us. Epistemologists often write about trustworthiness specifically in regard to testimony: a trustworthy testifier is both sincere and reliable. In this chapter, I have in mind a different type of epistemic trustworthiness, one not specifically related to virtuous testifying. Generally, in epistemic trustworthiness, the motivation is to not betray others' trust in us to take care of their epistemic goods. Annette Baier models trust as a three-place relation in which the truster (*A*) trusts the trustee (*B*) with valued good (*C*) (Baier 1996, 101). In the kind of epistemic trust I have in mind, we place our epistemic goods (e.g., our possession of true beliefs, or our epistemic communities) in the hands of those we trust (Zagzebski 1996, 161). In doing so, we make ourselves vulnerable to being betrayed and our epistemic goods harmed by those we trusted to care for them in various ways. The epistemically trustworthy person is motivated to avoid taking advantage of that vulnerability and to care for the epistemic goods entrusted to them. Epistemic trustworthiness is an other-regarding epistemic virtue in that it aims at the epistemic flourishing of others (cf. Kawall 2002). That said, even though it aims at the flourishing of others, epistemic trustworthiness can also produce epistemic benefits for oneself. For example, living up to others' trust in you to not disrupt the online spaces for dialogue that produce knowledge certainly aims at the epistemic flourishing of others who use those spaces, but it also promotes one's own epistemic flourishing if one also uses those epistemic spaces to unlearn one's own prejudices and socially constructed ignorance. Thus, epistemic trustworthiness is a useful epistemic virtue for lurkers, because it can motivate users to protect networks and spaces of trust that help agents produce and disseminate knowledge.

At this point, one might ask whose trust is at stake here. To whom should lurkers aim to be trustworthy? The answer is that lurkers should aim to be trustworthy to the members of online epistemic communities, even though the lurkers may be largely invisible to the community members. This is an interesting form of trustworthiness, and I should clarify that I have two different aspects of the full virtue of trustworthiness in mind. First, there is the straightforward feature of trustworthiness outlined in the previous paragraph: the motivation to avoid betraying the trust of those particular others who trust you. This aspect of trustworthiness is relevant when members of marginalized communities trust privileged lurkers to take a back seat in the conversation and not derail or disrupt the conversation. Since trust comes in degrees, this trust does not have to be complete trust in privileged lurkers. Nonetheless, marginalized groups often choose open platforms which are accessible to members of dominant groups. For example, an open blog comment thread or a public conversation among self-identified members of Black Twitter is open to white people. There may be many reasons why marginalized people choose platforms that are open in these ways, while still expecting some distance and selective interaction by dominant groups. It may simply be easiest to connect with other members of marginalized groups via open platforms (e.g., the ease of communication with large groups via Twitter). Another reason is that some marginalized people may have a dual purpose in online conversation—opting for a conversation among themselves which is open to the public as an educational opportunity (perhaps in order to provide an opportunity for privileged lurkers to unlearn their ignorance). Sometimes people choose an open platform for a conversation which, if one is paying attention to the conversational cues, is clearly intended to be between a smaller group than the public at large.[5] Additionally,

---

[5] Catherine Knight Steele provides a useful analysis of African American bloggers in this context. As she writes, "The bloggers are operating within a medium that is accessible to anyone, yet the content is created specifically for a Black audience. Black art and media, in this discussion, exists for the maintenance of group identity and the strengthening of institutions. The blog then functions as a satellite public, fostering protected space to do this work" (Steele 2018, 219). Steele charts some of the strategies African American bloggers use to create spaces separate from mainstream culture, while still operating technically in open spaces. Similarly, André Brock notes how the cultural knowledge required to fully engage in Black Twitter enables Black users to "signal their cultural affiliations to a like-minded audience" (Brock 2020, 81). Brock observes that "[w]hile there are a number of non-Black and people of color Twitter users who have been 'invited to the cookout,' so to speak, participating in Black Twitter requires a deep knowledge of Black culture, commonplaces, and digital practices" (Brock 2020, 81).

some of the marginalized subjects who choose this open platform may do so with an attitude of some trust of outsiders. People making this choice may allow outsiders to lurk, but trust them, to some degree, not to disrupt the conversation. This is a type of generalized trust in which people trust strangers not to take advantage of them (cf. Govier 1997, 33; Frost-Arnold 2016a). Trustworthy agents are motivated to live up to the expectations that others are trusting them to uphold. So when marginalized subjects signal that they are trusting privileged subjects to merely lurk in the conversation (and not disrupt it), then the trustworthy privileged agent will be motivated to lurk and avoid ontologically expansive disruption. This is the first sense in which cultivating the virtue of trustworthiness can help privileged people avoid doing epistemic harm through derailing.

But it is important not to overstate the degree of trust that marginalized subjects have in dominant groups. Marginalized people are often all too familiar with the dominating and ontologically expansive tendencies of privileged people, so they may have little faith that privileged people will stay as silent lurkers; they may fully expect that they will have to constantly deal with disruptive behaviors by the privileged. To reduce their vulnerability in the face of such threats, marginalized users may make plans for how to deal with disruptions from privileged users. These may include setting up blog comments to go through moderation before being published or using tools like Twitter block lists. Thus, while marginalized users may make themselves vulnerable in their choice of public platforms, they may do so with an attitude of low levels of trust, or complete distrust. Taking steps to reduce one's vulnerability, such as making back-up plans in case the trustee fails to follow through, can be signs of distrust (Jones 2004; Frost-Arnold 2014b). Florini notes that vulnerability to intrusion from outsiders varies among media (Florini 2019, 79). For example, Black podcast networks are easier to enclave than Black Twitter because podcasts are not searchable. So if many marginalized users distrust (or have extremely low levels of trust in) members of privileged groups, what is the role for trustworthiness as a virtue?

This is where the second aspect of the full virtue of trustworthiness comes in. This is trustworthiness as an aspiration to be worthy of others' trust, should it materialize. Even if others distrust me, I may aspire to be worthy of their trust. By developing the relevant habits and motivations (e.g., sensitivity to the particularity of others) and by signaling to others that I have these dispositions, I endeavor to make myself worthy of others' trust (cf.

Potter 2002, 26–32). As Nancy Potter argues, this involves cultivating other virtues and taking my epistemic responsibilities seriously so that I am less likely to betray the trust of others who come to trust me, by, for example, misunderstanding what they are trusting me to do (Potter 2002). A fully virtuous privileged lurker will cultivate trustworthiness, even though they may be aware that many marginalized people have justified distrust in privileged people in general.

This trustworthiness has the potential to promote good epistemic consequences. As more privileged people cultivate and demonstrate trustworthiness by refraining from disrupting marginalized epistemic communities, trust has room to develop across lines of difference. As I have discussed previously, practices of distrust are epistemically costly. Marginalized communities could be more efficient and epistemically productive if marginalized people did not have to expend resources on mechanisms to protect them from outside disruption. Cultivating and sharing Twitter block lists takes time and emotional energy. If more privileged people were more trustworthy, they could earn the trust of those communities in which they lurk, and those communities, in turn, would not need to divert their efforts so much toward defensive methods.

Open-mindedness, curiosity, inquisitiveness, and humility are also relevant virtues because they can motivate reading and interacting with online content in order to unlearn one's prejudices and become privilege-cognizant. Jason Baehr provides a useful and nuanced account of open-mindedness:

> An open-minded person is characteristically (a) willing and (within limits) able (b) to transcend a default cognitive standpoint (c) in order to take up or take seriously the merits of (d) a distinct cognitive standpoint. (Baehr 2011, 152)

Open-mindedness involves a motivation and ability to step back from or detach from one's own cognitive standpoint, but it is more than simply getting some distance from one's own doxastic commitments. Open-mindedness also demands that we take seriously other cognitive standpoints. This involves learning about them, weighing their merits, and fairly adjudicating disputes between them and our default standpoints. It is with this first part of taking up or taking seriously other standpoints (i.e., learning about distinct standpoints) that lurking can be useful. An open-minded person of privilege may be motivated to lurk in online spaces primarily for marginalized people in order to learn more about viewpoints different to their own. Note that I am not saying that all lurkers are open-minded. Certainly many people lurk in online spaces in order to "learn about the enemy" or for purely non-epistemic reasons. My point is that open-mindedness is an intellectual virtue that can motivate lurking for beneficial epistemic reasons.

One of the useful features of Baehr's account of open-mindedness is that it is broad enough to include people who are taking seriously views with which they initially disagree as well as people who are neutral or undecided about the views (Baehr 2011, 148). This is important for the epistemology of prejudice and privilege, since as Mills points out, privilege has a tendency to produce both false beliefs and the absence of true beliefs (Mills 2007). So, for example, a white person who is aware of the problem of white ignorance may recognize that they are likely to have some false beliefs about racism in America and also that there will be issues relating to racism of which they are completely oblivious. Someone who recognizes this and also has the epistemic virtue of open-mindedness may be motivated to seek out distinct standpoints on racial oppression that will help remedy these two types of ignorance. As we have seen, lurking in online spaces for people of color can be one way of achieving this.

Similarly, inquisitiveness and curiosity are closely connected in that they both consist in a desire to learn. This motivation to learn (or unlearn, in the case of one's prejudices) can lead people to both lurk and engage in online dialogue in epistemically beneficial ways. Inquisitiveness is a type of curiosity marked by questioning. On Lani Watson's account, the inquisitive person is "characteristically motivated to engage sincerely in good questioning" (Watson 2016). Engaging in dialogue across difference by questioning can be an excellent way to gain epistemic friction and learn while 'world'-traveling. Thus, done at the right time and in the right way, questioning can be epistemically virtuous (cf. Medina 2016). But done in the wrong way, inquisitiveness can be ontologically expansive. Asking questions with the sincere desire to learn is a common way that white people derail conversations among people of color.

Intellectual humility is also implicated in practices of lurking and interaction. The intellectually humble person knows that there are things they might not know—they recognize the possibility of their ignorance, and they question whether they know (Hazlett 2016, 76). More specifically, intellectual humility involves regulating and calibrating one's confidence levels in one's own cognitive capacities, skills, and experiences (Kidd 2016). The intellectually humble person is motivated to seek out evidence that they are excessively confident in their beliefs and abilities. As with open-mindedness, curiosity, and inquisitiveness, this motivation can be one of the reasons why people lurk or engage with online dialogue across difference.[6]

A final relevant virtue is intellectual courage, which involves engaging in intellectual activity in the face of perceived risks. More precisely, Baehr characterizes it as "a disposition to persist in or with a state or course of action aimed at an epistemically good end despite the fact that doing so involves an apparent threat to one's own well-being" (Baehr 2011, 177). Intellectual courage might involve persisting with a belief, inquiry, or communication of knowledge (or belief) (Baehr 2011, 173–76). And the perceived threats to one's well-being could include threats to one's safety, reputation, mental health, and so on. As I have argued, sometimes merely lurking is insufficient to gain the kinds of epistemic benefits required to fully unlearn one's prejudices. Sometimes interaction is necessary. Thus, interaction can be aimed at an epistemically good end (the first part of Baehr's definition of intellectual courage). But engagement in online dialogue across lines of difference can be perceived as threatening (the second part of Baehr's definition), especially to those with privileged identities. Having lived with privilege, they may be used to having their beliefs and worldview unchallenged. And being surrounded with a social imaginary that often paints marginalized people as aggressive, threatening, and scary, privileged people may perceive challenges by people with marginalized identities as a potential threat. They may fear that their reputations will be publicly sullied forever on the internet; for example, many white people have excessive fear of being publicly called a racist. Thus, in light of these habits (e.g., seeking safety) and the surrounding social imaginary (e.g., the stereotypes), it may take intellectual courage for people of privilege to engage in online dialogue. They may need courage to share their thoughts despite the threats they perceive. Overcoming this perceived threat by going beyond merely lurking can be an act of courage. Heersmink's account of the virtue of courage online suggests that simply lurking in online spaces which challenge one's biases takes a degree of intellectual courage (Heersmink 2018). I do not discount this type of courage, but, as I have shown, it often takes more courage to engage in discussion.

Notice that on Baehr's account of intellectual courage, the perceived risks do not have to be actual risks. All that it takes is for there to be a perceived

---

[6] For a useful argument for the value of intellectual humility in a digital age, see Lynch 2019.

threat. This means that I am not saying that privileged people's fears are rational or well-founded. In fact, since many of the perceived threats are due to stereotypes, they are likely to be the result of epistemic vice or irresponsibility (cf. Fricker 2007). Thus, on this approach, one can be epistemically courageous despite having other epistemic vices that lead one to making inaccurate or poorly grounded judgments of threats. Although some may balk at attributing the virtue of courage to some privileged people in the grips of prejudice and stereotypes, I think it is helpful in showing how flawed, imperfect people who have been epistemically damaged by their social position of privilege can leverage what degree of virtue they do have in order to pull themselves out of positions of ignorance. Of course, this is not usually an accomplishment of the individual alone; unlearning one's ignorance often requires support and resources from the surrounding community.

5.6.2. The Importance of Practical Wisdom

As we saw in Chapter 3, practical wisdom is a unifying and sorting virtue that helps us determine which virtue to exhibit in the situation at hand, and how to find the appropriate mean for the relevant virtue. Recall that Zagzebski provides two relevant theoretical reasons why practical wisdom is necessary to make sense of our moral and epistemic lives. First, since some virtues are Aristotelian means between extremes, we need practical wisdom to determine the mean (Zagzebski 1996, 220). For example, we can be excessively courageous (foolhardy) or insufficiently courageous (cowardly). The person of practical wisdom finds the amount of courage appropriate to the situation (Zagzebski 1996, 221). Second, practical wisdom is the "ability to mediate between and among the individual moral virtues" (Zagzebski 1996, 222). Virtues may conflict. When they do, we need practical wisdom to identify the virtuous course of action.

Both of these features of practical wisdom are necessary for dealing with the challenges we have seen with lurking. First, many of the virtues relevant to these challenges have a mean, and failure to find the mean often causes problems. Excessive lurking and failure to interact can result from failing to find the mean with respect to courage. If I lurk because I am afraid to be attacked, I am deficient in intellectual courage. The person of practical wisdom can avoid these problems by better locating the right amount of courage to participate when they should. Additionally, excessive curiosity or inquisitiveness can lead white users to ontological expansiveness by entering online spaces for people of color so that they can unlearn their white privilege or prejudices. The example of the first white commenter on the blog for women of color illustrates this. She appears to have a genuine desire to learn how to be a better white ally. But perhaps her excessive curiosity and inquisitiveness lead her to derail a conversation, which is epistemically damaging.

Second, some ontologically expansive acts are caused by failures to properly adjudicate conflicts between virtues. Another way of analyzing the problem of online ontological expansiveness is that it often results from failure to properly resolve the conflict between trustworthiness and humility (which may require staying out of a conversation), and the virtues that motivate participation (i.e., curiosity, inquisitiveness, open-mindedness, humility, and courage). Curiosity, inquisitiveness, open-mindedness, and humility may motivate me to interact so that I can gain the full epistemic benefits of epistemic friction and 'world'-traveling. Courage may also motivate participation, since I am brave enough to deal with any pushback I receive to the views I post online. But if I am also a trustworthy person, I may feel reluctant to participate, since I know the people of color in this space are trusting white allies to take a back seat and not derail the conversation toward their educational needs. So with conflicting virtues pulling me in opposite directions, I need practical wisdom to sift through the courses of action and make a good judgment about whether (and how) to participate in the way a virtuous person would.

Practical wisdom is also needed in those situations when one virtue seems to call for conflicting courses of action, depending on the specifics of the situation. In some respects, it seems that humility calls for engagement in online dialogue across difference. Suppose I am aware enough of my socially constructed ignorance to have an epistemically humble attitude toward my own beliefs about my privilege, and I am humble enough to have some distrust toward my stereotypes about other groups (perhaps because I have learned something about implicit bias) (cf. Jones 2002). Then epistemic humility may motivate participation to gain those benefits of epistemic friction and 'world'-traveling that may help me further unlearn my ignorance. But on the other hand, intellectual humility may make me acutely aware of how little I know and how little value my contributions to the dialogue about racial oppression, for example, may have to other members of a particular epistemic community. Being humble enough to know that the main person who would benefit from my participation is me, I may feel reluctant to take up space in the conversation. So what should I do in this particular situation? Answering this question requires wrestling with the particularities of the situation and making a good judgment, with practical wisdom, about what to do. In all these ways, we can see how practical wisdom is necessary for navigating the difficult epistemic challenges online lurking presents.

It is also clearly necessary for dealing with the *ethical* challenges involved in deciding when to engage in an online conversation. As Wittkower (2016) argues, jumping into some online conversations can be a disrespectful and creepy privacy violation. My epistemic argument here could be extended to call for *phronesis* in the ethical choices we make to respect others' privacy. There are complex considerations that the person of practical wisdom should attend to. For example, Wittkower argues that

> we must recognize that not all conversations to which we are party on SNS [social networking sites], through the not-entirely customizable architectures of sharing and posting, are conversations in which we are in fact welcome. Care and respect for others demand that we not treat contingent non-denial of access as equivalent to consent, but that we are instead mindful of the limits architectures may place on choice, treading lightly or seeking out explicit consent when it is unclear whether we have been invited, whether we have failed by oversight to be disinvited, or whether our dis-invitation was simply impractical or impracticable. (Wittkower 2016)

Phronesis is also implicated in the way a virtuous person experiences and handles their emotions. On an Aristotelian approach, the emotions also have a mean. Aristotle says, "to feel these feelings at the right time, on the right occasion, towards the right people, for the right purpose and in the right manner, is to feel the best amount of them, which is the mean amount—and the best amount is of course the mark of virtue" (Aristotle 1926, 1106b11). And emotional virtue is also part of virtuous lurking. It involves wrestling with the emotions that may pull us in harmful directions. When I feel defensive, do I have a tendency to lash out and thereby derail a conversation with my anger and frustration? If so, I need *phronesis* and virtues of emotional self-control to rein myself in. But what if I have the opposite tendency? What if when I feel defensive, I hide and disengage? If my failure to handle my defensive emotions causes me to disengage when I should continue the conversation because I am at the cusp of learning something important, then I need *phronesis* and virtues of courage to push me past my fears. Becoming a virtuous lurker requires appropriate handling of one's feelings of discomfort. As Sullivan says:

> Complementing the realization that there are some spaces that white people should not enter and do not have legitimate authority to enter, fighting whiteliness vis-à-vis space also means that white people must recognize that it is not inappropriate or unjust for them to feel uncomfortable when they do enter spaces that are predominantly non-white. . . . The lack of comfort and feeling of illegitimacy are entirely appropriate responses to the recognition that space is not racially neutral or empty and that white people do not have a legitimate claim to all space. (Sullivan 2006, 164–65)

Thus, this virtue epistemology is helpful in identifying the need for practical wisdom to handle the cognitive and affective elements of virtuous lurking.

5.7. Applying the Virtue Epistemology of Lurking

Thinking through this virtue epistemology also helps us both diagnose and see as inadequate one of the common defensive reactions white people often have to challenges to their ontological expansiveness. It is common to see white people claim that they are being unfairly attacked when their habits of ontological expansiveness are pointed out. Whites often feel that they are being told that they are a bad person, and this seems unfair to them because they believe that their attempts to engage in cross-racial online dialogue are motivated by good intentions. They claim that their motive was to learn, and they believe that their acts of participation are acts of virtue. So it seems unfair to them to attack their acts of participation because it ignores their virtuous motives.

The virtue epistemology I've outlined helps us both understand and critique this defensive response. We can recognize, in agreement with those who feel unfairly attacked, that there may be some degree of particular virtues behind their actions. Open-mindedness, curiosity, inquisitiveness, humility, and courage are valuable virtues pushing white people to engage in online discourse. But we can disagree with them that this excuses their action. Virtue comes in degrees, and for those without full practical wisdom, acts which are motivated by some virtue may nonetheless not be fully virtuous. Recognizing that some degree of curiosity, humility, and courage motivated the interaction, we can still critique whites who derail conversations about race for lack of practical wisdom in deciding whether this was this was the right time, the right space, and the right way to engage in cross-racial dialogue. The derailer may be deficient in practical wisdom (i.e., by failing to find the mean of open-mindedness, curiosity, inquisitiveness, or courage), or they may fail to be motivated by trustworthiness (i.e., they are not motivated to live up to the trust of people of color to take a back seat in the conversation at hand). This is, I think, a charitable, but nonetheless critical evaluation of *some* ontologically expansive allies. Note that I have qualified this claim, because many acts of white ontological expansiveness are not remotely acts of virtue. Whites may blunder into spaces for people of color and simply feel entitled to say whatever is on their mind. Such people may not have had virtuous motives, but when challenged may claim post hoc to have had them as a way of deflecting critique of their thoughtlessness. And other acts of ontological expansiveness are just disruptive sealioning. So my charitable critique of some ontologically expansive whites is not supposed to be a defense of them all. Instead, my analysis gives us theoretical tools to avoid indiscriminately lumping together all forms of epistemically damaging white habits, but it does not let white derailers off the hook.

An important consideration that will be salient to the virtuous agent is whether this particular online space is an appropriate community in which to pursue inquisitive acts of online engagement. For example, white people should carefully consider whether the same spaces where they lurk are appropriate venues for them to engage. Virtuous white users will pay attention to signals provided by the community about whether it welcomes cross-racial dialogue or whether the community, while being open to lurkers, is targeted at a specific audience of participants.

A virtue approach to epistemology of the internet is helpful in identifying users as moral agents with varying degrees of virtue that can change and grow over time. Instead of focusing on individual acts and assessing their epistemic merits, we can talk about habits and how good habits can be encouraged and entrenched and bad habits unlearned. Instead of getting in often fruitless debates about whether particular acts were motivated by good intentions, we can talk about practical wisdom and the need for 'allies' to continually develop their good judgment to help them navigate the challenges of finding the mean and sifting through competing virtues.

I think this approach could go some way in helping whites (and other privileged groups) move away from what Lugones calls the "infantilization of judgment." A common pattern she sees among whites/Anglos is that "[t]hey have turned into children, incapable of judgment, avoiding all commitment except against racism in the abstract, paralyzed as responsible beings, afraid of hostility and hostile in their fear, wedded to their ignorance and arrogant in their guilty purity of heart" (Lugones 2003, 48). While whites often react with fear to being told they said something racist and defensively claim that they should not be attacked since they did not know any better, Lugones maintains that as adults we should all recognize that we need good judgment and that we cannot be frozen and unwilling to grow. I think the tools provided in this chapter help us both critique those who are lacking in good judgment and talk about the need to grow in our practical wisdom.

I conclude this section by summarizing the practical applications of this analysis. Without some of the philosophical jargon, what does virtue epistemology tell us about lurking? What kinds of considerations will be salient to the person with practical reason? I now make explicit the considerations that will be salient to the *phronimos*, as I have explicated them in this chapter. As Baehr argues, analyses that simply appeal to the notion of practical reason are often of limited value if they do not spell out the normative considerations that form the basis for the *phronimos*' choice of a particular course of action (Baehr 2011, 187). Simply saying that a problem will be solved by agents cultivating practical reason does not help us see how to solve the problem. What is needed is to point out some of the normative considerations that will become salient to us as we grow our practical reason.

I put this summary in the first person to demonstrate how a white person might try to be a better member of online communities. This theory tells me that to act epistemically virtuously online, I need to be motivated to use online conversations to unlearn my prejudices, and I need to be motivated to do so in responsible ways that live up to the trust of others who use those spaces. If I'm doing this well, I'll be motivated to seek out blogs, Facebook conversations, and Twitter threads that challenge my prejudices and show me things that my white privilege might hide from me. Before I enter these spaces, I will determine whether lurkers are welcome in these spaces, and I will stay out of any spaces marked as only for people of color. When lurking is welcome, I'll be attentive to the ways in which sometimes I hide from interaction with others as a way of protecting myself from being personally challenged, and I'll notice when feelings of defensiveness are encouraging me to lurk when I should participate. But I'll also be sensitive to the tendency I have as a white person to derail conversations people of color are having among themselves and to hijack conversations in ways that attend to my own needs rather than the needs of those experiencing racial oppression. I'll recognize when others are trusting me to stay out of a conversation or to curtail my contributions appropriately, and I'll be motivated to live up to that trust. In sum, developing these habits of epistemically virtuous lurking helps individual agents live up to their epistemic responsibility to unlearn their socially constructed ignorance without damaging the fabric of trust necessary for knowledge production in marginalized communities.

5.8. Objections and Replies

I conclude by addressing two pressing objections to the argument of this chapter. A first objection maintains that there is nothing new in my analysis. On this objection, lurking is just another name for reading or listening to others' speech in a relatively passive way, modes of education that do not depend on the internet. The objector doubts that there are new epistemic benefits provided by online lurking that are not available from reading print media, watching television, or simply sitting quietly in conversations between marginalized people. Similarly, the objector suspects that the challenges posed by online ontological expansiveness are not significantly different than its offline manifestations. So what is new here?

Much of my response to this objection is already implicit in the argument throughout the chapter, but I want to make explicit how online lurking provides epistemic benefits different to these other modes of education. First, for curious lurkers, online lurking provides faster access to a more diverse community of speakers than does print media. Just consider the speed with which news and analysis of events in one part of the world can be disseminated to people far away via Twitter. In addition to the benefit of speed, the internet provides access to a wider diversity of speakers who might otherwise not make it past the gatekeepers of publishers and editors of print media. Furthermore, print media cannot provide a window into ongoing conversations within marginalized communities in the same way that online spaces give lurkers real-time insight into the pace, flow, and intensity of these conversations. For lurkers who pay attention, much can be learned from watching the conversational norms and direction of community formation (and dissolution) in online spaces. Such insights are much harder to gain from print media. Second, television and radio may improve upon print media in these respects, but they nonetheless have many of the same limitations, such as less speed, more gatekeepers, and somewhat less insight into ongoing conversation and community formation than online spaces. Third, while sitting in on offline conversations between marginalized people has the speed, can have the diversity, and provides access to ongoing conversations and community developments, it lacks the anonymity of online lurking. This anonymity is epistemically rich, and it prevents many practical harms as well. As I discussed in section 5.3, privileged people often do harm when they enter conversations between marginalized people. But even if they are silent, the presence of privileged people in the room often changes the conversation. Testimonial smothering occurs, and other dynamics of the community are changed (cf. Dotson 2011). In contrast, when privileged lurkers are part of the invisible online audience (cf. boyd 2011), they are much less disruptive.

One additional benefit of online lurking which I have not previously discussed is the searchability of online content (cf. boyd 2011, 46). Due to segregation (both offline and online), privileged people interested in unlearning their ignorance are likely, especially at early stages in this process, to have social networks that lack diversity. Thus, they may not know about epistemically beneficial online spaces where they could lurk. Search engines can help with this. By googling terms of interest or following hashtags and using them to find people to follow on Twitter, privileged people can locate epistemic sources that they would not otherwise identify. Thus, online lurking has many epistemic benefits that other media lack, even though this is often a difference in degree, not kind.

This objection also raised a concern that the challenges of online ontological expansiveness are not particularly novel. In response, I grant that many of the same dynamics that mar offline dialogue across lines of difference appear in our online interactions. In fact, one of the goals of this book is to show that race, class, gender, sexual orientation, and so on matter online in many of the same ways that they do offline. There were many early idealistic visions of an online world free of racism, sexism, ableism, and so on (cf. Daniels 2015). Failure to take seriously the ways in which power and privilege shape online interactions has led to an epistemically damaging epistemology of ignorance that maintains hierarchies of knowledge production. Failure to recognize that social inequalities shape online interactions has led to problems being ignored, such as the problem of online harassment of marginalized groups. So I take it as an advantage, rather than a drawback, that this chapter shows a continuity between online and offline problems in these areas of lurking and interaction.

That said, there are some differences between the ways that ontological expansiveness manifests itself online and offline. Platform design and algorithms shape the nature of online ontological expansiveness in ways that have no easy analogy in offline contexts. Consider the different ways that conversations are threaded or organized in different platforms. It is very easy to derail blog comments that are tightly chronologically threaded. While the conversation may start off on one track with commenters replying to comments posted above them, one derailing comment can start the conversation off on another topic, and it can be awkward to return the conversation to the earlier topic, since finding earlier contributions requires effort to scroll up and up to find previously forgotten comments. The linear structure of the platform design makes it vulnerable to derailing. But Twitter conversations are less tightly threaded, and users often have multiple, branching, simultaneous conversations. These conversations are harder to derail due to the different platform design.

Algorithms also shape derailing. Facebook's algorithm that determines which posts appear in one's newsfeed has significant power over what we know and which events in our community are made salient to us (Tufekci 2017, 154–63; Vaidhyanathan 2018). Like many important social media algorithms, Facebook's is designated as proprietary and not made transparent. There is no public knowledge of how the algorithm prioritizes posts. However, some aspects of it have been inferred from Facebook's public statements and documents released by whistleblowers: it prioritizes posts that have more "likes," emoji reactions, and comments on them (Tufekci 2017, 156; Vaidhyanathan 2018; Merrill and Oremus 2021). This has the somewhat contradictory effect of biasing the content of users' newsfeeds toward more feel-good posts as well as controversial posts that garner many comments. It is this last point that illustrates how algorithms shape ontological expansiveness. Controversial and disruptive acts of ontological expansiveness can dominate users' attention. Consider an example I witnessed on a Facebook group created by members of a marginalized community and devoted to organizing and promoting an event (details of this Facebook group and event have been obscured as part of my privacy-respecting research ethics practice). This group had repeated problems with people who did not belong to the marginalized group disrupting and derailing the conversation, moves which were actively denounced by members of the marginalized group and 'allies.' The posts in which controversy erupted appeared much more often in my newsfeed than the organizational, motivational, or other posts by the marginalized organizers that did not feature comment threads populated by controversy over problematic acts of privileged people. While I cannot be sure, I suspect that it was the fact that Facebook's algorithm favors posts with more comments that gave the acts of ontological expansiveness extra space on my newsfeed. What this means is that the secret, corporate algorithms of social media platforms can make privileged people's acts of ontological expansiveness widely known while hiding the speech of marginalized groups. These issues are certainly worthy of further exploration, since they are one of the features of online interaction that distinguish it from offline discourse (cf. Miller and Record 2013). So while many of the same dynamics of power and privilege are at issue in online and offline ontological expansiveness, there are interesting differences, which bear further investigation.

A second objection is that I paint an overly rosy picture of lurking. This objector points out that lurking can be a means of epistemic appropriation and theft of intellectual labor, especially the labor of marginalized groups. Consider Twitter mining. This is the practice by which journalists lurk in Twitter looking for interesting tweets, which they then turn into articles. Journalists may steal ideas for stories from Twitter (Honey 2017) or republish screenshots of someone's tweets along with some commentary (Thériault 2015). While some maintain that there is nothing unethical about this practice (since the tweets used are public), others argue that this is exploitative. As Anne Thériault puts it, "The problem isn't that Twitter is public; the problem is that media outlets are making a profit off the work of people . . . while simultaneously giving them a hyper-visibility that is tantamount to placing a target on their backs" (Thériault 2015). There are two epistemic problems here. First, there is the problem of theft of intellectual labor. Second, there is the problem of exposing private citizens to public attention and online harassment. I have discussed the second problem elsewhere as one of the epistemic problems of online context collapse (Frost-Arnold 2021), and I will return to this problem in the research ethics Appendix. When the words of marginalized people are shared by others in broader contexts, they are often exposed to online harassment and threats, which has a chilling effect on epistemically valuable speech (McMillan Cottom 2016; Frost-Arnold 2021).

In this chapter, I focus on the first problem of the theft of intellectual labor for which Emmalon Davis has coined the useful term 'epistemic appropriation' (E. Davis 2018). Davis identifies two harms of epistemic appropriation: epistemic detachment and epistemic misdirection. In epistemic detachment, "the participatory role of marginalized contributors in the process of knowledge production is obscured" (E. Davis 2018, 705). Epistemic misdirection happens "when epistemic resources developed within, but detached from, the margins are utilized in dominant discourses in ways that disproportionately benefit the powerful" (E. Davis 2018, 705). I find it helpful to think of epistemic appropriation through the lens of Iris Young's account of exploitation as one of the five faces of oppression (I. Young 2001). Exploitation "occurs through a steady process of the transfer of the results of the labor of one social group to benefit another" (I. Young 2001, 39). This form of oppression occurs via lurking on Twitter through a steady process of journalists from privileged groups taking ideas and tweets from marginalized groups and receiving the profit and reputational benefits from their labor. Ijeoma Oluo's experience illustrates these problems:

> Popular websites have created entire articles that are nothing but my tweets. . . . An inflammatory headline, an intro sentence, and then all my tweets. Bam, someone just made a couple of hundred dollars and I'm flooded with angry messages from strangers. . . . As a writer who is a woman of color, it's frustrating to see others making money off of my work when I get nothing from it but harassment. It's also often done in a way that is a misrepresentation of my work, with my words presented without context or given a new, inaccurate context.[7] (qtd. in Thériault 2015)

Epistemic appropriation is a type of exploitative epistemic injustice. But the epistemic problems go deeper than just the transfer of the fruits of epistemic labor. As Thériault points out (Thériault 2015), when media outlets rely on Twitter mining for their reporting, they are not hiring women of color to do the reporting themselves (cf. Florini 2019, 216). This means that women of color are denied the access to resources that would help them produce and share more knowledge. This perpetuates a system in which members of privileged groups have access to the means of knowledge production and marginalized groups do not. This is veritistically damaging, since the community is denied the truths that members of marginalized groups would

---

[7] The epistemic problems with sharing others' words out of context are also discussed in Frost-Arnold 2021.

contribute were they to have the resources. The community is also denied the opportunity for members of marginalized groups to detect errors and biases in the beliefs circulating in the community (cf. Frost-Arnold 2014c).

With these accounts of exploitation and epistemic appropriation in mind, one might pose the following objection to my argument that lurking can be an epistemically valuable practice: endorsing lurking by privileged users will encourage more privileged people to spend time in spaces for marginalized people where the privileged people will be tempted to engage in practices akin to Twitter mining, which are epistemic injustices that maintain a veritistically harmful system of epistemic hierarchy.

I am completely sympathetic to this objection. Twitter mining and epistemic appropriation are some of the many downsides of lurking, when practiced unethically and in epistemically damaging ways. Just as online discussion can be done harmfully through ontological expansiveness, online lurking can be exploitative. In some ways, this objection echoes concerns raised in section 5.4 about lurking as a form of epistemic irresponsibility that treats marginalized people as tools rather than ends in themselves. I address this objection here not to defend lurking as a practice that is epistemically beneficial no matter how it is practiced, but instead to remind us of one of the themes of this book: we have to be careful about *how* we live our epistemic lives online. While lurking can have epistemic benefits, it can also be epistemically harmful when practiced unethically.

I think the tools developed in the virtue epistemology section of this chapter are useful for thinking through how to avoid perpetrating these epistemic harms. Cultivating the virtue of epistemic trustworthiness, a fundamentally non-exploitative virtue, and growing one's practical reason are steps one can take to avoid the temptation to engage in Twitter mining. Lurkers need to recognize that members of marginalized groups often tweet publicly while trusting that others will respect their rights over the products of their own intellectual labor. Trustworthy lurkers who recognize this trust will be motivated to avoid stealing others' tweets for their own profit. Practical wisdom helps us determine when and how to ask for permission to use someone's tweet in another context (Frost-Arnold 2021).

Of course, the social and economic context matters here. As we have discussed elsewhere in the book, unjust social and institutional arrangements place constraints on our attempts to live virtuous lives (Potter 2002). Journalists working under pressure at corporate media outlets that place little value on ethical reporting, or who promote face-saving rationalizations for intellectual theft (e.g., "Everything publicly posted on Twitter is fair game" [cf. Chittal 2012]), confront difficult ethical dilemmas. As Nancy Potter argues, people in mid-level positions of power often face situations where, in order to be trustworthy to those more powerful than they are, they feel compelled to betray the trust of those less powerful (Potter 2002). Journalists can be torn between their employers and their online sources. But Potter provides a forceful argument that resistance is always possible. Trustworthy agents need to resist pressure to betray the trust of the less powerful. Thus, while the social and economic pressures on journalists are real, morally and epistemically virtuous agents can attempt to cultivate virtues and practices of resistance that will avoid the harms of Twitter mining. Finally, these problems cannot be fully addressed by acts of individual responsibility alone. Significant structural changes need to be made to the distribution and compensation for online labor.

In conclusion, I hope to have uncovered some of the complex epistemic promises and challenges of online lurking. The internet affords a new kind of anonymous lurking, which I have shown can provide significant epistemic benefits for those trying to unlearn their ignorance of privilege and prejudice. But lurking has its limits, both epistemic and ethical. Often, we need to question whether we have the right to enter the spaces of others. Sometimes engagement and relationship with others is required to more fully unlearn one's ignorance. But finding the right balance between lurking and engagement, while performing each of them in an epistemically responsible and non-oppressive manner, requires us to avoid ontological expansiveness and exploitative appropriation. The virtue theory I have provided here outlines some of the relevant virtues we need to cultivate to avoid these harms, and it explains the role of practical wisdom in tailoring our actions to the situations at hand.

6
Conclusion

My goal in this book has been to demonstrate the value of a socially situated approach to epistemology of the internet. Much is lost when we adopt an "*S*-knows-that-*p*" approach to social epistemology. Internet users are not merely a collection of identical Cartesian cognizers with smartphones; we are differently embodied beings interacting within systems of dominance. Our social identities and global inequalities shape who we are and who we can be online. And recognizing the social situatedness of online knowledge (and ignorance) is crucial for answering the normative question: who should we be online? Who each of us should be, how we should act, what habits we should cultivate, which structures should we collectively transform—all of these questions depend on the particular contexts at issue. The social situatedness of online knowledge matters.

I have argued that race, gender, sexuality, and colonialism matter in epistemology. In Chapter 2, we saw how racist and sexist stereotypes shape moderators' decisions and how structural hermeneutical ignorance leads to the speech of people of color (and others) being misunderstood and censored. We also saw how neocolonial exploitation of the epistemic labor of moderators in the Global South dumps toxic content on low-wage workers. In Chapter 3, I argued that colonial modes of identity tourism encourage damaging online imposture that disrupts trust networks necessary for objectivity and truth acquisition. In Chapter 4, we saw how white ignorance fuels and is fueled by fake news. In Chapter 5, I argued that white habits of ontological expansiveness make privileged people feel entitled to encroach upon online marginalized epistemic communities.

I have argued that capitalism matters in internet epistemology. Chapter 2 revealed how the corporate drive to maximize profits has led social media companies to exploit moderators and create an epistemic nightmare of biased moderation. Chapter 3 discussed the ever-increasing data collection and surveillance by social media companies as major drivers of demands for problematic modes of online authenticity. Chapter 4 summarized the many ways in which the search for ad revenue has led individual fakers, search engine providers, and social media companies to take actions that have exacerbated the fake news problem. And that chapter shows how Facebook's fear of losing conservative customers fueled its flight to neutral objectivity and algorithmic moderation of the trending topics feature. Chapter 5 exposed the harms of Twitter mining and the exploitation of the labor of marginalized people.

In the research ethics Appendix, I argue that positionality and power matter for how we conduct internet epistemology. As scholars, we have power to violate the privacy of research subjects, exploit their labor, and expose them to online harassment. We need to be aware that the people we study and quote are not generic users; they are particular subjects whose social positions make them differently vulnerable to exposure by our research. As researchers, we are also differently embodied, and we need our institutions and colleagues to recognize the disproportionate harassment of marginalized scholars and to set up systems to protect risky research.

In sum, social identities, economic conditions, power, and positionality all matter for internet epistemology. Of course, these are not the only things that matter. But I hope that demonstrating the value of socially situated social epistemology through these examples will suggest future lines of research beyond the "S-knows-that-p" approach.

This book has demonstrated the power of several social epistemological frameworks for analyzing the internet. In Chapter 1, I argued that feminist accounts of objectivity, veritistic systems-oriented social epistemology, epistemologies of ignorance, virtue epistemology, and the epistemic injustice literature provide mutually supporting epistemological frameworks. I gave the combination of these frameworks the catchy acronym: the FOVIVI approach—for Feminist accounts of Objectivity, Veritism, Ignorance, Virtues, and Injustice. Throughout the following chapters, I gave examples of how the frameworks can be applied to central problems of internet epistemology.

Chapter 2 drew on virtue epistemology and the epistemologies of ignorance literature in its analysis of epistemic injustice in online content moderation. The virtues of testimonial justice and hermeneutical justice are important virtues that moderators need so that they can avoid biased moderation decisions. This chapter showed how epistemically damaging social structures can make the cultivation of these virtues practically impossible for commercial content moderators. The policies put in place by social media companies encode hermeneutical ignorance, and the labor model denies moderators the resources to build the relationships necessary to correct for their biases (and the biases of the policies that guide their decisions). Social media companies have pursued an epistemology of ignorance by hiding the labor of commercial content moderators from scrutiny. Toiling in the shadows, these workers are subject to epistemic exploitation as the worst of the internet (including much toxic epistemic trash) is dumped on them. Content moderation is often traumatic and also unrespected, low-status work. To make content moderation less damaging for workers and more epistemically reliable will take a radical re-envisioning of the labor model. A mere flight to algorithmic moderation will not solve all the problems. Difficult questions about the limits of monopolistic digital capitalism need to be at the forefront of future discussions of the epistemology of content moderation.

In Chapter 3, I applied feminist accounts of objectivity, veritism, and the epistemologies of ignorance to provide an account of the virtue of trustworthiness on the internet. Trust is necessary for practices of objectivity and truth acquisition to function. These practices are valued by feminist epistemologists and veritists alike. If marginalized people do not trust themselves to share their knowledge, if they are not trusted by others, and if people do not trust the practices through which knowledge is shared, then biases and errors are less likely to be detected in online discussions. Internet imposters undermine trust, which means that trustworthiness is a key virtue for online agents. But trustworthiness is a complex virtue. Living up to others' expectations of authenticity is often a valuable habit to cultivate because it protects vulnerable epistemic agents. However, sometimes expectations of authenticity are oppressive, and betrayal of oppressive norms is often virtuous. In fact, the epistemologies of ignorance help us see ways in which tricking epistemic agents often has epistemic benefits. Online hoaxes are one tool that activists can use to trick people into questioning their biases and learning important truths that are often hidden by systems of dominance.

Chapter 4 used veritism, the epistemologies of ignorance, and feminist accounts of objectivity to reveal the complexity of the fake news problem. I centered veritism in my analysis of the epistemic harms of fake news. Resisting nostalgic narratives for a time when truth and trust reigned, my analysis heeds the lessons of epistemologists of ignorance who have shown that oppressive ignorance has persisted throughout history. Nonetheless, the hybrid media system spreads ignorance through many different causes, some of which are novel to a digital age. I showed how fake news often shapes (and is shaped by) white ignorance. This account extends Mills's work on white ignorance in new directions and shows how dealing with the fake news problem means addressing systemic racism throughout society. This chapter used feminist accounts of objectivity to present one solution to the fake news problem—instead of clinging to problematic notions of neutral objectivity, we can adopt feminist recommendations for preventing and weeding out bias in news curation. Truth and objectivity are crucial epistemic goods, but we will not achieve these goals by pretending that technology, journalism, or corporations are neutral. Instead, we need to heed decades of feminist recommendations to create diverse epistemic communities in which knowledge production and dissemination are grounded in the standpoint of the oppressed.

In Chapter 5, I used virtue epistemology to tackle one of the thorniest questions of the epistemologies of ignorance: how can people unlearn their ignorance? I showed how the internet provides opportunities for unlearning socially constructed ignorance of privilege and prejudice. Lurking can be a form of unintrusive listening. One of the epistemically valuable features of the internet is that online anonymity affords us the opportunity to listen to voices that challenge our prejudices. Cultivating habits of subjecting ourselves to epistemic friction through online lurking can help us unlearn ignorance in ways that reduce the epistemic burden on marginalized people to constantly teach privileged people about oppression. However, there are epistemic limits and dangers of lurking. Virtuous agents are sensitive to these problems. They avoid voyeurism that treats marginalized people as exotic objects. They stay out of marginalized online communities when they are not welcome. Virtuous agents pay attention to when they are using lurking in a cowardly way to hide from building real relationships across lines of difference. But virtue also requires knowing to avoid ontologically expansive acts of derailing conversations among marginalized people. This chapter emphasizes the virtue of practical wisdom as central to living an epistemically virtuous life online. We need to pay attention to the power dynamics of online communities and find the mean and balance of virtues of trustworthiness, open-mindedness, curiosity, inquisitiveness, humility, and courage.

In conclusion, this book shows how the FOVIVI epistemological frameworks help us untangle several difficult problems of internet epistemology. It is by no means an exhaustive analysis—there are many questions left to ask and problems to address. It is my hope that the frameworks provided here, and the interdisciplinary approach to epistemology of the internet I have attempted, provide some suggestions for future work. So much of our epistemic lives is lived online, and it will take significant collective action to make our online communities more just and trustworthy. There is much work left to be done.

APPENDIX

Internet Research Ethics for Philosophers: Privacy, Positionality, and Power

A.1. Purpose of This Appendix

Research about the internet faces some of the perennial problems of research ethics, as well as new challenges. Issues of justice, privacy, informed consent, and duty to avoid harm to research subjects (among others) arise for scholars of the internet just as they do for other disciplines. But these issues also manifest themselves in new ways online. For example, online life has created new, conflicting, and constantly shifting conceptions of privacy. Internet studies scholars have long recognized the need to think carefully about research ethics.[1] This is unsurprising, since many internet studies scholars work in disciplines (e.g., social sciences) where there is an ongoing tradition of formal research ethics procedures, and students are routinely trained in procedures for navigating institutional ethics committees, such as Institutional Research Boards (IRBs) in the United States. However, human subject research ethics is not a standard part of the training of academic philosophers. Most philosophy graduate students do not engage in human subjects research, and thus most philosophers (with the exception of experimental philosophers) do not have to submit their research to IRBs for approval. This means that while philosophers may learn and teach about research ethics as ethicists themselves or as IRB members, few philosophers are regularly called upon to articulate and account formally for their own research ethics.

This is not to say that philosophers never think about the ethics of scholarship; feminist philosophers, philosophers of race, and transgender philosophers (among many others) have been thinking for decades about their own positionality and the power relations inherent in academic scholarship (Hale 1997; Hoagland 2001; Ortega 2006; Townley 2006; Mills 2007; Ahmed 2013; Bettcher 2018). Questions of justice and bias loom large in these fields: Whose interests are served? Which questions are asked, and which are ignored? Who is authorized to speak, and whose voices are silenced? How does privilege encourage some scholars to theorize arrogantly about the lives of others in reckless and oppressive

---

[1] For example, the Association of Internet Researchers (AoIR) created its first set of ethical guidelines in 2002 (Ess and AoIR Ethics Committee 2002). And AoIR produced significant updates in 2012 and 2020 (A. Markham, Buchanan, and AoIR Ethics Committee 2012; franzke et al. 2020). For a history of internet research ethics, see Buchanan 2017.

ways? How does philosophy as a field and profession center the lives, interests, and knowledge of privileged groups and marginalize others? These are both ethical and epistemological questions. Justice and the responsibility to produce philosophy that does not serve structural racism, sexism, homophobia, ableism, transphobia, class exploitation, and other forms of oppression are an important part of research ethics.

With this background in mind, when I first started writing about the epistemology of the internet in 2011, I was only thinking about issues of positionality as the main ethical decisions relevant to my work. For example, questions arose, such as, What was I going to study?, How did my own social location shape those choices of topic?, and What steps could I take to manage and acknowledge any biases stemming from my social location? At the time, I shared the view (common to many academics) that there were no serious privacy issues with quoting or referring to publicly available online content.[2] However, as I began to delve more deeply into the interdisciplinary research in internet studies scholarship, I learned more about two issues that changed my conception of the ethical issues relevant to my work as a philosopher: privacy and online harassment. I now believe that there are a wide range of serious ethical considerations that social epistemologists must consider when studying the internet. Many of these same ethical questions need to be addressed by other philosophers who use online content (e.g., people's tweets) as examples in philosophical work about other topics (e.g., philosophy of language).

This appendix has two purposes: (1) to outline some of these ethical concerns, and some of the leading proposals for addressing these concerns, in the hopes that an overview of these issues may be helpful to others in my field, and (2) to explain my own research practice in this book. My hope for this appendix is that it prompts conversation about research ethics in my field—a conversation in which I want to be transparent about my own practices, so that I can be held accountable for any mistakes, make amends, and learn along with others.

In thinking through these issues, I have tried to practice reflexivity by considering how my own social position shapes this work in order to become the kind of researcher I want to be. Annette Markham argues for reflexivity as a "method of looking recursively and critically at the self in relation to the object, context, and process of inquiry" (A. Markham 2008, 135). The appendix contains more personal narrative than the rest of this book precisely because I take reflexivity to be a crucial part of research ethics. I take seriously both the adage of feminist epistemology that all knowledge is socially situated as well as the feminist move to see the connections between epistemology and ethics. Whether the claims in this book are oppressive or harmful is as important to me as whether they are false or unjustified. Reflecting on my social location (e.g., my race, class, gender) as well as my academic training (i.e., I am a philosopher engaged in interdisciplinary work between philosophy and an established field [internet studies] outside my academic training) has been central to my research process. Additionally, I have spent time thinking not only

---

[2] I will use the phrase "publicly available" or "publicly accessible" to refer to online content which is generally unrestricted so that researchers can see the content and potentially use it in their work. I do not mean to imply that it is 'public' in the sense in which that is contrasted with content over which the creator has some legitimate privacy claims. In other words, the goal of section A.2 is to show that even content which appears publicly available might raise privacy considerations for researchers. As I will argue, many researchers believe that there is a prima facie difference between an unrestricted tweet and a private Facebook message, and they may feel more entitled to quote the tweet but hesitant to quote the Facebook message. My goal here is to show that there are privacy considerations even for publicly available content.

about who I am and how that shapes the work but also about who I want to be. Heidi McKee and James Porter argue that internet studies scholars ought to develop a 'researcher ethos,' which is "a particular character or identity for oneself as a researcher" (McKee and Porter 2009, 145). This is a character that is "constructed, perhaps even modified, through the course of a research project" (McKee and Porter 2009, 145). There have been significant changes in my approach throughout this project. As I was finishing this appendix, I read Sarah Florini's "Methodological Appendix" to *Beyond Hashtags: Racial Politics and Black Digital Networks*, and I found it incredibly helpful to find another white scholar writing about race online who also wrote personally about her methodological choices. One of the things I admire about Florini's appendix is her statement that "while I believe my intentions were in the right place, this does not mean that my research is unproblematic" (Florini 2019, 211). Recognizing that scholarship takes place within many overlapping unjust systems of dominance, Florini argues that "we often have only bad choices and somewhat less bad choices" (Florini 2019, 211). Florini outlines her methodology and shows how at each step she worked to resist perpetuating oppression. Often this means opting for the somewhat less bad option. Similarly, I do not pretend that the researcher ethos I have tried to cultivate in this project is pure or untainted by systems of oppression. While the researcher ethos that I have settled upon at this point may not be a good fit for others in my field, I think it may be helpful for other philosophers to engage with some of the questions that I have wrestled with here.

A.2. Respecting Privacy

There is a common presumption that it is permissible to cite online content without seeking permission of the author because the internet is a public space. Some researchers view the internet as analogous to a "public park," that is, a public space where consent is not required to cite overheard speech (Buchanan and Zimmer 2018). For example, Matthew Williams, Pete Burnap, and Luke Sloan note that the "follower model and mode of posting facilitated by Twitter . . . may lead to the assumption that 'these are public data'" (M. L. Williams, Burnap, and Sloan 2017, 1151). But this public-park view of online content is not universal. As McKee and Porter put it, "probably all researchers believe in researcher rights to quote public text, but the difference would be in how they determine what is 'public'" (McKee and Porter 2009, 84–85). While there may be a lack of consensus about which types of online content are public and which types should receive privacy protections, several themes emerge in the internet research ethics literature.

A.2.1. Complications for the 'Public Data' Presumption

The risk of significant harm to users is the primary reason for researchers to be cautious about quoting online content they take to be public. The principle of "Do no harm" applies to internet research as much as other scholarship (McKee and Porter 2009, 145). Scholars can be significant agents of context collapse, which can harm users. Context collapse is the blurring or merging of multiple contexts or audiences into one (boyd 2008, 2011; Marwick and boyd 2011; Frost-Arnold 2021). Danah boyd is credited with first observing that context collapse is one of the key features of the internet by noting that "the lack of spatial, social, and temporal boundaries makes it difficult to maintain distinct social contexts" (boyd 2011, 49). Context collapse is often a problem because users rarely post online content while keeping in mind the full scope of the potential audience (Marwick and boyd 2011). Instead, a user imagines an audience that they expect to view the content. For example, a user may imagine that she is speaking to an audience of friends and family members who follow her on Twitter. But a scholar who quotes her tweet potentially exposes this user's tweet to a whole new audience who would not have read it otherwise. As McKee and Porter put it, "when online communications—be they posts, blog entries, or social networking messages—are quoted in other publications, those quotations are then made more public in a way that they were not before. There is a sense in which publication potentially *brings* a readership to a forum which otherwise would not have that readership" (McKee and Porter 2009, 107). Context collapse through research can both violate the privacy expectations of users and also expose users to harassment. I tackle each of these problems in turn.

First, while a scholar may view online content as public data, studies have shown that the public often does not share the view that online content is fair to quote without consent (M. L. Williams, Burnap, and Sloan 2017; Fiesler and Proferes 2018). Casey Fiesler and Nicholas Proferes found that "the majority of Twitter users in [their] study do not realize that researchers make use of tweets, and a majority also believe researchers should not be able to do so without permission" (Fiesler and Proferes 2018, 2), and Williams, Burnap, and Sloan found that "[j]ust under 80 per cent of respondents agreed that they would expect to be asked for their consent before their Twitter posts were published in academic outputs" (M. L. Williams, Burnap, and Sloan 2017, 1156). Two important points arise from these studies. First, users may be unaware that their content is regularly studied by scholars. Second, many users have expectations of privacy over their content, even though it is publicly available on platforms, such as Twitter. This means that as potential agents of context collapse, researchers can violate users' expectations by quoting text without consent.

To expand on this connection between users' expectations and privacy protections in research, I turn to the work of Michael Zimmer and Helen Nissenbaum. Zimmer argues that Nissenbaum's account of privacy as contextual integrity is useful for incorporating user expectations into discussions of internet research ethics (Nissenbaum 2004, 2010; Zimmer 2018a, 2018b). Nissenbaum argues that our expectations of privacy are highly contextual. Different social contexts are characterized by different norms of which information it is appropriate to reveal within that context, and how information should be transferred from one party to another (Nissenbaum 2004, 138–39). Privacy is violated when there is a breach of the norms of the context in which the content at issue was shared. One of the implications of Nissenbaum's account is that information is always tagged to a context, and it is a violation of privacy to share information outside that context when doing so flouts the norms of information transfer constitutive of that context (Nissenbaum 2004, 142). For example, I share sensitive information with my doctor, and I have expectations about how and with whom she will share that information. It would be a violation of the norms of information flow for the health care context for my doctor to post my medical information on social media or send it to my employer without my consent. People trust each other to follow the norms of information sharing relevant to the context of their interaction. Sharing information outside that context in ways that violate those norms is a betrayal of trust and a privacy violation. Applying this to research ethics, a scholar can betray trust and violate privacy when the scholar shares online content in a context outside the one(s) within which the author expected the content to remain. This presents a serious challenge to the public data presumption.

One might be tempted to dismiss this concern by arguing for a buyer-beware approach to privacy: users ought to be better educated about the publicity of their content so that they can apply privacy settings or avoid posting content they would prefer not be available to researchers. But there are several problems with this response. First, many users find the privacy settings of various platforms confusing or hard to navigate. Often the full privacy implications of using an app are hidden in the legal jargon of the terms of service, a problematic practice for which tech companies should be held accountable (cf. Beninger et al. 2014). Second, returning to the pervasiveness of context collapse, "users are often required [by platforms] to place friends, lovers, colleagues, and minor acquaintances within the same singular category of 'friends'" (Buchanan and Zimmer 2018). Under such conditions, it is easy for a user to simply forget the full array of social connections who can view a post. Thus, as Buchanan and Zimmer argue, users may inadvertently post something they consider to be relatively private (e.g., something they would only want their close friends to read) in a manner which is, in fact, much more public and accessible to distant acquaintances, or even anyone (Buchanan and Zimmer 2018). Another problem is when retweeting becomes a mechanism of context collapse. This can happen even for users who attempt to restrict their audience:

> Users who have been granted access to restricted accounts can easily retweet private tweets by copying and pasting into their own, unprotected feed, violating the privacy protections enacted by the original author. In a study of over 80 million Twitter accounts, nearly 250,000 protected accounts had at least one restricted tweet retweeted by a public user (Meeder et al. 2010). If such retweets of private tweets are included in research databases, the original author's expectations of privacy might have been breached. (Zimmer and Proferes 2014, 258)

If a researcher quotes such a post, they may act as a vehicle of context collapse by exposing information that can be both damaging to the user and contrary to the user's intentions. Another common problem on Facebook is due to users being confused about or forgetting the privacy settings on their posts and not realizing that making one post public means that future posts will be public by default. In sum, not only are users' intentions and their own conceptions of the privacy of their online content difficult for researchers to discern (Acquisti and Gross 2006; Buchanan and Zimmer 2018), but also the design of online platforms often makes it difficult for users to protect their privacy. Thus, researchers should be extremely cautious about simply assuming that because a post or tweet is available to the researcher that the author intended it to be public or that the author would feel comfortable with it being quoted in a research context.

Online harassment is another important consequence of context collapse by researchers. Anna Lauren Hoffmann and Anne Jonas argue that researchers need to pay attention to online harassment, particularly because it presents issues of justice: "Because marginalized people experience more online harassment, they shoulder more of the burden of online participation; this means researchers have an obligation to avoid replicating those existing injustices but to also foreground the needs and safety of vulnerable users" (Hoffmann and Jonas 2017, 3–4). Online harassment is disproportionately targeted against marginalized users (Pew Research Center 2014; Citron 2014; Jeong 2015; Amnesty International n.d.), and researchers should avoid taking actions that expose marginalized users to additional harassment. The problem is that, as Anne Thériault puts it, "Increased visibility means an increased chance of harassment" (Thériault 2015). In

Chapter 5, I discussed the ethical problems of Twitter mining by journalists, focusing on the epistemic appropriation involved. Another problem with Twitter mining is that it can also expose marginalized users to harassment (Thériault 2015; Florini 2019, 213). And this problem is not just caused by journalists. When scholars quote online content, they expose new audiences to content and its authors. For marginalized users, harassment by the crowds of online trolls, white supremacists, men's rights activists, transphobes, and so on can follow. For example, Zoë Quinn, a game developer and activist who was the initial target of GamerGate harassment, recounts, "Occasionally, I get a spike in harassment that seems to come from nowhere. Sometimes it's caused by a well-meaning academic publishing a paper that features my story and getting a lot of the facts wrong" (Quinn 2017, 164). Victims of harassment often work for years to put their lives back to 'normal,' hoping that eventually the abusers' interest will wane. New attention to a victim, prompted by an academic publication, can spark another wave of harassment. Not only can context collapse through academic research exacerbate harm for ongoing victims of online harassment, it can also draw abusers' attention to marginalized people who had previously flown under the harassers' radar. Thus, to avoid harm, researchers should be particularly careful about quoting texts by marginalized people under the presumption that all publicly available data are fair game.[3]

Finally, a feminist commitment to non-oppressive knowledge practices provides another reason to be suspicious of the public data presumption (Townley 2006; Bruckman, Luther, and Fiesler 2015; franzke 2020). Assuming that researchers can legitimately take the content of users without consent is a manifestation of what Cynthia Townley calls the "spectator-collector model" of knowledge production—a way of knowing that ignores the agency of research subjects (Townley 2006, 43). Townley argues that when we turn people into mere objects of study, we are following a colonial, spectator-collector mode of knowledge production: "Colonialism often imposes practices and procedures on an individual (or group) who becomes an object for others' knowledge, assessment, and even manipulation" (Townley 2006, 43). Researchers often treat subjects as mere tools, rather than viewing research subjects as partners (i.e., as agents who have expertise to contribute and who can, and have the right to, question the researchers' methods and analysis). Townley argues that it is morally and epistemically irresponsible to treat humans the way we treat thermometers—as mere objects from which we can collect data. She shows that even feminists who are committed to fighting oppression can fall into these practices: "Treating members of nonprivileged groups as exotic informants who 'supply the colorful life stories' (hooks 1984, 30) for theorizing and reporting even for self-consciously feminist projects is something to beware of" (Townley 2006, 47). As I will explicate further later, Townley provides a picture of an alternative mode of knowledge production, based on an empathetic relationship with research subjects. She argues that "[k]nowing through empathy requires being a participant as well as an observer, interacting, responding, developing understanding with her, not just observing and drawing conclusions about her" (Townley 2006, 44). I worry that collecting quotes and examples from the internet and citing it in research without consent enacts this oppressive mode of simply "observing and drawing conclusions" about users, rather than "interacting, responding, [and] developing understanding" with them. In a similar vein, Susannah Stern asks these provocative questions:

---

[3] I discuss these issues and other epistemic challenges of context collapse further in Frost-Arnold 2021. See also McMillan Cottom 2016.

Why should we, as researchers, get to decide what the parameters of consideration are? Given that people have such varying understandings of privacy, why should the researcher's perspective be privileged? In an age in which notions of privacy shift ceaselessly, it is important that our decisions about our research be guided increasingly by those we wish to study, as our own conceptions may be expanded or even challenged in this process. (Stern 2008, 97)

In sum, many considerations should make researchers pause before assuming that online content is public data that is fair game to cite without consent. We need to do the following: (1) recognize that many users have expectations of privacy over their content (even though they may struggle to protect this privacy due to the limitations—and the intentional design—of platforms), (2) appreciate the harms to users for exposing content to new contexts, especially the harms to marginalized users who are disproportionately targeted for harassment, and (3) reflect on the objectifying nature of the spectator-collector model of knowledge production. So what are the alternatives to the public data presumption?

A.2.2. Alternatives to Simply Quoting Material One Can Access Online

A common recommendation is for researchers to ask permission before quoting online content in publications (Stern 2008; McKee and Porter 2009; A. Markham, Buchanan, and AoIR Ethics Committee 2012; M. L. Williams, Burnap, and Sloan 2017; Buchanan and Zimmer 2018; Fiesler and Proferes 2018; franzke et al. 2020). This approach addresses the three concerns raised in the previous subsection. It recognizes that users may have expectations of privacy that conflict with the researcher's presumption of publicity,[4] it decreases the chances of harm to subjects because victims of harassment are more likely to know whether increased exposure through the research might prompt renewed harassment, and asking for permission also creates the possibility for a relationship between researcher and subject that respects the agency of the subject. I endorse this recommendation to ask for permission to cite in most situations.

To elaborate on my reasons for asking for permission to cite, I want to quote extensively from two authors whose writing has significantly informed my thinking on these issues: Quinn and Townley. Both authors emphasize partnership, humility, and respect for people about whom one is producing knowledge. As a survivor of vicious online harassment and an activist with years advocating for victims of harassment, Quinn argues:

> When it comes to conducting research that focuses on those who are targeted by online abuse, researchers have to treat us as partners more than subjects. Someone speaking about their experiences publicly, whether it's through social media, blog posts, or interviews, should not be treated as if they are automatically consenting to anything an academic might want to do with their words. The nature of online abuse centers on violating the target's boundaries and ability to control their digital life;

---

[4] Stern argues that "Researchers who endeavor to study people online have a responsibility to investigate the privacy expectations of their research subjects/participants. One practical way to do this is by asking them, or people like them, directly" (Stern 2008, 96).

without centering the consent of the people whom researchers study, research itself can be another violation. (Quinn 2017, 164–65)

More generally, Townley's account of epistemic responsibility provides a model of humility that has informed how I approach people whose life experiences I would like to discuss in my work. For Townley, "Epistemic responsibility means maintaining a space for others to speak, and in many contexts, holding the paradoxical position that even as I claim to know, I allow that you can tell me that I am wrong, and I am prepared to take that seriously, not defensively, arrogantly, or dismissively" (Townley 2006, 50). Offering people the opportunity to read a draft of my work follows Townley's approach:

> Making it a priority to communicate information back to those it concerns most directly might be difficult, involving translations, new concepts, new theoretical frameworks, and the like, but perhaps this is the most important audience for a new fruitful analysis, and, arguably, respect for these epistemic agents requires that they have first opportunity to consider, discuss, and contest how they appear in it. (Townley 2006, 49)

Similarly, Bruckman, Luther, and Fiesler argue for sharing research with research subjects: "To treat people as ends in themselves suggests that they are entitled to respond to our representations of them" (Bruckman, Luther, and Fiesler 2015, 246).

So how did I put this approach into practice? First, following Hoffmann and Jonas's call to avoid replicating the injustice of disproportionate harassment of marginalized people and Quinn's call for partnership with victims of harassment, I have contacted marginalized people whose online content I wanted to quote to ask for their permission. I did this even when I was not collecting their words myself (e.g., by reading their own tweet myself), but when their experiences and words had been reported in a news article. While it is common in philosophy to take news stories as fair game for examples to illustrate theories, I decided to contact marginalized victims of harassment, even though their experiences had been discussed by journalists. One reason I chose to contact members of marginalized groups who had been covered in news articles is to respect their agency. Even if an individual had been quoted in a news article, I am aware that they may have been misquoted and misrepresented. As Quinn's experience shows, repeated misrepresentation can lead to new waves of harassment. Additionally, circumstances can change, and someone who was once comfortable discussing their experiences with a journalist may now face different circumstances that would make them vulnerable to harm from renewed attention. In contacting these individuals, I offered to send them a draft of the chapter in which they were discussed, and let them know that I would welcome hearing any criticisms or concerns they had about the work.[5] Thus, asking for consent to quote was an important part of my research process. If I was quoting someone's social media content (e.g., tweet, Facebook post, blog post), I reached out to ask them for permission.

That said, there are several exceptions and limitations to this informed consent model. There are many reasons why it would be unnecessary, impractical, or imprudent to ask someone's explicit permission to quote their online speech. First, it would, of

---

[5] Florini provides useful suggestions for ways to make it less onerous for someone to look over one's draft (e.g., providing the relevant quotes and page numbers) (Florini 2019, 217).

course, be too expansive of a principle to advocate contacting all individuals discussed in news stories to ask their permission to discuss the news article in academic research. Even if we restrict the suggestion to seek permission to cite to just individuals who had been subject to online harassment, the principle is still too broad; since, unfortunately, harassment of public figures is rampant, and it would be impractical to ask researchers to get permission from public figures in order to discuss their speech as covered in news articles. Thus, although this did not come up in this project, I would not contact Hillary Clinton to ask her permission to quote one of her tweets. When it came to micro-celebrities, I followed Florini's practice of reaching out to them to ask permission to cite them (Florini 2019). However, since celebrity comes in degrees, and it felt onerous to ask some prominent micro-celebrities to respond to me directly, I followed Williams, Burnap, and Sloan's recommendations for distinguishing between opt-in or opt-out consent (M. L. Williams, Burnap, and Sloan 2017, 1163). I contacted prominent micro-celebrities with a request for opt-out consent and offered to send them a draft. But for more private individuals, I waited until I had explicit opt-in consent to cite; if I never received such permission, I deleted the example. Second, the sensitivity of the content and its perceived privacy are also relevant in considering whether informed consent is necessary (A. Markham, Buchanan, and AoIR Ethics Committee 2012; McKee and Porter 2009, 21). Third, seeking permission to cite might be impractical because sometimes one might not be able to contact the author. For example, it may prove impossible to track down contact information for the author of an anonymous or pseudonymous comment on a blog post. Fourth, given the threat of online harassment faced by researchers (especially marginalized researchers), scholars need to also take into consideration whether contacting some individuals would be likely to expose the researcher herself to harassment. As Alice Marwick, Lindsay Blackwell, and Katherine Lo discuss, "Researchers conducting research into sensitive topics may face online harassment, social shaming, or other networked forms of abuse" (Marwick, Blackwell, and Lo 2016, 1). Researchers should think carefully about whether it is prudent to contact harassers (or other bad actors who are likely to mobilize an army of followers to harass the researchers).

Fifth, ethical treatment of research subjects does not require treating them identically; in fact, doing so can perpetuate hierarchies of dominance. Those who use the internet to spread hate speech and harassment might want to be asked permission for citation so that they can deny it and keep their bad actions hidden from broader scrutiny.[6] But that does not mean that it is ethical for a scholar to respect these wishes of bad actors. Florini nicely explains why she does not treat racist and homophobic users the same as the members of Black Twitter whom she studied: "The set of standards I created for myself were designed to minimize harm and prevent me from repeating historical patterns of misrepresentation and exploitation. [Racists and homophobes] did not warrant such consideration; in fact, to give them to such people would merely reinforce hierarchies I was seeking to undermine in this project" (Florini 2019, 219). Exposing injustice is important scholarly work, and considerations of privacy should not prevent it. In sum, no one-size-fits-all principle can be given for when one ought to contact someone to ask permission to cite their online content; rather researchers should take into consideration the details of each

---

[6] Sometimes bad actors threaten legal action against those who critique their online content. Claiming legal protection for one's tweets, for example, is one such suspect strategy. For useful discussion of the legal protections for researchers using Twitter, see franzke et al. 2020.

case, focusing on issues of privacy, justice, harassment, the public or private status of the individual, the sensitivity of the content, the practicality of contacting the author, the risk of harm to the researcher, the background social hierarchies, and one's commitment to social justice.

So what other options are available to philosophers when they might want to take steps to protect the privacy of an individual, but asking for permission to cite is inappropriate? One option is to anonymize the quote by not including identifying information about the author. However, this approach provides very limited protection. Online content is very difficult to anonymize. For example, one can often unmask the identity of anonymized quotes by looking them up on a search engine, which can quickly deliver original sources. Researchers who make good faith efforts to hide the identities of research subjects often find that their efforts are all too easily undone (Bruckman 2002; McKee and Porter 2009, 107; Zimmer 2010; Robson 2017). The use of search engines to de-anonymize by simply removing the author's name/username is particularly relevant to philosophers taking this approach. Thus, the main problem with anonymizing is that it can fail to provide significant privacy protections. This problem can be addressed, in cases where the exact wording is not of paramount importance, by taking the additional step to paraphrase the quote, thereby making it harder to locate. The researcher can then enter the new paraphrased quote into a search engine to check whether the source has been successfully hidden (Robson 2017, 196).

Going even further, a researcher can fabricate entirely new examples based on some original online content (A. Markham 2012). For example, instead of quoting directly from someone's blog, a researcher might write a fictional blog post based on the real blog; or one might present an example of a dialogue between two users by fabricating an example of dialogue based closely on an original online discussion (A. Markham 2012, 343). Fabrication in this sense is not simply paraphrase because some non-essential details of the blog or dialogue might be changed to prevent discovery though web search. For example, if the style of conversation is essential to the research, then the researcher might change the subject matter being discussed in order to present a new example that represents the conversational style but protects the privacy of the original author(s). Markham defends fabrication as a privacy-protecting methodology, and she analyzes techniques for creating fictional narratives or composite accounts that present the data (i.e., the original online content, such as the blog or dialogue) in illuminating ways without being traceable. Markham's suggestions for epistemically respectable ways to fabricate examples based on online content provide some very useful models for philosophers who may want to use an example to illustrate a point, but who want to protect the identity of the author. Markham systematically addresses concerns that fabrication involves an abdication of epistemic responsibilities to present the truth and avoid bias. Markham cites Karp to explain how researchers can implement this practice while still holding themselves accountable to the truth: "Everything we write is, in fact, a story we are telling. We are trying to tell a compelling story, but it is a story that is disciplined by your data. I mean, you just can't tell *any* story" (Karp 2011, 349). Thus, one method to protect the privacy of online users is to present a composite account of the content one wants to present as an example, ensuring that one's account is disciplined by (and accountable to) the content but also ensuring that identifying details are obscured.

That said, a problem with anonymizing, paraphrasing, and fabricating is that authors have legitimate expectations that they receive credit for their words and ideas (Bruckman 2002; Beninger et al. 2014, 7; Bruckman, Luther, and Fiesler 2015). Amy Bruckman provides a valuable analysis of the history of research ethics in the humanities, finding that humanities scholars are often particularly concerned with ensuring that authors of online content cited in their research receive credit for their creations (Bruckman 2002). This concern makes sense within a tradition of respect for artistic creation, intellectual property, and attention to copyright issues. Bruckman argues that thinking of online authors as 'amateur artists' provides a useful metaphor for humanities scholars. Like professional artists, online authors produce intellectual and artistic creations. In some countries, online authors have copyright over their content, and researchers have good reason to respect their ownership of their intellectual productions (Bruckman 2002, 227). Additionally, one might want to show respect for the status of some online authors as public intellectuals who are publishing in a legitimate space. No one has to ask me to cite my published articles, and one might argue that it shows a lack of respect to treat some online authors as private individuals who need to be asked to cite their tweets. That said, many online authors are not professionals; thus, they may not be as aware of the risks involved in sharing and promoting their work online (Bruckman 2002, 228). This means that amateur artists are more vulnerable as a group. This leaves researchers in a complicated position. There are many conflicting considerations here: potential harm to the user may suggest anonymizing or fabricating the content to hide authorship, but then the author is denied credit for their work. However, some argue that researchers have a responsibility to not just take the author's wishes at face value, since some authors may want credit for their words without fully understanding the risks involved (Bruckman 2002, 228; Bruckman, Luther, and Fiesler 2015). In sum, balancing the need to protect users and respect their wishes for authorship credit may require difficult reflections. The AoIR ethics 3.0 document suggests that "the researcher cannot assume [users] should be protected but must get their consent to protect them" by using anonymization or fabrication (franzke et al. 2020, 11).

I hope to have conveyed some of the complex, conflicting, and serious ethical considerations involved in using online content in philosophical research. There is no one, simple answer to the question of how a philosopher should proceed when they want to quote or discuss some online content. As the AoIR ethics committee writes, "[R]ather than one-size-fits-all pronouncements, ethical decision-making is best approached through the application of practical judgment attentive to the specific context (what Aristotle identified as phronesis)" (A. Markham, Buchanan, and AoIR Ethics Committee 2012). Keeping in mind the relevant ethical considerations and taking seriously the particularities of the context, philosophers will need to exercise their practical judgment about how to approach each piece of online content in their research. For this project, I have taken the approach of asking for authors' consent to cite, unless considerations of risk, impracticality, or justice make that impossible. When getting permission was impractical, I have used a combination of anonymization and fabrication to protect user privacy. The exception to this was when hiding the name of the author would perpetuate systems of dominance.

A.3. Protecting the Researcher in an Environment of Online Harassment

Research ethics requires not only thinking about potential harms to the research subject but also to the researcher. Online harassment can be a traumatizing, stressful experience that can significantly disrupt a scholar's career and personal life (Greyson et al. 2018). Both a scholar's work and their personal identity can make them a target for harassment (cf. American Association of University Professors, American Federation of Teachers, and Association of American Colleges and Universities 2017; Herbert 2018). This requires feminist scholars, scholars from marginalized groups, and others to consider carefully their choice of research topics. Prudence is a virtue, and self-protection may mean that a scholar chooses to avoid a particular topic, question, or case study in order to avoid exposing herself and her family to harassment. As Marwick, Blackwell, and Lo discuss, scholars who work on certain topics are routinely subjected to online harassment (Marwick, Blackwell, and Lo 2016). This means that scholars who decide to work on "risky" topics may need to deploy cybersecurity steps to protect their personal information (e.g., phone number and home address) from potential harassers. There are a number of online resources for how to protect oneself as a scholar or online author, and I recommend that philosophers share these resources widely as philosophy of the internet grows as a field (Marwick, Blackwell, and Lo 2016; J. Friedman, Sarkeesian, and Bracey Sherman n.d.; Crash Override Network n.d.; Honeywell 2018; franzke et al. 2020). Individual scholars have an ethical responsibility to themselves and their family to take steps to address the risks involved in scholarship in an era of pervasive online harassment (cf. Massanari 2018).

That said, if academic communities and institutions value justice and academic freedom, then protecting scholars should not be conceived of as just an individual responsibility (Massanari 2018; franzke et al. 2020). In an environment in which marginalized scholars are disproportionately targeted for online harassment, institutions need to seriously consider how they support scholars. A number of steps could be taken at various institutional levels to provide resources, training, and institutional protection for marginalized scholars and those working on risky topics. First, graduate programs should add training in online protection and cybersecurity competence to the list of skills provided to their students. Second, institutions need to provide training for supervisors, department chairs, and administrators concerning steps to take in the event a scholar is harassed. Marwick, Blackwell, and Lo provide several useful fact sheets that explain online harassment and outline steps administrators can take to protect scholars who are being harassed (Marwick, Blackwell, and Lo 2016). Third, institutions might consider investing in information technology infrastructure that provides basic cybersecurity for scholars (e.g., multifactor authentication for email, funding to help scholars afford online services that remove one's personal information from online archives). In sum, if philosophers are going to do more research about the internet and more research that gains attention from online publics, we need to collectively think about what infrastructure we need to put in place to support this work. This includes careful advising of graduate students and mentorship of junior faculty. We need to prevent scholars from feeling alone with these issues, and we should not expect them to shoulder the burdens (including financial burdens) of protecting themselves alone. We need to alert them to possible risks of their research, and we need to do what we can do prevent them from experiencing harassment as a result of their work. Not only does philosophy have a problem of harassment of philosophers by fellow philosophers, but all of us work within an online ecosystem of rampant online harassment from many corners. Research ethics requires us to protect scholars alongside our work to protect research subjects.

A.4. Avoiding Epistemic Appropriation

In Chapter 5 I discussed the problems of epistemic appropriation that can result from online lurking. For example, in the practice of Twitter mining, journalists lurk in Twitter looking for interesting tweets, which they then turn into articles. Journalists may steal ideas for stories from Twitter (Honey 2017) or republish screenshots of someone's tweets along with some commentary (Thériault 2015). In Chapter 5, I analyzed this as a form of epistemic appropriation. Recall that for Davis, epistemic appropriation is a type of epistemic injustice in which the epistemic contributions of marginalized people are obscured and their epistemic resources are used in dominant contexts to benefit the privileged (E. Davis 2018). In thinking through these problems with lurking, I had to confront whether my own lurking practices were ethically and epistemically responsible. It is important to me to cultivate a researcher ethos that avoids epistemic appropriation. One obvious way to avoid the most egregious cases of epistemic appropriation is to adopt the practices I discussed in section A.2 by asking users' permission before I quote online content or present others' ideas that I encountered online. This clearly goes some way to avoid the theft of intellectual labor inherent in Twitter mining.

That said, as I reflected on my lurking practices, I noticed that I was gaining epistemic benefits from the epistemic labor of marginalized people whose contributions did not fit cleanly into traditional academic citation practices and whose labor is helpfully theorized as unpaid reproductive labor by Nakamura (Nakamura 2015). For example, I follow some trans and disability activists on Twitter. There are many reasons why I follow each of these users; for example, I enjoy their writing, their sense of humor makes me laugh, I share their politics, and so on. But often one of the additional reasons I follow them is that I want to unlearn any transphobic or ableist prejudices I may have. I want to learn how I can better disrupt transphobic or ableist oppression around me. So I also have epistemic aims in lurking in these users' threads. If I got a particular idea from one of these users, or if I wanted to quote some of their content in this book, then I would contact them and ask for permission, thereby respecting their ownership over their intellectual content. But what about the ways in which my own worldview might be changed, often without my own awareness, through lurking in the online worlds of these users? Unlike a particular idea or piece of writing which one notices and can be careful to ask for permission to cite, subtle influences on one's epistemic orientation or worldview might not rise to the level of awareness. Of course, all scholars need to be vigilant to work to notice such influences and do our due diligence to give them credit. But there are limits on our ability to do this. Thus, I started to ask myself whether I was gaining some epistemic benefits from online authors in ways I was not noticing and might therefore be potentially exploitative.

One might argue that it is excessive to worry about exploitation and appropriation in these cases, because non-academics who perform this work are offering their labor for free. Many people enjoy sharing knowledge online for a variety of reasons, and many of them are not looking for any form of compensation for their labors. But this response is incomplete because (1) some users do seek compensation, respect, and protection for their online epistemic labor (Florini 2019, 216; Brock 2020, 2014–15); and (2) some lurking does seem to exploit the existence of online communities that do not primarily exist for educational purposes. First, some users ask followers to subscribe to content (e.g., a newsletter), to contribute via a crowdfunding platform (e.g., Patreon), or to compensate their labor in other forms. To consume free content while ignoring such requests for compensation in other ways seems potentially exploitative, especially given the ways in which social media function to extract unpaid labor from artists, entrepreneurs, and other content creators (cf. Terranova 2000; Ritzer and Jurgenson 2010). Cassius Adair and Lisa Nakamura argue for the resistant potential of compensation for women of color's online labor:

> If the vernacular writing and commentary that women of color produce online is not only producing free content for social networks but is resulting in violence being aimed at their persons, then these feminists are essentially paying to do what professional academics would consider "digital pedagogy." To argue that these forms of gendered and racial theft deserve remuneration and acknowledgement, then, is not a perpetuation of capital's commodification of everyday life but a resistant reordering of it. (Adair and Nakamura 2017, 265)

Similarly, discussing some marginalized people's demand for compensation for quoting their material, Florini argues that "Users from marginalized groups have long had little say in how they were written about and how their ideas were used. Demands for remuneration when they are quoted are both an amelioration of inequitable material circumstances and an assertion of agency" (Florini 2019, 216). Second, some privileged people lurk in online spaces primarily created for mutual support and conversation between marginalized people. These spaces are not created with the goal of educating privileged people, even though they can serve this additional purpose through lurking. When privileged people derive epistemic benefits from the creation and maintenance of such epistemic communities without contributing to their sustenance in any way, this also seems potentially exploitative.

To avoid committing such exploitative appropriation, I have developed the following habits throughout this book project, in addition to the habits of citation and asking for permission I discussed earlier. First, I pay attention to whether someone I am following is asking for compensation, and if I find myself learning from them and regularly consuming their content, I subscribe to their newsletter, contribute to their Patreon, buy their book, or support them in the requested ways. Second, I look for opportunities to support communities from which I derive epistemic benefits. For example, I pay attention to crowdsourcing requests, and I donate to non-profit organizations promoted by people whom I follow online. These are habits that I am developing and tweaking as my scholarship in this area develops. Of course, much depends on my own financial ability to support these content creators, and it would be classist to argue that all academics have a responsibility to make these financial commitments, especially given the rising precarity of academic labor. Additionally, these suggestions are limited, individualized solutions to what is a larger collective and economic set of issues in the landscape of digital capitalism. What I hope to do in this section is to raise the issue of epistemic appropriation by academics, outline some habits I have developed to try to minimize my own exploitation of others, and to potentially encourage future conversations about institutional and collective solutions to these problems. Adair and Nakamura suggest some avenues to pursue that include developing "an alternative model of citation and circulation, one based on a feminist politics of consent and safety"; petitioning institutions for compensation for online pedagogical work by non-academics; and building "digital platforms that do not lend themselves to harassment, that do not subsist on data extraction, that pay writers, and that do not sell advertising" (Adair and Nakamura 2017, 274–75). Pursing this work seems to me an important kind of epistemic responsibility. As Davis writes:

First, we might say that we have epistemic responsibilities not merely to use resources created by nondominantly situated knowers but also to publicly acknowledge nondominantly situated knowers as contributors in the processes of meaning making. . . . Second, the benefits associated with the epistemic contributions of the marginalized should not disproportionately advantage those already occupying advantaged social positions. (E. Davis 2018, 725)

A.5. Cultivating a "Traitorous Identity" as a Researcher

Given that this book draws heavily on standpoint epistemology, the epistemologies of ignorance literature, and work on epistemic injustice, I am painfully aware that as a white woman writing about race and racism I am liable to make mistakes. I cannot pretend that I am immune to the problems of white ignorance, implicit bias, willful hermeneutical ignorance, testimonial injustice, and loving, knowing, ignorance, and so on. This means that I have to acknowledge the possibility that white supremacy and white racist bias may have skewed my analysis, despite my good intentions and attempts to eradicate biases and achieve an anti-racist standpoint. The same is true for other aspects of my social location where I occupy positions of privilege. To give just two examples, as a cisgender scholar, I am at risk of being oblivious to transphobic bias in my work; as an able-bodied scholar, I am more likely to be unaware of ableist assumptions in my theorizing. In this section, I discuss how recognition of the epistemology of privilege and an awareness of the social-epistemic dynamics of the philosophy profession in an online world create responsibilities for privileged scholars to cultivate 'traitorous identities' (Bailey 1998) and take steps to mitigate the harm that may fall upon marginalized scholars who take on the labor of pointing out the flaws in privileged scholars' work.

To make the issue clear, I will explain how this issue has arisen for me in writing this book. I will focus on my position as a white woman writing about race and racism in internet epistemology. I have often had the following series of concerns: What if there's some racist assumption or racist problem in this chapter that I am not noticing? What if none of the peer reviewers catch these problems before the book is published? What if after publication, the book is rightly criticized for any problems with racism? And what if any people of color who make these criticisms are publicly attacked and harassed by people trying to defend me? It is the last question in the series of concerns that I want to focus on, because thinking about this question requires understanding the social epistemology of academia in a world where online and offline worlds are blurred and online harassment is pervasive. I also include this issue in this appendix because I believe the internet provides some opportunities for epistemic responsibility that were not previously available to scholars.

But first, I want to note that there are answers to the earlier questions in the series of concerns (i.e., What if there's some racist assumption or racist problem in this chapter that I am not noticing? What if none of the peer reviewers catch these problems and the book is published with them? What if after publication, the book is rightly criticized for any problems with racism?). These issues raise important questions for all philosophers, not only for those working in epistemology of the internet. I address them here because they are particularly important questions for philosophers of the internet to take when they follow the approach advocated in this book by taking seriously the social situatedness of online knowledge. Privileged scholars have an ethical and epistemic responsibility to do everything they can to bring to light and remove any biases and prejudices in their work. Much of the literature in social epistemology discussed in this book provides recommendations for how to do this. The piece that I have found most useful is Mariana Ortega's paper "Being Lovingly, Knowingly Ignorant: White Feminism and Women of Color" in which she analyzes the recommendations of Audre Lorde, Elizabeth Spelman, Marilyn Frye, and María Lugones. Some of these solutions include "recognizing differences among women of color" (Ortega 2006, 66; Lorde 1984, 122), being vigilant (Ortega 2006, 66; Lorde 1984, 140), knowing that "[i]magining isn't the same thing as knowing, nor tolerance the same as welcoming" (Ortega 2006, 67; Spelman 1991, 184), developing habits of recognizing difference "rather than indulge in a theoretical discussion on the problem of difference" (Ortega 2006, 67; Lugones 2003, 68), and engaging in playful 'world'-travel (Ortega 2006, 67; Lugones 2003, 97). So the first step in addressing these concerns is for white scholars writing on race and racism to do what they can pre-publication to prevent perpetuating white supremacy in their work (cf. Russell 2019).

The second step to answer the concern, What if after publication, the book is rightly criticized for any problems with racism? is for white scholars to make a commitment to responding to such criticism with humility and gratitude, by granting scholars of color due credibility for their criticisms, apologizing for mistakes, making amends, and attempting to learn from the criticisms. White scholars should avoid reacting with defensiveness or perpetrating a testimonial injustice against their critics. In sum, I think there are already some clear answers in the literature that give guidance to answer these concerns.

But what about the final concern I have faced in this project: What if any people of color who make these criticisms are publicly attacked and harassed by people trying to defend me? This concern stems from some of the social-epistemic issues discussed in Chapter 2 arising from testimonial injustice and hermeneutical injustice in epistemic communities. Recall this dynamic common in online spaces: a white person posts something racist and is rightly criticized by people of color for the racist speech, but then it is the people of color who are accused of aggressive racism (i.e., anti-white racism) and experience sanctions either from the broader white-dominated online community or the moderation system of the platform. Due to stereotypes that cast people of color as aggressive, violent, and irrationally emotional, people of color who criticize racism often experience testimonial injustice when their criticisms are not given proper epistemic authority. And due to hermeneutical injustice, the speech of people of color who criticize racism can often be misinterpreted. This dynamic occurs in academia as well. Problems of testimonial injustice and hermeneutical injustice shape in-person academic conversations. Additionally, as discussed in Chapter 1, we also live in a hybrid online/offline (onlife) world in which academic conversations, debates, and intellectual engagement happen not simply in paper journals but also in online journals, blogs, Facebook posts, and Twitter threads. Thus, many of the same dynamics that I discussed in Chapter 2 occur in online academic discussions about scholarship. A scholar belonging to a privileged group may publish an article which scholars from marginalized groups criticize for implicit bias or for perpetuating systems of oppression. But then those marginalized scholars who took on the labor of explaining the problems with the original piece may themselves be criticized for being aggressive or bullying, be described as hysterical or irrational, and their anger at the harm perpetrated by the original piece used as evidence that they are emotional, unreasonable, and unprofessional. Of course, this does not happen every time a privileged scholar's work is criticized, but it is a pattern that we need to acknowledge in our academic communities.

As a scholar with several privileged identities looking at these social-epistemic features of the landscape of academia, I ask myself, What is the ethically and epistemically responsible way to handle these issues? To make this concrete by thinking about racism in academia: if it is likely that as a white woman I may be unaware of some racial bias in my work, and if I inhabit an epistemic landscape in which any people of color who take on the labor of pointing out racial bias in my work may be subjected to the unjust treatment I described, what (if anything) can I (and ought I) do about this? This is a pressing question because white women should be cognizant of the racial norms that cast white femininity as fragile and deserving of protection, particularly protection by "gallant" white men.[7] These expectations that white men rise to the protection of white women can lead, in academia and public life, to unjust treatment of people of color who rightly criticize a white woman for racism. Defenders may rush to the aid of the white woman, attacking the credibility of individual critics of color or casting a collection of critics as an irrational, aggressive, censoring mob.[8] In this environment, white women who are criticized can choose to wrap themselves in the protection of white femininity and accept the "gallantry" of defenders. They can also encourage and contribute to the hostility against their critics by casting themselves as victims under attack by a censoring mob.

But another course of action is also available: white women can cultivate what Alison Bailey calls a "traitorous identity" (Bailey 1998). On Bailey's account, white race traitors are "privileged subjects who animate privilege-cognizant white scripts" (Bailey 1998, 33). White race traitors, of the kind Bailey endorses, are aware of white privilege and cultivate habits of disloyalty to the behavioral norms that uphold white supremacy, which Bailey calls "whitely scripts":

> Unlike whites who unreflectively animate whitely scripts, the traitor's task is to find ways to develop alternative scripts capable of disrupting the constant reinscription of whitely scripts. Privilege-cognizant whites actively examine their "seats in front" and find ways to be disloyal to systems that assign these seats. Some obvious examples include choosing to stop racist jokes, paying attention to body language and conversation patterns, and cultivating an awareness of how stereotypes shape perceptions of people of color. (Bailey 1998, 37)

In academia, a privilege-cognizant traitor's task is to be aware of the social-epistemic dynamics that bolster the credibility of white academics and protect them from criticism and reputational harm for their failings. But cultivating a traitorous identity involves more than mere awareness of privilege; it involves disloyalty and repeatedly acting to disrupt the systems that produce white privilege. Cultivating a traitorous identity, thus, involves a kind of virtue—cultivating habits of resistance to white racial domination.

How can one enact this traitorous identity as part of one's research ethics practice? This is where recognizing the complexity of the internet as an epistemic space is helpful. The internet both provides a platform for problems (such as online testimonial injustice and hermeneutical injustice, which run rampant throughout academic communities), but it also creates opportunities for solutions. Not only can I say here, in print, that I welcome

---

[7] On racist protection of white women that excluded enslaved Black women, see Truth 2010 and A. Davis 1972. Davis argues that the "alleged benefits of the ideology of femininity did not accrue to [the Black woman under slavery]. She was not sheltered or protected; she would not remain oblivious to the desperate struggle for existence unfolding outside the 'home'" (A. Davis 1972, 87).

[8] Again, I am focusing on race here to provide some concrete illustration, but similar dynamics hold for other identities; for example, people often rush to the defense of a cisgender woman to protect her from what is represented as a hoard of angry, irrational trans people.

criticism and do not want others to protect me from criticisms of any racist bias in this book, but I can also respond in real time to unjust treatment of my critics who are racially marginalized. Twitter, Facebook, and blogs all provide me with opportunities to reach out to the broader academic community to engage in ongoing disputes and to try to disrupt any harassment of marginalized scholars who have performed valuable labor in criticizing my work for bias. Of course, I cannot single-handedly change the epistemic landscape in which testimonial injustice and hermeneutical injustice thrive, but I can do the following: (1) use this appendix to point out the injustice prevalent in the epistemic landscape which this book will inhabit, (2) preemptively abjure defenses that attack marginalized people for useful criticisms of bias in my work—I can say clearly here that I do not want "gallant knights" to ride to my defense if I am rightly attacked for bias in my work, and (3) post-publication, I can use social media to publicly thank critics for helping me to learn, and to push back against anyone who harasses them. The internet, thus, provides real-time opportunities for resistance to epistemic oppression in academia.

To conclude, I raise these issues about post-publication research ethics with the following useful reminder from the Association of Internet Researchers (AoIR) guidelines in mind: "Ethical issues may arise and need to be addressed during *all* steps of the research process, from planning, research conduct, publication, and *dissemination*" (A. Markham, Buchanan, and AoIR Ethics Committee 2012, 5, emphasis added). As social epistemologists attuned to the various epistemic injustices prevalent in our hybrid offline/online epistemic communities, we should think about the ways that our work can reinforce hierarchies of domination and not only try to avoid contributing to this in our writing but also commit to resisting oppressive uses of our writing as it is disseminated. This book has argued that social epistemology has much to offer those who study the internet, and that studying the internet provides important insights for the field of social epistemology. This appendix has shown that understanding the social epistemic landscape of academia helps us to see more clearly the ethical challenges of studying the internet, and how we might use the internet responsibly to resist epistemic oppression in academic research.

References

Abbas, Faisal J. 2011. "Let Us Not Allow 'a Gay Girl in Damascus' to Discredit All Blogging." Huffington Post. June 24, 2011. http://www.huffingtonpost.com/faisal-abbas/let-us-not-allow-a-gay-gi_b_880215.html.

Abunimah, Ali. 2011. "New Evidence about Amina, the 'Gay Girl in Damascus' Hoax." The Electronic Intifada. June 12, 2011. https://electronicintifada.net/blogs/ali-abunimah/new-evidence-about-amina-gay-girl-damascus-hoax.

Acquisti, Alessandro, and Ralph Gross. 2006. "Imagined Communities: Awareness, Information Sharing, and Privacy on the Facebook." *Proceedings of the 6th Workshop on Privacy Enhancing Technologies* 4258: 36–58.

"Activists Come Clean." n.d. The Yes Men. https://theyesmen.org/article/cop15-activists-come-clean.

Adair, Cassius, and Lisa Nakamura. 2017. "The Digital Afterlives of This Bridge Called My Back: Woman of Color Feminism, Digital Labor, and Networked Pedagogy." *American Literature* 89 (2): 255–78. https://doi.org/10.1215/00029831-3861505.

AFP, CORRECTIV, Pagella Politica/Facta, Full Fact, and Maldita.es. 2020. "Infodemic COVID-19 in Europe: A Visual Analysis of Disinformation." https://covidinfodemiceurope.com.

Ahmed, Sara. 2012. *On Being Included: Racism and Diversity in Institutional Life*. Durham, NC: Duke University Press.

Ahmed, Sara. 2013. "Making Feminist Points." *Feministkilljoys* (blog). September 11, 2013. https://feministkilljoys.com/2013/09/11/making-feminist-points/.

Aikin, Scott F., and Robert B. Talisse. 2018. "On 'Fake News.'" *3 Quarks Daily* (blog). May 21, 2018. https://3quarksdaily.com/3quarksdaily/2018/05/on-fake-news.html.

Alcoff, Linda. 1991. "The Problem of Speaking for Others." *Cultural Critique*, no. 20 (December): 5–32. https://doi.org/10.2307/1354221.

Alfano, Mark, and Colin Klein. 2019. "Trust in a Social and Digital World." *Social Epistemology Review and Reply Collective* 8 (10): 1–8.

Alfano, Mark, and Joshua August Skorburg. 2016. "The Embedded and Extended Character Hypotheses." In *The Routledge Handbook of Philosophy of the Social Mind*, edited by Julian Kiverstein, 481–94. New York: Routledge.

American Association of University Professors, American Federation of Teachers, and Association of American Colleges and Universities. 2017. "Taking a Stand against Harassment, Part of the Broader Threat to Higher Education." https://www.aaup.org/sites/default/files/Statement%20on%20Harassment.pdf.

Amnesty International. n.d. "Troll Patrol Findings." Troll Patrol Report. Accessed April 4, 2019. https://decoders.amnesty.org/projects/troll-patrol/findings.

Anderson, Elizabeth. 2006. "The Epistemology of Democracy." *Episteme: A Journal of Social Epistemology* 3 (1): 8–22.

Anderson, Elizabeth. 2012. "Epistemic Justice as a Virtue of Social Institutions." *Social Epistemology* 26 (2): 163–73. https://doi.org/10.1080/02691728.2011.652211.

Anderson, Elizabeth. 2020. "Feminist Epistemology and Philosophy of Science." In *The Stanford Encyclopedia of Philosophy*, edited by Edward N. Zalta, Spring 2020. Metaphysics Research Lab, Stanford University. https://plato.stanford.edu/archives/spr2020/entries/feminism-epistemology/.

Anderson, Luvell. 2017. "Hermeneutical Impasses." *Philosophical Topics* 45 (2): 1–19. https://doi.org/10.5840/philtopics201745211.

Angwin, Julia, and Hannes Grassegger. 2017. "Facebook's Secret Censorship Rules Protect White Men from Hate Speech but Not Black Children." ProPublica. June 28, 2017. https://www.propublica.org/article/facebook-hate-speech-censorship-internal-documents-algorithms.

Aristotle. 1926. *Nicomachean Ethics*. Translated by H. Rackham. Cambridge, MA: Harvard University Press. http://www.loebclassics.com/view/aristotle-nicomachean_ethics/1926/work.xml.

Aristotle. 1969. *Nicomachean Ethics*. Translated by Terence Irwin. Indianapolis: Hackett.

Bady, Aaron. 2011. "'This Is the Face.'" *Zunguzungu* (blog). June 13, 2011. http://zunguzungu.wordpress.com/2011/06/13/this-is-the-face/.

Baehr, Jason. 2011. *The Inquiring Mind: On Intellectual Virtues and Virtue Epistemology*. New York: Oxford University Press.

Baier, Annette C. 1996. *Moral Prejudices: Essays on Ethics*. Cambridge, MA: Harvard University Press.

Bailey, Alison. 1998. "Locating Traitorous Identities: Toward a View of Privilege-Cognizant White Character." *Hypatia* 13 (3): 27–42. https://doi.org/10.1111/j.1527-2001.1998.tb01368.x.

Bailey, Alison. 2007. "Strategic Ignorance." In *Race and Epistemologies of Ignorance*, edited by Nancy Tuana and Shannon Sullivan, 77–94. Albany: SUNY Press.

Baker, Katie J. M. 2012. "No, Victoria's Secret Does Not Have a New Line of Anti-Rape Panties." Jezebel. December 3, 2012. http://jezebel.com/5965323/no-victorias-secret-does-not-have-a-new-line-of-anti-rape-panties.

Banet-Weiser, Sarah. 2012. *Authentic TM: The Politics of Ambivalence in a Brand Culture*. New York: New York University Press.

Barber, Bernard. 1983. *The Logic and Limits of Trust*. New Brunswick, NJ: Rutgers University Press.

Battaly, Heather. 2008. "Virtue Epistemology." *Philosophy Compass* 3 (4): 639–63.

Bell, Melissa, and Elizabeth Flock. 2011. "'A Gay Girl in Damascus' Comes Clean." *The Washington Post*, June 17, 2011. http://www.washingtonpost.com/lifestyle/style/a-gay-girl-in-damascus-comes-clean/2011/06/12/AGkyH0RH_story_1.html.

Beninger, Kelsey, Alexandra Fry, Natalie Jago, Hayley Lepps, Laura Nass, and Hannah Silvester. 2014. "Research Using Social Media; Users' Views." London: NatCen Social Research.

Benkler, Yochai, Rob Faris, and Hal Roberts. 2018. *Network Propaganda: Manipulation, Disinformation, and Radicalization in American Politics*. New York: Oxford University Press.

Benkler, Yochai, Robert Faris, Hal Roberts, and Ethan Zuckerman. 2017. "Study: Breitbart-Led Right-Wing Media Ecosystem Altered Broader Media Agenda." *Columbia Journalism Review* (blog). March 3, 2017. https://www.cjr.org/analysis/breitbart-media-trump-harvard-study.php.

Berenstain, Nora. 2016. "Epistemic Exploitation." *Ergo, an Open Access Journal of Philosophy* 3 (22): 569–90.

Bettcher, Talia Mae. 2007. "Evil Deceivers and Make-Believers: On Transphobic Violence and the Politics of Illusion." *Hypatia* 22 (3): 43–65. https://doi.org/10.1111/j.1527-2001.2007.tb01090.x.

Bettcher, Talia Mae. 2018. "'When Tables Speak': On the Existence of Trans Philosophy." *Daily Nous*. May 30, 2018. http://dailynous.com/2018/05/30/tables-speak-existence-trans-philosophy-guest-talia-mae-bettcher/.

Bichlbaum, Andy. 2020. "Creative Trickery Is Dead, Long Live Creative Trickery." *ConTactos* (blog). July 28, 2020. https://contactos.tome.press/creative-trickery-is-dead-long-live-creative-trickery/.

Bichlbaum, Andy, Mike Bonanno, and Laura Nix. 2014. *The Yes Men Are Revolting*. New York: The Orchard.

Bird, Sharon, Jacquelyn Litt, and Yong Wang. 2004. "Creating Status of Women Reports: Institutional Housekeeping as 'Women's Work.'" *NWSA Journal* 16 (1): 194–206.

Block, Hans, and Moritz Riesewieck. 2018. *The Cleaners (Im Schatten Der Netzwelt)*. Gebrueder Beetz Filmproducktion.

Booth, Robert, Matthew Weaver, Alex Hern, and Shaun Walker. 2017. "Russia Used Hundreds of Fake Accounts to Tweet about Brexit, Data Shows." *The Guardian*, November 14, 2017. http://www.theguardian.com/world/2017/nov/14/how-400-russia-run-fake-accounts-posted-bogus-brexit-tweets.

Bowden, Rasalyn. 2017. "CCM Workers: Tales from the Moderation Screen." Presented at the All Things in Moderation Conference, University of California, Los Angeles, December 7. https://atm-ucla2017.net/.

Bowman, John. 2015. "Facebook Flags Aboriginal Names as Not 'Authentic.'" CBC. February 25, 2015. https://www.cbc.ca/news/trending/facebook-flags-aboriginal-names-as-not-authentic-1.2970993.

boyd, danah. 2008. "Taken Out of Context: American Teen Sociality in Networked Publics." Ph.D. Thesis, University of California Berkeley.

boyd, danah. 2011. "Social Network Sites as Networked Publics: Affordances, Dynamics, and Implications." In *A Networked Self: Identity, Community, and Culture on Social Network Sites*, edited by Zizi Papacharissi, 39–58. New York: Routledge.

boyd, danah. 2017. "Did Media Literacy Backfire?" Data & Society: Points. January 5, 2017. https://points.datasociety.net/did-media-literacy-backfire-7418c084d88d.

Brandom, Russell. 2014. "Facebook's Report Abuse Button Has Become a Tool of Global Oppression." The Verge. September 2, 2014. https://www.theverge.com/2014/9/2/6083647/facebook-s-report-abuse-button-has-become-a-tool-of-global-oppression.

Brock, André L. 2020. *Distributed Blackness: African American Cybercultures*. New York: New York University Press.

Broderick, Ryan. 2017. "Trump Supporters Online Are Pretending to Be French to Manipulate France's Election." BuzzFeed. January 24, 2017. https://www.buzzfeed.com/ryanhatesthis/inside-the-private-chat-rooms-trump-supporters-are-using-to.

Brown, Etienne. 2019. "'Fake News' and Conceptual Ethics." *Journal of Ethics and Social Philosophy* 16 (2): 144–54. https://doi.org/10.26556/jesp.v16i2.648.

Brown, Kendrick T., and Joan M. Ostrove. 2013. "What Does It Mean to Be an Ally?: The Perception of Allies from the Perspective of People of Color." *Journal of Applied Social Psychology* 43 (11): 2211–22. https://doi.org/10.1111/jasp.12172.

Brown, Kristen V. 2014. "SF Drag Queens Pressure Facebook's Name Policy." *The Technology Chronicles* (blog). September 12, 2014. https://blog.sfgate.com/techchron/2014/09/12/sf-drag-queens-pressure-facebooks-name-policy/.

Brownstein, Michael, and Jennifer Saul, eds. 2016. *Implicit Bias and Philosophy, Volume 1: Metaphysics and Epistemology*. New York: Oxford University Press.

Bruckman, Amy. 2002. "Studying the Amateur Artist: A Perspective on Disguising Data Collected in Human Subjects Research on the Internet." *Ethics and Information Technology* 4 (3): 217–31. https://doi.org/10.1023/A:1021316409277.

Bruckman, Amy, Kurt Luther, and Casey Fiesler. 2015. "When Should We Use Real Names in Published Accounts of Internet Research?" In *Digital Research Confidential: The Secrets of Studying Behavior Online*, edited by Eszter Hargittai and Christian Sandvig, 243–58. Cambridge, MA: MIT Press.

Buchanan, Elizabeth A. 2017. "Internet Research Ethics: Twenty Years Later." In *Internet Research Ethics for the Social Age: New Challenges, Cases, and Contexts*, edited by Michael Zimmer, XXIX–XXXIII. New York: Peter Lang.

Buchanan, Elizabeth A., and Michael Zimmer. 2018. "Internet Research Ethics." In *The Stanford Encyclopedia of Philosophy*, edited by Edward N. Zalta, Fall 2018. Metaphysics Research Lab, Stanford University. https://plato.stanford.edu/archives/fall2018/entries/ethics-internet-research/.

Butler, Judith. 1993. *Bodies That Matter: On the Discursive Limits of "Sex."* New York: Routledge.

"Canada Freaks out the World." n.d. The Yes Men. https://theyesmen.org/project/cop15.

Carlson, Matt. 2018. "Facebook in the News: Social Media, Journalism, and Public Responsibility Following the 2016 Trending Topics Controversy." *Digital Journalism* 6 (1): 4–20.

Chadwick, Andrew. 2017. *The Hybrid Media System: Politics and Power*. 2nd ed. New York: Oxford University Press.

Chen, Adrian. 2014. "The Laborers Who Keep Dick Pics and Beheadings Out of Your Facebook Feed." *Wired*, October 23, 2014. https://www.wired.com/2014/10/content-moderation/.

Chen, Adrian. 2017a. "The Human Toll of Protecting the Internet from the Worst of Humanity." *The New Yorker*, January 28, 2017. https://www.newyorker.com/tech/elements/the-human-toll-of-protecting-the-internet-from-the-worst-of-humanity.

Chen, Adrian. 2017b. "The Fake-News Fallacy." September 4, 2017. http://www.newyorker.com/magazine/2017/09/04/the-fake-news-fallacy.

Chittal, Nisha. 2012. "How to Decide What Can Be Published, What's Private on Twitter and Facebook." Poynter. March 29, 2012. http://www.poynter.org/2012/how-to-decide-what-can-be-published-whats-private-on-twitter-and-facebook/167704/.

Chun, Wendy Hui Kyong. 2006. *Control and Freedom: Power and Paranoia in the Age of Fiber Optics*. Cambridge, MA: The MIT Press.

Chun, Wendy Hui Kyong. 2016. *Updating to Remain the Same: Habitual New Media*. Cambridge, MA: The MIT Press.

Citron, Danielle Keats. 2014. *Hate Crimes in Cyberspace*. Cambridge, MA: Harvard University Press.

Coady, David. 2012. *What to Believe Now: Applying Epistemology to Contemporary Issues*. Malden, MA: Wiley-Blackwell.

Coady, David. 2017. "Epistemic Injustice as Distributive Injustice." In *The Routledge Handbook of Epistemic Injustice*, edited by Ian James Kidd, José Medina, and Gaile Pohlhaus Jr., 61–69. New York: Routledge.

Coady, David. 2019. "The Trouble with 'Fake News.'" *Social Epistemology Review and Reply Collective* 8 (10): 40–52.

Code, Lorraine. 1987. *Epistemic Responsibility*. Hanover, NH: Published for Brown University Press by University Press of New England.
Code, Lorraine. 1995. *Rhetorical Spaces: Essays on Gendered Locations*. New York: Routledge.
Code, Lorraine. 2006. *Ecological Thinking: The Politics of Epistemic Location*. New York: Oxford University Press.
Coleman, Gabriella. 2014. *Hacker, Hoaxer, Whistleblower, Spy: The Many Faces of Anonymous*. New York: Verso.
Collins, Ben, and Joseph Cox. 2017. "Jenna Abrams, Russia's Clown Troll Princess, Duped the Mainstream Media and the World." *The Daily Beast*, November 3, 2017. https://www.thedailybeast.com/jenna-abrams-russias-clown-troll-princess-duped-the-mainstream-media-and-the-world.
Collins, Patricia Hill. 1986. "Learning from the Outsider Within: The Sociological Significance of Black Feminist Thought." *Social Problems* 33 (6): S14–32. https://doi.org/10.2307/800672.
"Community Standards." n.d. Facebook. Accessed April 1, 2018. https://www.facebook.com/communitystandards/#hate-speech.
Constine, Josh, and Sarah Buhr. 2016. "Facebook Now Directly Denies Report of Biased Trends, Says There's No Evidence." *TechCrunch* (blog). May 9, 2016. http://social.techcrunch.com/2016/05/09/facebook-workers/.
Cope, Sophia, Jillian York, and Jeremy Gillula. 2017. "Industry Efforts to Censor Pro-Terrorism Online Content Pose Risks to Free Speech." Electronic Frontier Foundation. July 12, 2017. https://www.eff.org/deeplinks/2017/07/industry-efforts-censor-pro-terrorism-online-content-pose-risks-free-speech.
Cox, Chris. 2014. "Facebook Status Update." October 1, 2014. https://www.facebook.com/chris.cox/posts/10101301777354543.
Crash Override Network. n.d. "Crash Override Network // Online Abuse Helpline and Advocacy Organization." Accessed January 31, 2019. http://www.crashoverridenetwork.com/index.html.
Crasnow, Sharon. 2013. "Feminist Philosophy of Science: Values and Objectivity." *Philosophy Compass* 8 (4): 413–23. https://doi.org/10.1111/phc3.12023.
Crawford, Kate, and Tarleton Gillespie. 2016. "What Is a Flag for? Social Media Reporting Tools and the Vocabulary of Complaint." *New Media & Society* 18 (3): 410–28. https://doi.org/10.1177/1461444814543163.
D'Ancona, Matthew. 2017. "There Must Be Free Speech, Even for Milo Yiannopoulos." *The Guardian*, February 6, 2017. http://www.theguardian.com/commentisfree/2017/feb/06/free-speech-milo-yiannopoulos-alt-right-far-right.
Daniels, Jessie. 2009a. *Cyber Racism: White Supremacy Online and the New Attack on Civil Rights*. Lanham, MD: Rowman & Littlefield.
Daniels, Jessie. 2009b. "Cloaked Websites: Propaganda, Cyber-Racism and Epistemology in the Digital Era." *New Media & Society* 11 (5): 659–83. https://doi.org/10.1177/1461444809105345.
Daniels, Jessie. 2013. "Race and Racism in Internet Studies: A Review and Critique." *New Media & Society* 15 (5): 695–719. https://doi.org/10.1177/1461444812462849.
Daniels, Jessie. 2015. "'My Brain Database Doesn't See Skin Color': Color-Blind Racism in the Technology Industry and in Theorizing the Web." *American Behavioral Scientist* 59 (11): 1377–93. https://doi.org/10.1177/0002764215578728.

Daukas, Nancy. 2006. "Epistemic Trust and Social Location." *Episteme: A Journal of Social Epistemology* 3 (1): 109–24.

Daukas, Nancy. 2011. "Altogether Now: A Virtue-Theoretic Approach to Pluralism in Feminist Epistemology." In *Feminist Epistemology and Philosophy of Science*, edited by Heidi E. Grasswick, 45–67. New York: Springer.

Davis, Angela. 1972. "Reflections on the Black Woman's Role in the Community of Slaves." *The Massachusetts Review* 13 (1/2): 81–100.

Davis, Emmalon. 2016. "Typecasts, Tokens, and Spokespersons: A Case for Credibility Excess as Testimonial Injustice." *Hypatia* 31 (3): 485–501. https://doi.org/10.1111/hypa.12251.

Davis, Emmalon. 2018. "On Epistemic Appropriation." *Ethics* 128 (4): 702–27. https://doi.org/10.1086/697490.

Davis, Jenny L. 2012. "Accomplishing Authenticity in a Labor-Exposing Space." *Computers in Human Behavior* 28 (5): 1966–73. https://doi.org/10.1016/j.chb.2012.05.017.

Davis, Jenny L., and Nathan Jurgenson. 2014. "Context Collapse: Theorizing Context Collusions and Collisions." *Information, Communication & Society* 17 (4): 476–85. https://doi.org/10.1080/1369118X.2014.888458.

Dickey, Megan Rose. 2016. "Facebook Temporarily Banned a Social Justice Activist for Commenting on Racism." *TechCrunch* (blog). December 22, 2016. http://social.techcrunch.com/2016/12/22/facebook-ban-leslie-mac/.

DiResta, Renée. 2020. "Virus Experts Aren't Getting the Message Out." *The Atlantic*, May 6, 2020. https://www.theatlantic.com/ideas/archive/2020/05/health-experts-dont-understand-how-information-moves/611218/.

DiResta, Renée, Kris Shaffer, Becky Ruppel, David Sullivan, Robert Matney, Ryan Fox, Jonathan Albright, and Ben Johnson. 2018. "The Tactics & Tropes of the Internet Research Agency." New Knowledge. https://cdn2.hubspot.net/hubfs/4326998/ira-report-rebrand_FinalJ14.pdf.

Domino, Jenny. 2020. "Why Facebook's Oversight Board Is Not Diverse Enough." Just Security. May 21, 2020. https://www.justsecurity.org/70301/why-facebooks-oversight-board-is-not-diverse-enough/.

Domonoske, Camila. 2016. "Students Have 'Dismaying' Inability to Tell Fake News from Real, Study Finds." NPR.Org. November 23, 2016. http://www.npr.org/sections/thetwo-way/2016/11/23/503129818/study-finds-students-have-dismaying-inability-to-tell-fake-news-from-real.

Donovan, Joan. 2020. "Social-Media Companies Must Flatten the Curve of Misinformation." *Nature*, April. https://doi.org/10.1038/d41586-020-01107-z.

Donovan, Joan, and danah boyd. 2019. "Stop the Presses? Moving from Strategic Silence to Strategic Amplification in a Networked Media Ecosystem." *American Behavioral Scientist*, September, 1–18. https://doi.org/10.1177/0002764219878229.

Dotson, Kristie. 2011. "Tracking Epistemic Violence, Tracking Practices of Silencing." *Hypatia* 26 (2): 236–57. https://doi.org/10.1111/j.1527-2001.2011.01177.x.

Dotson, Kristie. 2012. "A Cautionary Tale: On Limiting Epistemic Oppression." *Frontiers: A Journal of Women Studies* 33 (1): 24–47.

Dotson, Kristie. 2014. "Conceptualizing Epistemic Oppression." *Social Epistemology* 28 (2): 115–38.

Douek, Evelyn. 2020. "What Kind of Oversight Board Have You Given Us?" The University of Chicago Law Review Online. May 11, 2020. https://lawreviewblog.uchicago.edu/2020/05/11/fb-oversight-board-edouek/.

Douglas, Heather E. 2009. *Science, Policy, and the Value-Free Ideal*. Pittsburgh: University of Pittsburgh Press.

Driver, Julia. 2000. "Moral and Epistemic Virtue." In *Knowledge, Belief, and Character: Readings in Virtue Epistemology*, edited by Guy Axtell, 123–34. New York: Rowman & Littlefield.

Driver, Julia. 2001. *Uneasy Virtue*. New York: Cambridge University Press.

Duarte, Natasha, and Emma Llansó. 2017. "Mixed Messages? The Limits of Automated Social Media Content Analysis." Center for Democracy & Technology. https://cdt.org/insights/mixed-messages-the-limits-of-automated-social-media-content-analysis/.

Duffy, Brooke Erin, and Emily Hund. 2015. "'Having It All' on Social Media: Entrepreneurial Femininity and Self-Branding Among Fashion Bloggers." *Social Media + Society* 1 (2): 1–11. https://doi.org/10.1177/2056305115604337.

Duguay, Stefanie. 2018. "Social Media's Breaking News: The Logic of Automation in Facebook Trending Topics and Twitter Moments." *Media International Australia* 166 (1): 20–33. https://doi.org/10.1177/1329878X17737407.

Dwoskin, Elizabeth, and Nitasha Tiku. 2020. "Facebook Sent Home Thousands of Human Moderators Due to the Coronavirus. Now the Algorithms Are in Charge." *Washington Post*, March 24, 2020. https://www.washingtonpost.com/technology/2020/03/23/facebook-moderators-coronavirus/.

Dwoskin, Elizabeth, Nitasha Tiku, and Heather Kelly. 2020. "Facebook to Start Policing Anti-Black Hate Speech More Aggressively than Anti-White Comments, Documents Show." *Washington Post*, December 3, 2020. https://www.washingtonpost.com/technology/2020/12/03/facebook-hate-speech/.

Eckersley, Peter, and Yomna Nasser. n.d. "Measuring the Progress of AI Research." Electronic Frontier Foundation. Accessed July 9, 2018. https://www.eff.org/files/AI-progress-metrics.html#Reading-Comprehension.

El Kassar, Nadja. 2018. "What Ignorance Really Is. Examining the Foundations of Epistemology of Ignorance." *Social Epistemology* 32 (5): 300–310. https://doi.org/10.1080/02691728.2018.1518498.

El Kassar, Nadja. 2020. "The Place of Intellectual Self-Trust in Theories of Epistemic Advantages." *Journal of Social Philosophy* 51 (1): 7–26. https://doi.org/10.1111/josp.12300.

Elgin, Catherine Z. 2017. *True Enough*. Cambridge, MA: MIT Press.

Elish, M. C., and danah boyd. 2018. "Situating Methods in the Magic of Big Data and AI." *Communication Monographs* 85 (1): 57–80.

Ess, Charles, and AoIR Ethics Committee. 2002. "Ethical Decision-Making and Internet Research: Recommendations from the AoIR Working Committee." https://aoir.org/reports/ethics.pdf.

"Facebook's Civil Rights Audit—Final Report." 2020. https://about.fb.com/wp-content/uploads/2020/07/Civil-Rights-Audit-Final-Report.pdf.

Fallis, Don. 2007. "Epistemic Value Theory and the Digital Divide." In *Information Technology and Social Justice*, edited by Emma Rooksby and John Weckert, 29–46. Hershey, PA: Idea Group.

Fallis, Don. 2011. "Wikipistemology." In *Social Epistemology: Essential Readings*, edited by Alvin I. Goldman and Dennis Whitcomb, 297–312. New York: Oxford University Press.

Fallis, Don, and Kay Mathiesen. 2019. "Fake News Is Counterfeit News." *Inquiry*, November, 1–20. https://doi.org/10.1080/0020174X.2019.1688179.

Farkas, Johan, and Jannick Schou. 2018. "Fake News as a Floating Signifier: Hegemony, Antagonism and the Politics of Falsehood." *Javnost–The Public* 25 (3): 298–314.

Farkas, Johan, Jannick Schou, and Christina Neumayer. 2018. "Platformed Antagonism: Racist Discourses on Fake Muslim Facebook Pages." *Critical Discourse Studies* 15 (5): 463–80. https://doi.org/10.1080/17405904.2018.1450276.

Fehr, Carla. 2011. "What Is in It for Me? The Benefits of Diversity in Scientific Communities." In *Feminist Epistemology and Philosophy of Science*, edited by Heidi E. Grasswick, 133–55. New York: Springer.

Fiesler, Casey, and Nicholas Proferes. 2018. "'Participant' Perceptions of Twitter Research Ethics." *Social Media + Society* 4 (1): https://doi.org/10.1177/2056305118763366.

Florini, Sarah. 2019. *Beyond Hashtags: Racial Politics and Black Digital Networks*. New York: New York University Press.

Foucault, Michel. 1978. *The History of Sexuality, Volume 1: An Introduction*. Translated by Alan Hurley. New York: Vintage Books.

franzke, aline shakti. 2020. "Feminist Research Ethics." In *Internet Research: Ethical Guidelines 3.0*, edited by aline shakti franzke, Anja Bechmann, Michael Zimmer, Charles Ess, and the Association of Internet Researchers, 64–75. https://aoir.org/reports/ethics3.pdf.

franzke, aline shakti, Anja Bechmann, Michael Zimmer, Charles Ess, and the Association of Internet Researchers. 2020. *Internet Research: Ethical Guidelines 3.0*. https://aoir.org/reports/ethics3.pdf.

Fraser, Nancy. 1990. "Rethinking the Public Sphere: A Contribution to the Critique of Actually Existing Democracy." *Social Text*, no. 25/26: 56–80. https://doi.org/10.2307/466240.

Freelon, Deen, Michael Bossetta, Chris Wells, Josephine Lukito, Yiping Xia, and Kirsten Adams. 2022. "Black Trolls Matter: Racial and Ideological Asymmetries in Social Media Disinformation." *Social Science Computer Review* 40 (3): 560–78.

Freelon, Deen, and Tetyana Lokot. 2020. "Russian Disinformation Campaigns on Twitter Target Political Communities across the Spectrum. Collaboration between Opposed Political Groups Might Be the Most Effective Way to Counter It." *Misinformation Review* 1 (1). https://dash.harvard.edu/handle/1/42401973.

Freelon, Deen, and Chris Wells. 2020. "Disinformation as Political Communication." *Political Communication* 37 (2): 145–56.

Frenkel, Sheera. 2016. "Renegade Facebook Employees Form Task Force to Battle Fake News." BuzzFeed. November 14, 2016. https://www.buzzfeed.com/sheerafrenkel/renegade-facebook-employees-form-task-force-to-battle-fake-n.

Fricker, Miranda. 2007. *Epistemic Injustice: Power and Ethics in Knowing*. New York: Oxford University Press.

Fricker, Miranda. 2016. "Epistemic Injustice and the Preservation of Ignorance." In *The Epistemic Dimensions of Ignorance*, edited by Rik Peels and Martijn Blaauw, 160–77. New York: Cambridge University Press.

Friedberg, Brian, and Joan Donovan. 2019. "On the Internet, Nobody Knows You're a Bot: Pseudoanonymous Influence Operations and Networked Social Movements." *Journal of Design and Science*, no. 6 (August). https://doi.org/10.21428/7808da6b.45957184.

Friedman, Jacklyn, Anita Sarkeesian, and Renee Bracey Sherman. n.d. "Speak Up & Stay Safe(r):—A Guide to Protecting Yourself from Online Harassment." Accessed January 31, 2019. https://onlinesafety.feministfrequency.com/en.

Friedman, Uri. 2011. "MacMaster Recasts Gay Girl in Damascus as Fiction." *The Atlantic*, June 23, 2011. https://www.theatlantic.com/international/archive/2011/06/macmaster-recasts-gay-girl-damascus-fiction/352076/.
Frost-Arnold, Karen. 2014a. "Imposters, Tricksters, and Trustworthiness as an Epistemic Virtue." *Hypatia* 29 (4): 790–807. https://doi.org/10.1111/hypa.12107.
Frost-Arnold, Karen. 2014b. "The Cognitive Attitude of Rational Trust." *Synthese* 191 (9): 1957–74. https://doi.org/10.1007/s11229-012-0151-6.
Frost-Arnold, Karen. 2014c. "Trustworthiness and Truth: The Epistemic Pitfalls of Internet Accountability." *Episteme* 11 (1): 63–81. http://dx.doi.org/10.1017/epi.2013.43.
Frost-Arnold, Karen. 2016a. "Social Media, Trust, and the Epistemology of Prejudice." *Social Epistemology: A Journal of Knowledge, Culture, and Policy* 30 (5–6): 513–31. https://doi.org/10.1080/02691728.2016.1213326.
Frost-Arnold, Karen. 2016b. "Willful Ignorance." *Metascience* 25 (2): 323–26. https://doi.org/10.1007/s11016-016-0068-7.
Frost-Arnold, Karen. 2018. "Wikipedia." In *Routledge Handbook of Applied Epistemology*, edited by David Coady and James Chase, 28–40. New York: Routledge.
Frost-Arnold, Karen. 2021. "The Epistemic Dangers of Context Collapse Online." In *Applied Epistemology*, edited by Jennifer Lackey, 437–56. New York: Oxford University Press.
Frye, Marilyn. 1983. *The Politics of Reality: Essays in Feminist Theory*. Trumansburg, NY: Crossing Press.
Fusco, Coco. 1995. *English Is Broken Here: Notes on Cultural Fusion in the Americas*. New York: New Press.
"Gay Girl in Damascus: Tom MacMaster Defends Blog Hoax." 2011. BBC News. June 13, 2011. http://www.bbc.co.uk/news/uk-scotland-13747761.
Gelfert, Axel. 2018. "Fake News: A Definition." *Informal Logic* 38 (1): 84–117.
Giddens, Anthony. 1990. *The Consequences of Modernity*. Stanford, CA: Stanford University Press.
Gillespie, Tarleton. 2010. "The Politics of 'Platforms.'" *New Media & Society* 12 (3): 347–64. https://doi.org/10.1177/1461444809342738.
Gillespie, Tarleton. 2018. "Facebook and YouTube Just Got More Transparent. What Do We See?" *Nieman Lab* (blog). May 3, 2018. http://www.niemanlab.org/2018/05/facebook-and-youtube-just-got-more-transparent-what-do-we-see/.
Global Internet Forum to Counter Terrorism. 2019. "About Our Mission." 2019. https://perma.cc/44V5-554U.
Goldman, Alvin I. 1992. *Liaisons: Philosophy Meets the Cognitive and Social Sciences*. Cambridge, MA: MIT Press.
Goldman, Alvin I. 1999. *Knowledge in a Social World*. New York: Clarendon Press.
Goldman, Alvin I. 2008. "The Social Epistemology of Blogging." In *Information Technology and Moral Philosophy*, edited by Jeroen van den Hoven and John Weckert, 111–22. New York: Cambridge University Press.
Goldman, Alvin I. 2011. "A Guide to Social Epistemology." In *Social Epistemology: Essential Readings*, edited by Alvin I. Goldman and Dennis Whitcomb, 11–37. New York: Oxford University Press.
Gorwa, Robert, Reuben Binns, and Christian Katzenbach. 2020. "Algorithmic Content Moderation: Technical and Political Challenges in the Automation of Platform Governance." *Big Data & Society*, February: 1–15 https://doi.org/10.1177/2053951719897945.

Gottfried, Jeffrey, and Elisa Shearer. 2016. "News Use across Social Media Platforms 2016." *Pew Research Center's Journalism Project* (blog). May 26, 2016. http://www.journalism.org/2016/05/26/news-use-across-social-media-platforms-2016/.

Govier, Trudy. 1997. *Social Trust and Human Communities*. Buffalo, NY: McGill-Queen's University Press.

Grasswick, Heidi E. 2004. "Individuals-in-Communities: The Search for a Feminist Model of Epistemic Subjects." *Hypatia* 19 (3): 85–120. https://doi.org/10.1111/j.1527-2001.2004.tb01303.x.

Grasswick, Heidi E. 2017. "Feminist Responsibilism, Situationism, and the Complexities of the Virtue of Trustworthiness." In *Epistemic Situationism*, edited by Abrol Fairweather and Mark Alfano, 216–34. Oxford: Oxford University Press.

Graves, Lucas. 2016. *Deciding What's True: The Rise of Political Fact-Checking in American Journalism*. New York: Columbia University Press.

Gray, Mary L., and Siddharth Suri. 2019. *Ghost Work: How to Stop Silicon Valley from Building a New Global Underclass*. New York: Houghton Mifflin Harcourt.

Greyson, Devon, Nicole Cooke, Amelia Gibson, and Heidi Julien. 2018. "Online Targeting of Researchers/Academics: Ethical Obligations and Best Practices." *PRA2 Proceedings of the Association for Information Science and Technology* 55 (1): 684–87.

Grimmelmann, James. 2018. "The Platform Is the Message." Presented at the Governance and Regulation of Internet Platforms, Washington, DC, Georgetown University Law Center, February 23. https://james.grimmelmann.net/files/articles/platform-message.pdf.

Gunn, Hanna, and Michael P. Lynch. 2021. "The Internet and Epistemic Agency." In *Applied Epistemology*, edited by Jennifer Lackey, 389–409. New York: Oxford University Press.

Habgood-Coote, Joshua. 2019. "Stop Talking about Fake News!" *Inquiry: An Interdisciplinary Journal of Philosophy* 62 (9–10): 1033–65.

Habgood-Coote, Joshua. 2020. "Fake News, Conceptual Engineering, and Linguistic Resistance: Reply to Pepp, Michaelson and Sterken, and Brown." *Inquiry*, May, 1–29. https://doi.org/10.1080/0020174X.2020.1758770.

Haimson, Oliver L., Avery Dame-Griff, Elias Capello, and Zahari Richter. 2021. "Tumblr Was a Trans Technology: The Meaning, Importance, History, and Future of Trans Technologies." *Feminist Media Studies* 21 (3): 345–61. https://doi.org/10.1080/14680777.2019.1678505.

Haimson, Oliver L., and Anna Lauren Hoffmann. 2016. "Constructing and Enforcing 'Authentic' Identity Online: Facebook, Real Names, and Non-Normative Identities." *First Monday* 21 (6). https://doi.org/10.5210/fm.v21i6.6791.

Halbwachs, Maurice. 1992. *On Collective Memory*. Edited and translated by Lewis A. Coser. Chicago: University of Chicago Press.

Hale, Jacob. 1997. "Suggested Rules for Non-Transsexuals Writing about Transsexuals, Transsexuality, Transsexualism, or Trans ____." 1997. https://sandystone.com/hale.rules.html.

Hamera, J. 2006. "Performance, Performativity, and Cultural Poiesis in Practices of Everyday Life." In *The Sage Handbook of Performance Studies*, edited by D.S. Madison and J Hamera, 46–64. Thousand Oaks, CA: Sage.

Hampton, Rachelle. 2019. "Years Ago, Black Feminists Worked Together to Unmask Twitter Trolls Posing as Women of Color. If Only More People Paid Attention." *Slate*

Magazine, April 23, 2019. https://slate.com/technology/2019/04/black-feminists-alt-right-twitter-gamergate.html.

Hara, Kotaro, Abi Adams, Kristy Milland, Saiph Savage, Chris Callison-Burch, and Jeffrey Bigham. 2017. "A Data-Driven Analysis of Workers' Earnings on Amazon Mechanical Turk." *ArXiv:1712.05796 [Cs]*, December. http://arxiv.org/abs/1712.05796.

Haraway, Donna. 1988. "Situated Knowledges: The Science Question in Feminism and the Privilege of Partial Perspective." *Feminist Studies* 14 (3): 575–99. https://doi.org/10.2307/3178066.

Hardiman, Alex. 2018. "Removing Trending from Facebook." *About Facebook* (blog). June 1, 2018. https://about.fb.com/news/2018/06/removing-trending/.

Harding, Sandra G. 1991. *Whose Science? Whose Knowledge? Thinking from Women's Lives*. Ithaca, NY: Cornell University Press.

Harding, Sandra G. 1992. "Rethinking Standpoint Epistemology: What Is 'Strong Objectivity?'" *The Centennial Review* 36 (3): 437–70.

Harding, Sandra G. 1995. "'Strong Objectivity': A Response to the New Objectivity Question." *Synthese* 104 (3): 331–49.

Harding, Sandra G. 2015. *Objectivity and Diversity: Another Logic of Scientific Research*. Chicago: The University of Chicago Press.

Hazlett, Allan. 2016. "The Civic Virtues of Skepticism, Intellectual Humility, and Intellectual Criticism." In *Intellectual Virtues and Education: Essays in Applied Virtue Epistemology*, edited by Jason Baehr, 71–92. New York: Routledge.

Heersmink, Richard. 2018. "A Virtue Epistemology of the Internet: Search Engines, Intellectual Virtues and Education." *Social Epistemology* 32 (1): 1–12. https://doi.org/10.1080/02691728.2017.1383530.

Heldke, Lisa. 1997. "In Praise of Unreliability." *Hypatia* 12 (3): 174–82. https://doi.org/10.1111/j.1527-2001.1997.tb00011.x.

Hendricks, Vincent F., and Pelle G. Hansen. 2014. *Infostorms: How to Take Information Punches and Save Democracy*. New York: Springer.

Herbert, Cassie. 2018. "Women in Philosophy: Online Misogyny and Our Profession." *Blog of the APA* (blog). July 4, 2018. https://blog.apaonline.org/2018/07/04/women-in-philosophy-online-misogyny-and-our-profession/.

Hicks, Daniel. 2011. "Is Longino's Conception of Objectivity Feminist?" *Hypatia* 26 (2): 333–51.

Hill, Benjamin Mako, and Aaron Shaw. 2013. "The Wikipedia Gender Gap Revisited: Characterizing Survey Response Bias with Propensity Score Estimation." *PLoS ONE* 8 (6): e65782. https://doi.org/10.1371/journal.pone.0065782.

Hoagland, Sarah Lucia. 1988. *Lesbian Ethics: Toward New Value*. Palo Alto, CA: Institute of Lesbian Studies.

Hoagland, Sarah Lucia. 2001. "Resisting Rationality." In *Engendering Rationalities*, edited by Nancy Tuana and Sandra Morgen, 125–50. Albany: State University of New York Press.

Hoagland, Sarah Lucia. 2007. "Denying Relationality: Epistemology and Ethics and Ignorance." In *Race and Epistemologies of Ignorance*, edited by Nancy Tuana and Shannon Sullivan, 95–118. Albany: State University of New York Press.

Hoffmann, Anna Lauren, and Anne Jonas. 2017. "Recasting Justice for Internet and Online Industry Research Ethics." In *Internet Research Ethics for the Social Age: New Challenges, Cases, and Contexts*, edited by Michael Zimmer and Katharina Kinder-Kurlanda, 3–18. New York: Peter Lang.

Honey, Minda. 2017. "When WaPo Steals Your Twitter Thread." The Establishment. April 10, 2017. https://theestablishment.co/when-wapo-steals-your-twitter-thread-b7c8e19ef32e.

Honeywell. 2018. "Staying Safe When You Say #MeToo." American Civil Liberties Union. February 12, 2018. https://www.aclu.org/blog/privacy-technology/internet-privacy/staying-safe-when-you-say-metoo.

hooks, bell. 1984. *Feminist Theory from Margin to Center*. Boston: South End Press.

Hoskins, Andrew, ed. 2018a. *Digital Memory Studies: Media Pasts in Transition*. New York: Routledge.

Hoskins, Andrew. 2018b. "Memory of the Multitude: The End of Collective Memory." In *Digital Memory Studies: Media Pasts in Transition*, edited by Andrew Hoskins, 85–109. New York: Routledge.

Howard, Philip N., Bharath Ganesh, Dimitra Liotsiou, John Kelly, and Camille François. 2018. "The IRA, Social Media and Political Polarization in the United States, 2012–2018." Computational Propaganda Research Project, University of Oxford. https://comprop.oii.ox.ac.uk/wp-content/uploads/sites/93/2018/12/IRA-Report-2018.pdf.

Ingraham, Christopher. 2020. "New Research Explores How Conservative Media Misinformation May Have Intensified the Severity of the Pandemic." *Washington Post*, June 25, 2020. https://www.washingtonpost.com/business/2020/06/25/fox-news-hannity-coronavirus-misinformation/.

Intemann, Kristen. 2010. "25 Years of Feminist Empiricism and Standpoint Theory: Where Are We Now?" *Hypatia* 25 (4): 778–96. https://doi.org/10.1111/j.1527-2001.2010.01138.x.

Intemann, Kristen. 2011. "Diversity and Dissent in Science: Does Democracy Always Serve Feminist Aims?" In *Feminist Epistemology and Philosophy of Science*, edited by Heidi E. Grasswick, 111–32. New York: Springer.

Intemann, Kristen. 2017. "Feminism, Values, and the Bias Paradox Why Value-Management Is Not Sufficient." In *Current Controversies in Values and Science*, edited by Kevin Christopher Elliott and Daniel Steel, 130–44. New York: Routledge.

"Internet Users in the World 2021." 2021. Statista. 2021. https://www.statista.com/statistics/617136/digital-population-worldwide/.

Irani, Lilly C., and M. Six Silberman. 2016. "Stories We Tell About Labor: Turkopticon and the Trouble with 'Design.'" In *Proceedings of the 2016 CHI Conference on Human Factors in Computing Systems*, 4573–86. New York: Association for Computing Machinery. https://dl.acm.org/doi/abs/10.1145/2858036.2858592.

Jack, Caroline. 2017. "Lexicon of Lies: Terms for Problematic Information." Data & Society Research Institute. https://datasociety.net/output/lexicon-of-lies/.

Jack, Caroline, Becca Lewis, and Kinjal Dave. 2018. "'Viewpoint Diversity' and the Illusion of an Impartial Center." *Medium* (blog). April 19, 2018. https://medium.com/@MediaManipulation/viewpoint-diversity-and-the-illusion-of-an-impartial-center-3bb69b949c8d.

Jaggar, Alison M. 1983. *Feminist Politics and Human Nature*. Totowa, NJ: Rowman & Allanheld.

Jaggar, Alison M. 1989. "Love and Knowledge: Emotion in Feminist Epistemology." *Inquiry* 32 (2): 151–76. https://doi.org/10.1080/00201748908602185.

Jaggar, Alison M. 2004. "Globalizing Feminist Ethics." In *Setting the Moral Compass: Essays by Women Philosophers*, edited by Cheshire Calhoun, 233–55. New York: Oxford University Press.

James, William. 2007. *The Will to Believe and Other Essays in Popular Philosophy*. New York: Cosimo.

Jeong, Sarah. 2015. *The Internet of Garbage*. Jersey City, NJ: Forbes.
Johnson, Amy. 2016. "The Multiple Harms of Sea Lions." In *Perspectives on Harmful Speech Online*, 13–15. Berkman Klein Center for Internet & Society. https://dash.harvard.edu/handle/1/33746096.
Johnson, Gabbrielle M. 2021. "Algorithmic Bias: On the Implicit Biases of Social Technology." *Synthese*, 198: 9941–61. https://doi.org/10.1007/s11229-020-02696-y.
Jones, Karen. 2002. "The Politics of Credibility." In *A Mind of One's Own: Feminist Essays on Reason and Objectivity*, edited by Louise Antony and Charlotte Witt, 154–76. Boulder, CO: Westview Press.
Jones, Karen. 2004. "Trust and Terror." In *Moral Psychology: Feminist Ethics and Social Theory*, edited by Peggy DesAutels and Margaret Urban Walker, 3–21. New York: Rowman & Littlefield.
Jones, Karen. 2012a. "The Politics of Intellectual Self-Trust." *Social Epistemology* 26 (2): 237–51.
Jones, Karen. 2012b. "Trustworthiness." *Ethics* 123 (1): 61–85.
Joseph, Tiffany D., and Laura E. Hirshfield. 2011. "'Why Don't You Get Somebody New to Do It?' Race and Cultural Taxation in the Academy." *Ethnic and Racial Studies* 34 (1): 121–41. https://doi.org/10.1080/01419870.2010.496489.
June, Audrey Williams. 2015. "The Invisible Labor of Minority Professors." *The Chronicle of Higher Education*, November 8, 2015. https://www.chronicle.com/article/The-Invisible-Labor-of/234098.
Kahn, Kimberly, Katherine Spencer, and Jack Glaser. 2013. "Online Prejudice and Discrimination: From Dating to Hating." In *The Social Net: Understanding Human Behavior in Cyberspace*, edited by Yair Amichai-Hamburger, 201–16. New York: Oxford University Press.
Kang, Cecilia. 2016. "Fake News Onslaught Targets Pizzeria as Nest of Child-Trafficking." *The New York Times*, November 21, 2016. https://www.nytimes.com/2016/11/21/technology/fact-check-this-pizzeria-is-not-a-child-trafficking-site.html.
Kantrowitz, Alex. 2016. "Mark Zuckerberg: I Know Many Conservatives Don't Trust Our Platform Is Unbiased." BuzzFeed. May 18, 2016. https://www.buzzfeed.com/alexkantrowitz/mark-zuckerberg-i-know-many-conservatives-dont-trust-our-pla.
Kantrowitz, Alex. 2017. "Facebook Says Pages Sharing Fake News Can't Buy Ads." BuzzFeed. August 28, 2017. https://www.buzzfeed.com/alexkantrowitz/facebook-cracks-down-on-fake-news-with-new-ad-rules.
Karp, David. 2011. "Behind the Scenes with David Karp." In *The Practice of Qualitative Research*, edited by S. Heese-Biber and P. Leavy, 2nd ed., 349–50. Thousand Oaks, CA: Sage.
Kawall, J. 2002. "Other–Regarding Epistemic Virtues." *Ratio* 15 (3): 257–75.
Kaye, David. 2019. *Speech Police: The Global Struggle to Govern the Internet*. New York: Columbia Global Reports.
Khondker, Habibul Haque. 2011. "Role of the New Media in the Arab Spring." *Globalizations* 8 (5): 675–79. https://doi.org/10.1080/14747731.2011.621287.
Kidd, Ian James. 2016. "Educating for Intellectual Humility." In *Intellectual Virtues and Education: Essays in Applied Virtue Epistemology*, edited by Jason Baehr, 54–70. New York: Routledge.
Kidd, Ian James, José Medina, and Gaile Pohlhaus Jr. 2017a. "Introduction to the Routledge Handbook of Epistemic Injustice." In *The Routledge Handbook of Epistemic

Injustice, edited by Ian James Kidd, José Medina, and Gaile Pohlhaus Jr., 1–9. New York: Routledge.

Kidd, Ian James, José Medina, and Gaile Pohlhaus Jr, eds. 2017b. *The Routledge Handbook of Epistemic Injustice*. New York: Routledge.

King, Hope. 2016. "Facebook Will Require Political Bias Training for All Employees." CNNMoney. June 23, 2016. https://money.cnn.com/2016/06/23/technology/facebook-political-bias-training/index.html.

Klonick, Kate. 2018. "The New Governors: The People, Rules, and Processes Governing Online Speech." *Harvard Law Review* 131 (6): 1599–670.

Klonick, Kate, and Thomas Kadri. 2018. "How to Make Facebook's 'Supreme Court' Work." *The New York Times*, November 17, 2018. https://www.nytimes.com/2018/11/17/opinion/facebook-supreme-court-speech.html?smid=nytcore-ios-share.

Koebler, Jason, and Emanuel Maiberg. 2019. "How Facebook Trains Content Moderators." *Motherboard* (blog). February 25, 2019. https://motherboard.vice.com/en_us/article/43z7gj/how-facebook-trains-content-moderators.

Kreps, Sarah, and Douglas Kriner. 2020. "Good News and Bad News about COVID-19 Misinformation." *Scientific American Blog Network* (blog). June 10, 2020. https://blogs.scientificamerican.com/observations/good-news-and-bad-news-about-covid-19-misinformation/.

Krimsky, Sheldon. 2003. *Science in the Private Interest: Has the Lure of Profits Corrupted Biomedical Research?* Lanham, MD: Rowman & Littlefield.

Kvanvig, Jonathan L. 2003. *The Value of Knowledge and the Pursuit of Understanding*. New York: Cambridge University Press.

Kvanvig, Jonathan L. 2005. "Truth Is Not the Primary Epistemic Goal." In *Contemporary Debates in Epistemology*, edited by Matthias Steup, John Turri, and Ernest Sosa, 285–96. New York: Blackwell.

Laat, Paul B. de. 2008. "Online Diaries: Reflections on Trust, Privacy, and Exhibitionism." *Ethics and Information Technology* 10 (1): 57–69. http://dx.doi.org/10.1007/s10676-008-9155-9.

Lacey, Hugh. 2005. *Is Science Value Free? Values and Scientific Understanding*. New York: Routledge.

LaPlante, Rochelle. 2017. "CCM Workers: Tales from the Moderation Screen." Presented at the All Things in Moderation Conference, University of California, Los Angeles, December 7. https://atm-ucla2017.net/.

Lazar, Shira. 2011. "'A Gay Girl in Damascus' Bravely Blogs and Builds Online Following from Syria." CBS News. May 6, 2011. http://www.cbsnews.com/8301-504943_162-20060462-10391715.html.

Lee, Emily S. 2011. "The Epistemology of the Question of Authenticity, in Place of Strategic Essentialism." *Hypatia* 26 (2): 258–79. https://doi.org/10.1111/j.1527-2001.2011.01165.x.

Levy, Neil. 2017. "The Bad News about Fake News." *Social Epistemology Review and Reply Collective* 6 (8): 20–36.

Levy, Steven. 2020. "Facebook Names the 20 People Who Can Overrule Mark Zuckerberg." *Wired*, May 6, 2020. https://www.wired.com/story/facebook-names-20-people-overrule-mark-zuckerberg/.

Liao, Shen-yi, and Bryce Huebner. 2021. "Oppressive Things." *Philosophy and Phenomenological Research* 103 (1): 92–113. https://doi.org/10.1111/phpr.12701.

Llansó, Emma. 2020. "Understanding Automation and the Coronavirus Infodemic: What Data Is Missing?" *Center for Democracy and Technology* (blog). April 22, 2020.

https://cdt.org/insights/understanding-automation-and-the-coronavirus-infodemic-what-data-is-missing/.

Llansó, Emma, Joris van Hoboken, Paddy Leerssen, and Jaron Harambam. 2020. "Artificial Intelligence, Content Moderation, and Freedom of Expression." Transatlantic Working Group on Content Moderation Online and Freedom of Expression. https://www.ivir.nl/publicaties/download/AI-Llanso-Van-Hoboken-Feb-2020.pdf.

Lloyd, Elisabeth A. 1995. "Objectivity and the Double Standard for Feminist Epistemologies." *Synthese: An International Journal for Epistemology, Methodology and Philosophy of Science* 104 (3): 351–81.

Longino, Helen E. 1990. *Science as Social Knowledge: Values and Objectivity in Scientific Inquiry*. Princeton, NJ: Princeton University Press.

Longino, Helen E. 2002. *The Fate of Knowledge*. Princeton, NJ: Princeton University Press.

Lorde, Audre. 1984. *Sister Outsider: Essays and Speeches*. Berkeley, CA: Crossing Press.

Lorenz, Taylor. 2017. "Facebook Is Banning Women for Calling Men 'Scum.'" *The Daily Beast*, December 4, 2017. https://www.thedailybeast.com/women-are-getting-banned-from-facebook-for-calling-men-scum.

Lugones, María. 2003. *Pilgrimages/Peregrinajes: Theorizing Coalition against Multiple Oppressions*. New York: Rowman & Littlefield.

Lugones, María, and Elizabeth Spelman. 1983. "Have We Got a Theory for You! Feminist Theory, Cultural Imperialism and the Demand for 'the Woman's Voice.'" *Women's Studies International Forum* 6 (6): 573–81. https://doi.org/10.1016/0277-5395(83)90019-5.

Lynch, Michael P. 2018. "Fake News and the Internet Shell Game." *The New York Times*, January 20, 2018. https://www.nytimes.com/2016/11/28/opinion/fake-news-and-the-internet-shell-game.html.

Lynch, Michael P. 2019. *Know-It-All Society: Truth and Arrogance in Political Culture*. New York: Liveright.

MacAulay, Maggie, and Marcos Daniel Moldes. 2016. "Queen Don't Compute: Reading and Casting Shade on Facebook's Real Names Policy." *Critical Studies in Media Communication* 33 (1): 6–22. https://doi.org/10.1080/15295036.2015.1129430.

MacMaster, Tom. 2011. "'A Gay Girl in Damascus': An Illusion: Apology to Readers." *A Gay Girl in Damascus* (blog). June 13, 2011. http://damascusgaygirl.blogspot.com/2011/06/apology-to-readers_13.html.

Markham, Annette. 2008. "How Can Qualitative Researchers Produce Work That Is Meaningful across Time, Space, and Culture?" In *Internet Inquiry: Conversations about Method*, edited by Annette Markham and Nancy K. Baym, 131–55. Los Angeles: Sage.

Markham, Annette. 2012. "Fabrication as Ethical Practice: Qualitative Inquiry in Ambiguous Internet Contexts." *Information, Communication & Society* 15 (3): 334–53.

Markham, Annette, Elizabeth A. Buchanan, and AoIR Ethics Committee. 2012. "Ethical Decision-Making and Internet Research: Recommendations from the AoIR Ethics Working Committee (Version 2.0)." Association of Internet Researchers. https://aoir.org/reports/ethics2.pdf.

Marwick, Alice E. 2015. *Status Update: Celebrity, Publicity, and Branding in the Social Media Age*. New Haven, CT: Yale University Press.

Marwick, Alice E, Lindsay Blackwell, and Katherine Lo. 2016. "Best Practices for Conducting Risky Research and Protecting Yourself from Online Harassment." New York: Data & Society Research Institute. https://datasociety.net/pubs/res/Best_Practices_for_Conducting_Risky_Research-Oct-2016.pdf.

Marwick, Alice E., and danah boyd. 2011. "I Tweet Honestly, I Tweet Passionately: Twitter Users, Context Collapse, and the Imagined Audience." *New Media & Society* 13 (1): 114–33. https://doi.org/10.1177/1461444810365313.

Marwick, Alice E., and Rebecca Lewis. 2017. "Media Manipulation and Disinformation Online." Data & Society Research Institute. https://datasociety.net/output/media-manipulation-and-disinfo-online/.

Mason, Rebecca. 2011. "Two Kinds of Unknowing." *Hypatia* 26 (2): 294–307. https://doi.org/10.1111/j.1527-2001.2011.01175.x.

Massanari, Adrienne L. 2018. "Rethinking Research Ethics, Power, and the Risk of Visibility in the Era of the 'Alt-Right' Gaze." *Social Media + Society* 4 (2): 1–9. https://doi.org/10.1177/2056305118768302.

Matamoros-Fernández, Ariadna. 2017. "Platformed Racism: The Mediation and Circulation of an Australian Race-Based Controversy on Twitter, Facebook and YouTube." *Information, Communication & Society* 20 (6): 930–46. https://doi.org/10.1080/1369118X.2017.1293130.

Matthews, Paul, and Judith Simon. 2012. "Evaluating and Enriching Online Knowledge Exchange: A Socio-Epistemological Perspective." In *Virtual Communities, Social Networks and Collaboration*, edited by Athina Lazakidou, 35–59. New York: Springer.

McGarity, Thomas O., and Wendy Wagner. 2010. *Bending Science: How Special Interests Corrupt Public Health Research*. Cambridge, MA: Harvard University Press.

McKee, Heidi A., and James E. Porter. 2009. *The Ethics of Internet Research: A Rhetorical, Case-Based Process*. New York: Peter Lang.

McKinney, Rachel Ann. 2016. "Extracted Speech." *Social Theory & Practice* 42 (2): 258–84. https://doi.org/10.5840/soctheorpract201642215.

McKinnon, Rachel. 2017. "Allies Behaving Badly: Gaslighting as Epistemic Injustice." In *The Routledge Handbook of Epistemic Injustice*, edited by Ian James Kidd, José Medina, and Gaile Pohlhaus Jr., 167–74. New York: Routledge.

McLeod, Kembrew. 2020a. "An Interview with the Yes Men." In *Fake News: Understanding Media and Misinformation in the Digital Age*, edited by Melissa Zimdars and Kembrew McLeod, 307–14. Cambridge, MA: The MIT Press.

McLeod, Kembrew. 2020b. "An Oral History of the Yes Men." In *Fake News: Understanding Media and Misinformation in the Digital Age*, edited by Melissa Zimdars and Kembrew McLeod, 209–306. Cambridge, MA: The MIT Press.

McMillan Cottom, Tressie. 2016. "Twitter's New @Replies Re-Design Isn't Just Stupid; It's Really Stupid." Medium. October 30, 2016. https://medium.com/@tressiemcphd/twitters-new-replies-re-design-isn-t-just-stupid-it-s-really-stupid-c471ca254f0a#.15w402250.

Medina, José. 2011. "The Relevance of Credibility Excess in a Proportional View of Epistemic Injustice: Differential Epistemic Authority and the Social Imaginary." *Social Epistemology* 25 (1): 15–35.

Medina, José. 2012. "Hermeneutical Injustice and Polyphonic Contextualism: Social Silences and Shared Hermeneutical Responsibilities." *Social Epistemology* 26 (2): 201–20.

Medina, José. 2013. *The Epistemology of Resistance: Gender and Racial Oppression, Epistemic Injustice, and Resistant Imaginations*. New York: Oxford University Press.

Medina, José. 2016. "Ignorance and Racial Insensitivity." In *The Epistemic Dimensions of Ignorance*, edited by Rik Peels and Martijn Blaauw, 178–201. New York: Cambridge University Press.

Medina, José. 2017. "Varieties of Hermeneutical Injustice." In *The Routledge Handbook of Epistemic Injustice*, edited by Ian James Kidd, José Medina, and Gaile Pohlhaus Jr., 41–52. New York: Routledge.

Meeder, Brendan, Jennifer Tam, Patrick Gage Kelley, and Lorrie Faith Cranor. 2010. "RT @IWantPrivacy: Widespread Violation of Privacy Settings in the Twitter Social Network." Paper presented at *Web 2.0 Security and Privacy Workshop, IEEE Symposium on Security and Privacy*, Oakland, CA. http://www.cs.cmu.edu/~bmeeder/papers/Meeder-SNSP2010.pdf.

Mejia, Robert, Kay Beckermann, and Curtis Sullivan. 2018. "White Lies: A Racial History of the (Post)Truth." *Communication and Critical/Cultural Studies* 15 (2): 109–26. https://doi.org/10.1080/14791420.2018.1456668.

Merrill, Jeremy B., and Will Oremus. 2021. "Five Points for Anger, One for a 'Like': How Facebook's Formula Fostered Rage and Misinformation." *Washington Post*, October 26, 2021. https://www.washingtonpost.com/technology/2021/10/26/facebook-angry-emoji-algorithm/.

Metzger, Miriam J., Andrew J. Flanagin, and Ryan B. Medders. 2010. "Social and Heuristic Approaches to Credibility Evaluation Online." *Journal of Communication* 60 (3): 413–39. https://doi.org/10.1111/j.1460-2466.2010.01488.x.

Miller, Boaz. 2021. "Is Technology Value-Neutral?" *Science, Technology, & Human Values* 46 (1): 53–80. https://doi.org/10.1177/0162243919900965.

Miller, Boaz, and Isaac Record. 2013. "Justified Belief in a Digital Age: On the Epistemic Implications of Secret Internet Technologies." *Episteme* 10 (2): 117–34. https://doi.org/10.1017/epi.2013.11.

Mills, Charles. 1997. *The Racial Contract*. Ithaca, NY: Cornell University Press.

Mills, Charles. 2007. "White Ignorance." In *Race and Epistemologies of Ignorance*, edited by Nancy Tuana and Shannon Sullivan, 26–31. Albany, NY: SUNY Press.

Mills, Charles. 2018. "Global White Ignorance." In *Routledge International Handbook of Ignorance Studies*, edited by Matthias Gross and Linsey McGoey, 217–27. New York: Routledge.

Mohanty, Chandra Talpade. 2003. "Under Western Eyes: Feminist Scholarship and Colonial Discourses." In *Feminism without Borders: Decolonizing Theory, Practicing Solidarity*, 17–42. Durham, NC: Duke University Press.

Morales, Lymari. 2011. "Majority in U.S. Continues to Distrust the Media, Perceive Bias." Gallup.Com. September 22, 2011. https://news.gallup.com/poll/149624/Majority-Continue-Distrust-Media-Perceive-Bias.aspx.

Mukerji, Nikil. 2018. "What Is Fake News?" *Ergo, an Open Access Journal of Philosophy* 5 (35). http://dx.doi.org/10.3998/ergo.12405314.0005.035.

Murphy, Carla. 2015. "Can 'Black Wikipedia' Take Off Like 'Black Twitter'?" Colorlines. February 4, 2015. http://www.colorlines.com/articles/can-black-wikipedia-take-black-twitter.

Mustafaraj, Eni, and Panagiotis Takis Metaxas. 2017. "The Fake News Spreading Plague: Was It Preventable?" *ArXiv:1703.06988 [Cs]*, March. http://arxiv.org/abs/1703.06988.

Nakamura, Lisa. 1995. "Race In/For Cyberspace: Textual Performance and Racial Passing on the Internet." *Works and Days* 13 (1/2): 181–93.

Nakamura, Lisa. 2002. *Cybertypes: Race, Ethnicity, and Identity on the Internet*. New York: Routledge.

Nakamura, Lisa. 2011. "Syrian Lesbian Bloggers, Fake Geishas, and the Attractions of Identity Tourism." July 15, 2011. https://hyphenmagazine.com/blog/2011/07/syrian-lesbian-bloggers-fake-geishas-and-attractions-identity-tourism.

Nakamura, Lisa. 2015. "The Unwanted Labour of Social Media: Women of Colour Call Out Culture as Venture Community Management." *New Formations* 86 (Winter): 106–12. https://doi.org/info:doi/10.3898/NEWF.86.06.2015.

Nassar, Daniel. 2011a. "From Damascus with Love: Blogging in a Totalitarian State." LGBT Asylum News. June 12, 2011. http://madikazemi.blogspot.com/2011/06/from-damascus-with-love-blogging-in.html.

Nassar, Daniel. 2011b. "Foreign Policy: Damascus Still Has Gay Girls." NPR.Org. June 17, 2011. http://www.npr.org/2011/06/16/137217280/foreign-policy-damascus-still-has-gay-girls.

"New TSA Policy Codifies Discrimination Against Transgender People." 2016. *National LGBTQ Task Force* (blog). March 5, 2016. https://www.thetaskforce.org/new-tsa-policy-codifies-discrimination-against-transgender-people/.

Newton, Casey. 2019a. "The Secret Lives of Facebook Moderators in America." The Verge. February 25, 2019. https://www.theverge.com/2019/2/25/18229714/cognizant-facebook-content-moderator-interviews-trauma-working-conditions-arizona.

Newton, Casey. 2019b. "Facebook Will Increase Pay for Its Contractors in North America." The Verge. May 13, 2019. https://www.theverge.com/2019/5/13/18617997/facebook-moderator-pay-raise-contractor-content-working-conditions.

Newton, Casey. 2020. "Facebook Will Pay $52 Million in Settlement with Moderators Who Developed PTSD on the Job." The Verge. May 12, 2020. https://www.theverge.com/2020/5/12/21255870/facebook-content-moderator-settlement-scola-ptsd-mental-health.

Nguyen, C. Thi. 2020. "Echo Chambers and Epistemic Bubbles." *Episteme* 17 (2): 141–61. https://doi.org/10.1017/epi.2018.32.

Nguyen, C. Thi. 2021. "How Twitter Gamifies Communication." In *Applied Epistemology*, edited by Jennifer Lackey, 410–36. New York: Oxford University Press.

Nickerson, Raymond S. 1998. "Confirmation Bias: A Ubiquitous Phenomenon in Many Guises." *Review of General Psychology* 2 (2): 175–220. http://dx.doi.org/10.1037/1089-2680.2.2.175.

Nissenbaum, Helen. 2004. "Privacy as Contextual Integrity." *Washington Law Review* 79: 119–57.

Nissenbaum, Helen. 2010. *Privacy in Context: Technology, Policy, and the Integrity of Social Life*. Stanford, CA: Stanford Law Books.

Noble, Safiya Umoja. 2013. "Google Search: Hyper-Visibility as a Means of Rendering Black Women and Girls Invisible." *InVisible Culture; Rochester*, no. 19 (Fall). https://search.proquest.com/docview/1771536966/abstract/4D987D0E30204B9DPQ/1.

Noble, Safiya Umoja. 2017. "CCM Workers: Tales from the Moderation Screen." Presented at the All Things in Moderation Conference, University of California, Los Angeles, December 7. https://atm-ucla2017.net/.

Noble, Safiya Umoja. 2018. *Algorithms of Oppression: How Search Engines Reinforce Racism*. New York: New York University Press.

Nunez, Michael. 2016a. "Want to Know What Facebook Really Thinks of Journalists? Here's What Happened When It Hired Some." Gizmodo. May 3, 2016. http://gizmodo.com/want-to-know-what-facebook-really-thinks-of-journalists-1773916117.

Nunez, Michael. 2016b. "Former Facebook Workers: We Routinely Suppressed Conservative News." Gizmodo. May 9, 2016. http://gizmodo.com/former-facebook-workers-we-routinely-suppressed-conser-1775461006.
Nussbaum, Martha Craven. 1999. *Sex & Social Justice*. New York: Oxford University Press.
Nyhan, Brendan, and Jason Reifler. 2010. "When Corrections Fail: The Persistence of Political Misperceptions." *Political Behavior* 32 (2): 303–30. https://doi.org/10.2307/40587320.
O'Connor, Cailin, and James Owen Weatherall. 2018. *The Misinformation Age: How False Beliefs Spread*. New Haven, CT: Yale University Press.
Ohlheiser, Abby. 2013. "Sorry, No, Playboy Didn't Write an Anti-Rape College Guide." The Wire. September 17, 2013. http://www.thewire.com/national/2013/09/sorry-no-playboy-didnt-write-anti-rape-college-guide/69525/.
Okereke, Caleb, and Stephanie Burari. 2020. "She Was Cropped out of a Photo of White Climate Activists. Now, She Says It's Time to Stop Erasing African Voices." CNN. February 5, 2020. https://www.cnn.com/2020/01/30/africa/uganda-activist-vanessa-nakate-cropped-intl/index.html.
Ollman, Dan, Sarah Price, and Chris Smith. 2003. *The Yes Men*. United Artists.
Oreskes, Naomi, and Erik M. Conway. 2010. *Merchants of Doubt: How a Handful of Scientists Obscured the Truth on Issues from Tobacco Smoke to Global Warming*. New York: Bloomsbury Press.
Ortega, Mariana. 2006. "Being Lovingly, Knowingly Ignorant: White Feminism and Women of Color." *Hypatia* 21 (3): 56–74. https://doi.org/10.1111/j.1527-2001.2006.tb01113.x.
"Oversight Board." n.d. Accessed June 22, 2020. https://www.oversightboard.com/.
Papacharissi, Zizi. 2016. "Affective Publics and Structures of Storytelling: Sentiment, Events and Mediality." *Information, Communication & Society* 19 (3): 307–24. https://doi.org/10.1080/1369118X.2015.1109697.
Pariser, Eli. 2011. *The Filter Bubble: How the New Personalized Web Is Changing What We Read and How We Think*. London: Penguin Books.
Pellegrino, Edmund D., Robert M. Veatch, and John Langan, eds. 1991. *Ethics, Trust, and the Professions: Philosophical and Cultural Aspects*. Washington, DC: Georgetown University Press.
Pepp, Jessica, Eliot Michaelson, and Rachel Sterken. 2019a. "What's New about Fake News?" *Journal of Ethics and Social Philosophy* 16 (2): 67–94. https://doi.org/10.26556/jesp.v16i2.629.
Pepp, Jessica, Eliot Michaelson, and Rachel Sterken. 2019b. "Why We Should Keep Talking about Fake News." *Inquiry*, November, 1–17. https://doi.org/10.1080/0020174X.2019.1685231.
Pew Research Center. 2014. "Online Harassment." http://assets.pewresearch.org/wp-content/uploads/sites/14/2014/10/PI_OnlineHarassment_72815.pdf.
Phillips, Whitney. 2015a. *This Is Why We Can't Have Nice Things: Mapping the Relationship between Online Trolling and Mainstream Culture*. Cambridge, MA: The MIT Press.
Phillips, Whitney. 2015b. "We're the Reason We Can't Have Nice Things on the Internet." *Quartz* (blog). December 29, 2015. https://qz.com/582113/were-the-reason-we-cant-have-nice-things-online/.
Phillips, Whitney. 2018. "The Oxygen of Amplification." Data & Society Research Institute. https://datasociety.net/output/oxygen-of-amplification/.

Phillips, Whitney, Jessica Beyer, and Gabriella Coleman. 2017. "Trolling Scholars Debunk the Idea That the Alt-Right's Shitposters Have Magic Powers." Motherboard. March 22, 2017. https://www.vice.com/en_us/article/z4k549/trolling-scholars-debunk-the-idea-that-the-alt-rights-trolls-have-magic-powers.

Phillips, Whitney, and Ryan M. Milner. 2017. *The Ambivalent Internet: Mischief, Oddity, and Antagonism Online*. Malden, MA: Polity.

Phillips, Whitney, and Ryan M. Milner. 2020. *You Are Here: Mapping Network Pollution*. Cambridge, MA: MIT Press. https://you-are-here.pubpub.org/.

Pohlhaus Jr., Gaile. 2012. "Relational Knowing and Epistemic Injustice: Toward a Theory of Willful Hermeneutical Ignorance." *Hypatia* 27 (4): 715–35. https://doi.org/10.1111/j.1527-2001.2011.01222.x.

Pohlhaus Jr., Gaile. 2017. "Varieties of Epistemic Injustice." In *The Routledge Handbook of Epistemic Injustice*, edited by Ian James Kidd, José Medina, and Gaile Pohlhaus Jr., 13–26. New York: Routledge.

Potter, Nancy Nyquist. 2002. *How Can I Be Trusted? A Virtue Theory of Trustworthiness*. Lanham, MD: Rowman & Littlefield.

Powers, Elia. 2017. "My News Feed Is Filtered?" *Digital Journalism*, February. http://www.tandfonline.com/doi/abs/10.1080/21670811.2017.1286943.

Proctor, Robert. 1995. *Cancer Wars: How Politics Shapes What We Know and Don't Know about Cancer*. New York: Basic Books.

Proctor, Robert, and Londa L. Schiebinger, eds. 2008. *Agnotology: The Making and Unmaking of Ignorance*. Stanford, CA: Stanford University Press.

Punsmann, Burcu Gültekin. 2018. "Three Months in Hell: What I Learned from Three Months of Content Moderation for Facebook in Berlin." *SZ Magazin*, January 6, 2018. https://sz-magazin.sueddeutsche.de/internet/three-months-in-hell-84381.

Quinn, Zoë. 2017. *Crash Override: How Gamergate (Nearly) Destroyed My Life, and How We Can Win the Fight against Online Hate*. New York: PublicAffairs.

Rachels, James. 1975. "Why Privacy Is Important." *Philosophy & Public Affairs* 4 (4): 323–33.

Rashid, Neha. 2017. "The Emergence of the White Troll behind a Black Face." NPR.Org. March 21, 2017. https://www.npr.org/sections/codeswitch/2017/03/21/520522240/the-emergence-of-the-white-troll-behind-a-black-face.

Read, Max. 2011. "'A Gay Girl in Damascus' Is Actually a Married Guy in Edinburgh." Gawker. June 12, 2011. http://gawker.com/5811169/a-gay-girl-in-damascus-is-actually-a-married-guy-in-edinburgh.

Reilly, Ian. 2013. "From Critique to Mobilization: The Yes Men and the Utopian Politics of Satirical Fake News." *International Journal of Communication* 7: 1243–64.

Ridder, Jeroen de. 2019. "So What If 'Fake News' Is Fake News?" *Social Epistemology Review and Reply Collective* 8 (10): 111–13.

Rini, Regina. 2017. "Fake News and Partisan Epistemology." Kennedy Institute of Ethics Journal. July 20, 2017. https://kiej.georgetown.edu/fake-news-partisan-epistemology/.

Ritzer, George, and Nathan Jurgenson. 2010. "Production, Consumption, Prosumption: The Nature of Capitalism in the Age of the Digital 'Prosumer.'" *Journal of Consumer Culture* 10 (1): 13–36. https://doi.org/10.1177/1469540509354673.

Roberts, David. 2017. "America Is Facing an Epistemic Crisis." Vox. November 2, 2017. https://www.vox.com/policy-and-politics/2017/11/2/16588964/america-epistemic-crisis.

Roberts, Robert Campbell, and W. Jay Wood. 2007. *Intellectual Virtues: An Essay in Regulative Epistemology*. New York: Oxford University Press.

Roberts, Sarah T. 2014. "Behind the Screen: The Hidden Digital Labor of Commercial Content Moderation." PhD Thesis, University of Illinois at Urbana-Champaign.

Roberts, Sarah T. 2016. "Digital Refuse: Canadian Garbage, Commercial Content Moderation and the Global Circulation of Social Media's Waste." *Wi: Journal of Mobile Media* 10 (1): 1–18.

Roberts, Sarah T. 2017a. "Content Moderation." In *Encyclopedia of Big Data*, 1–4. Cham, Switzerland: Springer International. https://doi.org/10.1007/978-3-319-32001-4_44-1.

Roberts, Sarah T. 2017b. "Social Media's Silent Filter." *The Atlantic*, March 8, 2017. https://www.theatlantic.com/technology/archive/2017/03/commercial-content-moderation/518796/.

Roberts, Sarah T. 2017c. "CCM Workers: Tales from the Moderation Screen." Presented at the All Things in Moderation Conference, University of California, Los Angeles, December 7. https://atm-ucla2017.net/.

Roberts, Sarah T. 2018. "Digital Detritus: 'Error' and the Logic of Opacity in Social Media Content Moderation." *First Monday* 23 (3). http://firstmonday.org/ojs/index.php/fm/article/view/8283.

Roberts, Sarah T. 2019. *Behind the Screen: Content Moderation in the Shadows of Social Media*. New Haven, CT: Yale University Press.

Roberts, Sarah T. 2020. "Over*Flow: Digital Humanity: Social Media Content Moderation and the Global Tech Workforce in the COVID-19 Era." *FLOW* (blog). March 19, 2020. https://www.flowjournal.org/2020/03/digital-humanity/.

Robson, James. 2017. "Participant Anonymity and Participant Observations: Situating the Researcher within Digital Ethnography." In *Internet Research Ethics for the Social Age: New Challenges, Cases, and Contexts*, edited by Michael Zimmer and Katharina Kinder-Kurlanda, 195–202. New York: Peter Lang.

Rolin, Kristina. 2006. "The Bias Paradox in Feminist Standpoint Epistemology." *Episteme: A Journal of Social Epistemology* 3 (1): 125–36.

Rolin, Kristina. 2017. "Can Social Diversity Best Be Incorporated into Science by Adopting the Social Value-Management Ideal?" In *Current Controversies in Values and Science*, edited by Kevin Christopher Elliott and Daniel Steel, 113–29. New York: Routledge.

Rooney, Phyllis. 2011. "The Marginalization of Feminist Epistemology and What That Reveals About Epistemology 'Proper.'" In *Feminist Epistemology and Philosophy of Science*, edited by Heidi E. Grasswick, 3–24. New York: Springer.

Roose, Kevin, and Kate Conger. 2019. "YouTube to Remove Thousands of Videos Pushing Extreme Views." *The New York Times*, June 5, 2019. https://www.nytimes.com/2019/06/05/business/youtube-remove-extremist-videos.html.

Rosenberg, Eli. 2018. "Trump Admitted He Attacks Press to Shield Himself from Negative Coverage, Lesley Stahl Says." *Washington Post*, May 22, 2018. https://www.washingtonpost.com/news/the-fix/wp/2018/05/22/trump-admitted-he-attacks-press-to-shield-himself-from-negative-coverage-60-minutes-reporter-says/.

Russell, Camisha. 2019. "On Black Women, 'In Defense of Transracialism,' and Imperial Harm." *Hypatia* 34 (2): 176–94. https://doi.org/10.1111/hypa.12470.

Salisbury, Meredith, and Jefferson D. Pooley. 2017. "The #nofilter Self: The Contest for Authenticity among Social Networking Sites, 2002–2016." *Social Sciences* 6 (1): 10. https://doi.org/10.3390/socsci6010010.

Sample, Ruth J. 2003. *Exploitation: What It Is and Why It's Wrong*. Lanham, MD: Rowman & Littlefield.

"Santa Clara Principles on Transparency and Accountability in Content Moderation." 2018. Santa Clara Principles. 2018. https://santaclaraprinciples.org/.

Sap, Maarten, Dallas Card, Saadie Gabriel, Yejin Choi, and Noah A. Smith. 2019. "The Risk of Racial Bias in Hate Speech Detection." In *Proceedings of the 57th Annual Meeting of the Association for Computational Linguistics*, 1668–78. Florence, Italy.

Scheman, Naomi. 2001. "Epistemology Resuscitated: Objectivity as Trustworthiness." In *Engendering Rationalities*, edited by Nancy Tuana and Sandra Morgen, 23–52. Albany: State University of New York Press.

"Search FYI: An Update to Trending." 2016. *Facebook Newsroom* (blog). August 26, 2016. https://newsroom.fb.com/news/2016/08/search-fyi-an-update-to-trending/.

Sedgwick, Eve Kosofsky. 1990. *Epistemology of the Closet*. Berkeley: University of California Press.

Sessions, Lauren F. 2009. "'You Looked Better on MySpace': Deception and Authenticity on the Web 2.0." *First Monday* 14 (7). https://doi.org/10.5210/fm.v14i7.2539.

Shao, Chengcheng, Giovanni Luca Ciampaglia, Onur Varol, Kai-Cheng Yang, Alessandro Flammini, and Filippo Menczer. 2018. "The Spread of Low-Credibility Content by Social Bots." *Nature Communications* 9 (1): 1–9. https://doi.org/10.1038/s41467-018-06930-7.

Shayne, Julie. 2017. "The Importance of Recognizing Faculty for Their Emotional Support of Students." Inside Higher Education. September 15, 2017. https://www.insidehighered.com/advice/2017/09/15/importance-recognizing-faculty-their-emotional-support-students-essay.

Sherman, Benjamin R, and Stacey Goguen. 2019. *Overcoming Epistemic Injustice: Social and Psychological Perspectives*. Lanham, MD: Roman & Littlefield.

Shu, Kai, Amy Sliva, Suhang Wang, Jiliang Tang, and Huan Liu. 2017. "Fake News Detection on Social Media: A Data Mining Perspective." *ACM SIGKDD Explorations Newsletter* 19 (1): 22–36. https://doi.org/10.1145/3137597.3137600.

Siapera, Eugenia. 2019. "Organised and Ambient Digital Racism: Multidirectional Flows in the Irish Digital Sphere." *Open Library of the Humanities* 5 (1): 13.

Silverman, Craig. 2016a. "These Two Teenagers Keep Fooling the Internet with Justin Trudeau Hoaxes." BuzzFeed. August 9, 2016. https://www.buzzfeed.com/craigsilverman/teen-trudeau-hoaxes.

Silverman, Craig. 2016b. "Facebook Must Either Innovate or Admit Defeat at the Hands of Fake News Hoaxsters." BuzzFeedNews. August 30, 2016. https://www.buzzfeed.com/craigsilverman/how-facebook-fell-into-a-fake-news-trap-of-its-own-making?utm_term=.eaJ4LLkngz#.wr9E55VKwa.

Silverman, Craig. 2016c. "Here's Why Facebook's Trending Algorithm Keeps Promoting Fake News." BuzzFeed. October 26, 2016. https://www.buzzfeed.com/craigsilverman/can-facebook-trending-fight-off-fake-news.

Silverman, Craig, and Lawrence Alexander. 2016. "How Teens in the Balkans Are Duping Trump Supporters with Fake News." BuzzFeed. November 3, 2016. https://www.buzzfeed.com/craigsilverman/how-macedonia-became-a-global-hub-for-pro-trump-misinfo.

Silverman, Craig, Lauren Strapagiel, Hamza Shaban, Ellie Hall, and Jeremy Singer-Vine. 2016. "Hyperpartisan Facebook Pages Are Publishing False and Misleading

Information at an Alarming Rate." BuzzFeed. October 20, 2016. https://www.buzzfeed.com/craigsilverman/partisan-fb-pages-analysis.

Simon, Judith. 2015. "Distributed Epistemic Responsibility in a Hyperconnected Era." In *The Onlife Manifesto: Being Human in a Hyperconnected Era*, edited by Luciano Floridi, 145–59. New York: Springer. https://doi.org/10.1007/978-3-319-04093-6_17.

Simpson, Thomas W. 2012. "Evaluating Google as an Epistemic Tool." *Metaphilosophy* 43 (4): 426–45. https://doi.org/10.1111/j.1467-9973.2012.01759.x.

Sinders, Caroline. 2018. "Machine Learning Harassment." XYZ. June 27, 2018. https://xyz.informationactivism.org/en/machine-learning-harassment.

Singh, Spandana. 2019. "Everything in Moderation." New America. http://newamerica.org/oti/reports/everything-moderation-analysis-how-internet-platforms-are-using-artificial-intelligence-moderate-user-generated-content/.

Solomon, Miriam. 2006. "Norms of Epistemic Diversity." *Episteme* 3 (1): 23–36.

Solon, Olivia. 2017. "Underpaid and Overburdened: The Life of a Facebook Moderator." *The Guardian*, May 25, 2017. http://www.theguardian.com/news/2017/may/25/facebook-moderator-underpaid-overburdened-extreme-content.

Spelman, Elizabeth V. 1991. *Inessential Woman: Problems of Exclusion of Feminist Thought*. Boston: Beacon Press.

Spelman, Elizabeth V. 2007. "Managing Ignorance." In *Race and Epistemologies of Ignorance*, edited by Shannon Sullivan and Nancy Tuana, 119–31. Albany: State University of New York Press.

Spivak, Gayatri Chakravorty. 1988. "Can the Subaltern Speak?" In *Marxism and the Interpretation of Culture*, edited by Cary Nelson and Lawrence Grossberg, 271–316. Urbana: University of Illinois Press.

Squires, Catherine R. 2002. "Rethinking the Black Public Sphere: An Alternative Vocabulary for Multiple Public Spheres." *Communication Theory* 12 (4): 446–68. https://doi.org/10.1111/j.1468-2885.2002.tb00278.x.

Starr, Terrell Jermaine. 2017. "How Russia Used Racism to Hack White Voters." The Root. August 9, 2017. http://www.theroot.com/how-russia-used-racism-to-hack-white-voters-1797582833.

Steele, Catherine Knight. 2018. "Black Bloggers and Their Varied Publics: The Everyday Politics of Black Discourse Online." *Television & New Media* 19 (2): 112–27. https://doi.org/10.1177/1527476417709535.

Stern, Susannah R. 2008. "A Response to Malin Sveningsson." In *Internet Inquiry: Conversations about Method*, edited by Annette N. Markham and Nancy K. Baym, 94–98. Los Angeles: Sage.

Subramanian, Samanth. 2017. "Meet the Macedonian Teens Who Mastered Fake News and Corrupted the US Election." *Wired*, February 15, 2017. https://www.wired.com/2017/02/veles-macedonia-fake-news/.

Sullivan, Shannon. 2006. *Revealing Whiteness: The Unconscious Habits of Racial Privilege*. Bloomington: Indiana University Press.

Sullivan, Shannon, and Nancy Tuana. 2012. *Race and Epistemologies of Ignorance*. Albany: State University of New York Press.

Sunstein, Cass R. 2006. *Infotopia: How Many Minds Produce Knowledge*. New York: Oxford University Press.

Sunstein, Cass R. 2008. "Democracy and the Internet." In *Information Technology and Moral Philosophy*, edited by Jeroen van den Hoven and John Weckert, 93–110. New York: Cambridge University Press.

Sveningsson, Malin. 2004. "Ethics in Internet Ethnography." In *Readings in Virtual Research Ethics: Issues and Controversies*, edited by Elizabeth A. Buchanan, 45–61. Hershey, PA: Information Science.

Swift, Art. 2016. "Americans' Trust in Mass Media Sinks to New Low." Gallup.Com. September14,2016.http://news.gallup.com/poll/195542/americans-trust-mass-media-sinks-new-low.aspx.

Swire-Thompson, Briony, Joseph DeGutis, and David Lazer. 2020. "Searching for the Backfire Effect: Measurement and Design Considerations." *Journal of Applied Research in Memory and Cognition* 9 (3): 286–99. https://doi.org/10.1016/j.jarmac.2020.06.006.

Swisher, Kara. 2020. "Can a Facebook Oversight Board Push Back the Ocean?" *The New York Times*, May 6, 2020. https://www.nytimes.com/2020/05/06/opinion/facebook-independent-oversight-board.html?auth=login-google.

Taber, Jane. 2009. "Environment Canada Hit by 'Damn Clever' Climate Stunt." *The Globe and Mail*, December 14, 2009. https://www.theglobeandmail.com/news/politics/ottawa-notebook/environment-canada-hit-by-damn-clever-climate-stunt/article1346364/.

Terranova, Tiziana. 2000. "Free Labor: Producing Culture for the Digital Economy." *Social Text* 18 (2): 33–58.

Thagard, Paul. 1997. "Collaborative Knowledge." *Noûs* 31 (2): 242–61. https://doi.org/10.1111/0029-4624.00044.

The Onlife Initiative. 2015. "The Onlife Manifesto." In *The Onlife Manifesto: Being Human in a Hyperconnected Era*, edited by Luciano Floridi, 7–13. New York: Springer. https://doi.org/10.1007/978-3-319-04093-6_2.

The Telegraph. 2011. "'A Gay Girl in Damascus': How the Hoax Unfolded." June 17, 2011. http://www.telegraph.co.uk/news/worldnews/middleeast/syria/8572884/A-Gay-Girl-in-Damascus-how-the-hoax-unfolded.html.

Thériault, Anne. 2015. "The Dubious Ethics of Twitter Mining." The Establishment. November 4, 2015. https://theestablishment.co/the-dubious-ethics-of-twitter-mining-ce13e56e9fcb.

Timberg, Craig, and Elizabeth Dwoskin. 2017. "Russian Content on Facebook, Google and Twitter Reached Far More Users than Companies First Disclosed, Congressional Testimony Says." *Washington Post*, October 30, 2017. https://www.washingtonpost.com/business/technology/2017/10/30/4509587e-bd84-11e7-97d9-bdab5a0ab381_story.html.

Tirosh, Noam. 2017. "Reconsidering the 'Right to Be Forgotten'—Memory Rights and the Right to Memory in the New Media Era." *Media, Culture & Society* 39 (5): 644–60. https://doi.org/10.1177/0163443716674361.

Todd, Bridget. n.d. "How Black Women Tried to Save Twitter." There Are No Girls on the Internet. https://www.tangoti.com/ep004-how-black-women-tried-to-save-twitter.

Toole, Briana. 2019. "From Standpoint Epistemology to Epistemic Oppression." *Hypatia* 34 (4): 598–618. https://doi.org/10.1111/hypa.12496.

Townley, Cynthia. 2006. "Toward a Revaluation of Ignorance." *Hypatia* 21 (3): 37–55. https://doi.org/10.1111/j.1527-2001.2006.tb01112.x.

Townsend, Leanne, and Claire Wallace. n.d. "Social Media Research: A Guide to Ethics." http://www.dotrural.ac.uk/socialmediaresearchethics.pdf.

"Trending Review Guidelines." 2016. Facebook Newsrooms. https://fbnewsroomus.files.wordpress.com/2016/08/trending-review-guidelines.pdf.

Tripodi, Francesca. 2018. "Searching for Alternative Facts." Data & Society Research Institute. https://datasociety.net/output/searching-for-alternative-facts/.
Truth, Sojourner. 2010. "Ain't I a Woman?" In *Feminist Theory: A Reader*, edited by Wendy K. Kolmar and Frances Bartkowski, 3rd ed., 75. New York: McGraw-Hill.
Tuana, Nancy. 2004. "Coming to Understand: Orgasm and the Epistemology of Ignorance." *Hypatia* 19 (1): 194–232.
Tucker, Ian. 2013. "Evgeny Morozov: 'We Are Abandoning All the Checks and Balances.'" *The Guardian*, March 9, 2013. http://www.theguardian.com/technology/2013/mar/09/evgeny-morozov-technology-solutionism-interview.
Tucker, Joshua Aaron, Andrew Guess, Pablo Barbera, Cristian Vaccari, Alexandra Siegel, Sergey Sanovich, Denis Stukal, and Brendan Nyhan. 2018. "Social Media, Political Polarization, and Political Disinformation: A Review of the Scientific Literature." William & Flora Hewlett Foundation. https://hewlett.org/wp-content/uploads/2018/03/Social-Media-Political- Polarization-and-Political-Disinformation-Literature-Review.pdf.
Tufekci, Zeynep. 2017. *Twitter and Tear Gas: The Power and Fragility of Networked Protest*. New Haven, CT: Yale University Press.
Tufekci, Zeynep. 2018. "How Social Media Took Us from Tahrir Square to Donald Trump." *MIT Technology Review*. https://www.technologyreview.com/2018/08/14/240325/how-social-media-took-us-from-tahrir-square-to-donald-trump/.
Tynan, Dan. 2016. "How Facebook Powers Money Machines for Obscure Political 'News' Sites." *The Guardian*, August 24, 2016. http://www.theguardian.com/technology/2016/aug/24/facebook-clickbait-political-news-sites-us-election-trump.
Uski, Suvi, and Airi Lampinen. 2016. "Social Norms and Self-Presentation on Social Network Sites: Profile Work in Action." *New Media & Society* 18 (3): 447–64. https://doi.org/10.1177/1461444814543164.
Vaidhyanathan, Siva. 2012. *The Googlization of Everything: And Why We Should Worry*. Updated edition. Berkeley: University of California Press.
Vaidhyanathan, Siva. 2018. *Antisocial Media: How Facebook Disconnects Us and Undermines Democracy*. New York: Oxford University Press.
Vaidhyanathan, Siva. 2020. "Facebook and the Folly of Self-Regulation." *Wired*, May 9, 2020. https://www.wired.com/story/facebook-and-the-folly-of-self-regulation/.
Vallor, Shannon. 2016. *Technology and the Virtues: A Philosophical Guide to a Future Worth Wanting*. New York: Oxford University Press.
Vimes, Benny. 2016. "Invasion of the Cisgender Heterosexuals." *Scrappy Deviation* (blog). August 14, 2016. http://the-orbit.net/scrappy/2016/08/14/invasion-cisgender-heterosexuals/.
Wagner, Kurt. 2016. "Facebook Refutes Gizmodo Report That It Was Censoring Conservative News." Recode. May 10, 2016. https://web.archive.org/web/20160511122206/http://www.recode.net/2016/5/10/11647738/facebook-refutes-gizmodo-report-that-it-was-censoring-conservative-news.
Walker, Margaret Urban. 2006. *Moral Repair: Reconstructing Moral Relations after Wrongdoing*. New York: Cambridge University Press.
Wanderer, Jeremy. 2017. "Varieties of Testimonial Injustice." In *The Routledge Handbook of Epistemic Injustice*, edited by Ian James Kidd, José Medina, and Gaile Pohlhaus Jr., 27–40. New York: Routledge.
Watson, Lani. 2016. "Why Should We Educate for Inquisitiveness?" In *Intellectual Virtues and Education: Essays in Applied Virtue Epistemology*, edited by Jason Baehr, 38–53. New York: Routledge.

Watts, Clint. 2017. *Statement Prepared for the U.S. Senate Select Committee on Intelligence Hearing: "Disinformation: A Primer in Russian Active Measures and Influence Campaigns."* https://www.intelligence.senate.gov/sites/default/files/documents/os-cwatts-033017.pdf.

West, Sarah Myers. 2017. "Raging Against the Machine: Network Gatekeeping and Collective Action on Social Media Platforms." *Media and Communication* 5 (3): 28–36.

"What Is the WTO?" n.d. Accessed August 9, 2020. https://www.wto.org/english/thewto_e/thewto_e.htm.

"What Names Are Allowed on Facebook?" n.d. Facebook Help Center. Accessed June 3, 2019. https://www.facebook.com/help/112146705538576.

"What Types of ID Does Facebook Accept?" n.d. Facebook Help Center. Accessed June 3, 2019. https://www.facebook.com/help/159096464162185?helpref=faq_content.

Whittle, Stephen. 1998. "The Trans-Cyberian Mail Way." *Social & Legal Studies* 7 (3): 389–408.

Williams, Matthew L, Pete Burnap, and Luke Sloan. 2017. "Towards an Ethical Framework for Publishing Twitter Data in Social Research: Taking into Account Users' Views, Online Context and Algorithmic Estimation." *Sociology* 51 (6): 1149–68. https://doi.org/10.1177/0038038517708140.

Williams, Patricia J. 1995. *The Alchemy of Race and Rights.* Cambridge, MA: Harvard University Press.

Winner, Langdon. 1980. "Do Artifacts Have Politics?" *Daedalus* 109 (1): 121–36.

Wittkower, Dylan Eric. 2016. "Lurkers, Creepers, and Virtuous Interactivity: From Property Rights to Consent and Care as a Conceptual Basis for Privacy Concerns and Information Ethics." *First Monday* 21 (10). http://firstmonday.org/ojs/index.php/fm/article/view/6948.

Wu, Tim. 2016. *The Attention Merchants: The Epic Scramble to Get inside Our Heads.* New York: Alfred A. Knopf.

Wylie, Alison. 2003. "Why Standpoint Matters." In *Science and Other Cultures: Issues in Philosophies of Science and Technology,* edited by Robert Figueroa and Sandra G. Harding, 26–48. New York: Routledge.

Yan, Holly, Sheena Jones, and Steve Almasy. 2017. "Chicago Torture Video: 4 Charged with Hate Crimes, Kidnapping." CNN. January 5, 2017. http://www.cnn.com/2017/01/05/us/chicago-facebook-live-beating/index.html.

Yiannopoulos, Milo. 2016. "Why Women Should Leave the Internet." Breitbart. July 5, 2016. https://www.breitbart.com/milo/2016/07/05/solution-online-harassment-simple-women-log-off/.

York, Jillian. 2018. "More Than Words: The Complexities of Platforms Responding to Online Harassment." XYZ. May 9, 2018. https://xyz.informationactivism.org/en/more-than-words-complexities-platforms-responding-online-harassment.

York, Jillian. 2021. *Silicon Values: The Future of Free Speech under Surveillance Capitalism.* Brooklyn: Verso Books.

Young, Iris. 2001. "The Five Faces of Oppression." In *Readings for Diversity and Social Justice,* edited by Maurianne Adams, Warren J. Blumenfeld, Rosie Castañeda, Heather W. Hackman, Madeline L. Peters, and Ximena Zúñiga, 35–49. New York: Routledge.

Young, Virginia Alvino. 2020. "Nearly Half of the Twitter Accounts Discussing 'Reopening America' May Be Bots." Carnegie Mellon School of Computer Science. May 20, 2020. https://www.scs.cmu.edu/news/nearly-half-twitter-accounts-discussing-reopening-america-may-be-bots.

Zagzebski, Linda Trinkaus. 1996. *Virtues of the Mind: An Inquiry into the Nature of Virtue and the Ethical Foundations of Knowledge.* New York: Cambridge University Press.

Zimmer, Michael. 2010. "'But the Data Is Already Public': On the Ethics of Research in Facebook." *Ethics and Information Technology* 12 (4): 313–25. http://dx.doi.org/10.1007/s10676-010-9227-5.

Zimmer, Michael. 2018a. "Addressing Conceptual Gaps in Big Data Research Ethics: An Application of Contextual Integrity." *Social Media + Society* 4 (2): 1–11 https://doi.org/10.1177/2056305118768300.

Zimmer, Michael. 2018b. "How Contextual Integrity Can Help Us with Research Ethics in Pervasive Data." *Medium* (blog). July 25, 2018. https://medium.com/pervade-team/how-contextual-integrity-can-help-us-with-research-ethics-in-pervasive-data-ef633c974cc1.

Zimmer, Michael, and Nicholas John Proferes. 2014. "A Topology of Twitter Research: Disciplines, Methods, and Ethics." *Aslib Journal of Information Management* 66 (3): 250–61. http://dx.doi.org/10.1108/AJIM-09-2013-0083.

Zuckerman, Ethan. 2011. "Understanding #amina." *My Heart's in Accra* (blog). June 13, 2011. http://www.ethanzuckerman.com/blog/2011/06/13/understanding-amina/.

Zuckerman, Ethan. 2017. "Stop Saying 'Fake News'. It's Not Helping." *My Heart's in Accra* (blog). January 30, 2017. http://www.ethanzuckerman.com/blog/2017/01/30/stop-saying-fake-news-its-not-helping/.

Index

For the benefit of digital users, indexed terms that span two pages (e.g., 52–53) may, on occasion, appear on only one of those pages.

4chan, 71–72
2016 US presidential election
    Clinton's online supporters during, 127
    Facebook and, 127, 141, 148–49
    fake news and, 112–13, 115–16, 122–24, 126, 128, 141–42
    Russian interference in, 71–72, 112–13, 115–16, 128, 141
    Trump's online supporters during, 126–27
    Twitter and, 127–28, 141
2020 US presidential election, 4–5

Adair, Cassius, 221–22
algorithms
    bias and, 66–68, 157
    content moderation and, 39n.4, 63–70, 198–99, 204–5
    ethical limitations of, 69
    Facebook and, 121, 148–50, 152–54, 156–57, 198–99, 204
    fake news and, 113, 121, 123–24, 127, 152–54, 156–57
    Google and, 121, 148–50, 152–54, 156–57, 198–99, 204
    lack of transparency regarding, 144–45, 198–99
    ontological expansiveness and, 198–99
    racism perpetuated by, 142–44
    technological limitations of, 68–69
    Twitter and, 66, 121
allies and allyship, 172–74, 191, 193–94, 198–99
alt-right groups, 124–25, 140–41, 146, 159–60
Anansi, 97

Arab Spring (2011)
    A Gay Girl in Damascus blog hoax and, 1–2, 71, 78–79, 85–86, 107–8, 133–34
    social media's positive impact during, 80–81, 85–86, 87–88
    Syria's authoritarian regime and, 85–86
    Western media's reliance on social media to cover, 107–8
Aristotle, 94–95, 96–97, 99, 192–93, 219
Arraf, Amina Abdullah, 1–2, 71. *See also* MacMaster, Tom
artificial intelligence (AI), 41–42, 66, 68–69. *See also* algorithms
authenticity. *See also* imposture; trickery
    amateurism and, 83
    blog audiences and, 86–87
    consistency and, 83–85, 88, 93–94, 95–96
    corporate interests and, 93
    epistemic harms of, 73, 82–83, 84, 88–94, 95–96, 205–6
    epistemic value of, 73, 84–88, 93
    "epistemology of outing" and, 90–91
    experimentation foreclosed by norms of, 91–92, 93–94, 95
    Facebook's "real-name" policy and, 88–90
    imposture's violation of, 82, 83–84
    investigative accountability and, 90–91
    online authenticity and, 82–84, 86–87, 88–91
    prescriptive norms of, 82
    privacy and, 91, 95–96
    protective function of, 84
    sharing of personal details and, 83
    spontaneity and, 83

256 INDEX

authenticity (*cont.*)
  surveillance cultures' preoccupation
    with, 89–90, 93–94, 95, 203–4
  testimonial injustice and, 85
  trickery and, 97
  trust and, 85, 87
  trustworthiness and, 84, 95–96, 205
  virtue epistemology and, 95–97

Baehr, Jason, 20–22, 187–88, 189–90
Baier, Annette, 82, 184–85
Bailey, Alison, 17–18, 225
Banet-Weiser, Sarah, 82
Beckermann, Kay, 135–36
Belgian Congo atrocities, 139–40
Belsky, Marcia, 29
Benkler, Yochai, 115, 127
Berenstain, Nora, 50, 62, 170–71
#BernieSoBlack, 181–82
betrayal
  ability to detect, 87
  epistemic benefits of, 99–101, 109–11
  epistemic harms of, 87–88, 99
  trickery and, 98–101
  trust and, 87–88, 99–100, 109–10
Bhopal disaster (1984), 102–3
Bichlbaum, Andy, 102–3, 106, 108–9, 110.
  See also Yes Men
"Black Lives Matter Kidnapping"
  (#BLMKidnapping, 2017), 112–13,
  124, 141, 143–44
Black Lives Matter movement, 4–5, 59–
  60, 181–82
Black Twitter, 107–8, 146, 169–70, 177,
  185–86, 217–18
Blackwell, Lindsay, 216–17, 219–20
Bonanno, Mike, 102–3, 104–5. *See also*
  Yes Men
bots, 71–72, 113, 122–23, 146
Bowden, Rasalyn, 52
boyd, danah, 82, 126–27, 141–42, 211–12
Brexit vote (United Kingdom,
  2016), 112–13
Brock, André, 39, 169–70, 185n.5
Bruckman, Amy, 216, 218–19
Buchanan, Elizabeth, 213
Burnap, Pete, 211–12, 216–17
Butler, Judith, 92

Canada, 56–57, 104, 106–7
Cardeno, Ryan, 49
Cartesian epistemology, 7–8, 25, 136–39,
  146–47, 203
Chadwick, Andrew, 4, 116–17
Chandia, Kodili, 104
Chun, Wendy, 90–91
The Cleaners (documentary film), 41–42
Clinton, Hillary, 141–42
Coady, David, 115–17
Code, Lorraine, 7–8
Coleman, Gabriella, 97
commercial content moderation (CCM).
  See also content moderation
  algorithms and, 63–70
  Amazon Mechanical Turk as source of
    workers for, 41–43, 53–54, 67–68
  The Cleaners documentary film
    about, 41–42
  conditions among workers engaged in,
    30–32, 41–44, 45–46, 48–50, 52–54,
    63–65, 69–70, 204–5
  COVID-19 epidemic's impact on, 68–69
  digital capitalism and, 30, 44, 203–5
  epistemic injustice and, 30–31, 44, 49–
    56, 63–65, 203–5
  epistemic trash and, 56–57, 63–65, 204–5
  epistemologies of ignorance and, 55–
    56, 204–5
  Facebook and, 29–30, 38–39, 41–42,
    43n.5, 45–48, 49, 54, 69, 148–54,
    156–57, 158–61, 162, 204
  global nature of online communication
    and, 42–44
  The Philippines as source of workers
    engaged in, 31–32, 41, 48–49, 56–57
  post-traumatic stress disorder among
    workers engaged in, 30, 48–49, 52
  terrorism-related content and, 49, 66
  Twitter and, 31, 47, 66
  virtue epistemology and, 30–31, 44–45
confirmation bias, 86–87, 119–21, 136–
  37, 141
content moderation. *See also* commercial
  content moderation (CCM)
  algorithms and, 39n.4, 63–70, 198–
    99, 204–5
  ambiguity of online content and, 35

censorship debates regarding, 32
definition of, 29–30
epistemic dumping and, 26, 56–57
epistemic injustice and, 25–26, 203
flagging of content performed by users and, 33–35, 66, 89–90
gender discrimination and, 29
hermeneutical justice and, 24–26, 36–41, 43–44, 45–48, 66–68, 203, 204–5
interactive objectivity and, 154–57, 161
"Nazi Problem" and, 158–62
racism and, 29, 34–35, 38–39, 158
sexual harassment and, 35–36
testimonial justice and, 25–26, 35–36, 38–39, 43–44, 45–46, 66–68, 204–5
virtue epistemology and, 30–33, 35, 44–45, 48, 204–5
context collapse, 211–14
COP15 hoax (Copenhagen UN Climate Change Conference, 2015), 104–6
COVID-19 pandemic, 1, 68–69, 71–72, 112–13
Cox, Chris, 96
Crawford, Kate, 33–34
cyborgs, 122–23

"Daily Me," 127, 144–45
Daniels, Jessie, 142–43
Davis, Emmalon, 62, 199–200, 221, 222–23
Delgado, Didi, 29, 38–39
Descartes, René. *See* Cartesian epistemology
digital capitalism
    commercial content moderation and, 30, 44, 203–5
    corporate social media monopolies and, 12–13
    epistemic appropriation and, 222
    epistemologies of ignorance and, 16–17
    fake news and, 123–25, 131–32, 142–43, 203–4
    internet epistemology and, 4–5, 12–13, 16–17
    misogyny and, 117–18, 142–43
    racism and, 117–18, 142–43
digital detritus, 30, 56–57, 65
Doctrine of the Mean, 95, 99, 190, 192–93

Dotson, Kristie, 16, 24, 36–37, 40, 183
Douglas, Heather, 150–52, 154
Dow Chemical, 72, 102–3
Driver, Julia, 22

enclave publics, 182–83
#EndFathersDay, 71–72, 108n.11
endingthefed.com, 153
epistemic appropriation, 23–24, 199–201, 204, 210, 221–23
epistemic dumping, ix–x, 26, 56–58, 60–65
epistemic injustice
    ally epistemology and, 173–74
    Cartesian epistemology and, 25
    commercial content moderation and, 30–31, 44, 49–56, 63–65, 203–5
    definition of, 23–24, 63
    epistemic agential injustices and, 50
    epistemic dumping and, 61–63
    epistemic labor exploitation and, 50–56, 51n.6
    hermeneutical injustice, 24–26, 36–37, 40, 59–60
    knowledge production and, 50
    testimonial injustice and, 24, 25–26, 173–74
    testimonial smothering and, 24
epistemic trash
    in academic contexts, 57–58, 61–64
    conspiracy theories as, 60
    definition of, 57–59
    epistemic dumping and, 26, 56–57, 60–65
    false beliefs as, 59–60
    homophobia and transphobia as, 61–62
    interest relativity and, 59–60
    moral trash compared to, 58–59
    racism as, 61–62
    toxicity of, 59–63
    white ignorance as, 59–60
    willful hermeneutical ignorance and, 59–60
epistemic value pluralism, 15–16
epistemologies of ignorance
    commercial content moderation and, 55–56, 204–5
    digital capitalism and, 16–17
    epistemic friction and, 168–69

epistemologies of ignorance (*cont.*)
    epistemic trash and, 60–61
    epistemophilia and, 17–19
    fake news and, 16–17, 142–43
    logic of opacity and, 55
    ontological expansiveness and, 197–98
    privileged people's habits of turning away from the truth and, 16
    strategic ignorance and, 17–19
    trickery and, 18–19, 108–9, 205
    veritism, 17–19
    "world traveling" and, 98, 168–69, 223–24
epistemophilia, 17–19

Facebook
    2016 US presidential election and, 127, 141, 148–49
    algorithms used by, 121, 148–50, 152–54, 156–57, 198–99, 204
    community standards statement at, 38–39
    conservatives' accusations regarding ideological bias at, 149–50, 152, 156–57, 204
    content moderation at, 29–30, 38–39, 41–42, 43n.5, 45–48, 49, 54, 69, 148–54, 156–57, 158–61, 162, 204
    corporate interest in users' online identity at, 93
    fake news and, 113–14, 122, 141, 148–49, 151–54, 156–57, 158–59
    gender discrimination and, 29
    Gizmodo story (2016) about content management at, 149–50, 151–52
    harassment on, 96
    interactive objectivity and, 156–57, 162
    "Nazi Problem" and, 158–61
    neutral/biased binary at, 149–52, 154, 204
    ontological expansiveness and, 198–99
    Oversight Board at, 45–46
    privacy and, 213
    racism and, 29, 38–39
    real-name policy at, 88–90, 91–92, 93–94, 96–97
    social media market share of, 148–49
    Trending Topics on, 113–14, 148–54, 156, 158, 203–4

fake news
    2016 US presidential election and, 112–13, 115–16, 122–24, 126, 128, 141–42
    algorithms and, 113, 121, 123–24, 127, 152–54, 156–57
    alt-right groups and, 124–25, 140–41, 146
    ambiguity of online communication and, 126
    blurring of journalistic boundaries and, 115–16
    bots and, 113, 122–23, 146
    Cartesian epistemology and, 136–37, 146–47
    cognitive heuristics and, 120, 122–23, 128–29, 130, 141–42
    confirmation bias and, 119–20, 136–37, 141
    corporate media's censoring of political speech and, 117–18
    COVID-19 pandemic and, 112–13
    definitions of, 114–17
    digital capitalism and, 123–25, 131–32, 142–43, 203–4
    distrust of mainstream media and, 124, 134, 147
    epistemic damage of, 128–36
    epistemic double bind facing the media and, 125–26
    epistemologies of ignorance and, 16–17, 142–43
    Facebook and, 113–14, 122, 141, 148–49, 151–54, 156–57, 158–59
    false beliefs and, 128–33
    Google and, 121–22, 123–24, 127, 141–44
    intentional misleading of audiences and, 115, 117
    mainstream news sources and, 115–16
    media literacy and, 113, 127
    misogyny and, 132
    objectivity and, 147, 149–50, 162–63
    online advertising market dynamics and, 123–24
    polarization and, 108–9, 120–21, 127, 136–37

"post-truth society" arguments regarding, 135–36, 205–6
right-wing authoritarians' capture of the term, 117–18, 131–32
right-wing media and, 131–32
search engines and, 116–17, 121–24, 141–46
social causes of, 124–28
social memory and, 141–42, 144–45
technological design issues facilitating, 120–24, 130
trickery compared to, 106, 108–9
Trump's disingenuous use of the term, 117–18, 131–33
trust undermined by, 133–36, 162–63
trustworthiness of internet harmed by, 133–36, 162–63
Twitter and, 112, 122, 124, 128, 141, 146
veritism and, 12–13, 128–33, 135, 162–63, 205–6
white ignorance and, 27, 113–14, 136–47, 161, 162–63, 203
white racism and, 27, 132, 140–44, 145–46, 162–63, 205–6
false beliefs
as epistemic trash, 59–60
fake news and, 128–33
hermeneutical ignorance and, 25
white racism and, 138–40, 188
Farkas, Johan, 117–18, 131–33
Fehr, Carla, 61–62
feminist epistemology
bias identification and, 69–70
empiricism and, 10–11, 73–75, 99–100, 157–58, 162
internet epistemology and, 1–2, 5, 11
"Nazi problem" and, 157–62
objectivity and, 8–11, 27, 73–75, 99–100, 147–49, 154–57, 162–63, 205–6
philosophy of science and, 147–48
public data presumption and, 214
scientific communities and, 9–10, 13, 155, 157–58
standpoint epistemology and, 10–11, 73–75, 99–100, 136–37, 157–58, 160–62
veritism and, 13, 15, 75, 205
Fiesler, Casey, 212, 216

Florini, Sarah, 135–36, 181–82, 186, 210–11, 216–18, 222
FORCE: Upsetting Rape Culture (artist collective), 72
Foucault, Michel, 90–91
FOVIVI approach (Feminist accounts of Objectivity, Veritism, Ignorance, Virtues, and Injustice), 2–3, 6, 25, 26, 113–14, 204, 206–7
Freelon, Deen, 128
Fricker, Miranda, 24–26, 46, 63
Frost-Arnold, Karen, 75, 164–65
Frye, Marilyn, 173–74
Fusco, Coco, 98–101, 110

Gamergate (2014), 71–72, 213–14
gaslighting, 18–19, 23–24, 172–74, 183
A Gay Girl in Damascus (blog hoax, 2011), 1–2, 71, 78–79, 133–34. *See also* MacMaster, Tom
Gelfert, Axel, 115–16
Gillespie, Tarleton, 33–34, 66, 147–48
Global South, 56–57, 104–5, 203
Goldman, Alvin
on goals of veritism, 19–20, 75
on true belief and knowledge, 12
on veriphobia, 13–15, 129–30
veritistic perspective on fake news and, 128–29
on veritism and feminist epistemology, 13, 75
on veritism and questions of interest, 106
Gómez-Peña, Guillermo, 98–101, 110
Google
AdSense service of, 123–24
algorithms used by, 121, 123–24, 127, 142–45
digital capitalism and, 142–43
fake news and, 121–22, 123–24, 127, 141–44
racism and, 142–44
Grasswick, Heidi, 7–8
Gray, Mary, 41–43

Habgood-Coote, Joshua, 63–64
Haimson, Oliver, 88–89
Hale, Jacob, 177–78

harassment
  of academic researchers, 216–17, 219–20
  context collapse and, 213–14
  cybersecurity against, 219–20
  Gamergate (2014) and, 71–72, 213–14
  marginalized populations disproportionately targeted by, 6–7, 213–15, 216, 219–20
  of public figures, 216–17
  research ethics and, 210, 213–14, 219–20
  unintentional exposure through academic research and, 213–14, 215, 216
Harding, Sandra, 9–10, 74–75
Heldke, Lisa, 87
hermeneutical injustice
  active listening and, 40–41
  African Americans online and, 39
  content moderation online and, 24–26, 36–41, 43–44, 45–48, 66–68, 203, 204–5
  epistemic justice and, 24–26, 36–37, 40, 59–60
  individual agency and, 40, 46–48
  LGBTQ individuals and, 177–79
  open-mindedness and, 40
  structural injustice and, 46–48
  willful hermeneutical ignorance and, 36–39, 59–60, 177–78
Hicks, Daniel, 157–60
Hoagland, Sarah, 17–18, 98
hoaxes. *See also* imposture; trickery
  COP15 hoax (2015) and, 104–6
  Dow Chemical hoax and, 102–3
  A Gay Girl in Damascus blog and, 1–2, 71, 78–79, 133–34
  Yes Men and, 102–9
Hochschild, Adam, 139–40
Hoffmann, Anna Lauren, 88–89, 213–14, 216

imposture. *See also* hoaxes
  2016 US presidential election and, 71–72
  authenticity violated by, 82, 83–84
  bots and, 71–72
  definition of, 73
  epistemic harms of, 72–73, 87–88, 101, 133–34, 178–79
  "identity tourism" and, 79–80, 91–92, 203
  investigative accountability and, 90–91
  MacMaster's *A Gay Girl in Damascus* blog and, 1–2, 71, 72, 73, 78–79, 80–81, 83–84, 93–94, 99, 101, 108, 133–34, 178–79
  objectivity undermined by, 77–81
  online gaming and, 79–80, 91–92
  racism and, 107–8, 146
  sockpuppetry and, 71–72
  stereotypes promoted by, 79–80, 86–87, 178–79
  trust undermined by, 26–27, 77–81, 111, 203, 205–6
  Twitter and, 71–72, 107–8, 128, 146
  veritism and, 75
Instagram, 45–46
Intemann, Kristen, 11, 73–75, 160–62
internet epistemology
  blurring of offline and online lives and, 4–5
  Cartesian epistemology and, 7–8
  digital capitalism and, 4–5, 12–13, 16–17
  epistemologies of ignorance and, 16
  feminist epistemology and, 1–2, 5, 11
  FOVIVI approach and, 2–3, 6, 204
  power relations and, 6
  situated knowledge thesis and, 6–8, 204
  social epistemology and, 4–5, 22–23
  testimonial injustice and, 25
  veritism and, 12–13, 15–16
  virtue epistemology and, 20–23
investigative accountability, 90–91
Iraq War (2003–12), 115–16
Ivy, Veronica, 172–73

Jack, Caroline, 126
James, William, 135
January 6 insurrection (2021), 1
Jeong, Sarah, 56–57
Johnson, Amy, 180–81
Jonas, Anne, 213–14, 216

Karp, David, 218
Kawall, Jason, 22–23
Kaye, David, 47
Kelly, Megyn, 153
Kidd, Ian James, 63
King, Jr., Martin Luther, 143–44

LaPlante, Rochelle, 53–54, 55–56
Lewis, Rebecca, 124–25, 140–41
LGBTQ communities
    Facebook's "real-name" policy and, 88–90, 96
    hermeneutical injustice and, 177–79
    homophobia and transphobia at academic institutions and, 61–62
    in the Middle East, 77–80
    online harassment of, 6–7
    ontological expansiveness and, 180
    testimonial injustice and, 35
    trickery and, 98
Lo, Katherine, 216–17, 219–20
Longino, Helen, 154–55, 157–62
Lugones, María, 97–98, 168–70, 176–77, 179n.3, 194–95, 223–24
lurking
    ally epistemology and, 172–73, 193–94
    anonymity and, 166–67, 174, 196–97, 202, 206
    blogs and, 166–67
    as oppressive mode of knowledge production, 166, 168, 174–76, 179, 201, 206
    context cues regarding appropriateness of, 175, 194, 195–96, 206
    cowardice and, 166, 177, 179, 206
    curiosity and, 188, 206
    definitions of, 27, 165, 166–67
    engagement compared to, 175–76, 189
    epistemic appropriation and, 199–202, 204, 213–14, 221
    epistemic benefits of, 165, 167–74, 196–97, 202, 221
    epistemic friction and, 169–70, 177–78, 179, 206
    epistemic harms of, 166, 174–75, 177, 179, 199–202, 204, 206
    hermeneutical justice and, 177–78
    intellectual courage and, 189–90, 206
    intellectual humility and, 188–89, 191–92, 206
    internet's facilitation of, 165, 166–67, 171–72, 174, 196–97, 202, 206
    as means to unlearn ignorance and prejudice, 165, 168–72, 174, 177, 178–79, 185–86, 189–90, 195–96, 202, 206, 221
    objections to, 196–202
    ontological expansiveness and, 166, 181, 191, 193–94, 197–98, 202, 203, 206
    open-mindedness and, 187–88, 191, 193–94, 206
    persistence and, 166–67
    polarization and, 167–68
    practical wisdom and, 190–94, 195
    reduction of epistemic burden on marginalized groups and, 165, 170–72
    search engines' facilitation of, 197
    in transgender spaces, 177–79, 221
    trustworthiness and, 184–87, 193–94, 201
    on Twitter, 166–67, 169–70, 177, 185–87, 196–97, 198
    virtue epistemology and, 27, 166, 168, 184–90, 193–96, 201–2
    voyeurism and, 166–68
    "world traveling" and, 169–70, 177, 179, 191–92
Luther, Kurt, 216
Lynch, Michael, 115–16

Mac, Leslie, 29, 38–39
MacAulay, Maggie, 89–90, 96
MacMaster, Tom
    defenses of imposture offered by, 77, 85
    epistemic harm caused by, 73, 77, 78–81, 85–88, 93–94, 101, 107–8, 133–34
    identity tourism and, 79–80
    imposter status of, 1–2, 71, 72, 73, 78–79, 80–81, 83–84, 93–94, 99, 101, 108, 133–34, 178–79
    LGBTQ critics of, 77–78
    media interviews given under false identity by, 79
    stereotypes promoted by, 79–80, 86–87
    trust undermined by, 77–81, 133–34

Markham, Annette, 210–11, 218
Marwick, Alice
  authenticity defined by, 82
  on corporate interests in users' online authenticity, 93
  on dangers of authenticity norms for oppressed groups, 91
  on digital capitalism and fake news, 124–25
  on epistemic double bind facing journalists confronting fake news, 125
  on harassment of academic researchers, 216–17, 219–20
  on racism and fake news, 140–41
McKee, Heidi, 210–12
McKinney, Rachel, 50
Medina, José, 24, 40, 46, 63, 146, 168–70
Mejia, Robert, 135–36
Metaxas, Panagiotis Takis, 122–24
#MeToo movement, 29
Microsoft, 30, 49
Mills, Charles
  on Cartesian epistemology, 7–8, 138
  on privilege and false belief, 188
  on racism as a norm, 14–15
  on social memory and racism, 139–40, 141–42
  white ignorance and, 16–17, 113–14, 136–47, 162–63, 205–6
Milner, Ryan, 126
Moldes, Marcos, 89–90, 96–97
Morozov, Evgeny, 65
Morrow, Rod, 181–82
Mustafaraj, Eni, 122–24
MySpace, 52

Nakamura, Lisa, 78–80, 91–92, 221–22
Native Americans, 89–90
"Nazi problem," 157–62
Nissenbaum, Helen, 212–13
Noble, Safiya Umoja, 142–44, 145–46, 162–63
Nussbaum, Martha, 51–52

objectivity
  epistemic *versus* metaphysical forms of, 73–74
  fake news and, 147, 149–50, 162–63
  feminist epistemology and, 8–11, 27, 73–75, 99–100, 147–49, 154–57, 162–63, 205–6
  imposture's undermining of, 77–81
  interactive objectivity and, 154–57, 161
  neutral/biased binary and, 149–52, 154, 162, 204
  scientific objectivity and, 150–51
  standpoint epistemology and, 74–75
  trickery and, 103–5
  trust and, 26–27, 75–81, 87, 95–96, 205
  trustworthiness and, 81, 87–88, 154
Oluo, Ijeoma, 199–200
ontological expansiveness
  algorithms and, 198–99
  ally epistemology and, 181
  definition of, 180
  epistemic harms of, 182–83
  epistemologies of ignorance and, 197–98
  hijacking of online spaces and, 180–82, 183
  lurking and, 166, 181, 191, 193–94, 197–98, 201, 203, 206
  online *versus* offline forms of, 197–98
  practical wisdom and, 191
  sealioning and, 180–81, 193–94
  straight-queer relations and, 180
  trust disrupted by, 182–83
  Twitter and, 181–82
  white privilege and, 180–82, 193–94
open-mindedness
  as character trait, 21–22
  content moderation and, 35
  definition of, 187
  hermeneutical justice and, 40
  internet epistemology and, 21–22
  lurking and, 187–88, 191, 193–94, 206
Ortega, Mariana, 87, 173–74, 177, 223–24

Papacharissi, Zizi, 86n.6, 91–92
Phillips, Whitney, 126
phronesis (practical wisdom), 94, 192–93, 219. *See also* practical wisdom
Pizzagate conspiracy theory, 112–13, 141–42

Pohlhaus, Jr., Gaile
    on categories of epistemic injustice and knowledge production, 50
    epistemic injustice defined by, 63
    on *To Kill a Mockingbird*, 39–40
    on "willful hermeneutical ignorance," 36–37, 39–40, 46
polarization
    asymmetric polarization and, 127–28, 136–37
    fake news and, 108–9, 120–21, 127, 136–37
    group polarization and, 120, 127
    lurking and, 167–68
    racism and, 128
    technological design of the internet and, 127
    Trump's role in promoting, 127
Pooley, Jefferson, 82–83
Porter, James, 210–12
Potter, Nancy, 96–97, 186–87, 201–2
practical wisdom
    Aristotle's *phronesis* and, 94, 192–93, 219
    defining qualities of, 94
    Doctrine of the Mean and, 95, 99, 190, 192–93
    justice and, 94–95
    lurking and, 190–94, 195
    trickery and, 94–95, 99–100
    trustworthiness and, 93–97
privacy
    anonymization of quoted material and, 218–19
    buyer-beware approach to, 213
    citation of online content and, 211–18, 221–22
    contextual nature of, 211–13
    fabrication as means of protecting, 218–19
    Facebook and, 213
    harassers' expectations regarding, 217–18
    online settings for, 213
    research ethics and, 209–10, 211–19
    Twitter and, 211–13, 216
Proferes, Nicholas, 212, 213
Punsmann, Burcu Gültekin, 41–42, 63–64

Quinn, Zoë, 213–14, 215–16

racism
    in academic contexts, 61–62
    algorithms' role in perpetuating, 142–44
    alt-right groups and, 140–41, 146
    content moderation and, 29, 34–35, 38–39, 158
    epistemic harms of, 162–63
    Facebook and, 29, 38–39
    fake news and, 27, 132, 140–44, 145–46, 162–63, 205–6
    false beliefs and, 138–40, 188
    imposture and, 107–8, 146
    norms of, 14–15
    online harassment and, 6–7
    polarization and, 128
    search engines and, 142–46
    social memory and, 138–42, 143–45
    white racism and, 16–17, 34–35, 138–40, 141–42, 144, 145–46
Ramadan, Danny (aka Daniel Nassar), 77–78
research ethics
    citation of online content and, 211–18, 221–22
    empathic relationships with research subjects and, 214, 215–16, 218–19
    epistemic appropriation as issue in, 221–23
    harassment and, 210, 213–14, 219–20
    privacy and, 209–10, 211–19
    reflexivity and, 210–11
    remuneration issues and, 221–22
    "traitorous identity" and, 225–26
Roberts, David, 135–36
Roberts, Sarah
    on algorithms' limitations, 68–69
    content moderation defined by, 29–30
    on "digital detritus," 30, 56–57
    on social invisibility of commercial content managers, 54–55
    on working conditions among commercial content moderators, 41–43
Rousseau, Jean-Jacques, 82
Russian Internet Research Agency disinformation, 71–72

Salisbury, Meredith, 82–83
Sample, Ruth, 49–54
Sandberg, Sheryl, 151–52
Sanders, Bernie, 181–82
Sap, Maarten, 66–67
satellite publics, 182–83
Schou, Jannick, 117–18, 131–33
sealioning, 180–81, 193–94
searchability, 122, 141–42, 197
Sedgwick, Eve Kosofsky, 90–91
self-trust, 75–77, 80, 99–100, 109–10
Servin, Jacques, 102–3. *See also* Yes Men
Shao, Chengcheng, 113, 122–23
Sheikh, Naheed, 55–56
Silverman, Craig, 153–54
Simon, Judith, 45
Sinders, Caroline, 66–67
Sloan, Luke, 211–12, 216–17
social bots. *See* bots
social memory, 138–42, 143–45
sockpuppetry, 71–72
Soto, Henry, 30, 48, 52
Spelman, Elizabeth, 176–77, 179n.3
Squires, Catherine, 182–83
Stahl, Lesley, 132–33
Stern, Susannah, 214–15
Stocky, Tom, 152
Sullivan, Curtis, 135–36
Sullivan, Shannon, 166, 180–81, 192–93
Sunstein, Cass, 144–45
Suri, Siddharth, 41–42, 43
Sveningsson, Malin, 166–67

TallBear, Kimberly, 89–90
technological solutionism, 65
terrorism, 49, 66, 89–90
testimonial injustice
  authenticity and, 85
  content management and, 25–26, 35–36, 38–39, 43–44, 45–46, 66–68, 204–5
  LGBTQ individuals and, 35
  white ignorance and, 146
Thériault, Anne, 199–201, 213–14
Tirosh, Noam, 141–42
To Kill a Mockingbird (Lee), 39–40
Townley, Cynthia, 17–19, 174–75, 214, 216

trickery
  authenticity and, 97
  benign forms of, 85
  betrayal and, 98–101
  definition of, 73, 97
  epistemic benefits of, 72–73, 98–101, 205
  epistemologies of ignorance and, 18–19, 108–9, 205
  fake news and, 106, 108–9
  identity correction and, 103, 104–5
  the internet as a venue for, 101–8, 111
  museums and, 98–101, 110
  objectivity and, 103–5
  practical wisdom and, 94–95, 99–100
  privileged groups' ignorance and, 97–99, 100–1
  resistance and, 26–27, 97, 98–99, 100–1
  stereotypes challenged by, 105
  trustworthiness and, 97, 105, 110
  veritism and, 105–7
  virtue epistemology and, 26–27, 72
  Yes Men and, 72–73, 102–9
Trump, Donald
  desensitization of American public to racism by, 108–9
  "fake news" term used disingenuously to attack media by, 117–18, 131–33
  online supporters during 2016 election of, 126–27
  polarization of American politics and, 127
trust. *See also* trustworthiness
  authenticity and, 85, 87
  betrayal and, 87–88, 99–100, 109–10
  epistemophilia and, 17–19
  exclusion of oppressed groups from networks of, 76–77
  imposture's undermining of, 26–27, 77–81, 111, 203, 205–6
  objectivity and, 26–27, 75–81, 87, 95–96, 205
  ontological expansiveness and, 182–83
  in others, 75–76, 84, 109–10
  in practices, 75–76, 80–81, 109–10
  self-trust and, 75–77, 80, 99–100, 109–10
  sharing and, 164
  truth and, 26–27

vulnerability and, 87
trustworthiness
  as aspiration, 186–87
  authenticity and, 84, 95–96, 205
  Doctrine of the Mean and, 95, 99
  epistemic trustworthiness and, 184–86, 201
  epistemic virtue of, 26–27, 81–97, 111, 184–85
  fake news and, 133–36, 162–63
  lurking and, 184–87, 193–94, 201
  normative expectations and, 81–82
  objectivity and, 81, 87–88, 154
  practical wisdom and, 93–97
  reliance and, 81–82
  trickery and, 97, 105, 110
  vulnerability and, 184–85
Tufekci, Zeynep, 134
Twitter
  2016 US presidential election and, 127–28, 141
  algorithms used by, 66, 121
  Black Twitter, 107–8, 146, 169–70, 177, 185–86, 217–18
  confirmation bias and, 120–21
  content moderation at, 31, 47, 66
  experimentation with identity on, 91–92
  fake news and, 112, 122, 124, 128, 141, 146
  imposture and fake accounts on, 71–72, 107–8, 128, 146
  lurking and, 166–67, 169–70, 177, 185–87, 196–97, 198
  "mining" by journalists of, 199–202, 204, 213–14, 221
  ontological expansiveness and, 181–82
  privacy expectations and, 211–13, 216
  trickery and, 104
  "Two Undiscovered Amerindians Visit . . ." (Fusco and Gómez-Peña), 98–101, 110

Uganda, 104–5
United Kingdom, 112–13

Vamos, Igor, 102–3. *See also* Yes Men
veritism
  epistemic value pluralism and, 15–16

  epistemologies of ignorance and, 17–19
  error-avoiding veritism *versus* truth-seeking veritism, 135
  fake news and, 12–13, 128–33, 135, 162–63, 205–6
  feminist epistemology and, 13, 15, 75, 205
  imposture and, 75
  internet epistemology and, 12–13, 15–16
  objectivity and, 75
  power relations and, 14–15
  veriphobia and, 13–15
virtue epistemology
  authenticity and, 95–97
  character virtues and, 21–22
  content moderation and, 30–33, 35, 44–45, 48, 204–5
  internet epistemology and, 20–23
  lurking and, 27, 166, 168, 184–90, 193–96, 201–2
  trickery and, 26–27, 72
  true belief formation and, 21–23

Watson, Lani, 188
Wheeler, Ed, 139–40
white ignorance
  bots' influence on online discourse and, 146
  fake news and, 27, 113–14, 136–47, 161, 162–63, 203
  Mills on, 16–17, 113–14, 136–47, 162–63, 205–6
  testimonial injustice and, 146
Wikipedia, 8, 31–32, 127
Williams, Matthew, 211–12, 216–17
Williams, Patricia, 180
Wittkower, D. E., 166–67, 182n.4, 192
World Trade Organization (WTO), 72, 102–3
Wu, Tim, 123–24

Yes Men
  as anti-corporate activists, 72, 102–3, 106–8
  COP15 hoax and, 104–6
  documentary film about, 104

Yes Men (*cont.*)
   Dow Chemical hoax and, 102–3
   identity correction and, 103, 104–5
   objectivity and, 103–5
   as tricksters, 72–73, 102–9
   veritism and, 105–7
Yiannopoulos, Milo, 159–60

York, Jillian, 47
#YourSlipIsShowing, 71–72, 108n.11
YouTube, 30, 31, 33, 47, 65–66

Zagzebski, Linda Trinkhaus, 94, 190
Zimmer, Michael, 212–13
Zuckerberg, Mark, 149